MUSIC: HISTORY AND THEORY

MUSIC
HISTORY AND THEORY

WILLIAM R. CLENDENIN, Ph.D.

Associate Professor of Music
University of Colorado

A COLLEGE COURSE GUIDE

Doubleday & Company, Inc., Garden City, New York

Library of Congress Catalog Card Number 64–16251

Printed in the United States of America

Illustrations by Marta Cone

Grateful acknowledgment is made for permission to include the following material.

AMERICAN BOOK COMPANY. *"Frère Jacques,"* from *The American Singer,* second edition, Book 4, by John W. Beattie, *et al.,* copyright © 1960 by American Book Company. Reprinted by permission of the publisher.

ASSOCIATED MUSIC PUBLISHERS, INC. From "Jephte" by Giacomo Carissimi from *Geschichte der Musik in Beispielen* by Schering. Copyright 1931 by Breitkopf & Härtel, Leipzig. Renewed 1959. Reprinted by permission of the original copyright owners and their U.S. representatives, Associated Music Publishers, Inc.

BOOSEY & HAWKES, INC. From *String Quartet, Opus 74—No. 3,* by Franz Joseph Haydn. Hawkes Pocket Scores; from *Mikrokosmos—Volume 2* by Béla Bartók. Copyright 1940 by Hawkes & Son (London) Ltd.; from *Petrouchka,* by Igor Stravinsky. Copyright by Édition Russe de Musique. All rights assigned to Boosey & Hawkes, Inc. Revised edition copyright 1947 by Boosey & Hawkes, Inc. All reprinted by permission of Boosey & Hawkes, Inc.

DESCLÉE & CIE. From the *Liber usualis.* Reprinted by permission of Desclée & Cie, Tournai, Belgium.

DOVER PUBLICATIONS, INC. From *The Gift to Be Simple,* by Edward D. Andrews. Published by Dover Publications, Inc. Reprinted by permission of the publisher and author.

DURAND & CIE. From *Quatuor à cordes* by Claude Debussy; from *La Fille aux cheveux de lin* by Claude Debussy. Both reprinted by permission of Durand & Cie, editors-proprietors.

GALLIARD, LTD. From *Les Oeuvres de Arcangelo Corelli,* edited by Joachim and Chrysander. Published by Galliard, Ltd.

WILHELM HANSEN MUSIK-FORLAG. From *Fünf Klavierstücke* by Arnold Schoenberg, Op. 23. Copyright © 1923 and 1951 by Wilhelm Hansen, Copenhagen. Reprinted by permission of the publishers.

HARPER & ROW, PUBLISHERS, INC. From "Prout's Tune," from *Understanding Music* by Newman. Reprinted by permission of Harper & Row, Publishers, Inc.

HARVARD UNIVERSITY PRESS. From *Historical Anthology of Music: Baroque, Rococo, and Pre-Classical Music,* by Archibald T. Davison and Willi Apel. Copyright 1950 by the President and Fellows of Harvard College. Reprinted by permission of Harvard University Press.

EDWIN F. KALMUS, MUSIC PUBLISHERS. From Schubert's *"Fantasie,* Op. 15," from *Franz Schubert Impromptus, Moments Musicaux, Phantasies, Allegretto, Andante, March, Scherzos.* Reprinted by permission of Edwin F. Kalmus, Music Publishers.

W. W. NORTON & COMPANY, INC., and FABER & FABER, LTD. From *Masterpieces of Music before 1750,* compiled and edited by Carl Parrish and John F. Ohl. Copyright 1951 by W. W. Norton & Company, Inc. From *A Treasury of Early Music,* compiled and edited with notes by Carl Parrish. Copyright © 1958 by W. W. Norton & Company, Inc. Both reprinted by permission of W. W. Norton & Company, Inc., and Faber & Faber, Ltd.

NOVELLO & COMPANY, LTD. From Mozart's string quartets in B♭ Major and in C Major, from *W. A. Mozart, The Ten Celebrated String Quartets,* a Paul Hirsch Music Library Publication. Reprinted by permission of Novello & Company, Ltd.

C. F. PETERS CORPORATION. From *Symphonie fantastique,* by Hector Berlioz, score by Eulenberg Pocket Scores; from *Till Eulenspiegels lustige Streiche,* by Richard Strauss. Copyright by C. F. Peters Corporation. Both reprinted by permission of C. F. Peters Corporation, sole American agents of Eulenberg Pocket Scores.

G. SCHIRMER, INC. From *Wagner Selections from the Operas Arranged for the Piano;* from "Passacaglia in C Minor," by J. S. Bach, from *Johann Sebastian Bach, Complete Organ Works,* edited by Widor and Schweitzer. Both reprinted by permission of G. Schirmer, Inc.

SIMON & SCHUSTER, INC. From *Opera Themes and Plots,* by Rudolph Fellner. Copyright © 1958 by Rudolph Fellner. Reprinted by permission of Simon & Schuster, Inc.

STAINER & BELL, LTD. From "As Vesta Was Descending," from Vol. XIII of *The English Madrigal School,* edited by Fellowes. Reprinted by permission of Stainer & Bell, Ltd., London.

UNIVERSAL EDITION, LTD. From Mahler's use of *"Frère Jacques,"* from *Symphony No. 1,* by Gustav Mahler. Reprinted by permission of Universal Edition, Ltd.

To Albert T. Luper

with sincere appreciation

Preface

Music: History and Theory is a concise yet comprehensive survey of the art of music, of its forms and development through the ages, and of the contributions of individual composers. The book is intended for all who are interested in learning about music. It is my hope that it will be useful for classroom study, for review purposes, and as an introducton to music for the layman.

Part One, "The Elements of Music," is devoted to such fundamentals as rhythm, melody, and harmony, and to texture, style, and basic forms.

Parts Two through Five present the history of music, commencing with primitive and ancient music in various parts of the world. The successive chapters then give careful attention in turn to each of the great periods of music: the Middle Ages, the Renaissance, the Baroque period, the Classical period, the Romantic period, post-Romanticism, Impressionism, and the music of the twentieth century. Despite the broad scope, it has been possible to present each period in some detail and to provide a real acquaintance with composers and their works.

Various important musical instruments, both early and in present use, are discussed, and in most cases shown in the illustrations. The range of the human voice is also considered.

At many points in the book, passages of music are reproduced as especially illustrative of the topic being considered. In so far as possible, references to compositions are to works that are readily available on phonograph records.

In citing examples we have followed the standard practice of referring in many cases to certain major collections of published music, and have designated these by the customary abbreviations. The names of the basic collections and the abbreviations always used for them appear in a list on the page following the Table of Contents.

It is my hope that readers of this book will find that it brings to them much to enhance their appreciation and understanding of music.

Finally, may I express my gratitude for the editorial assistance of Copeland & Lamm, Inc., and especially Lawrence W. Lamm, Lewy Olfson, and Harry L. Wagner; and also to Marta Cone for her illustrations.

W.R.C.

Boulder, Colorado
July 1964

Contents

PART THREE

THE RENAISSANCE AND BAROQUE PERIODS

PART FOUR

THE CLASSICAL AND ROMANTIC PERIODS

Source Abbreviations

Numerous references have been made in this book to compositions given or listed in musical anthologies, thematic catalogues, etc., and to instruments pictured in one particular publication. These sources have been indicated by abbreviations, the key to which is given below:

BWV Schmieder, Wolfgang, ed. *Thematisch-systematisches Verzeichnis der musikalischen Werke von Johann Sebastian Bach*. Leipzig: Breitkopf & Härtel, 1950.

D. Deutsch, Otto Erich. *Schubert: Thematic Catalogue of All His Works*. London: Dent, 1951.

EM Gleason, Harold, ed. *Examples of Music before 1400*. New York: Crofts, 1946.

GMB Schering, Arnold, ed. *Geschichte der Musik in Beispielen*. Leipzig: Breitkopf & Härtel, 1931. Reprint, *History of Music in Examples*. New York: Broude Brothers, 1950.

HAM I Davison, Archibald T., and Apel, Willi, eds. *Historical Anthology of Music*, Vol. I: *Oriental, Medieval, and Renaissance Music*. Cambridge, Mass.: Harvard University Press, 1946, 1949.

HAM II Davison, Archibald T., and Apel, Willi, eds. *Historical Anthology of Music*, Vol. II: *Baroque, Rococo, and Pre-*

Classical Music. Cambridge, Mass.: Harvard University Press, 1950.

K. Köchel, Ludwig Ritter von. *Chronologisch-thematisches Verzeichnis sämtlicher Tonwerke Wolfgang Amade Mozarts,* third edition (1937), revised by Alfred Einstein. Ann Arbor: Edwards, 1947.

LU *The Liber usualis*. Tournai: Desclée, 1950.

MITA Buchner, Alexander. *Musical Instruments Through the Ages*. London: Batchworth Press, 1961.

MM Parrish, Carl, and Ohl, John F. *Masterpieces of Music before 1750*. New York: Norton, 1951.

TEM Parrish, Carl. *A Treasury of Early Music*. New York: Norton, 1958.

PART ONE

The Elements of Music

CHAPTER 1

The Fundamentals

THE VALUE OF MUSICAL KNOWLEDGE

The appreciation of music can be a continuing source of pleasure to everyone. Many people enjoy listening to music without any special background of knowledge about its forms and techniques or its history, but there seems to be little question that some acquaintance with the methods of musical composition and the characteristics of individual composers enhances one's musical experience. Music can and does have an important place in our lives.

Medieval man did not find it strange, or even unscientific, to believe that the heavenly bodies in their courses throughout space emitted musical tones that were in perfect harmony. This "music of the spheres" was to him only another manifestation of the perfect order of the universe; and what could be a better way of representing the divine order than as harmonious music? Our present age may reject the astronomy implied, but the essential rightness of the image remains. Indeed, we find that each and every society–no matter how primitive–has created its own order in sound, and this sound is a basic reflection of the society itself. The creation of music, then, is not only the creation of a succession of melodious sounds; it is also the expression of a people's response to the rhythms, patterns, and sounds of the world as they see it. The Gregorian chant, the Baroque harpsichord sonata, the Classical symphony, the Romantic opera, and the modern experimental music are all expressions of their cultures, and it is impossible to listen to them without experiencing some of the original feelings that went into them. The sound an age makes is perhaps the freshest and clearest expression of its identity.

As to the role of music in our own time, we are in grave danger of not seeing the forest for the trees. Music is everywhere in our society, and its uses run the gamut from the sublime to the ridiculous. It is presented in concert halls and opera houses; it is also used to quiet nerves in tedious places like factories and elevators; it stimulates shopping, reduces tension, and masks background noises like rattling dishes and loud talkers; and, in spite of or possibly because of all this, it offers a greater amount of serious art than ever before. The repertoire available to the general public on records, tapes, and radio is far more extensive today than even the most knowledgeable musicologist of earlier times was able to command. Thus today's listener, faced with almost too wide a choice, must remain at once sophisticated and open-minded, receptive yet discriminating.

In order to do this the listener should not make the common mistake of underrating his own inherent taste. Most people know more about music than they think they do, and the best way to increase one's knowledge in this field is to follow one's likes. Familiarity in music breeds appreciation, not contempt, and the one sure way to achieve greater understanding in music is to enjoy it. The alternative is to like a piece of music because somebody else likes it, a policy that will not provide much in the way of lasting gain, for if one surrenders his judgments to outside influences too often, he loses forever the possibility of forming his own tastes and reactions. Nothing could be more inimical to the true appreciation of music.

The actual listening to music may be divided broadly into three levels: the sensual, the emotional, and the intellectual. The sensual manner of listening requires little effort or concentration; it is only the sound itself that matters, and the listener makes no attempt to understand the intent or meaning of the music.

Emotional listening requires some thought about the music, but it does not demand any special study of music as an art, for the listener here is primarily concerned with his own personal, emotional reactions to the piece. A composition heard in this manner may well provoke different responses from different people, yet composers consider this a valid artistic reaction and are much concerned with it.

The intellectual approach—really less forbidding than it sounds—is the most difficult and the most rewarding, because it includes the emotional and sensual way of listening, and in addition demands a modicum of musical knowledge for the listener to have a wider and deeper appreciation of what pleases him. Naturally, in order to gain this knowledge it is necessary to shed old prejudices and listening habits. One must listen to a piece of music on its own terms and no others; expecting the music of Mozart to conform to the ideas of Tchaikovsky is unfair to both composers and can only prevent the listener from hearing the real values of each. It is only the intellectual approach to music that allows one to listen with a "relativistic" ear.

Thus we see that a knowledge of some of the technical features of music, a familiarity with different textures, styles, forms, and composers, is indispensable; and while there are people who maintain that this spoils their inherent appreciation of music, the evidence all points the other way. One might just as well say that a knowledge of the rules and method of scoring spoils a spectator's appreciation of a football game.

Therefore, this chapter and the next will deal with the elements of musical composition in order that this basic knowledge may be acquired and readily used. From that point on the book will devote itself to the development of music through the ages and the contributions of individual composers.

RHYTHM

The English word "rhythm" stems from the Greek word "*rhythmos*" meaning "measured motion," which in turn is derived from the base of *"rheein,"* meaning "to flow." Thus the definition of rhythm may be expanded to mean a flow or movement characterized by a regularly recurring element, such as a beat or accent, that is interspersed with periods of relaxation.

Man lives in a rhythmical world of days and nights and changing seasons, in all of which he finds nature's capricious habits ultimately controlled by an over-all rhythmic pattern. Man himself sleeps, breathes, eats, walks, and works in a rhythmic pattern; and, of course, he owes his very life to the continuance of the steady, measured beat of his heart. Now as man finds his vital activities bound so closely to rhythmic patterns, it should come as no surprise to him that music, which is intimately bound up with his emotional make-up, has for its basic element a large amount of rhythmical association. Therefore, the general definition of rhythm given above can be revised slightly for musical application as follows: RHYTHM is the gathering or arrangement of successive tones according to their relative accentuation and duration.

Music is a time art (the tones or pitches in music exist only as related to time); and it is necessary to discuss the element of rhythm under three important factors: meter, rhythmic patterns, and tempo. These three factors together produce the rhythmic element of music.

METER. Meter is the organizing force of rhythm. It may be described as a certain regularity of accents or beats in given units of time. These units of time are called MEASURES or BARS, and the beats are grouped within them in twos, threes, fours, etc., with the first beat normally bearing the strongest accent. The meter of a composition is indicated by a fraction-like sign called the meter signature (to be discussed later). In the meter signature (see Table I, below) the upper figure shows the number of beats or counts in a measure, and the lower figure represents the note value to receive a single beat or count. The duple, triple, and quadruple meters (two, three, and four beats to the measure, respectively) are known as simple meters, and all the others are either combinations of simple meters or compound meters.

TABLE I

SIMPLE METERS

Beat Note Value	*Duple*	*Triple*	*Quadruple*
eighth note (♪)	2/8	3/8	4/8
quarter note (♩)	2/4	3/4	4/4 = C
half note (𝅗𝅥)	2/2 = ¢	3/2	4/2

COMPOUND METERS

Beat Note Value	*Duple*	*Triple*	*Quadruple*
sixteenth note (𝅘𝅥𝅯)	6/16	9/16	12/16
eighth note (♪)	6/8	9/8	12/8
quarter note (♩)	6/4	9/4	12/4

It may be seen from Table I that a composition with a 3/4 meter signature would be in simple triple meter, and that another, with the meter signature 9/8, would be in compound triple meter. In performing compound meters, it is often more convenient to reduce the count to two, three, or four beats in a measure as heard in the simple meters; thus 9/8 meter might be counted as three beats to the measure instead of nine.

Meters as discussed above are found in superabundance in music, especially in the compositions of the 17th century through the 19th. Table II illustrates a few of the simple and compound meters as found in musical literature.

A few composers have tried using simple meters by adding them together to produce COMBINATION meters. Such a meter is 5/4 (2 + 3 or 3 + 2) or 7/8 (4 + 3, 3 + 4, or 2 + 3 + 2). Perhaps the most famous example of a combination meter is the flowing 5/4 found in the second movement of Tchaikovsky's *Symphony No. 6 ("Pathétique")*.

In contemporary or modern music, composers have introduced two new uses of meter called POLYMETRIC and MULTI-

TABLE II

Meter Signature	*Composer*	*Composition*
2/4	Haydn	*Symphony No. 101* ("The Clock"), second movement
4/4	Haydn	*Symphony No. 101,* fourth movement
3/4	Haydn	*Symphony No. 101,* third movement
4/4	Prokofiev	March from *The Love for Three Oranges*
6/8	Beethoven	*Symphony No. 6,* fifth movement
9/8	Debussy	*"Clair de lune,"* from *Suite bergamasque*
12/8	Beethoven	*Symphony No. 6,* second movement

METRIC. The former means the simultaneous use of more than one meter in a composition. Jazz pieces, or musical numbers in a jazz style, have made use of this technique; an excellent example is George Gershwin's "Fascinating Rhythm," in which the opening five measures of the melody, with beats grouped to correspond to the meters 2/2, 3/4, 2/2, 2/4, and 3/4, respectively, are set against four measures of the accompaniment in 2/2. In multimetric compositions, composers deliberately disturb the regularity of the forward flow of the music by frequent changes of meter, often within a short span of measures. Debussy, in his *Prelude to the Afternoon of a Faun,* changed meters nineteen times in a composition 110 measures in length.

A certain amount of music in the Western world has been composed without meter or measured rhythm. The outstanding example of this would be the whole body of Gregorian chant—the basic service music of the Roman Catholic Church. This music is NONMETRIC in that it is written without a meter signature and has no regularly recurring accent. This type of music draws its rhythm from the prose rhythm of the Latin text to which it is set.

Rhythmic Patterns. The second factor in this discussion of rhythm–rhythmic patterns–concerns the duration of tones, or note value, and displaced accents. Rhythmic patterns formed by an arrangement of notes of different values often serve as a kind of overlay to the basic (metrical) pulse of the music. An elementary illustration of this idea is shown in Example 1. Here,

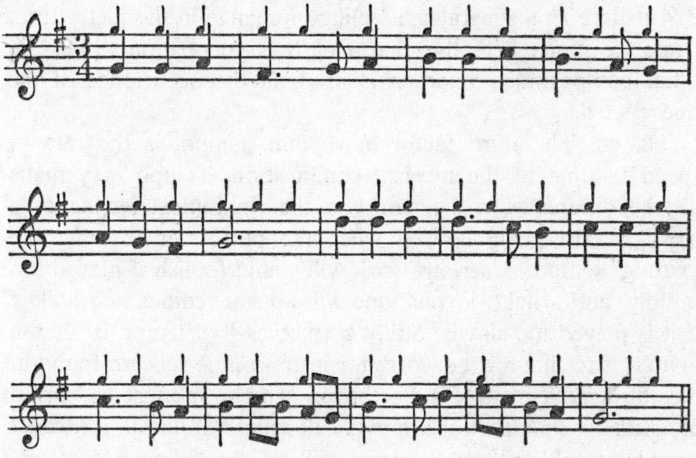

Example 1

in the tune "America," the meter is indicated by a constant symbol (♩) above the staff. It is clear that in the first measure the notes of the melody coincide with the metrical pulse, but in the second measure, where the rhythmic pattern is ♩. ♪ ♩ (each note having a different duration), a slight impulse is given to the forward flow of the tune. Jazz, of course, is famous for this overlay of rhythmic impulse. Indeed, much of the excitement of jazz is produced by the often complex number of rhythmic patterns superimposed on the basic duple meter. Moreover, the systematic use of a rhythmic pattern throughout a piece may characterize the forward motion of the composition; thus the pattern ♫ ♩♩♩ 𝅗𝅥 may be considered the vital, plunging element of "The Star-Spangled Banner."

The name given to one popular usage of the displaced accent, SYNCOPATION, is defined as the use of a strong accent in an unexpected place within the measure. This technique is aptly illustrated in measures 248–79 of the first movement of Beethoven's *Symphony No. 3,* where a combination of notational devices and dynamic indications tends to remove a number of the strong accents from the first beat of the measures written in 3/4 meter. This generates a feeling of change in the meter from triple to duple; here the charm of the syncopation lies, as in other compositions where it is used, in the occurrence of the unexpected.

TEMPO. The third factor in rhythm, tempo, is the rate or speed in time of the musical composition. Tempo may make all the difference in the world in the rhythmical feeling of a work, a fact easily noticed when the performer is using the "wrong" tempo. A serious work will sound foolish if played too rapidly, and a light, joyous tune will appear tedious and hollow if it is played too slowly. Still, "correctness" of tempo is often a matter of feeling for the work; for instance, the scherzo found in the third movement of a Beethoven symphony must be played much faster than the third-movement minuet found in a Mozart symphony, although both pieces will be notated in 3/4 meter.

Notational practices in music may indicate the desired tempo, but sometimes notation alone is not enough, so composers have adopted Italian words to specify further the correct tempo. Table III illustrates some commonly used tempo indications.

TABLE III

Largo = slow ("broadly")
Adagio or lento = slow
Andante = a leisurely pace
Allegro = fast
Presto or vivace = very fast
Prestissimo = as fast as possible

Finally, since invention of the metronome by Johann Mälzel in 1816, composers have sometimes used its indications to suggest tempi for their compositions. For example, ♩ = 80 would mean a quarter note to be played to each tick of the metronome when that instrument is set at the 80 mark. At this setting the metronome would tick eighty times a minute.

MELODY

If rhythm is the first element in the construction of music, melody is surely the second. In fact, for many people the two elements are practically inseparable. Melody is, perhaps, the most direct communication link between the composer and the listener, for melody is the part of the music that is heard and comprehended first, and it is the last part to be forgotten. Anyone—without outside help—can hum, whistle, or sing a single line of music, in other words, a melodic line or melody.

Definition of Melody. In one sense melody might be considered a pleasing succession of tones. But this is hardly a broad enough definition, as different historical periods have advanced quite different opinions as to what may be considered "pleasing." In Example 2 a succession of tones is given that was once

Example 2

submitted by the eminent English theorist and teacher Ebenezer Prout (1835–1909) as not having melodic substance; it was not, to him, a pleasing succession. Yet if these tones are adjusted, as in Example 3, the group might gain some credence

Example 3

as a "pleasing" melodic formula in 20th-century music. Perhaps, then, a more comprehensive definition of melody is that it is a succession of tones related to one another and to the whole in such a way as to express a satisfying and coherent musical idea or entity.

TERMS APPLIED TO MELODIES. Such words as "tune," "air," "theme," and "subject" are often used interchangeably with melody; and musicians frequently speak of "melodic lines" or just "lines." In spite of this free interchange of terminology, it is possible to be more specific in the use of these terms. A TUNE or AIR represents a self-contained melody organized in a few simple phrases; church hymns are tunes and, indeed, are identified by a title called a tune. The melodies of symphonic movements are called THEMES, whereas the melody of a fugue is known as its SUBJECT. Both theme and subject imply a melody that is capable of development or manipulation throughout the course of the musical composition.

A melody may be discussed in terms of its shape. A rising melodic line brings a feeling of tension, possibly due to the fact that tones building to a higher range actually require greater physical effort on the part of the singer or wind instrument player, and also, perhaps, for psychological reasons. In the opposite manner, a line falling into a resting place, or CADENCE (not to be confused with the metrical cadence used by a marching band), implies relaxation. A melody that moves horizontally in a line is called STATIC, and is often associated with, and complemented by, a second theme, known as a COUNTERMELODY. Thus the rather staid opening melody of the second movement of Beethoven's *Symphony No. 7* is soon joined by a second, flowing theme or countermelody. These melodies are identified by (a) and (b), respectively, in Example 4.

CHARACTERISTICS OF MELODIES. Melodies also exhibit certain styles or characteristics. According to the predominating feature, they may be classed as DIATONIC (closely allied to the prevailing scale) or CHROMATIC (with added accidentals not found in the prevailing scale); CONJUNCT (mostly stepwise) or DISJUNCT (mostly by skip); as being in a NARROW RANGE

Example 4

OR WIDE RANGE; as being SHORT AND TERSE or LONG AND FLOWING. By way of illustration, the melody of "America" may be described as a basically diatonic, conjunct, smooth line in a narrow range, whereas that of "The Star-Spangled Banner" is a diatonic, disjunct, angular, bold line in a wide range.

Frequently melodies are called upon through their very sound or activity to express a mood or to enhance the concept of a word (or words) in a text. This is called MOOD PAINTING and TEXT PAINTING. For instance, in the song "Home on the Range" it is not difficult to hear in the music the cowboy's longing that is explicit in the text. Composers of the Middle Ages and the Renaissance, when setting the text of the Creed in the Ordinary of the Mass, were very careful to accompany the phrases "*descendit de coelis*" and "*ascendit in coelum*" by descending and ascending melodic lines, respectively.

In the final analysis, a good melody must be correct in its proportions, function in a fitting rhythmical pattern, attain a climax of some sort, and provide an expressive quality suitable to the composition that it heads. To conceive melodies of this sort, the composer must rely on his native genius alone, for good melodies come by inspiration or they come not at all.

HARMONY

Harmony is the third basic element of music, and it has played an especially large role in the Western tradition of music. It began with the addition of a second line of music, which was to be played simultaneously with the melody, a major achievement of musical composition in the Western world. Harmony originated with a style of sacred music called ORGANUM (or′gȧ-num) in approximately the 9th century A.D. In musical notation (which will be discussed later) melody is seen as the horizontal element of music, and harmony as the vertical; using painting as a comparison, melody would be the painter's line on the canvas and harmony would be the depth or perspective of the painting.

As harmony began in two voice parts, we will first consider

the association of a pair of simultaneously sounded tones, known as a HARMONIC INTERVAL, and also the way in which these intervals are built into chords of three or more tones (see below in connection with Example 5). Then, considering the average music listener and the music most frequently heard today, we will discuss the system known as TRADITIONAL OR FUNCTIONAL harmony, which was in use from the 17th century to the 19th. This system, also designated by the name TONALITY, or TONAL SYSTEM, is based on the major and minor scales, and relies on the I, IV, and V degrees of the scale as strong focal points, with I the tonic, or tonal center (see Example 6).

HARMONIC INTERVAL. Emotion in varying degrees is an inseparable element of musical art, and emotion in music is closely linked to a state of tension or relaxation which in turn is induced by harsh and clashing sounds—DISSONANCE—or gentle and blending ones—CONSONANCE. In the tonal system the consonant intervals of a key (KEY is defined as the organization of the tones of the major or minor scale around a center called the tonic) are called perfect (unison, fourth, fifth, octave) and imperfect (major and minor thirds and sixths). Of some special importance is the octave, which is that interval between the first and eighth notes of a diatonic scale and with the simplest

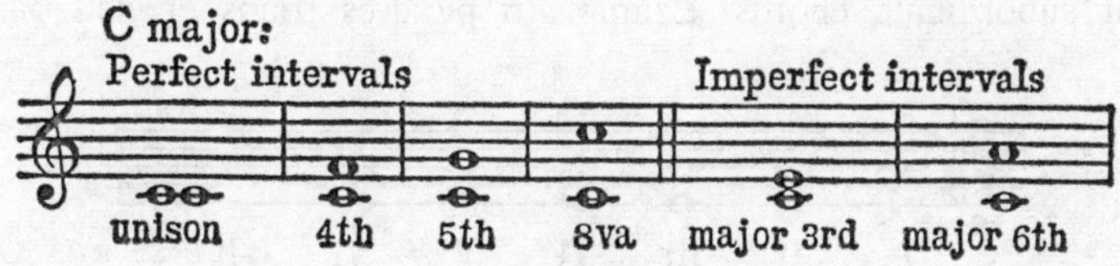

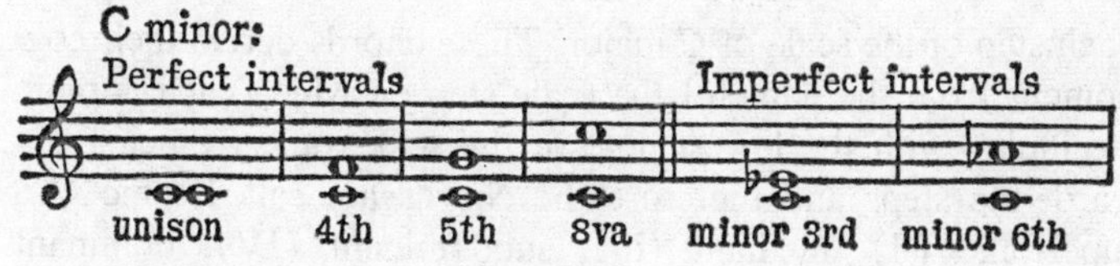

Example 5

possible vibration ratio 1:2; composers often make use of this interval both melodically and harmonically for reinforcement of a tone. For a notated illustration of these basic intervals see Example 5. The other twenty intervals possible within the octave would be considered dissonant; however, these twenty as a group must be judged in context—that is, with regard to the key in use in the composition—for some of these intervals may have a consonant quality when sounded alone or "out of context."

CHORD. Although two simultaneous lines of music marked the beginning of harmony, the study of this element is more closely connected with the chord than with the interval. A CHORD in tonal theory is defined as an association of three or more tones consisting of a root with superimposed thirds. Such a chord with three tones is called a TRIAD; four tones a SEVENTH CHORD; five tones a NINTH CHORD, and so on, according to the intervallic relationship between the bottom and top tones of the chord. This terminology is rarely carried beyond the chord of the thirteenth.

Chords erected on the first, fourth, and fifth degrees of the scale (and identified as I, IV, V) are designated as the primary chords of the key, and those built on the second, third, sixth, and seventh steps (ii, iii, vi, vii) are known as secondary or subordinate chords. Example 6 pictures triads erected on

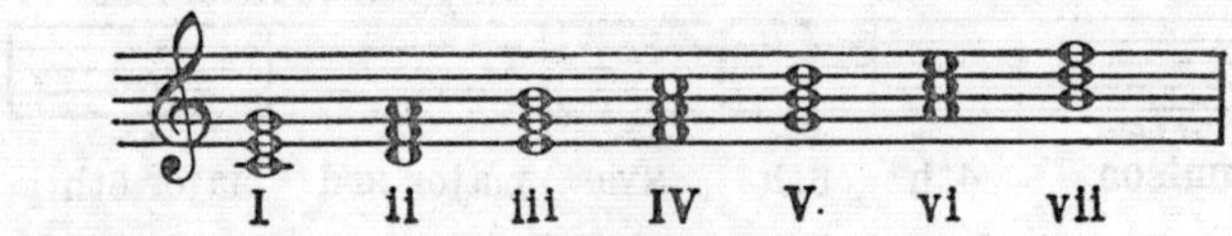

Example 6

each step of the scale of *C* major. These chords derive their cognomens from the name of the scale step on which each is built. Beginning with the lowest note of the scale and advancing upward, the steps and therefore the chords are called tonic (I), supertonic (ii), mediant (iii), subdominant (IV), dominant (V), submediant (vi), and subtonic or leading tone (vii).

The basic harmonic structure of the entire tonal system lies in the primary chords called tonic, subdominant, and dominant. This may be seen quite readily in the simple harmonizations of folk melodies, hymns, and popular songs, where the structure is easily broken down into the I, IV, and V chords, and it is possible, at least in a general way, to present even complex and extended tonal compositions in terms of tonic, subdominant, and dominant areas. However, to add color and variety to the harmony, a composer is often willing to sacrifice some of the strength of the primary chords and to replace them with subordinate chords that bring him additional harmonic resources.

A second feature of harmonic study, aside from the vertical associations of tones in a chord, is that of functional analysis, or the consideration of the movement from one chord to another. As the composer draws on an ever-increasing vocabulary of chords, he faces the problem of joining these chords together and moving the entire progression toward a position of rest and fulfillment—the cadence—which in tonal theory will eventually be the tonic chord of the key.

Table IV demonstrates six strong root movements of subordinate and primary chords from a position of unrest and lesser stability toward the ultimate position of stability known as the tonic. Subordinate chords always exhibit the factor of instability to a much greater degree than do the primary chords IV and V.

TABLE IV

1. vii–iii–IV–V–I
2. vi–ii–V–vi–IV–V–I
3. iii–vi–iii–IV–V–I
4. ii–V–vi–V–I
5. IV–ii–V–vi–ii–V–I
6. V–vi–iii–IV–V–I

Although a tonal composition usually begins and ends in the same key, it is quite possible that several keys will be used during the course of a piece of music. This change of key involves a process called MODULATION, and it is accomplished in the most satisfying way through (1) a pivot chord, which can be defined as a member of both the old and the new keys, and (2) the absolute establishment of the new key, probably through a dominant-tonic chord relationship in the new key. In modulation, the pivot chord furnishes a substantial and positive liaison between keys; the V-I cadence, being the strongest functional chord progression, when used in the new key turns the thoughts of the listener from the old key to the new. Modulation by the circle of fifths (given below) provides the listener with movement through a related series of keys and is thus quite acceptable to the ear.

The main key of a work is of course indicated on the score by the KEY SIGNATURE at the beginning, consisting of all the SHARPS (written "♯" and understood to raise the pitch of a note one half step, or semitone) and all the FLATS (written "♭" and understood to lower a note one half step) that occur in that particular key. Once the key is established by the key signature, the individual notes need not have sharp and flat signs next to them. When modulation occurs, however, the change in key obviously calls for new sharps and flats or the obliteration of old ones; and so directly before each of the notes in question the sharp or flat sign is added as needed. When a sharp or flat is to be cancelled, a NATURAL sign (♮) is inserted in the same way. These added sharps, flats, and naturals are called ACCIDENTALS.

Composers of the 17th and 18th centuries confined modulation for the most part to near-related keys, i.e., keys the signature of which differs by not more than one accidental from the initial key. Figure 1 shows the relationship of the major and minor keys one to another as presented in the famous "circle of fifths"; in the illustration the major key is shown by a capital letter, with the related minor key (which always bears the same key signature) designated by a lower-case letter.

A glance at Figure 1 reveals the near-related keys of *C* major to be: *a* minor, *G* major, *e* minor, *F* major, and *d* minor.

The many-voiced music written from the 9th century through the 16th was composed under a system called MODALITY. In the Middle Ages there existed eight modes, identified as the Church, or ecclesiastical, modes; four of these were authentic modes

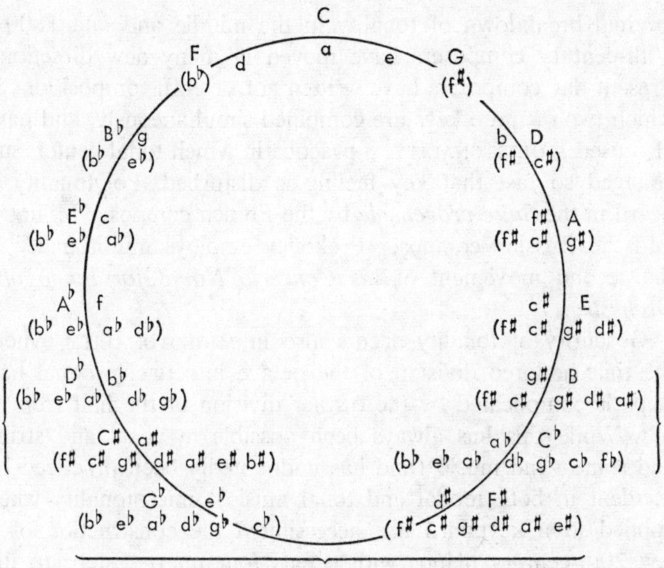

Fig. 1: The Circle of Fifths.

called Dorian, Phrygian, Lydian, and Mixolydian, each of which had a related plagal mode known in turn as Hypodorian, Hypophrygian, Hypolydian, and Hypomixolydian. (For a discussion of these see Chapter 4.) Two new authentic modes –Ionian and Aeolian–and their plagal forms were recognized by theorists (though never by the Church) in Renaissance times, and completed the modal system as used. (See Chapter 5.) Actually, the vertical association of tones in the modal system is more of an intervallic theory than a harmonic one; moreover, the functional movement of "chords" in modality is scarcely apparent until the 16th century, and modulation plays no part in this system. Music of this type is not well known to the general listening public, but some truly great settings of the Mass, motet, chanson, Italian madrigal, and English madrigal from the Middle Ages and Renaissance are based on the modal system. These works will all be discussed in later chapters.

The Break with Traditional Tonality. Following the

gradual breakdown of tonality in the middle and late 1800's, 20th-century composers have moved in many new directions. Present-day composers have written POLYTONAL compositions in which two or more keys are combined simultaneously, and have also used MULTITONALITY, a practice in which tonal centers are changed so fast that key feeling is disturbed. Polytonality is heard in the *Suite provençale* by the French composer Milhaud, and the Russian composer Prokofiev employs multitonality in the second movement of his *Concerto No. 3 for Piano and Orchestra*.

Obscurity of tonality occurs also in MICROTONALITY, where the time-honored division of the octave into twelve equal half steps is complicated by the further division of the half step itself. While this has always been possible in vocal and string and some wind music (and has undoubtedly been practiced by accident in both modal and tonal music), microtonality when applied to a keyboard has necessitated the construction of a few 20th-century pianos with twenty-four quarter steps to the octave.

A complete break with the preceding tonal system was accomplished by the introduction of the TWELVE-TONE, OR SERIAL, TECHNIQUE. This is not properly a scale, but rather a technique or system of composition in which every one of the twelve chromatic tones of our scale is given equal importance. (In other systems the first and fifth [dominant] receive special weight, for instance.) Given the twelve tones, the composer then arranges them arbitrarily into a certain sequence that is called the *tone row* for the composition. Example 7 shows the row or

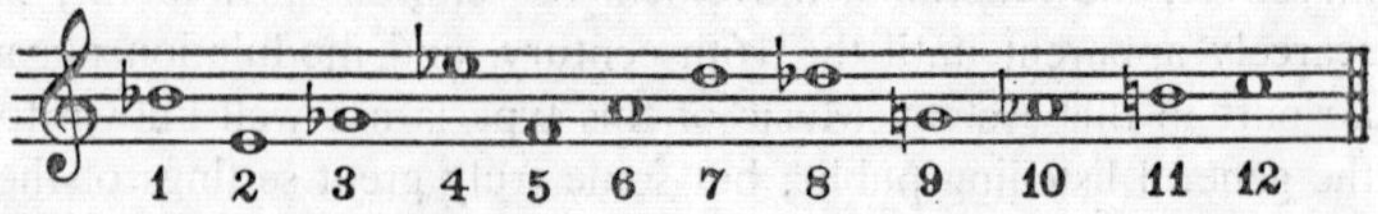

Example 7

arrangement of notes chosen by Arnold Schoenberg (the originator of the twelve-tone technique) for his *Variations for*

Orchestra, Opus 31. (A fuller explanation of twelve-tone composition will be found in the Schoenberg discussion in Chapter 10.)

Schoenberg's pupil, Alban Berg, brought a somewhat warmer approach to this style by retaining some vestiges of tonality, and the orchestral prelude to Act III, Scene 5, of his opera *Wozzeck* is an interesting example of movement from a tonal center into atonal sound. In his *Septet* of 1953, Igor Stravinsky adopted the serial technique, utilizing the sixteen-note tone row, noted in Example 8, in the "Passacaglia" and "Gigue" movements.

Example 8

MUSICAL NOTATION

As the basic components of music (rhythm, melody, and harmony) developed, it became increasingly clear that a system of notation was necessary to give exact pitch and time-duration values to each of the tones in a musical composition; this was indispensable to obtaining more correct performance practices and more accurate preservation for later generations. A number of notation systems were devised, but the one discussed here originated in the early 17th century, at the beginning of the Baroque period, and is still in use. Earlier systems will be introduced in their historical contexts later in the book.

THE STAFF. The staff as used today is a series of five horizontal lines, on and between which the musical notes are placed to indicate their pitch. Each line and each space on a staff represents one note, and of course the total number of different notes that can be played on all the various instruments is considerably larger than what can be covered on one five-line staff, so we have resorted to using various CLEF SIGNS to indicate which range of notes a particular staff is supposed to cover. By its position the clef sign points out one line on the staff that is then assigned a certain note, as follows:

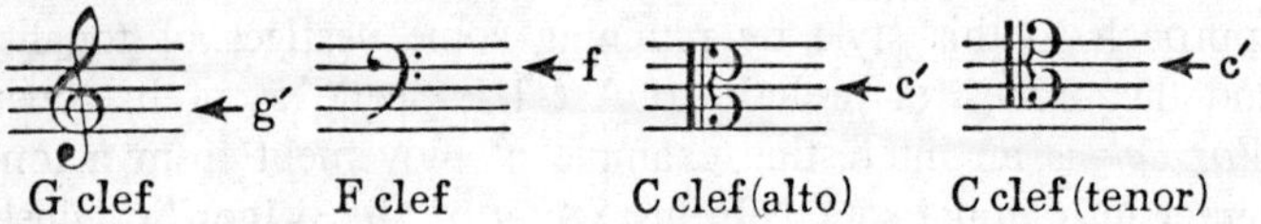

Example 9

The G clef ("violin clef" or "treble clef") indicates that a note placed on the second line from the bottom is to be understood as the pitch g′ (note also example below), so that e′ is then represented by the bottom line, f′ by the first space at the bottom, a′ by the second space from the bottom, b′ by the third line from the bottom, and so forth. The F clef ("bass clef") indicates that the second line from the top is understood as f; the C clef that focuses on the middle line (the "alto clef" or "viola clef") means that the middle line is understood as c′; and the C clef that focuses on the second line from the top (the "tenor clef") means that the second line from the top is understood as c′.

If the range usually covered by a staff must be extended, the very high and low notes can be indicated simply by adding small lines above and below the staff, and in extreme cases adding an "8" with a line over or under the notes to which it applies to mean another octave above or below, respectively. Thus, using two of our clefs and some added lines, we can make our musical notation indicate a wide range of octaves:

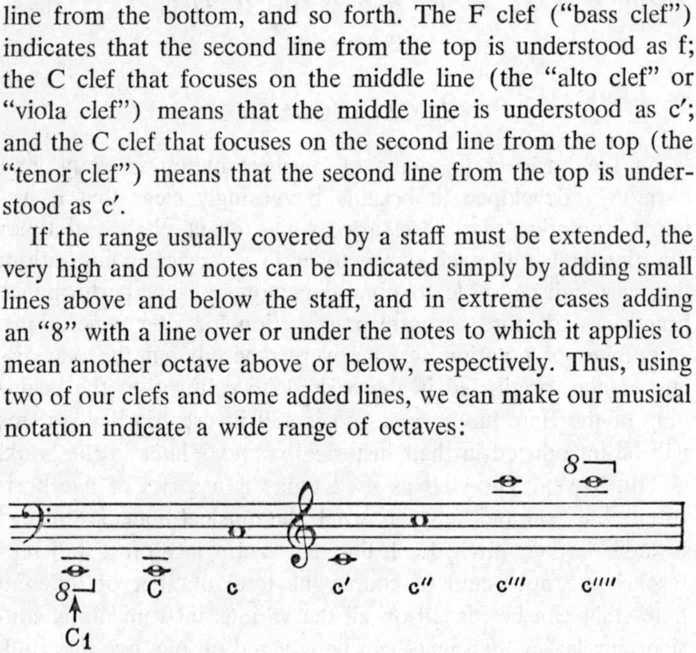

Example 9a

Moreover, by the use of the symbols for sharps and flats (discussed above under harmony) either as part of the key signature or as accidentals, we can indicate the semitones between the tones we have just discussed.

After the clef sign at the head of the staff, there come the key signature (discussed above) and, last, the METER SIGNATURE, often called the TIME SIGNATURE. The meter signature denotes the organization of strong and weak beats for the whole or part of a composition. As mentioned earlier, two, three, and four units to the measure are referred to, respectively, as duple meter (2/2, 2/4, 2/8), triple meter (3/2, 3/4, 3/8), and quadruple meter (4/2, 4/4, 4/8). These are known as simple meters. Groupings of simple meters through multiplication of the number of beats per measure by three give compound meters such as compound duple (6/4, 6/8, 6/16), compound triple (9/4, 9/8, 9/16), and compound quadruple (12/4, 12/8, 12/16). Since music in a compound meter is often of a flowing nature, this quality is more clearly indicated to the performer if the note value that represents one beat is made shorter; thus the bottom figure of a compound meter signature often appears double that of the corresponding simple meter signature. Table I has already presented meters in graphic form.

NOTES. The pitch and duration of a musical sound are indicated by a note placed upon the staff, which bears a certain clef and key signature at its head. On the other hand, a duration of time when a musical sound of any kind is *not* to occur is denoted by a REST OR RESTS. Table V illustrates the notes and their equivalent rests seen oftenest in musical scores.

SCALES. Every musical composition has as its background some sort of a scale formation. Much Oriental music is founded upon a five-note scale, the PENTATONIC SCALE (see Example 51c). Western music from about 1680–1880 made use of a system of DIATONIC SCALES, comprising certain arrangements of whole tones (T) and semitones (S) such as the MAJOR SCALE (T-T-S-T-T-T-S), the MELODIC MINOR (T-S-T-T-T-T-S ascending, and T-T-S-T-T-S-T descending), and the HARMONIC MINOR (T-S-T-T-S-T½-S). These major and minor

TABLE V

Name of Note	*Note Symbol*	*Rest Symbol*
whole	𝅝	𝄻
half	𝅗𝅥	𝄼
quarter	𝅘𝅥	𝄽
eighth	𝅘𝅥𝅮	𝄾
sixteenth	𝅘𝅥𝅯	𝄿
thirty-second	𝅘𝅥𝅰	𝅀
sixty-fourth	𝅘𝅥𝅱	𝅁

scales start on any one of twelve different pitches, and thus there are twelve major scales and twelve of each type of minor scale. Each of these scales has a key name, which is the name of the pitch on which it starts, and a mode name according to whether the whole-tone and semitone arrangement identifies it as major or minor. The twelve major, twelve melodic minor, and twelve harmonic minor scales are given in Example 38.

The seven different steps of these major and minor scales are often identified as SCALE DEGREES in the following manner: I = tonic; II = supertonic; III = mediant; IV = subdominant; V = dominant; VI = submediant; and VII = leading tone. (The eighth note merely duplicates the first or tonic note at a new pitch.) All the tones of the above scales may be combined in one scale of twelve semitones called the CHROMATIC OR DUODECUPLE SCALE, which forms the background for modern music (Example 9b).

Music written in the Middle Ages and the Renaissance had a background based on the EIGHT CHURCH SCALES, better called modes, since each had a different tone-semitone arrangement; four more such modes were added to the theoretical system in the 16th century (see Examples 23 and 34). There can, of

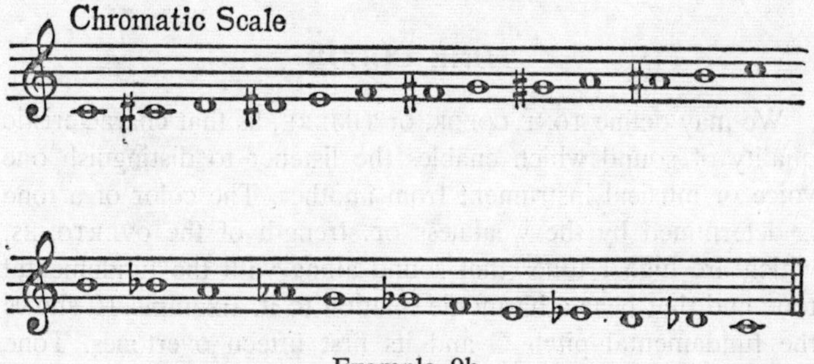

Example 9b

course, be any number of scale patterns of tones and semitones; and one well-known scale is without semitones and is called, appropriately enough, the WHOLE-TONE SCALE (see Example 51b).

OTHER SYMBOLS. In addition to the symbols just discussed, musical notation involves designations (usually in Italian) that indicate the TEMPO, or rate of speed at which the music is to be played, and the DYNAMICS, or the volume of sound to be used. Tempo has already been discussed, but the dynamic markings are usually word abbreviations or signs placed at or near a musical passage to specify the desired sound volume. Table VI illustrates those most commonly found in musical scores.

TABLE VI

Italian Name	*Abbreviation and Sign*	*English Translation*
fortissimo	ff	very loud
forte	f	loud
mezzo forte	mf	medium loud
mezzo piano	mp	medium soft
piano	p	soft
pianissimo	pp	very soft
crescendo	cresc., <	gradually louder
decrescendo	decr., >	gradually softer
diminuendo	dim., >	gradually softer

TONE COLOR

We may define TONE COLOR, or TIMBRE, as that characteristic quality of sound which enables the listener to distinguish one voice or musical instrument from another. The color of a tone is determined by the weakness or strength of the OVERTONES, which are higher tones that sound along with the fundamental tone and that bear a harmonic relation to it. Example 10 shows the fundamental pitch C and its first fifteen overtones. Tone

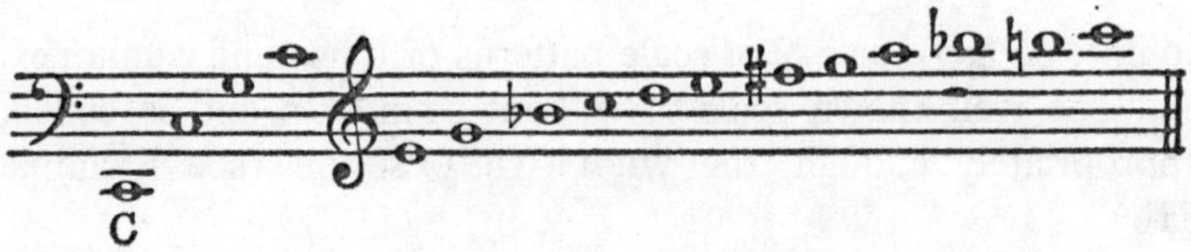

Example 10

color must be distinguished from the INTENSITY of the tone (degree of loudness or softness, produced by the amplitude of the vibration of the sound wave), from the PITCH of the tone (highness or lowness of sound, according to the frequency of the sound-wave vibration), and from the DURATION of the tone (the length of existence of the sound in time).

Although color is never lacking in composition, throughout the history of music composers have exhibited varying degrees of coloristic interest; some have been true colorists, while others have emphasized the development of melodic, rhythmic, and harmonic ideas. Perhaps it could be said of Bach that he lived in an age when individual colors were not overly important, for he shows no qualms about transcribing Italian string music for performance on the organ. However, with the advent in the late 18th century of the orchestra—truly an "instrument" that may be called a "coat of many colors"—composers became vitally interested in color. It is agreed that the 19th-century composer Rimsky-Korsakov was a supreme colorist; in fact, he wrote a very famous book on ORCHESTRATION—the art of most effectively combining the various tones of the orchestral instruments.

THE HUMAN VOICE. Perhaps the best place to start a discussion of tone color is with the instrument closest to each of us, the human voice. A singer's voice may be classified by range as soprano, mezzo-soprano, alto or contralto, tenor, baritone, or bass. However, it has become useful to classify further the basic soprano, alto, tenor, and bass voices (often abbreviated S.A.T.B.) by affixing before these names such titles as coloratura, lyric, dramatic, and the like.

The COLORATURA SOPRANO reveals a voice of utmost pliability, capable of the execution of rapid runs and trills, a quality often found in a high vocal register. The term LYRIC may be associated with either the soprano, tenor, or bass voice, and implies a smooth, melodic sound; presumably a brilliant, clear voice of light texture, the lyric type serves well in concert performance of the art song. DRAMATIC is a term frequently applied to the soprano and tenor voices, and signifies a strong and forthright voice capable of the full expression of emotion. Power and stamina are prime necessities in the DRAMATIC SOPRANO and HEROIC TENOR (or *heldentenor*) voices, especially when these singers appear in the long and difficult roles found in the Wagnerian operas. The BASSO PROFUNDO is a low and powerful bass voice that provides the perfect vehicle for the portrayal of certain "shady" characters. Table VII gives examples in musical literature of all these voice ranges.

TABLE VII

Vocal Range and Type	*Illustrating Compositions*
Coloratura soprano	"Jewel Song," from Act II of Gounod's *Faust*
Lyric soprano	Schubert's *"Heidenröslein"*
Dramatic soprano	Isolde's role in the Love Death (*Liebestod*): Act III, Scene 2 of Wagner's *Tristan und Isolde*
Mezzo-soprano	*"Habanera"* and *"Seguidilla"* as sung by Carmen in Bizet's *Carmen*
Contralto or alto	Brahms's *Alto Rhapsody*

TABLE VII–Continued

Vocal Range and Type	*Illustrating Compositions*
Lyric tenor	Aria "Every valley shall be exalted," from Handel's *Messiah*
Dramatic or heroic tenor	*"In fernem Land,"* from Wagner's *Lohengrin*
Baritone	*"Avant de quitter ces lieux,"* from Gounod's *Faust*
Lyric bass	"The people that walked in darkness," from Handel's *Messiah*
Basso profundo	"Mephisto's Serenade" from Gounod's *Faust*

MUSICAL INSTRUMENTS. The orchestra contains an astonishing array of color possibilities, and perhaps it is for this reason that orchestral literature has presently become the most admired and discussed form of musical art. In order to appreciate this variety it is necessary to consider carefully the families or instrumental divisions of the orchestra, and to examine the colors of the individual basic instruments. The four divisions of the orchestra are as follows: (1) string, (2) woodwind, (3) brass, and (4) percussion.

(1) The string section. This is the heart of the ensemble, for well over half of the membership of a modern orchestra plays an instrument of the string family, and most of the warmth of tone in a symphony orchestra is the result of this large body of strings. They are able to produce a sound that becomes even warmer still when the strings are played VIBRATO, that is, with a tremulous tone quality produced by vibrating the left hand at the wrist as the finger presses the string against the finger board, thus spreading the tone a bit on both sides of the pitch. Several other techniques used on all the string instruments are: PIZZICATO, a plucking (instead of bowing) of the strings; DOUBLE-STOPPING, the playing of two notes at one time; GLISSANDO, the sliding of a finger of the left hand along the string while the right hand bows; HARMONICS, high-pitched and pale tones produced by lightly pressing a string at a certain point so as to permit only a segment of the string to vibrate; ARCO SALTANDO, bouncing the bow on the strings; SPICCATO, the rapid playing of

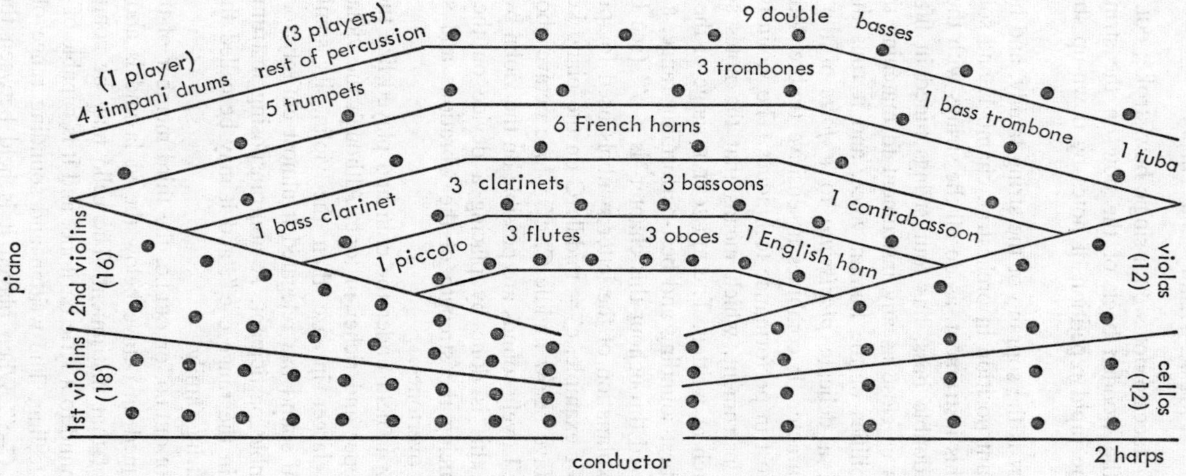

Fig. 2: Seating Arrangement of a World-famous Symphony Orchestra.

a number of staccato notes on a single bow-stroke; COL LEGNO, the use of the wooden back of the bow on the strings; and TREMOLO, the rapid repetition of notes by down-up strokes of the bow.

The VIOLIN is the soprano of the string family, and holds the most important position in orchestral, chamber, and solo string literature. This instrument, as do all the strings with the exception of the double bass, has four strings tuned in fifths. The violin comes as close as any instrument to matching the emotional possibilities of the human voice, and it runs the entire gamut from a delicate *pianissimo* to a *forte* of the highest dramatic character. It combines a sensitive timbre with agility and the utmost in performance techniques. The violin is a nontransposing instrument, which means that the notes sound at the same pitch as written. The EFFECTIVE range of the violin—that is, the best-sounding and best-performing range, a classification followed throughout this chapter—is g–b‴ (see Example 9a for an explanation of the letter symbols used for pitches in this book; for example, c′ = middle C on the piano keyboard, c = one octave below middle C, c″ = one octave above middle C, etc.). Lovely sounds are possible on the violin by muting the strings; this is done by placing a device on the bridge, thereby reducing the strength of the vibrations and subduing some of the overtones.

The VIOLA is held under the chin and played like the violin, but it is deeper and richer in tone. Although the viola is only one-seventh larger in size than the violin, its somber and slightly nasal sound has relegated it almost entirely to the role of an ensemble participant. A nontransposing instrument, the viola plays in the range c–c‴, and it may be called the tenor-alto of the string family.

The VIOLONCELLO, or CELLO, the third member of the string family, is tuned an octave below the viola and is about twice the length of that instrument. The cello may be compared in quality of sound to a lyric baritone, and it is capable of expressing intense feeling. The written and sounding range of the instrument is C–c″. When played it is held between the knees,

Fig. 3: The String Section. *Top* violoncello, viola; *bottom* violin, double bass.

resting on the floor by means of an adjustable end pin. The cello serves as the bass of the string quartet, but in the orchestra it gives over this position to the double bass.

The DOUBLE BASS, also known as the bass viol or contrabass, is the largest instrument in the string family. As one of its names suggests, it has retained certain characteristics of instruments called viols, predecessors of modern strings. These features include a flat back with rounded shoulders, and the four strings tuned in fourths instead of fifths (E_1, A_1, D, G; some double

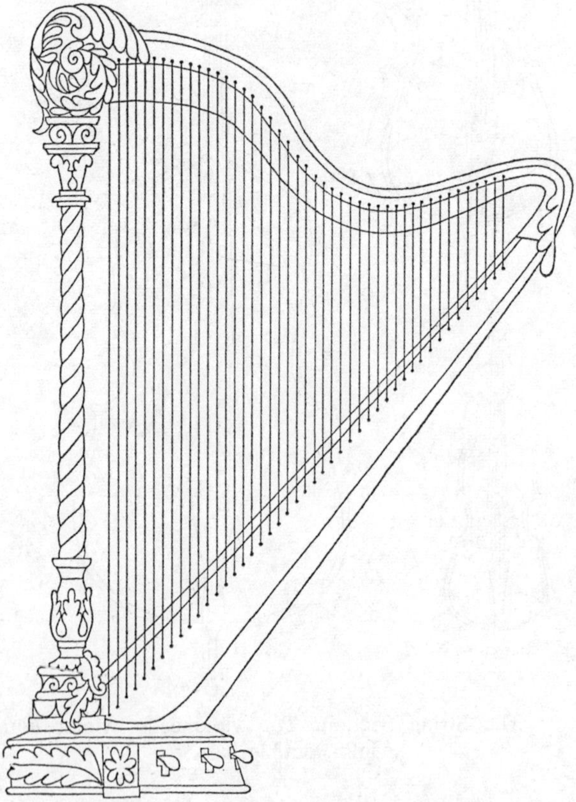

Fig. 4: The String Section. Harp.

basses now have a fifth string, tuned C_1). The string bass may be called a TRANSPOSING INSTRUMENT, meaning an instrument for which music is written in a key or octave other than that of the actual sound. The bass sounds an octave lower in sound, hence the name double bass. It is such a large instrument that the performer must play it either standing or seated on a high stool. Its low, weighty tone provides a sturdy bass to the string section of the orchestra.

The HARP, whose tone color is familiar to all, is included in the string section.

Table VIII gives information on the approximate number of each string instrument in the large orchestra, and an illustration of its effective use in orchestral literature.

TABLE VIII

Instrument	*Number in Orchestra*	*Illustrating Composition*
Violin	16 (1st violins) 14 (2nd violins)	Mendelssohn, *Concerto in e minor for Violin and Orchestra*
Viola	12	Berlioz, *Harold in Italy,* especially the first and third movements
Violoncello	10	Schubert, *Symphony No. 7* ("Unfinished"), second theme of first movement
Double bass	8	Beethoven, *Symphony No. 5,* Trio of the third movement
Harp	1	Debussy, *La Mer*

(2) The woodwinds. The problems of intonation and the playing of complete chromatic scales on woodwind instruments —so called because they were all once made of wood—were finally resolved in the 19th century by a keyed mechanical system. This made possible a more complete participation by the woodwinds in music that was becoming ever more complex in melodic and harmonic ideas.

The TRANSVERSE FLUTE serves as the soprano of the woodwind family. It is a cylindrical tube about twenty-six inches long, with a stopped parabolic head at one end. In the side of the head is a hole across which the performer blows; as the "transverse" part of the name indicates, the instrument is held horizontally, to the right of the mouth. The flute is very facile, with almost all trills and ornaments possible. It can also be liquid and light in cantabile (literally "singing") passages, although the color is rather bland, due to its lack of overtones. A nontransposing instrument, the transverse flute has a range d′–b♭‴.

The PICCOLO is very much like the flute except that it is only half as long. One of the clearest and most penetrating of instruments, its upper register is a bright and distinct top to the orchestral score. It is the highest-sounding instrument in the orchestra. The piccolo is a transposing instrument, its written range of g′–a‴ sounding an octave higher.

The DOUBLE-REED members of the woodwind family are the

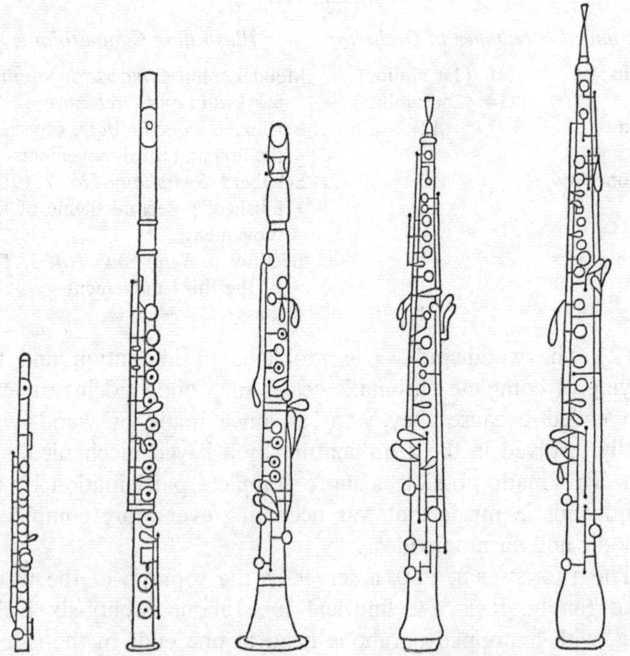

Fig. 5: The Woodwind Section. Piccolo, flute, clarinet, oboe, English horn.

oboe, English horn, bassoon, and contrabassoon. All these have tubes of conical bore, and mouthpieces made of two thin pieces of cane bound tightly together. It is from this double-reed mouthpiece that they draw their classification.

The OBOE is a soprano-like instrument of a curious and rather nasal color that remains constant throughout its entire range. Its sound is not easily covered in the orchestra, and for this and other reasons the oboe is quite useful in a solo capacity. A nontransposing instrument, it has a somewhat limited range of c'–d'''.

The ENGLISH HORN is neither English nor a horn. Perhaps the early French designation for this instrument as a bent or angled horn, *cor anglé,* may have been corrupted in time to *cor anglais.* Be that as it may, the English horn is an alto oboe, pitched a fifth lower than the oboe. A pear-shaped bell helps account for its somewhat dolorous color, and its soft, wistful timbre contrasts in its melodic usage with the more penetrating sound of the oboe. The English horn is a transposing instrument and sounds a perfect fifth below its written range of b–$b\flat''$. Both the oboe and English horn are frequently used to portray the shepherd's pipe in music representing pastoral themes.

The BASSOON has a transparent, hollow tone, a wide range, and the ability to play both a sustained legato line and staccato (sometimes humorous) figures. The instrument has eight feet of tubing bent back upon itself; the Italians call the bassoon a *fagotto,* quite appropriately, a "bundle of sticks." This woodwind plays in the written and sounding range $B\flat_1$–$b\flat'$.

The CONTRABASSOON is such a large and bulky affair that it must rest on the floor; it has a tube about sixteen feet long, doubled back on itself four times. This woodwind is an awkward tone-producing mechanism and is best suited for passages in slow or moderate tempi. It produces the lowest tone in the orchestra, and is noted for its dark but penetrating quality. The contrabassoon sounds an octave lower than its written range $B\flat_1$–$e\flat'$.

The CLARINET and the BASS CLARINET complete the basic woodwinds of the orchestra. These are cylindrical pipes made

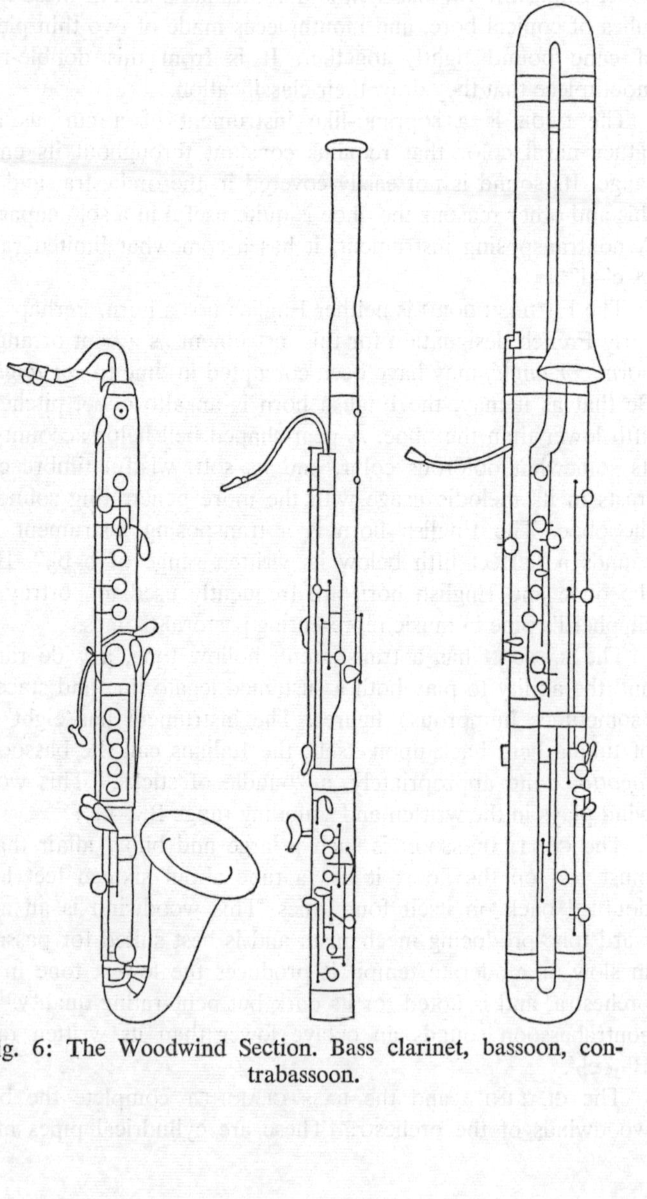

Fig. 6: The Woodwind Section. Bass clarinet, bassoon, contrabassoon.

of wood or ebonite, each with a beak mouthpiece to which a thin cane reed is attached; thus any member of the clarinet family is classified as a single reed. All clarinets are written in the range e–e‴. The most popular clarinet in use today is the one made in B♭, which sounds effectively d–d‴; however, much music has been written for the A clarinet, with a sounding range of c♯–c♯‴.

To complete the picture, the bass clarinet sounds D–d″. The B♭ clarinet is a shade more brilliant than the one in A, but loses little of the characteristic body of this family of instruments. The A clarinet is often chosen for music written in sharp keys and the B♭ clarinet for music in flat keys, primarily for ease of performance. Among wind instruments clarinets have the widest range and the greatest change in color and regulation of dynamics within this range. Along with this excellent dynamic control, the bass clarinet has lower tones of splendid resonance. Table IX provides illustrations of the woodwinds in orchestral settings.

TABLE IX

Instrument	*Number in Orchestra*	*Illustrating Composition*
Piccolo	1	Tchaikovsky, *Nutcracker Suite* ("Chinese Dance")
Flute	2	Debussy, *Prélude à l'après-midi d'un faune*
Oboe	2	Schubert, *Symphony in C Major* ("Great"), second movement
English Horn	1	Dovřák, *Symphony No. 9* ("From the New World"), second movement
Clarinet	2	Mozart, *Concerto in A Major for Clarinet and Orchestra,* K. 622
Bass Clarinet	1	Grofé, *Grand Canyon Suite* ("On the Trail")
Bassoon	2	Dukas, *The Sorcerer's Apprentice*
Contrabassoon	1	Ravel, *Mother Goose Suite* ("The Beast")

(3) The brasses. At the beginning of the 19th century only the slide-trombone players among all brass performers were able to produce satisfactorily all chromatic intervals within the octave. But with the year 1813 the playing of the other brasses was greatly facilitated by the invention of valves, and this invention elevated trumpet and French horn performers in particular to the position of soloist in the orchestra.

The TRUMPET, the soprano of the brass family, is made of a cylindrical bore that flares out into a moderate-sized bell at the end. The three valves make possible a dazzling technique that has been exploited in many orchestral compositions and that is, of course, the basis for the pyrotechnics of the trumpet in the jazz ensemble. The bright and shining timbre of the instrument has been found useful time and time again for that added brilliance at the climactic point in a symphonic work. The trumpet is made in several keys, including those of B♭, C, and D. The most widely used of the three is that in B♭, which sounds a major second lower than its written range of a–b♭″. The sound of the instrument may be softened and its color slightly changed by mutes of different types which are placed in the bell.

The CORNET, little used in the symphonic music today save for a few French scores, is much like the trumpet, and yet it is clearly distinguishable from that instrument. The cornet is shorter in length, of a slightly different shape, and has a mellower tone. But the two instruments have the same range, and what is possible on the one is possible on the other. The B♭ cornet is standard in band instrumentation.

The trombones found in the modern orchestra are the TENOR TROMBONE and the BASS TROMBONE. These instruments do not have valves; instead, their tube lengths are varied by means of a U-shaped slide, producing notes of different pitches. The trombone is best suited to music expressing a loud, heroic message, but it can also play softly. Muting on the trombone is done just as it is on the trumpet, and the result is relatively the same. The trombone is a nontransposing instrument, with the tenor

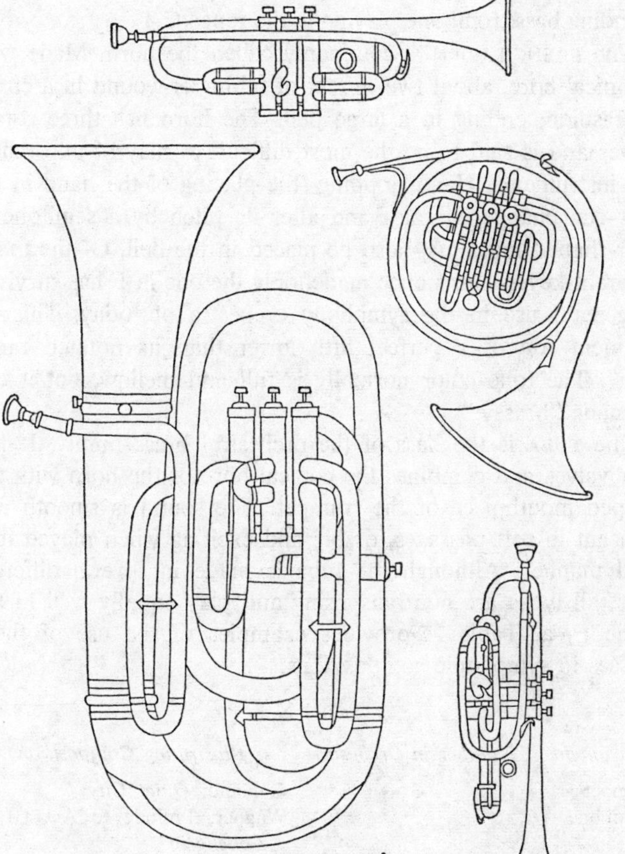

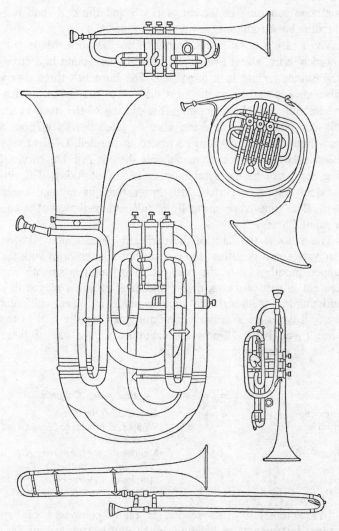

Fig. 7: The Brass Section. *Clockwise from top* trumpet, French horn, cornet, trombone, tuba.

trombone sounding in the range E–c″, and the dark and full-sounding bass trombone playing in the range C–f′.

The FRENCH HORN is commonly called the horn. Made with a conical bore, about twelve feet of tubing is wound in a circular fashion, ending in a large bell. The horn has three rotary valves and is said to be the most difficult to play of all orchestral instruments. Hand-stopping—the placing of the hand in the bell—can change its color and alter its pitch by a semitone; a pear-shaped mute may also be placed in the bell. Of the many different-keyed horns once made, only the one in F has survived in general use in the symphony orchestra of today. This instrument sounds a perfect fifth lower than its notated range A–g″. The tone color normally is full and mellow, but it can be made "brassy."

The TUBA is the bass of the orchestral brass family. It has four valves and combines the conical bore of the horn with the cupped mouthpiece of the trumpet. The sound is smooth and pleasant in soft passages, or big and exciting when played in a loud manner. Although the tuba is made in several different keys, all types are nontransposing and play equally well in the range F_1–a. Table X provides examples of the use of these brasses in symphonic compositions.

TABLE X

Instrument	*Number in Orchestra*	*Illustrating Composition*
Trumpet	3	Copland, *Quiet City*
Trombone	3	Wagner, Prelude to Act III of *Lohengrin*
French Horn	4	Mendelssohn, *Midsummer Night's Dream* ("Nocturne")
Tuba	1	Stravinsky, *Petrouchka,* Fourth Tableau ("Performing Bear")

(4) Percussion. This section is really composed of two groups: instruments of indefinite pitch and instruments of definite pitch. The question of the usefulness of instruments of indefinite pitch—the "noisemakers"—in the symphony orchestra sometimes arises, but when judiciously employed they serve a

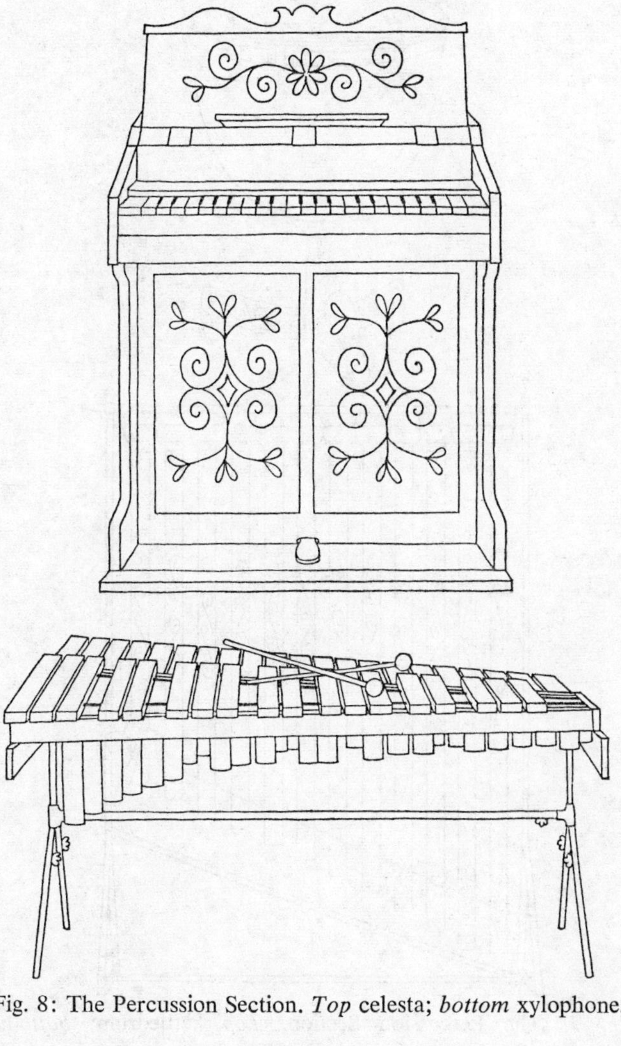

Fig. 8: The Percussion Section. *Top* celesta; *bottom* xylophone.

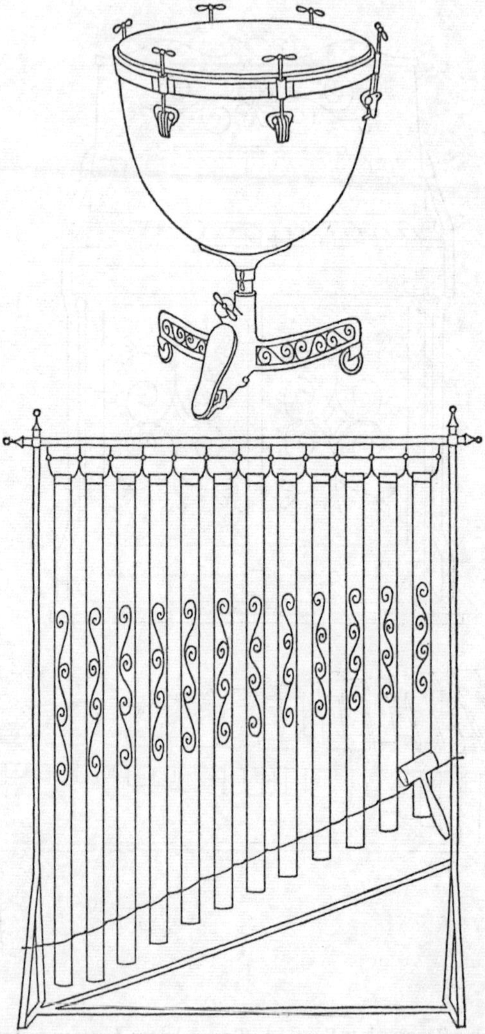

Fig. 9: The Percussion Section. *Top* kettledrum; *bottom* chimes.

real and vital purpose in the psychological and emotional effectiveness of the musical sound. In this category we find the SNARE or SIDE DRUM, BASS DRUM, CYMBALS, GONG or TAM-TAM, TRIANGLE, TAMBOURINE, CASTANETS, RATTLE, WHIP, and CHINESE BLOCKS.

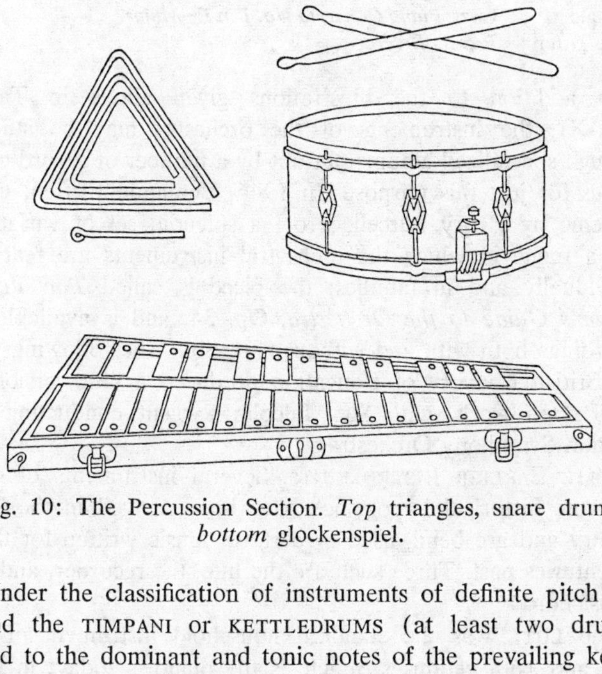

Fig. 10: The Percussion Section. *Top* triangles, snare drum; *bottom* glockenspiel.

Under the classification of instruments of definite pitch are found the TIMPANI or KETTLEDRUMS (at least two drums, tuned to the dominant and tonic notes of the prevailing key), CHIMES, CELESTA (tuned bars played from a keyboard), XYLOPHONE, GLOCKENSPIEL or ORCHESTRAL BELLS, and the MARIMBA. Musical examples of the more commonly used members of the percussion family are provided in Table XI below.

TABLE XI

Instrument	*Illustrating Composition*
Timpani	Haydn, *Symphony No. 103* ("Drum Roll"), first movement
Glockenspiel	Tchaikovsky, *Nutcracker Suite* ("Chinese Dance")

TABLE XI–Continued

Instrument	*Illustrating Composition*
Xylophone	Saint-Saëns, *Danse macabre*
Celesta	Tchaikovsky, *Nutcracker Suite* ("Dance of the Sugar-Plum Fairy")
Chimes	Tchaikovsky, *Overture 1812,* last section
Triangle	Liszt, *Piano Concerto No. 1 in E♭ Major*
Snare Drum	Ravel, *Boléro*

In addition to the illustrations given above in Tables VIII–XI, the instruments of the orchestra may be studied through specialized albums put out by a number of record companies for just this purpose. In 1946, Benjamin Britten, using a theme by Henry Purcell, wrote a splendid set of variations and a fugue in which the orchestral instruments are featured individually and in families; the piece is called *The Young Person's Guide to the Orchestra,* Op. 34, and is available on recordings both with and without narration. The following year the British Ministry of Education produced a film version of the Britten work, with Sir Malcolm Sargent conducting the London Symphony Orchestra.

SOME EARLIER INSTRUMENTS. Several instruments of considerable historical importance have been revived in the 20th century and are being used to perform music written for them in centuries past. Three such are the lute, the recorder, and the harpsichord.

The LUTE was the standard household instrument of the 15th and 16th centuries, much as the piano is today; in fact, performance on the lute was one important mark of a gentleman in the Renaissance age. It commonly had one single and five double strings tuned G-c-f-a-d′-g′, with a fretted neck and with a pegbox turned back at nearly a right angle. The strings of the lute were plucked with the fingers, producing a soft and gentle sound. The instrument, capable both of chords and runs, was used in solo performance or to accompany singing.

The RECORDER, OR STRAIGHT FLUTE–an end-blown flute with a "whistle" mouthpiece–played an important part in music of

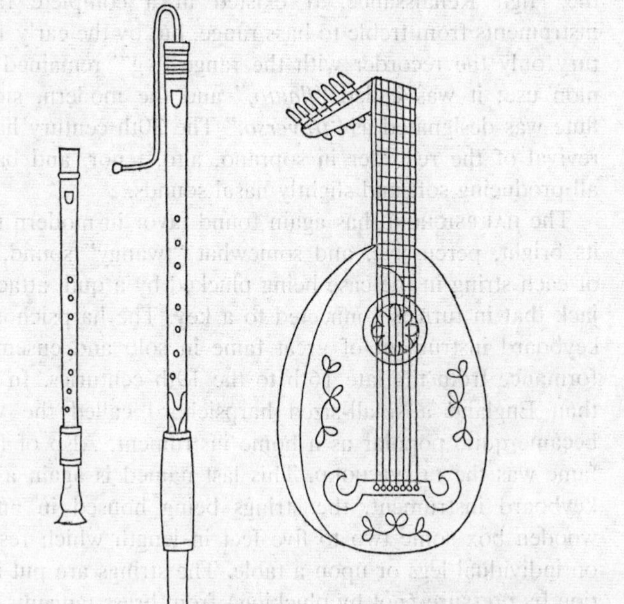

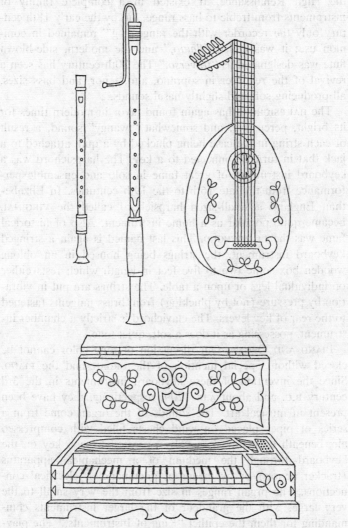

Fig. 11: Early Instruments. *Top* tenor recorder, bass recorder, lute; *bottom* clavichord.

the High Renaissance. It existed in a complete family of instruments from treble to bass range, but by the early 18th century only the recorder with the range f′–g‴ remained in common use; it was called "*flauto,*" and the modern, side-blown flute was designated as "*traverso.*" The 20th century has seen a revival of the recorder in soprano, alto, tenor, and bass sizes, all producing soft and slightly nasal sounds.

The HARPSICHORD has again found favor in modern times for its bright, percussive, and somewhat "twangy" sound, a result of each string in the case being plucked by a quill attached to a jack that in turn is connected to a key. The harpsichord was a keyboard instrument of great fame in solo and ensemble performance from the late 16th to the 19th centuries. In Elizabethan England a small-sized harpsichord called the VIRGINAL became quite popular as a home instrument. Also of historical fame was the CLAVICHORD. This last named is again a stringed keyboard instrument, the strings being housed in an oblong wooden box some two to five feet in length which rests either on individual legs or upon a table. The strings are put in vibration by pressure (not by plucking) from brass tangents fastened to the rear of key levers. The clavichord is strictly a chamber instrument, possessing as it does a soft, quiet tone.

PIANO AND ORGAN. Our discussion of tone color cannot be closed without special mention of the ORGAN and the PIANO. Since the invention of these keyboard instruments in the 3rd century B.C. and about A.D. 1709, respectively, they have been present in musical art. The sounds of the organ come from a series of pipes placed on wind chests filled with compressed air; beneath each pipe is a valve operated from a key on the keyboard through the medium of a mechanical apparatus (tracker action) or by means of pneumatic or electrical connections. The organ ranges in size from the very small to the very large, with the grandeur of the larger instruments commanding for them the epithet "King of Instruments." The playing console normally has from two to five keyboards for the fingers and a thirty-two-note pedal keyboard played by the feet.

The piano is also a stringed instrument, but, unlike the harp-

Fig. 12: Early Instruments. *Top* virginal; *bottom* harpsichord.

sichord or clavichord, the strings are put in vibration by being struck with felt hammers connected to an action controlled by the keys of the piano. The great success of the piano lies in its ability to regulate to a large extent the volume of sound produced, from *piano* (soft) to *forte* (loud); hence the full name of the piano: pianoforte.

CHAPTER 2

Texture and Style in Music

THE FABRIC OF MUSIC

The study of texture in music is concerned primarily with the number and disposition of voice parts in the composition. Many musical works have only a single line, while the other extreme can be found in Orazio Benevoli's polychoral Mass for fifty-three parts. These and other musical types will be discussed within the framework of the three species of musical texture: monophonic, polyphonic, and homophonic.

MONOPHONY. Monophony does not, strictly speaking, have a texture at all, since it is music of but a single line with no harmony present. However, custom decrees that it be treated as a textural type since the oldest music in the world is of the monophonic variety; primitive, Oriental, and Greek music all are monophonic. In the Western world monophony is represented in some three thousand melodic chants of the Roman Catholic Church; in the unaccompanied troubadour, trouvère, and minnesinger songs of the Middle Ages; and in the music of the medieval drama.

Certain presentations of monophonic music actually approach true textural possibilities through the use of DRONES (long sustained notes, usually found in the lowest part of a musical passage), and through HETEROPHONY, which may be described as an accidental or intentional decorative performance around and about the composed melodic line. What music of the monophonic type may lack, because of the absence of harmonic color, it makes up in the infinite rhythmic and ornamental procedures that may be applied to a single line unencumbered by accompanying parts.

POLYPHONY. The texture of many-voiced music (two or more voice parts) may be likened to the warp and the woof of a woven fabric, where the melodic, or horizontal, aspect of music is similar to the warp threads of the fabric, and the harmonic, or vertical, musical aspect is equivalent to the woof threads. It is this analogy that explains phrases like "the fabric of music" and "musical texture." Many-voiced, or polyphonic, music became a reality in Western culture after the 9th century A.D., and it has undergone a steady development since that time, with special emphasis during the Baroque era in the 17th century and again in our own contemporary music. Polyphony is also known as counterpoint or contrapuntal music. Counterpoint derives from an early Latin terminology *punctus contra punctum* ("point against point"), where the custom of using a point or dot to represent a note head led to the designation of "note against note."

Polyphonic, or contrapuntal, music is based on the idea that all the voices comprising the texture are of equal importance and should combine to form a unified whole. One very important technique used to achieve this unity is called IMITATION, and it is found in two styles, STRICT and FREE. The strict type, note-for-note and interval-for-interval, may first be seen in music of the late Middle Ages and is technically described as CANONIC IMITATION, which will be discussed further later. This type may perhaps be best illustrated through the round "Three Blind Mice," a round being a canon at the unison, which means that each successive initial imitative entry will begin on the very same pitch with which the first voice began.

FREE IMITATION (where the imitation is approximate, not exact) is a later and more useful procedure, and since its development in the late 15th and 16th centuries it has never ceased to play an important role in musical composition. Example 11 demonstrates free imitation as used in the opening of the Kyrie of William Byrd's *Mass for 4 Voices;* this entire ex-

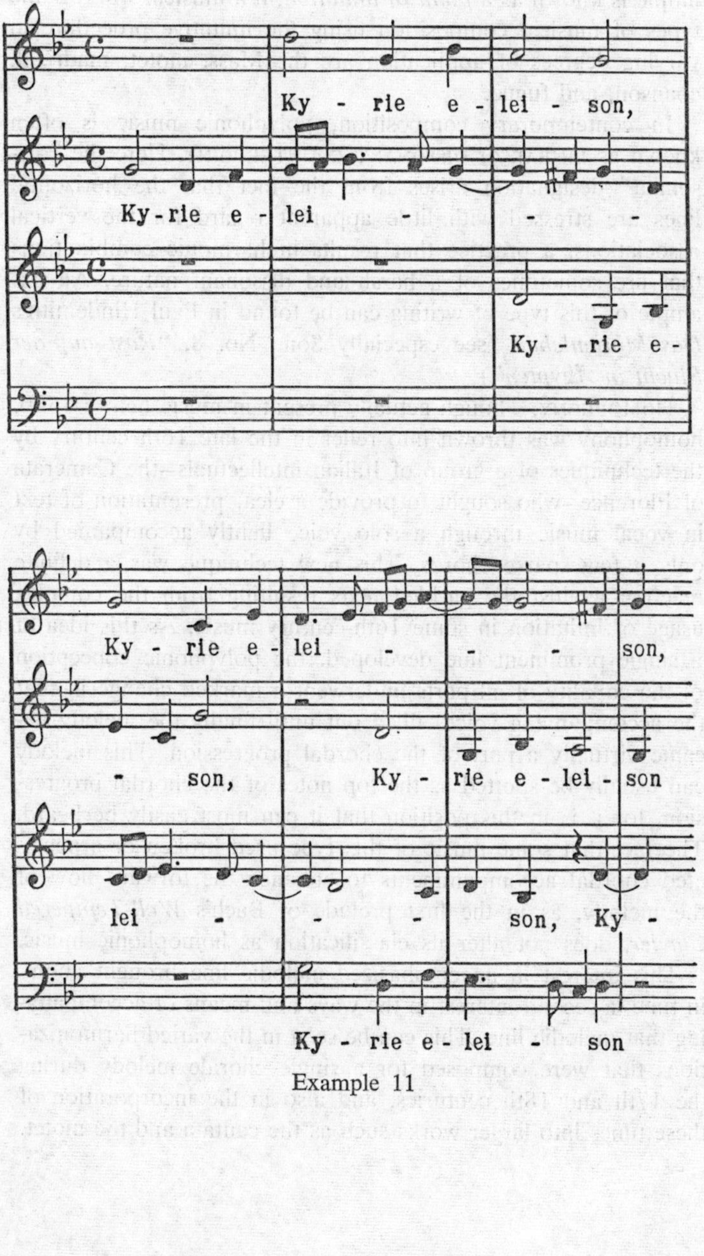
Ky - rie e - lei - son,
Ky - rie e - lei - - -
Ky - rie e -
Ky - rie e - lei - - son,
- son, Ky - rie e - lei - son
lei - - - son, Ky -
Ky - rie e - lei - son

Example 11

ample is known as a *point of imitation* in a musical work. Some types of musical composition using the imitative procedure in varying degrees of application are the Mass, motet, madrigal, chanson, and fugue.

In contemporary composition, polyphonic music is often known as LINEAR OR DISSONANT COUNTERPOINT. Here the "dissonant" designation arises from the fact that the horizontal lines are stressed with little apparent regard for the vertical associations, a practice that results in harmonic combinations that are sometimes of a harsh and dissonant nature. An example of this type of writing can be found in Paul Hindemith's *Das Marienleben* (see especially Song No. 8, "*Rast auf der Flucht in Ägypten*").

HOMOPHONY. Though actually present in music before 1500, homophony was thrown into relief in the late 16th century by the techniques of a group of Italian intellectuals–the Camerata of Florence–who sought to provide a clear presentation of text in vocal music through a solo voice lightly accompanied by only a few sparse chords. This new technique was a definite reaction against the garbled texts resulting from the complex usage of imitation in some 16th-century music. As this idea of a single prominent line developed, the polyphonic conception of the equality of all parts underwent a marked change in that the accompanying voices filled out until finally the melody became virtually a part of the chordal progression. This melody can usually be spotted as the top notes of the chordal progression, for it is in this position that it can most easily be heard. The fact that some music of this type used broken or arpeggiated chordal accompaniments to enhance the forward flow of the melody, as in the first prelude of Bach's *Well-Tempered Clavier,* does not alter its classification as homophonic music.

This interest in an emphasized melodic line brought about, in time, a second interest in the ways and means of accompanying that melodic line. This can be seen in the varied harmonizations that were composed for a single chorale melody during the 17th and 18th centuries, and also in the incorporation of these tunes into larger works such as the cantata and the motet.

Homophony may be found in such musical forms as hymns, opera, sections in certain symphonies, marches, folk songs, and indeed anywhere that a single, clear melody is desired within the texture. Example 12 illustrates homophonic texture as used

Example 12

by Joseph Haydn at the beginning of the second movement of his *Symphony No. 85* (*"La Reine"*). Writing here for the string section of the orchestra, Haydn assigns the borrowed melody of the French chanson *"La Gentile et jeune Lisette"* to the first violins, accompanying this melody with the rest of the strings.

Whereas some music may be classified as being specifically written in either a monophonic, polyphonic, or homophonic texture, a great deal of music combines two and perhaps all three of these types. Thus Example 13 demonstrates all three textures in excerpts from the one composition "As Vesta was from Latmos hill descending," a six-voice madrigal by Thomas Weelkes. The excerpt marked (a) shows briefly and appropriately the monophonic texture at the words "all alone"; (b) demonstrates polyphonic texture; and (c) illustrates homophonic texture.

SONORITY, a special attribute of texture, is based on the number, disposition, *tessitura* (see below), and color of the tones in the vertical association, and is related to the qualities of richness and resonance. With regard to NUMBER OF PARTS, vocal music of the 16th century, with its four to eight parts and

Example 13

a normal number of five, presents a more complete sonority than vocal music of the 15th century, where only three parts were normally used. Continuing with this reasoning, one can see that Benevoli's fifty-three-part Mass, mentioned above, should offer (and does) quite a sonorous sound.

Most essential to the type of sonority desired is the DISPOSITION OF TONES in the chordal pattern. This spacing is especially important at the cadences, where the music comes to rest and the harmony is more clearly presented to the listener. The four-part *Notre Dame Mass* by Guillaume de Machaut, written in the modal style of the 14th century, uses vertical fourth and fifth intervals that sound incomplete, vacant, and hollow; but a fuller sonority is attained at a later age by William Byrd in his *Mass for 4 Voices* when he uses harmonies erected in third intervals and builds his cadences with complete I-III-V triads.

Sonority becomes a problem at the extremes of range in both vocal and instrumental music. All voices and instruments have a certain TESSITURA—meaning a high, medium, or low pitch position in musical space—where they sound best; the study of vocal arrangements and of orchestration is based partly upon this fact. Textures tend to thin out and lose resonance in the higher registers, and to thicken and perhaps become "muddy" in the lower registers.

TIMBRE is the identifiable quality of a musical sound, such as bright, dull, thin, thick, etc. Any sonorous quality that is sought through the number of parts, their spacing, and their *tessitura* can be radically altered by the color of the voices or instruments used.

DENSITY, a condition relating to the thickness or compactness of sounds in music, is closely related to sonority. A dense or heavy texture can be observed and heard in the works of Brahms, Wagner, Richard Strauss, and Sibelius, whereas a less dense or lighter texture is apparent in the compositions of Couperin-le-Grand, Mozart, Mendelssohn, and in some music by Stravinsky. There is a current trend to refer to certain vertical conglomerates in modern music as densities rather than chords, since definition by chordal pattern in a logical sense is often difficult, indeed impossible, to establish in this kind of music.

THE QUALITY OF STYLE IN MUSIC

INDIVIDUAL STYLES. Style exists in any art as a characteristic manner or mode of expression; in music, style represents the total effect of a composition in a given situation at a given time.

In analyzing a piece of music for style one examines the handling of fundamentals (melody, rhythm, harmony, etc.) in relation to the intention of the music or the mood it seeks to invoke. As useful as this stylistic analysis is, and it does allow one to comprehend the piece as an artistic entity, it still is obvious that each work must be examined also in the light of its composer's whole body of work, its compositional and historical period, and its ostensible function. The knowledge gained from this extended manner of analysis reveals the stylistic differences between single works of a composer, a necessary step in tracing the relationship of the work to its historical age and to the entire history of the art. Thus a stylistic comparison of Beethoven's *Symphony No. 1,* written in the Classical style, with his *Symphony No. 9,* written in the Romantic style under the influence of the poet Schiller, will reveal both Beethoven's individual growth and the influences brought to bear upon him by historical changes in stylistic practices.

Unfortunately, it appears that the stylistic traits of the composer are more likely to be misinterpreted than those of creators in other fields. The style of a composer, made up as it is of his personality, his reaction to his environment, and other personal traits, is of course a style that is uniquely *his;* but whereas in letters (even drama), in painting, and in architecture the work from the artist's hand is directly available, in music so few people are able to read notation that a performer is needed to re-create the work before it can be appreciated. Clearly, the performer is responsible for studying style both in the larger and in the narrower sense, and also is obliged to acquaint himself with any special instruments, performance practices, or attitudes common to the age of the music he intends to perform. The listener, for his part, should acquire a knowledge of correct stylistic practices in order not to be deceived by a poor performance, and, naturally, in order to appreciate truly a good one.

Regional and national styles should also be taken into account. Oriental music, with its high development of melodic (often microtonal) and rhythmic ideas performed by instruments and vocal tones not in use in the Western world, presents a strange, exotic, and sometimes irritating sound to Occidental ears. Here style is a major problem, but it must be remembered that there are various styles in the Western tradition which are no less distinguishable, though less foreign. Spanish and Russian composers have maintained a musical idiom clearly bound up with the national heritage of their respective countries, and French, German, and Italian styles have a number of individual characteristics. For instance, there is a French technique in writing for and performing on woodwind instruments; the Italian *bel canto* method of singing is quite distinct; and the German concept of density and logical construction in symphonic works is not likely to be overlooked by even the casual listener.

STYLE DEFINED BY USE. In the Baroque era there arose a desire among composers to write specifically for a particular medium, in other words, to write one kind of music for a solo violin and another kind for an operatic soprano. Music before the 17th century had used voices and instruments more or less interchangeably on the polyphonic lines as the voice or instrument capable of singing or playing the particular line was available for use. But the rise of IDIOMATIC writing in the Baroque era created a new concept of style.

An immediate division that comes to mind when thinking about the different qualities of media is the one between vocal and instrumental music. The range, color, agility, and definite pitch of some instruments have given them the edge over the human voice in such functions as the use of an angular melodic line that requires wide and abrupt skips; musical patterns requiring great technical manipulation over a wide range; and the delineation of the more daring harmonic and rhythmic effects. On the other hand, a composer will write music of a highly ornamental nature in high *tessitura* for the light, flexible coloratura soprano, and will give the contralto a lower, smoother, less ornamental, more cantabile melody to fit her resonant, dark-hued voice. These examples show that style since the Baroque era has been definitely linked to the qualities of the medium used. A side-by-
4 side comparison of certain pieces from the *Fitzwilliam Virginal*

Book, performed first on a plucked string instrument played from a keyboard and then played on a piano, will quickly reveal that the virginal-type instrument is by far the best medium for this light-textured, highly ornamental music.

The textures of music discussed earlier in this chapter may also be interpreted in the light of stylistic practice. Thus monophonic, polyphonic, and homophonic textures may be just as freely discussed as MONOPHONIC, POLYPHONIC, and HOMOPHONIC STYLES, where the interest centers on the mode of presentation of music written in one or more of these textures.

Indeed, some musical "forms" are better discussed as STYLISTIC TYPES than as sectional forms. Under this category comes the FUGUE, the organization of which is described oftener as a contrapuntal procedure (style defined through texture) than as a form. It is next to impossible to find any two of Bach's fugues written in identical form, although they all follow a general contrapuntal technique. The TOCCATA, or "touch piece," consists of rapid passages to show off the organ or harpsichord performer's virtuosity, and it preserves the illusion of spontaneity with an extremely free formal organization. Despite the close association of recitative, arioso, and aria in opera, the first is of one style because of its declamatory nature; the aria is of another, which is dictated by the longer lyric phrases; and the arioso style stands somewhere in between. The rondo type (discussed more fully later) in instrumental music exists in a dual capacity. It is very definitely a sectional form, with its regular alternation of theme and diversion sections, and it is also very definitely a stylistic type, where its bubbling, playful, semiserious quality made it a happy choice for so many final movements of concertos and symphonies in the Classical period.

A style can also be influenced by the functional purpose of the music. As the serious musicians of the Middle Ages were invariably trained by the Roman Catholic Church, the Church saw to it that these educated talents composed music suitable for the various services of the Christian religion. In the 16th century considerable interest was expressed in court music, and much of the stylistic quality of English spinet, viol, and madrigal music was related to its courtly fashion in the reign of Elizabeth I. The work song is another interesting example of a functionally styled piece. Here the accent is on a single melody and form, with a strong, measured rhythm. When the railroads were first being built across the United States, music played a part in this giant venture through work songs; men laboring to fasten the rails to the ties used songs to provide the rhythm needed for them, working as a unit, to drive home the numerous spikes.

PERIOD STYLES. In the 20th century great stress has been laid upon the appreciation of music by period style, that is, the style that represents the sum total of political, religious, educational, economic, artistic, philosophic, and inventive forces in a given historical era. The historical periods in Western music are: Middle Ages, Renaissance, Baroque, Rococo, Classical, Romantic, Impressionistic, and Modern or 20th century or contemporary. Music scholars do not always agree on the specific terminal dates of these periods, mainly because of the difficulty in determining precisely the stylistic ending of one period and the beginning of the next; however, the terminology is still useful, and indeed necessary, as a point of departure in consideration of broad areas of musical style.

The MIDDLE AGES, dated from about A.D. 400 to 1400, can be said stylistically to have been dominated by two textural qualities; monophonic and polyphonic. Monophonic texture is represented, as mentioned earlier, by the chant of the Church and by the secular songs of the troubadour, trouvère, and minnesinger. Gregorian chant, so called after Pope Gregory the Great, is based on the eight Church modes and is ideally sung unaccompanied to Latin texts. This music, still part of a Roman Catholic service today, is nonmetrical, its rhythm deriving from association with the Latin text; the range of the chant is limited primarily to the octave. The secular monophonic types had melodies of wider range, were metrical in concept, used vernacular texts, and had a theoretical background prophetic of a much later age.

Polyphony, as previously noted, made its debut in church

music about the 9th century in a stylistic type called organum. Early organum, called "strict," began in two parts, with considerable parallel part movement. Later the style became freer, with the addition of oblique and contrary voice leadings. By the 12th century three voice parts were in common usage, with the octave, fifth, and fourth vertical intervals established as the correct consonances for strong beats. This construction produced the vacant, hollow sound typical of the harmonic element of the entire period. Triple meter was used almost exclusively in sacred polyphonic music, in deference to the Holy Trinity.

The 14th century brought about new and more involved rhythms, and also an interest in duple meter. Simple imitative patterns of a canonic type were used, and part songs of a secular nature developed. The harmonic interval of the third began to achieve theoretical standing as a consonance, and the fourth fell more and more into the dissonant category. Considering the period as a whole, the music is predominantly vocal and is based on the modal system. The polyphonal compositions of Léonin in the 12th century, of Pérotin in the late 12th and the 13th centuries, and of Machaut and Landini in the 14th century offer excellent illustrations of the part-music style of the Middle Ages.

In the RENAISSANCE, during the 15th and 16th centuries, vocal music, basically of a polyphonic texture, still prevailed, although instruments were freely used. Three voices were a favored combination in the first half of the 15th century, but after the establishment of a lower bass line about the middle of the century four voice parts were more commonly used; in the 16th century the parts reached a "norm" of five voices. Imitation, in the free manner, became a true element of style in the late 15th and 16th centuries. In the 16th century the octave, fifth, third, and sixth were the consonant harmonic intervals, and the dissonant second, fourth, and seventh intervals were given very special treatment under a system later dubbed the "Palestrina style," which made possible a free-flowing movement and a harmonious blend, still based on modality but showing obvious signs of the rapidly approaching tonal system. The Church remained the focal point of music, but the interests of the Renaissance man in the world about him produced entertaining madrigals and chansons in the secular literature of the period. Guillaume Dufay of Burgundy, Josquin des Prez and Orlandus Lassus of Flanders, Giovanni Pierluigi da Palestrina of Italy, and William Byrd of England were leading composers of the Renaissance.

The BAROQUE age (*c.* 1600–*c.* 1750) saw the establishment of the tonal system and the introduction of homophonic texture into music. As a matter of fact, polyphony and homophony joined hands within the tonal framework and brought about a new type of compositional style called HARMONIC COUNTERPOINT. Soprano and bass parts rose to cardinal importance, with melodies being the property of the soprano, and the bass line, called the *basso continuo,* regulating the harmonic structure. Freer dissonant treatment produced harmonies of dramatic intensity which found use in the new forms of opera, oratorio, and cantata. Instrumental music, characterized by discontinuity and short sections in the 17th century, achieved in the late Baroque a fuller and more complete unity, coupled with compelling rhythms of a strong and driving nature. The performance of string music was enhanced by the marvelous instruments made by artists such as the Amati family and Antonio Stradivari; indeed they made the finest stringed instruments the world has ever known. Musical literature of the period includes string works by Arcangelo Corelli and Antonio Vivaldi; English operas and service music for the Anglican Church by Henry Purcell; operas and oratorios by George Frederick Handel; and almost every form and type of music known in Baroque art (save that of opera) by Johann Sebastian Bach.

Before the end of the Baroque era a new style arose in France called the Rococo. The Rococo expression entertained the courtly life of the 18th century with its wit, gracefulness, polish, and ornamentation. Within its thin, delicate texture a highly decorated soprano line sang to the barest accompaniment of an inconsequential nature. In France the programmatic harpsichord and ensemble works of François Couperin stirred up fanciful titles; in Germany the corresponding style (*empfindsamer Stil*, "the basic and natural feelings") was heard in the works of Georg Telemann and Johann Quantz.

The fifty years from 1750 to 1800 produced the CLASSICAL period, which is vital for the development of symphonic, piano, and chamber music. The symphony orchestra was here standardized, and the string quartet conceived. Music underwent a change of emphasis from harmonic counterpoint to pure homophony; it is marked in this period by clear and regular musical phrases, simple but sound harmonic and rhythmic structure, and the development of closed musical forms, the most perfect of which was the sonata form. It was a period of objectivity in humanistic endeavors, revealed in music through the masterworks of Christoph Willibald Gluck, Franz Joseph Haydn, Wolfgang Amadeus Mozart, and Ludwig van Beethoven.

The great ROMANTIC age was the 19th century. Musicians of this period were impatient with the rules of the Classical era and showed instead an intense subjectivity in composition and performance. Homophonic texture remained in vogue along with some of the Classical forms, but when the latter were used they were expanded and varied, and with this expansion of formal treatment came the enlargement of the symphony orchestra. The Classical orchestra consisted of the full string family combined with a small group of wind instruments, numbering in all about thirty players, and to this the Romantic composers added quite a few more winds. New mechanisms such as the Boehm system for flute and clarinet, the Heckel system for bassoon, and the Lorée system for oboe permitted these instruments to assume a more important position in symphonic music. As a result of the increase in both the numbers and the importance of woodwinds and brasses, the latter now equipped with either piston or rotary valves, more string instruments were added to maintain a correct balance, and the size of the orchestra grew to some hundred or more players.

The Romantic artist emphasized the emotional quality in

art; he coupled a renewed interest in nature and the simple life with an apparent desire to escape from reality, by choosing, as he did, many of his themes from the remote past. The Romantic age was also an age of virtuosity in music, producing some of the first great concert pianists and violinists. The opera and symphony developed greatly, but not to the exclusion of the small forms (miniatures) in piano and song literature.

The color possibilities of the enlarged Romantic symphony orchestra were matched by increased harmonic resources; altered seventh and ninth chords were found with increasing frequency, along with a greater use of chromaticism and nonchordal tones. A flood of chromaticism near the end of the century was to break down tonality in much the same way that a similar flood had destroyed the modal system at the close of the 16th century. There are a great number of fine Romantic composers, but the height of Romantic style can be seen in the piano works of Frédéric Chopin, Robert Schumann, and Franz Liszt; the symphonic compositions of Hector Berlioz, Felix Mendelssohn, Schumann, and Liszt; and the music dramas of Richard Wagner.

The music of Claude Debussy launched the IMPRESSIONISTIC style, which was in vogue from about 1890 to 1920. It remained almost exclusively a French style, although some musicians in Italy, England, and the United States composed music of similar nature. Debussy and his followers employed whole-tone and pentatonic scales for coloristic effects; the modes again found favor, and the archaic practice of the consecutive movement of fourth and fifth harmonic intervals was revived. Traditional formal constructions and developmental techniques were abandoned, and the lightly touched dissonances of the Impressionistic harmonies tended to dissolve into one another and float away without resolution into consonant stability. Color was an important attribute of the style, as can be seen in the superb handling of the woodwinds, sounding in conjunction with the glitter of the harp.

Two terms, expressionism and neoclassicism, have been much used in connection with MODERN music. EXPRESSIONISM not only relates to music but also refers to drama, art, and the dance; it proposes to express by objective means the subjective feelings of an individual or group. This style has come to be associated with the 20th-century musical art that has shown a distinct and definite cleavage with the past, and it is best illustrated by the compositions of the Viennese school of Arnold Schoenberg (the founder) and his pupils Alban Berg and Anton Webern. NEOCLASSICISM implies simplification of material, form, and medium—Classical idealism clothed in 20th-century harmony, key schemes, orchestration, and melodic terseness. The French group "Les Six," of which the best known are Arthur Honegger, Darius Milhaud, and Francis Poulenc, abide by the principles of clear outlines and precise meanings in their art, and Igor Stravinsky, one of the greatest composers and pathfinders of the present century, was considered a member of the neoclassic camp from the time of his *Octet for Wind Instruments* (1923) until the 1950's.

A strong trend in national feeling in the modern age has been manifested in the use once again of folk material in serious music. The outstanding Hungarian composer Béla Bartók published nearly two thousand folk tunes drawn chiefly from Hungarian and Romanian sources, and used many of these melodies in his compositions along with new themes of his own. In like manner, Ralph Vaughan Williams successfully combined folk and art music in England, as has Aaron Copland in the United States.

Contemporary stylistic practices reveal how meter and rhythm have undergone really extensive development, resulting in a complexity of style and an increased difficulty of performance. Polymetric music, music without bar lines, and the frequent change of meter within the composition have altered a previous concept of regularity in rhythmic flow. Chord progressions are no longer bound to a functional plan, and modern counterpoint, using angular melodic lines, emphasizes linear movement with but little regard for the harmonic associations. The 20th century also brought about a move toward the destruction of the concept of a single immediate tonality. Polytonality was introduced early in the century and atonality followed soon after. The use of polytonality, atonality, extreme dissonant harshness, and at least the semblance of discontinuity are all manifestations of the age.

Most recently, interest in musical composition has been centered in TOTAL SERIALIZATION. This style seems to be a sequel to the twelve-tone method originated by Arnold Schoenberg around 1923. The Schoenberg procedure extended only to an ordering of twelve different pitches to be adhered to throughout the composition, whereas the new idca of serialism takes into account such additional musical qualities as timbre, articulation, dynamics, and time; that is, the duration of the individual sounding elements and their interrelation one with another. Also, electronic music, produced by mechanical means like the RCA Electronic Sound Synthesizer, has become a controversial topic of contemporary music.

THE FORMS OF MUSIC

Metaphorically speaking, form is the mold into which content is poured. This is not a true image, however, as artistic creation is a far more organic process than this simplified picture would indicate. Yet, granting that the separation of form from content is more a convenience than a reality, still it is helpful to speak about musical forms as a means to understanding the organization of music. Musical forms in general possess two basic qualities: repetition and contrast, or, put another way, unity and variety. As music is a time art, it needs repetition to establish unity and coherence, while at the same time it must provide contrast to prevent dullness.

When a text is set to music, the unity of the composition is more or less established by the association of words with the musical elements, and the formal problems are not so great, though even here repetition is often employed. Still, words do permit a style in which there is no repetition ("through-composed"), as in Schubert's *"Der Erlkönig,"* which is perhaps the most faithful way to render a text. As music for instruments alone (without text) became more popular, however, the problem of the retention of the musical scheme in the listener's mind presented itself more forcibly. The composer found that he needed something that would give shape to his ideas, as a painter's canvas gives dimension and limit to his ideas; he saw a sort of "mental canvas," or musical mold, if you will, as a basic necessity. Form was needed to ensure that a musical work would be both coherent and interesting, that it would in its completed state have unity, variety, coherence, balance, and proportion.

In almost every stylistic period of Western music certain schematic forms become established as compositional molds, and composers select from these to suit their musical ideas. Naturally, any one of these schemes marks only a point of departure, and serves to regulate only in broad terms the artistic desires of a composer. For ease and clarity in discussion, we will examine the many conceivable forms under a few broad categories. Musical works may be classed as written in OPEN form, where no section of the piece is repeated with any exactitude later in the composition, or in CLOSED form, which implies a repetition of a preceding part; works in open form are also said to be in CONTINUATION OR ADDITIVE form. In speaking of continuation form, it has become the custom to use the word "procedure" for "form," and this designation will be adopted here; thus the forms to be discussed in the rest of the chapter are: procedural method, variation forms, sectional forms, compound forms, and free forms.

THE PROCEDURAL METHOD: IMITATIVE TYPES. The two general classes to be described here as "procedures" are called imitative types and *cantus firmus* types. The first of the imitative group is the CANON, from the Greek word for "rule." (The reader is referred to the discussion on "strict imitation" earlier in this chapter.) Canon is a polyphonic construction in which all voice parts employ the same melody throughout; the intervals of the lead voice are exactly repeated in another part at a later time in the same or a different pitch, while the opening voice continues. This is the strictest type in the imitative procedure. The lead voice is called *dux,* and the following voice or voices, *comes.*

Here is a list of ways by which canons can be identified:

1. Interval of imitation of *comes*.

2. Augmentation (*comes* in notes of doubled value) or diminution (*comes* in notes of halved value). See the two-voiced canons each at the interval of the octave in Example 14 and Example 15.

Example 14

Example 15

3. Contrary motion or inversion. See the two-voiced canon at the third in Example 16.

Example 16

4. Retrograde, cancrizans, or crab (the crab walks backward), where the *comes* sings the melody from end to beginning.

5. Round (*comes* at the unison).

6. Mixed, in which notes not directly related to the *dux* and *comes* are added. Many examples may be found in Bach's *Goldberg Variations* (BWV988).

Canons have been used in music from about the 13th century onward. Composers do not often write them as separate compositions, but generally employ them as sections of larger works, since the strict style usually forbids extensive development. However, the beautiful, free-flowing canon between the two instruments in the last movement of César Franck's *Sonata for Violin and Piano in A Major* demonstrates how the supposed limitations of the procedure can be transcended.

The 15th and 16th centuries saw other types of composition which were written in imitative style; they were the motet, the Italian and English madrigal, the French chanson, and the German lied. These polyphonic vocal works were sung "ideally" without accompaniment (although instruments may double, or substitute for, voice lines) and were primarily dependent on their words for the formal scheme. The texts were of vital importance, not only in the organization of the music, but also for their association with the music in tone painting (text painting)—that is, the heightening of the text through pictorially related musical phrases, a feature all these Renaissance types had in common. It was a happy period for the combination of good literature and good music.

The 16TH-CENTURY MOTET is a short religious composition, with a Latin text drawn usually from the Book of Psalms; it is used in the Roman Catholic service, chiefly at Vespers, but it is nonliturgical in that it is not assigned a specific position in the Christian church ritual. Toward the end of the 15th century, the imitative treatment of certain portions of the text resulted in points of imitation throughout the composition. This important technique, along with a forward-moving flow achieved through overlapping cadences, gave rise to the designation "motet style," a term to be applied later to any music of any form written in this manner. Josquin des Prez's *Ave Maria* (see MM, No. 19) depicts this motet style clearly, with points of imitation in all four voices beginning in measures 1, 13, 23, 29, 46, and 58. When the motet form later acquired English words, it became known as the ANTHEM.

During the Renaissance a great many Flemish musicians

traveled to Italy, where they were charmed by the simple Italian folk-song-like pieces called *frottole;* to these the Flemings applied their advanced knowledge of contrapuntal techniques and thus created the ITALIAN MADRIGAL. These secular songs of high quality, with Italian texts, became one of the principal musical types of the early 16th century. By nature they were less severe than the motet, and the delightfulness of their imitative procedure and the skill with which their composers used text painting have ensured the popularity of the madrigal down to the present day. The Italian madrigal was the direct inspiration for the ENGLISH MADRIGAL, of the late 16th and early 17th centuries. The polyphonic and homophonic styles alternate freely in the madrigal, as may be seen in Thomas Weelkes's famous English madrigal "As Vesta was from Latmos hill descending," from which a few excerpts have been seen in Example 13. The English madrigal has been written and published also under other titles, such as songs, ayres, canzonets, and sonets.

The chanson and polyphonic lied are the French and German counterparts, respectively, of the madrigal. They exhibit the same close union of music and poetry found in the other Renaissance vocal types. The CHANSONS, composed chiefly on amorous subjects, display sections in imitative style as well as homophonic passages utilizing repeated chords, and are also noted for their sharp, clear rhythms. One characteristic rhythmic formula of considerable importance is the pattern 𝅗𝅥♩♩, with which most of these songs begin. The voice parts are constructed in short, sectional phrasings that, unlike the motet, often end together in well-defined cadences. These cadences, like those of the late English madrigals, frequently demonstrate inclination toward the soon to be realized tonal system. Thomas Crequillon's *"Pour ung plaisir"* (MM, No. 20) is a good example of many of these points.

A special type of chanson called the DESCRIPTIVE OR PROGRAM CHANSON became quite popular in the early 16th century. The program chanson utilized many notes in quick, repeated-note patterns and, as the name indicates, was adept in describing many activities of daily life in the 16th century. Of considerable fame was Clément Janequin's *"La Guerre,"* supposedly written about the Battle of Marignano (1515), which became the model of many succeeding "battle" pieces of the 16th century and later times.

The German POLYPHONIC LIED ("Lied" in general specifies German solo song literature and is not under discussion here) never achieved the lightness of texture and style of the madrigal and chanson, as steady, robust melodies and sturdy harmonies combined with the heavy, guttural sounds of the German language gave greater weight to the music. This solemnity of purpose is shown in the German part song *"Zwischen Berg und tiefem Tal"* (HAM I, No. 87), composed by Henricus Isaac.

Two imitative types not so well known or so often heard today are the instrumental *ricercare* and *canzona.* Both merit attention here on their use in the 17th century, and for the fact that they serve as the forerunners of later forms of great importance.

The RICERCARE, the immediate predecessor of the fugue, was the instrumental reincarnation of the motet. This is not surprising when one realizes that the *ricercare* is an early instrumental form, and that all music of this type developed out of the established song and dance literature of the preceding centuries. In adopting motet procedure, the *ricercare* made use of three or four themes in a succession of imitative points, using either the instrumental ensemble or a keyboard instrument. Composers using a keyboard instrument gradually reduced the number of themes employed until finally a monothematic *ricercare* evolved in a style displaying the scholarly and dignified attributes of the motet. The stately *ricercari* of the great organist of St. Peter's, Girolamo Frescobaldi, laid the true groundwork for the fugue, as may be seen in his *Ricercar dopo il Credo* (MM, No. 34); the name indicates that this piece was to be played after the Creed in the Roman Catholic Mass.

The CANZONA is derived from the French chanson, and also appears under such names as *canzona francese* and *canzona alla francese;* it is styled also for keyboard or ensemble. The *canzona,* stemming from the secular chanson, reveals in comparison with the *ricercare* a livelier and sunnier style; the beginning 𝅗𝅥♩♩ pattern of the chanson is retained by the *canzona.* In contradistinction to the *ricercare,* the *canzona* is a more sectionalized form, and therefore serves as the progenitor of the multimovement plan of the later *sonata da chiesa,* or church sonata. A *canzona* by Andrea Gabrieli is based on Crequillon's chanson *"Pour ung plaisir";* this derivation is aptly illustrated in MM Nos. 20 and 21, where the two compositions are arranged side by side. This illustration also reveals the manner of ornamentation idiomatic to the keyboard—ornamentations that are added to the original vocal lines and are mainly neighboring notes, passing tones, turns, and divisions in lesser-note values.

The last imitative type to be given here is the FUGUE. Unlike the earlier forms discussed, the fugue is a purely instrumental form. It is the acme of imitative procedure. (It has long been used in musical examinations to determine the doctoral candidate's ability to write in the contrapuntal style.) The "fugue" comes from the Latin *fuga,* meaning "flight," and may be interpreted as the flight of a theme through a maze of contrapuntal lines. The structure of a fugue may be broadly viewed as two asymmetrical parts: exposition and development. In a monothematic fugue the EXPOSITION opens with the SUBJECT (theme) announced alone in any voice part, immediately succeeded by the ANSWER in another voice at the interval of a fifth above or a fourth below. While the answer is played, the first voice continues as a counterpoint to it. If this continuing counterpoint assumes a character of importance and remains consistently allied with the theme throughout the fugue, it is called a COUNTERSUBJECT. Normally, when all the voices for which the fugue is written have stated the theme once, the exposition is closed. However, two circumstances may extend the exposition proper: (1) an EXTRA or REDUNDANT ENTRY, or (2) a COUNTEREXPOSITION. The extra entry occurs when there still is a desire to state the subject in the original, tonic key before the development begins. A counterexposition is a second exposition, immediately following the first, in which the voices enter in a different order; this second exposition may be partial or complete, according to whether only a part or all of the voices participate. As an illustration, a normal exposition of a three-voiced fugue is given in Example 17.

Example 17

The rest of the fugue after the exposition is called the DEVELOPMENT; it is by far the larger of the two parts. In this section the fugue theme usually appears in keys other than the tonic, but generally in near-related keys. Here, also, the theme may be subjected to the contrapuntal devices of augmentation, diminution, and inversion, as described earlier in connection with the canon. Near the end of the fugue the theme will reappear in the tonic key. This is usually a signal for a building of intensity, at which time a STRETTO, meaning "close" or "contracted" in Italian, may be introduced. In the fugue it is a passage where the theme is imitated in close succession, a second voice entering before the first voice has completed the theme (see Example 18). Also near the end a dominant or tonic PEDAL POINT may be introduced in which the dominant or tonic notes of the original key hold for quite some time without much regard for the harmonic associations (except at the beginning and the close of the passage). The composition may be lengthened at the very end by a CODA; the word is derived from the Latin *cauda,* meaning "tail," and it signifies the addition of a few bars or a passage of music to the end of a piece to make a more effective and satisfying conclusion. In the fugue the coda follows a final statement of the subject in the tonic key.

Any passage in the fugue which does not state the theme is called an EPISODE. Such passages may draw bits of material or ideas from the subject or countersubject, and may, especially in the development section, exhibit sequential treatment (a sequence being a few immediate repetitions of a short musical phrase at pitches other than the original). The primary function of the episode is to change keys and to render afresh the theme upon its restatement. Bach's *Well-Tempered Clavier* (BWV846–93) contains fugues that have long been the models for fugal study, but it must not be thought from this discussion that fugues are necessarily dry or pedantic; of those in the *Well-Tempered Clavier,* some have a gaiety and charm that make them a real pleasure to listen to.

THE PROCEDURAL METHOD: CANTUS FIRMUS TYPES. Most

Example 18

of the CANTUS FIRMUS musical types—the second classification under procedural method—arose in sacred music through the use in larger works of either Gregorian chant or the Protestant chorale. A *cantus firmus* (literally, "firm song") is a pre-existent melody that is used as the basis of a polyphonic composition. It can be considered a melody line (in earliest form a fragment of Gregorian chant was used) to which other, freely composed parts are added. The use of a *cantus firmus* starts with the beginning of part music, in the already mentioned organum.

The meaning of the word itself is obscure, but the style began with a plain-song phrase in the tenor voice paralleled note-against-note by a second voice, at the lower fifth or fourth. This strict organum could be performed in a four-voice composite manner by doubling the parts at the octave. The use of the melody in the tenor voice actually gave that part its name, for "tenor" is from the Latin *tenere,* meaning "to hold"—that is, to hold the melody.

In the 11th and early 12th centuries the style became freer, with the second voice (*duplum*) still following note-against-note but introducing oblique and contrary motion. In the late 12th and early 13th centuries schools of music at St. Martial and at the Cathedral of Notre Dame in Paris cast the *cantus firmus* in long-note values in the tenor, writing the upper voice or voices (up to three added voices were sometimes used) with each syllable extended in long, florid, stepwise, melodic lines ("melismas"). As the complexities of part writing increased, a plan of rhythmic control was devised under a system of rhythmic modes, and the whole procedure became an orderly and often quite graceful composition.

Out of the organum style of the 13th century arose the first authentic musical form—the MEDIEVAL MOTET. This was accomplished by the addition of *mots* ("words") to the *duplum;* through this process the *duplum* acquired also the designation of *motetus,* a name finally adopted for the entire composition. The tenor still employed a *cantus firmus,* usually a chant from a gradual, alleluia, or responsorium which was identified by the first word or syllable of the Latin text of the borrowed chant phrase. All voices were now subjected to the control of the rhythmic modes, but whereas the principal type of 13th-century motet was a religious, three-voiced, polytextual form with two different (yet related) Latin texts, there gradually developed a use of a French text in one of the upper voices, bringing about a polylingual, secularly tinged piece. This eventually spread to a freely composed (not borrowed) tune in the tenor and the use of a vernacular text in all voices, and in this form the motet became a completely secularized composition. This entire development of music from the beginning of organum through the establishment of the medieval motet can be seen by observing the examples in HAM I, Nos. 25–35.

The establishment of the Protestant Church in the 16th century provided its musicians with *cantus firmi* in the nature of chorale tunes for use in their extended musical compositions. Improvisations by Lutheran organists on chorale melodies, prior to the singing of these tunes by the congregation, finally developed into written-down versions called chorale preludes. These gradually formed into a number of specific types as used in the Baroque period, five of which are given below:

1. Motet style, where each line of the chorale tune serves as the subject of a short fugal development.
2. Pachelbel style, so named after the composer who made such great use of this procedure. His practice was to write a lengthy beginning in fugal style, using only the first line of the chorale melody as a subject. Later in the composition he would introduce the entire chorale tune in long-note values as a *cantus firmus* accompanied by the other voices of the prelude.
3. Ornamental style. Here the chorale melody is used throughout, but ornamented with added notes and figures, and is often intertwined in an almost unrecognizable manner with the accompanying parts.
4. Figured style, that is, the chorale tune presented clearly as a *cantus firmus* without alteration, but accompanied in the other parts by a rhythmic figuration not related by motive to the chorale tune.
5. Partita style, where the harmonized chorale serves as the basis for a series of well-marked variations.

The chorale prelude has remained in the organist's repertoire since its inception, and Protestant organists still make great use of it in their church services.

Variation Forms. Variation forms, like those of the procedural type, may also be classed as open forms, with each variation in the nature of an added section. This type of writing, established as a form in the 16th century (perhaps derived from Oriental dances, which still use the variation technique today), has always enjoyed great popularity, and it was so widely used during Baroque times that that period has been called the "Age of the Variation." Modern composers have again found the variation forms ideal for organizing their compositions in the linear contrapuntal style.

Many Baroque compositions used the technique of variations written over a BASSO OSTINATO (literally, "obstinate bass") or GROUND BASS. This consisted of a melody being repeated again and again in the bass voice, the composer using his ingenuity in contriving new harmonies, or variations, over repetitions of the bass. The name GROUND was given to such a composition, as Henry Purcell's piece for harpsichord *A New Ground,* where five different melodies are written over ten statements of the *ostinato* (MM, No. 38).

Two special types of Baroque variations were the PASSACAGLIA and the CHACONNE. Composers have used these titles interchangeably, but the forms are perhaps best illustrated and explained by Bach's organ *Passacaglia in c minor* (BWV582) and his chaconne from the *Partita No. 2 in d minor* (BWV-1004) for unaccompanied violin. The passacaglia begins with an eight-bar theme given out alone in the bass voice in 3/4 meter. There follow twenty statements of the theme, each accompanied by a different harmony; however, the theme is not always heard in the bass, and it appears several times in a highly ornamented fashion. In the chaconne the harmonized four-bar theme is stated at the outset in a dotted, sarabande rhythm in triple meter. Some sixty-three variations are based on the harmonic functions of this theme. The variations appear in three large groupings: the first in *d* minor, the second in the parallel key of *D* major, and the third again *d* minor. Viewed in the light of these two compositions, the passacaglia would seem to be based on a melody or ground, and a chaconne on a harmonic series; but not all passacaglias or chaconnes lend themselves to such an easy classification.

The THEME AND VARIATIONS form is yet another variation type based upon the principle of a clearly presented melodic theme with accompanying harmonies modified by either a few or many following variations. This form differs from the types just discussed in that it is more decisively sectionalized; the theme and each succeeding variation is more of a unit, each having its own conclusive ending cadence. The theme-and-variations form developed in the Spanish and English 16th-century keyboard schools, and later it was much used and much admired in the homophonic music of the late 18th and 19th centuries.

The themes used as the basis of this form in the Classical period were usually not longer than thirty-two measures consisting of simple, harmonized melodies cast in either binary or ternary form (see below for a discussion of these forms). The homophonic-styled themes build up from musical motives through phrases and periods (and sometimes double periods) into parts or sections. A motive is only a few notes in a characteristic rhythmic pattern; motives expand into the phrase, which is commonly four or eight measures in length; a period is a symmetrical balance of one phrase (antecedent) against a second (consequent) and a double period is a balancing of two periods.

As an example, consider the theme and variations found in the second movement of Haydn's *Symphony No. 85* (*"La Reine"*). The theme is the first twenty-two measures of the movement. The very first two measures of the piece show two motives—one of three notes and the other of five—that are essential to the construction of every phrase in the entire theme. Again at the beginning, the two motives expand into a four-bar antecedent phrase that is followed by a four-measure consequent phrase; this two-phrase period is the whole first part of the theme. A six-bar phrase begins the second part with a little reworking of the first phrase of Part 1, following which a period construction completes the theme.

The theme of a theme-and-variations scheme may be modified by any musical variation, but some means of identification with the original theme must be maintained. Until the end of the 18th century this was done by retaining the same key, or at least the parallel major or minor key, and by retaining the shape of the theme in a number of measures. The common means of thematic variation included melodic, harmonic, rhythmic, and coloristic changes; tempo alterations also were often used, and a march or dance pattern might be imposed upon the theme to give it a special character. In the Haydn movement mentioned above, the first variation is a rhythmic one; the second is modal (the key changes to the parallel minor); the third is a patterned modification in which the flute adds an obbligato figure or accompanying part, and the fourth and last variation is a melodic one with ten bars of coda at the end. The structure of the theme is basically retained in all variations, and the tonic key of *E*♭ major is used in all save the second variation. This form was said to be Haydn's favorite among musical schemes.

SECTIONAL FORMS. Two of the simple structures among sectional forms are the binary and ternary. The BINARY (two parts) uses a scheme represented by the letters AB, with both sections repeated. Thus the binary plan may be heard as AABB, but this does not alter the basic two-part scheme of the form. The harmonic formula, particularly after 1700, involves a modulation from the tonic key to the dominant (or to the relative major if the tonic key is minor); the second half begins in the dominant and, working with thematic or rhythmic material related to the first part, eventually finds its way back to the tonic. The two parts may be symmetrical, with both approximately equal in length; or asymmetrical, in which case the second part is considerably longer; or they may be constructed in such a manner that a portion of the first part reappears in the second without a very noticeable change, which gives the entire form the name ROUNDED BINARY.

The TERNARY scheme can be represented as ABA, but this may be heard, through repetition markings, as AABABA. In this form each section assumes more status as an independent unit, with the B part standing in sharper contrast to the A sections, and the second A part making a complete and unmistakable return to the material of the first A part. Because of the great use of this form in song literature, it is often called a SONG form. The distinction between the ternary and the rounded binary lies primarily in the degree of contrast in the B section and in the ternary form's complete return of the second A to the first. As an example, the courante (a quick dance measure) in J. J. Froberger's *Suite in e minor* (MM, No. 35) is in a symmetrical binary form, whereas the *Sonata in c minor* by Domenico Scarlatti (MM, No. 42) is clearly in rounded binary (as can be seen by comparing the last three measures each of the A and B sections). The tenor aria "If with all your hearts," from Mendelssohn's *Elijah,* is a short and easily understood ABA, albeit the return of A is somewhat modified and shortened. In it the contrasting B section begins at measure 20 and moves into a new key, and the returning A section at measure 37 goes back to the tonic key.

The sectional forms known as rondo and sonata form are more complex in their make-up. The RONDO form involves a regular return of the opening theme (REFRAIN) following each of several contrasting sections called EPISODES. Two schemes common to the 18th and 19th centuries were ABACA and ABACABA. Each letter represents a section of the piece, these sections often being cast in either binary or ternary form in their own right. A coda usually completes the work, and the final A generally extends into the coda as thematic material for the ending. The whole is generally arranged in a duple meter and has a rollicking rhythm, the refrain sounding in the tonic key and the episodes in near-related keys. The episodic material may or may not be related to the refrain, and the refrain may sometimes return in a modified repetition. The joining of the sections is an important feature of the rondo, and one of the delights for the listener lies in recognizing the manner by which the composer works from the episodes back into the refrain.

The ABACA scheme can be demonstrated by turning again to Haydn's *Symphony No. 85,* this time to the last movement. The theme, or refrain, is a symmetrical ternary form of 8-8-8 measures. The refrain returns are clearly heard at measures 70 and 164, and the episodes show dependence on the materials of the refrain. The linking passages between episodes and refrain are beautifully done, and the final A furnishes the thematic material for the coda, beginning at measure 190. The last movement of Beethoven's famous *Pathétique Sonata,* Op. 13, exemplifies the more extended scheme ABACABA. The refrain returns each time in the tonic key of *c* minor (at measures 62, 121, and 171), with the episodes in related keys; the return of B is cast in the parallel tonic key of *C* major. A coda begins in measure 193 and draws only briefly from the refrain theme.

The SONATA FORM is perhaps the most important of all single-movement musical forms. It has been estimated that over two-thirds of all movements of symphonies, concertos, and quartets written since the last quarter of the 18th century have been composed in some type of sonata form. It generally consists of three large sections: exposition, development, and recapitulation.

As the sonata form was developed in the last half of the 18th century in the homophonic tradition, the purpose of the EXPOSITION was to "expose" the themes of the movement in conjunction with their tonal associations, for the concept of duality of keys was as important a point as the contrast of the themes themselves. In the Classical period, if the opening theme of the exposition appeared in a major key, it was customary to write the second theme in the dominant major, but if the composition began in minor, the second theme was sounded in the relative major; passage between key centers was affected by a modulating transition or bridge section.

Also, it seemed appropriate to begin with a sturdy, energetic opening melody (a "masculine" theme), contrasting this with a graceful, songlike second melody ("feminine" theme). Sometimes the *same* theme was used in both positions, and the only contrast was one of key, proof that the use of two different tonal centers–duality-of-key concept–was of basic importance in the exposition. As the plan grew in scope, the first and second themes enlarged into groups of melodies, although retaining their first and second designations through the traditional key relationship. Frequently the final melody of the second group took on special importance as a closing theme, often working its way into a little codetta at the close of the exposition, much in the same manner that the final A dissolved into the coda in the rondo. The exposition is repeated in practically all the early works using this form, the purpose being to impress the thematic material of the movement upon the ear of the listener.

The DEVELOPMENT, or working-out, section allows the composer to show his ability to manipulate the themes of the exposition (particularly the first melody); and hence it is the real "idea" section of the form. Among the popular means of development are thematic fragmentation, the use of keys sometimes rather far removed from the tonic key, and the combination of themes or motives from the exposition or their treatment in a fugal style. Sequential formulas are also often used. On the whole, the developmental possibilities are limited only by the nature of the ideas the composer wishes to introduce and by the duration of the section.

Toward the close of the development section the way is prepared for the return of the tonic key and the RECAPITULATION. This final segment of the sonata form primarily restates the exposition, but with a few important differences. Probably the most important change is the return of the second theme or theme group in the tonic key, for plans must now be made to close the movement in the same key in which it began. Of course, the purpose of the transitional passage between first and second themes is not to modulate, or change from one key to another, but merely to connect. A coda of small or large dimensions is always possible (and very probable) for the concluding part of the movement, as is a slow INTRODUCTION at the very beginning of the movement. It should be again stressed that this and all musical forms are sketched here in only the broadest of outlines, and each such scheme is always subject to modification by the composer. Some 20th-century composers have exactly reversed the order of thematic entries in the recapitulation, producing a procedure called ARCH form or BOW form.

The classic example of sonata form is the opening movement of Mozart's *Symphony No. 40,* K. 550. The first theme begins immediately in *g* minor with a sturdy, rhythmic swing; a transitional passage begins in measure 28, terminating on the dominant chord of *B♭* major in bar 42. The second, feminine theme begins in measure 44 in the relative major key (*B♭*) and works into a codetta (at bar 72) utilizing a closing theme. The double bar and dots mark the exposition for repetition, at the conclusion of measure 100. Sequential treatment of the first theme, coupled with a long working-over of the opening motive of that theme, moves a splendid development from a beginning in the distant key of *f♯* minor to the recapitulation in the tonic key at measure 165. The main feature of the recapitulation is the contrapuntal material in the nonmodulating transitional passage between themes. The coda begins at measure 260 and completes the movement with an extended version of the exposition codetta.

Before leaving this discussion of structural forms, a word should be said about the combination of sonata form with the ABACABA rondo type. When this occurs, the C of the rondo takes on the nature of a development section and the exposition-development-recapitulation of the sonata form is expressed in the rondo scheme as ABA-C-ABA. This distinctive form is known as a SONATA-RONDO, and an example of it is the last movement of Beethoven's *Concerto No. 5 for Piano and Orchestra,* the "Emperor" concerto.

COMPOUND FORMS. The compound forms do not present any new structural schemes as such, but merely combine a number of single-movement forms into larger compositions of several movements. The most famous of such groupings is the SONATA. (This compound type in three or four movements is not to be confused with the single-movement sonata form, just discussed.) In the Classical period one use of the sonata is found in the four-movement works like the SYMPHONY and QUARTET. Table XII illustrates the possibilities of construction of these multimovement compositions.

TABLE XII

1st Movement (Allegro)	*2nd Movement* (Adagio)	*3rd Movement* (Dance)	*4th Movement* (Allegro)
Sonata form	Sonata form	Minuet-trio-minuet	Sonata form
	Binary	Scherzo-trio-scherzo	Rondo
	Ternary		Sonata-rondo
	Theme and variations		Theme and variations

The almost invariable use of the sonata form in the first movement of the sonata has given rise to its alternate names, FIRST-MOVEMENT FORM and SONATA-ALLEGRO FORM. The last name is derived from the combination of sonata form with a movement in ALLEGRO (fast) tempo, but this is actually a misnomer, for, as the table shows, this form may also be used in an ADAGIO (slow) second movement. The minuet-trio-minuet (or scherzo-trio-scherzo) is actually a compound of two minuets (the trio is only another minuet), each of which may be in a binary or ternary form. The repetition of the first minuet completes the large ABA pattern of the entire movement. Occasionally the second and third movements of the sonata may be switched in the four-movement sequence. Haydn wrote his *Symphony No. 85* in sonata form, theme and varations, minuet and trio, and rondo form with respect to the four movements.

The Classical SOLO CONCERTO is a compound work in three movements (fast-slow-fast), utilizing a soloist accompanied by an orchestra. The last movement is usually in rondo form; and the first movement in a modified sonata form as follows (each step is illustrated by the corresponding measure numbers of the first movement of Mozart's *Concerto in G Major for Piano and Orchestra,* K. 453):

1. First exposition by the orchestra alone, centering in the tonic key (measures 1–74).

2. A second, normal exposition involving both soloist and orchestra (measures 75–171).

3. An extension in the nature of a codetta by the orchestra (measures 171–81).

4. Normal development and recapitulation, as in a symphony, with soloist and orchestra (measures 182–319).

5. A second extension by the orchestra, coming to a pause on the tonic triad with the fifth of the chord in the bass, in other words on a second inversion of the tonic chord (measures 319–27).

6. A CADENZA, a section played by the soloist alone and used in the concerto to display the technical abilities of the performer. Early in the history of the form the cadenza was improvised by the performer; later the composer wrote it down, but it is still not included in the measure numbers.

7. A short coda for orchestra alone may be added (measures 328–49).

The concerto, as a three-movement type, does not use the dance form as employed in the symphony.

The Baroque CONCERTO GROSSO is a multimovement form without any set number or type of movements. The solo element is a group of performers (usually two violins, cello, and harpsichord, although other instruments may also be used) called the CONCERTINO; the accompanying unit is a small string orchestra, with perhaps a few winds added, variously called the *concerto grosso, tutti,* or *ripieno.* In the first and last movements *ripieno* and *concertino* more or less alternate in the use of thematic material, somewhat in the nature of a rondo, with the exception that the refrain (called here the *ritornello*) is apt to return in different keys. For an example see the first movement of Handel's *Concerto Grosso in C Major,* for oboes, strings, and *continuo* (MM, No. 43).

The SUITE is the last compound instrumental form to be discussed here. The Baroque suite consisted of a group of single-movement stylized dances, each in binary form and in the same key. The basic number was four: allemande (in a dignified duple meter), courante (fast triple meter), sarabande (slow and stately triple meter), and gigue (lively compound meter), as shown in Froberger's *Suite in e minor* for clavichord (MM, No. 35); between sarabande and gigue were often added optional dances such as the gavotte, minuet, and bourrée. Frequently a prelude preceded the entire suite. A different type of suite arose in the 19th century, in which the movements were arranged from operas and ballets—the composer's attempt to provide more opportunities to play, at least in part, his hard-to-stage larger works. Tchaikovsky's suite from his *Nutcracker* ballet music is a famous example of this.

COMPOUND VOCAL WORKS. The compound vocal works of music exist in large-scale compositions such as the Mass, the oratorio, the Passion, the cantata, and the opera. The MASS has been a prominent part of Western music since its establishment in the early history of the Roman Catholic Church. The ritual of the Mass, the most solemn service of the Church, is summarized in Table XIII.

TABLE XIII
HIGH (SUNG) MASS

Intoned or Spoken		*Sung or Chanted*	
Proper	*Ordinary*	*Proper*	*Ordinary*
		1. Introit	
			2. Kyrie
			3. Gloria*
4. Collect			
5. Epistle			
		6. Gradual	
		7. Alleluia or Tract	
8. Gospel			
			9. Credo
		10. Offertory	
11. Secret			
12. Preface			
			13. Sanctus and Benedictus
	14. Canon		
			15. Agnus Dei
		16. Communion	
17. Postcommunion			
			18. Ite, missa est or Benedicamus Domino
	19. Last Gospel		

* Omitted in seasons of Advent and Lent.

Except for the Gloria, as noted, Nos. 2, 3, 9, 13, and 15 of Table XIII would be sung at every High Mass throughout the year. Therefore, composers chose this group as the vehicle for their musical settings, and thus the Mass as a musical form contains the Kyrie, Gloria, Credo, Sanctus, Benedictus, and Agnus Dei.

The Mass was a form of major importance in the late Middle Ages and in the Renaissance. At that time it was often polyphonic in texture, involving a *cantus firmus* that borrowed one or more melodies from Gregorian chant or even from secular sources such as the French chanson. In the Baroque age and afterward, orchestral accompaniments were sometimes added, as well as movements in fugal style or as arias involving soloists. The length and number of sections increased, as may be seen in the twenty-five separate movements in Bach's great *Mass in b minor.* Fine musical settings of the Mass are still being written by composers today.

The oratorio, cantata, Passion (that is, as described below), and opera were all established in the 17th century. The first three of these are for the most part religious works performed without staging, scenery, or costumes. They may make use of recitatives, ariosos, arias, solo ensembles in the nature of duets, trios, quartets, etc., choruses, and the orchestra.

The ORATORIO is a large dramatic work, usually with a biblical story related by a narrator singing in recitative style. Extensive use of the chorus is a feature of this form. In the long line of oratorio composition stand such well-known works as Handel's *Messiah,* Haydn's *Creation,* and Mendelssohn's *Elijah.*

The CANTATA is shorter in length when compared with the oratorio, and is inclined to be more concerned with commentary than with narration. The cantata does appear in both sacred and secular types. Johann Sebastian Bach alone composed about three hundred cantatas, of which some two hundred are extant; most of these are sacred, *Cantata No. 140* (*Wachet auf*) being a famous example. However, approximately twenty of his cantatas are secular, written for weddings and civic, university, and court performances, and these were often staged in the manner of a Baroque operatic scene, as for instance Bach's "comic operetta" the "Coffee Cantata."

The PASSION is an oratorio type, but with a text based specifically on the writings of one of the biblical evangelists Matthew, Mark, Luke, or John. Both the sacred cantata and the Passion make great use of the Protestant chorale melodies in their compositional structures. Again, Bach's *St. Matthew Passion* is perhaps the finest work of its genre.

The OPERA is one of the most popular forms in the field of music. It is staged, often elaborately so, with splendid sets and costumes, and with actors and actresses who are some of the finest singers in the world of vocal music. Constructed in acts and often based upon dramas, the librettos can be legendary, historical, politically tinged, serious, or comic. The form offers a wealth of opportunities for singers in its solos and ensembles, as well as in its choruses. The ballet is an important part of numerous operas (particularly the French), and some of the orchestral music of opera has been of such quality as to find its way into the symphonic repertoire for concert performances.

FREE FORMS. There are still many pieces of music that build their schemes of unity and variety on means other than those already discussed. Only a few of these can be mentioned here. The PRELUDE, for example, has no set plan or procedure, but relies on some large, general idea of unity achieved perhaps by a motivic or rhythmic pattern maintained throughout the work (see Bach's preludes in the *Well-Tempered Clavier,* BWV-846–93). Sometimes an idea or a description of a person, place, or thing is all the unity that a composition needs. Quite a revealing (and not altogether impossible) piece of music is Marin Marais's *Tableau of a Gall Bladder Operation,* written to be played by a viola da gamba and harpsichord. A few sentences, spoken from time to time as the music unfolds, give a detailed account of the surgical procedure. Description became of major interest in 19th-century symphonic music when Franz Liszt introduced the SYMPHONIC POEM; here the object of the work was to present by musical sounds in mood or fact the outlines of a "program," or a story synopsis. Liszt's most famous orchestral work of this type was his *Les Préludes,* based on a program inspired by the composer's readings from the *Méditations poétiques* of Alphonse Lamartine.

PART TWO

Primitive Music and Music of the Middle Ages

CHAPTER 3

Primitive and Early Music

PRIMITIVE AND EARLY CIVILIZED CULTURES

BEGINNINGS OF MUSIC

The origin of music is lost in a maze of ancient myths and legends. However, a number of interesting theories have been advanced as to the nature of its beginnings.

First, although man has placed himself at the head of the animal kingdom, the primitive human being lived only a few notches above the next in line of the species. Therefore his interest in a musical interpretation of the sounds of other creatures, while natural, was essentially limited, for his next of kin does not sing even the slightest of melodic lines. Possibly the most tenable part of this theory is the emphasis it puts upon singing, for singing must be considered the initial method of music making. Man is born with the instrument for singing, and in the musical evolution of all high civilizations vocal music occupies first place.

Another and perhaps more tenable theory (involving also rudimentary singing) postulates the rise of music from the spoken language—intensified speech—and its association with bodily movements. We know that pitch was a factor in the meaning of early speech; the Bantu languages of Africa and the early spoken languages of China, India, and Japan show such a relationship. It seems likely that in associating language with some kind of melodic or rhythmic pattern, as in cantillation, or chant, the words receive added projection, staying power, and emotion. There can be little doubt that the poetry and music of primitive man hardly existed one without the other, and indeed they included bodily movements, too, as the dance also was of major importance in the origin of music. Admittedly, it is difficult to associate this theory of the language derivation of music with the whispering, humming, yelling, and general noisemaking inherent in the singing style of primitive man, and so all the theorizing about the origins of music must remain, for the present anyway, speculative and inconclusive, but the *relation* of music to primitive life points to another and perhaps more productive topic.

Music has long been associated with religion, and in primitive peoples it had a strong connection with magical forces. Early man employed music, too, in the community aspects of his work, play, and war. When he built his dwellings or performed other such group activities, music established a medium for the rhythmic effort necessary for the task at hand, and when the labors of the day ended, surely dancing and singing provided relaxation and a change of pace. Also, certain tribal dances, accompanied by instruments and singing, expressed definite ideas; for example, if war was imminent, there was a type of music designed to boost courage and stimulate desire for action. Thus music played an integral rather than an incidental role in the life of primitive man.

The earliest melodic formations can be distinguished by those that move along a scale and those that skip about in disjunct fashion. Examples of the former can be found among the songs of the Patagonian Indians and of the Botocudos of East Brazil, where a melody of two conjunct notes sounds in patterns indefinitely repeated. This idea of repetition, found also in primitive poetry, is a mark of all early music, and in fact it has never lost its place in the art, for it may be discovered in all music of the world down to the present day. Later a natural evolution brought about melodic patterns of three and four notes; when all such two- to four-note melodies embrace mainly conjunct relationships (with only a few narrow skips) and are sung without emotional stress, they are classified as LOGOGENIC, or word-born. On the other hand, as music was used to portray more passionate feelings, the ranges of melodies covered more or less a full octave and employed wide leaps quite freely. Such music, PATHOGENIC, has been found among primitive tribes in Australia and in music of the Hopi Indians in the United States. The wide middle range of melodies between the temperate logogenic and the emotional pathogenic types is known as MELOGENIC, music characterized by a flexible but even melody.

The rhythmic patterns of primitive music also range from the very strict to the very free. Strict rhythms are associated primarily with instruments and the dance, while free rhythms are employed in ceremonial rituals like the medicine man's driving out of evil spirits. The strict dance rhythms show varying degrees of sophistication from the simple, equal drum strokes used by the American Indians to the complicated cross-rhythms and dynamic shadings produced by African drummers.

It is commonly believed that primitive music consists of a single melodic line; heterophony, whether by chance or by intention, is admitted, but it is not meant to imply polyphony or homophony in the Western sense, nor is parallel singing at the octave taken as anything more than the simultaneous singing of the two adult sexes. However, it is difficult to discount fully the possibility of at least a rudimentary use of polyphonic practices, and investigation has produced evidence in Africa and the Caroline Islands of singing in parallel thirds, fourths, and fifths, and even short canonic passages.

The musical instruments of primitive man fall into three groups: those that can be beaten, scraped, or shaken; those that are plucked; and those that are blown. Among the first group are to be found the slit drum (see MITA, No. 25), stamping sticks used to beat the ground during a dance, a pair of bamboo tubes of different lengths to strike on sheets of water, and all types of rattles to be shaken by hand or affixed to the body. The earliest drums were constructed by binding a skin over a tube, gourd, or bowl.

Stringed instruments, which form the group to be plucked,

remained quite undeveloped in early music, though a very primitive type, the hunter's bow (MITA, No. 18), can be found. Finally, the wind-blown group includes flutes of bone and clay with three or four finger holes (MITA, No. 34), and long, trumpet-like instruments of wood or cane. These, together with the human voice, comprised the main musical instruments of primitive man.

ANCIENT MESOPOTAMIA

The beginnings of musical art among civilized people appear to have come in Mesopotamia (now Iraq). The Sumerians built a large temple in each of their cities and in these temples they sang hymns to the gods; by the 21st century B.C. there is some evidence that there was responsorial singing between priest and choir and alternate ("antiphonal") singing between choirs. Flutes, drums, and other percussion instruments were in use, and excavations in the royal tombs of Ur have revealed a lyre, a sistrum (a rattle-type instrument), a double cylindrical reed pipe, and two kinds of harps.

During the period of Babylonian rule the temple service was expanded (beginning around 2000 B.C.) from a single hymn or psalm into a complete liturgical service, and the services themselves began to include female singers and to make use of processional pomp. With Assyrian domination in the first millennium B.C. came the development of secular music. At that time musicians became members of royal households, performing at banquets and other functions, and they became persons of some repute because of their artistic abilities.

ANCIENT EGYPT

Egypt rivals Mesopotamia in the long line of civilization, and the use of common musical instruments in both lands indicates mutual contact from very early times. The Egyptians, too, gloried in their temples, where ceremonials were daily occurrences and priests accompanied by instruments chanted praises and supplications to the gods. Unfortunately the music was oral and none of it remains in notated form today. The harp was their most important musical instrument, and all sorts of clappers and rattles were used along with it.

Since the Pharaohs were priest-kings, temple music and court music were closely linked. All court musicians were highly respected, as in the Assyrian civilization, and they sang and danced to the harp, flutes, and reeds. Monophonic music was the rule, with the harp perhaps accompanying the melody with the octave, fourth, and fifth intervals.

During the last three centuries B.C. the Greek and Roman cultures penetrated into Egypt, and it is believed that the Alexandrians were the teachers of the Greeks in music.

JEWISH MUSIC

In the earliest times of civilization in Mesopotamia and Egypt, Semitic tribes of nomads and shepherds lived between these two countries. During the course of the 2nd millennium B.C., these Hebrew tribes were to make their way into Palestine by conquest and enter into a sedentary phase of agrarian life. This new life inspired work songs of field and vineyard and songs of war and triumph.

From the time of Saul, first king of Israel (1050–13 B.C.), the court had its musical performances; the Bible tells how David soothed Saul's troubled thoughts by singing songs accompanied by the lyre. Under King David's reign, which followed Saul's, Israel became a large and strong nation, with Jerusalem its capital. It was at Jerusalem, about the year 950 B.C., that David's son and successor, King Solomon, built the first temple. Although the Lord did not allow David to build the temple, tradition says that David, himself a composer, performer, and inventor of musical instruments, planned the ritual music for the morning and evening sacrifices and for the religious festivals throughout the year. He appointed the men of the Levi tribe to have jurisdiction over the music of the services, and the first psalms were probably sung in the temple by the Levites and the priests. This psalm singing may have been accompanied on the KINNOR, a lyre retained by the Jews from their nomadic days and known to the Greeks by the name *kithara.* The silver trumpets (HAZOZERAH) and the ram's-horn (SHOFAR) were used in the temple as signaling instruments—that is, instruments to announce the entrance of the priests or the beginning of the service. Other temple instruments were the angular harp (NEVEL), the timbrel (TOPH), and the copper cymbals (ZELZELIM or MEZILTAYIM).

There is reason to believe that some sort of responsorial and antiphonal styles existed in the temple psalm singing, if only in a minor way. Congregations may have responded quite simply at first to the priestly chant with an amen or an allelula, with refrains repeated later on. At least one psalm—Psalm xxiv—seems designed for antiphonal singing; here the setting calls for the posing of questions by one choir, stationed inside the temple, with the answers coming from a second choir, outside, waiting to be admitted. But all this came to a temporary halt with the destruction of the temple and the overthrow of the Jewish state by Nebuchadnezzar, king of the Chaldeans.

The Israelites came out of the Babylonian captivity and returned to Palestine during the time of Persian domination; a second temple was erected about 514 B.C., albeit this sanctuary had little of the glory of Solomon's former temple. Once again the old temple instruments were used, and in due time others were added to them: the double oboe (HALIL) and a small but powerful pipe organ called MAGREPHA (the Hebrew name for the Greek HYDRAULIS, invented in the 3rd century B.C.). The Levites and the congregation resumed and extended the singing of the psalms in the responsorial and antiphonal manner that was to serve as the forerunner of the chant style of the Christian church. However, since there was no royal court, there was no resumption of court music, and the final blow was dealt to Jewish temple music when the second temple was sacked and burned by the Romans, under Titus, in A.D. 70. Shortly thereafter began the dispersion of the Jews.

With the second and final destruction of the temple its instrumental music largely disappeared. However, the chanting of the prose sections of the Bible, known as cantillation, survived and became the foundation of the synagogical service. Signs (TA'-

AMIN, meaning "accents") written above or below the text indicated certain melodic formulas to be sung, and these symbols may have been the basis of the neumes (see Chapter 4, section on Gregorian chant) later used in the early Christian hymns.

The cantillation of the prayers is also quite ancient in practice, but the melodic formulas were not this time indicated by signs; rather for each service there existed a traditional melody type. This prayer motive, however, served only as the skeleton of the chant, and around this was woven a free and highly intricate vocalism. These freely extemporized songs are called HAZANUT, the word being derived from *hazan,* the name of the precentor who chants the prayers. This method of singing represents the embellished style commonly associated today with Jewish chant.

With the temple gone, the synagogue took over the functions of worship and a new liturgy gradually developed as the authority of the Levites slowly gave way to that of the rabbis. Besides the chanting of prose from the Holy Scriptures and the singing of psalms and prayers, there also existed the melismatic performance of spiritual songs. These must have been some sort of spontaneous outburst on the part of the congregation; it may have been the beginnings of the many songs based on the word "alleluia." The rabbis forbade the synagogical use of all instruments except the shofar (which is still in use in the synagogue today), ostensibly as a sign of mourning for the loss of the temple, but it may have also meant the fear of secular contamination. Whatever the reason, this ban was also applied to instrumental music in the services in the early centuries of the Christian church.

Neither the first synagogues nor the early Christian church used choirs in their services; an honorary precentor sang the music in the synagogue, with a PSALMISTA, or cantor, serving a like function in the church. Choirs did, however, become part of Judaism around the middle of the 7th century A.D., when students of the Talmudic academies of Babylon formed a chorus; and the monastic orders of Christendom accounted for a similar development in the Christian church.

A great Jewish culture involving hymn poetry arose in Spain following the Islamic conquest of that country. This hymnody proved to be a rich inspiration for synagogical composers and cantors from 900 to 1400. These Jewish musicians absorbed all the musical techniques of the late Middle Ages and entered with full confidence into the changing style of the 15th century. Their polyphonic compositions used melodies borrowed from a Roman Catholic background, and combined them with Jewish melodic formulas inherent in their own faith. Jewish motets of the mid-15th century were comparable to those of the great Guillaume Dufay. But the closing decade of the century saw the expulsion of the Spanish Jewry (Sephardim), and their dispersement overseas, to the Low Countries and along the Mediterranean coast, and thus what had promised to be a fruitful blend of Occidental and Oriental musical thought was brought to an end.

GREEK MUSIC

From the poetry, drama, and philosophy of ancient Greece we know that music played an important part in the lives of this people. Unfortunately there is almost no Greek music in existence from which we can build a history of its development.

Song and poetry were closely linked, and minstrels connected with aristocratic households sang in a recitative style. Their accompaniments were played on the lyre, also used as a solo instrument, and the aulos, a double-reed wind instrument. The late 6th century B.C. saw the rise of the Greek drama, musicodramatic works showing a close synthesis of poetry, music, and the dance, designed to be staged in outdoor amphitheaters. This music was primarily choral.

The early Greeks looked upon music as a cosmological phenomenon in which sounds and rhythms were controlled by the laws of all creation. During a later age—the time of Plato and Aristotle—the philosophers concerned themselves with the effect of music upon man's emotions—the basis for the Greek doctrine of ethos—and the way in which music could be used for the training of man's mind or soul.

Greek musical theory was some six hundred years in the making. The foundation of Greek theory is the tetrachord, which is composed of four notes in a descending pattern (rather than ascending, as in modern practice), of which the two outer notes always stand in the relationship of a perfect fourth; this interval provides the basis of nearly all musical systems, and it may have come to the Greeks, as we suggested earlier, from ancient Egypt. There were three types of tetrachords (GENERA): the DIATONIC, composed of two whole tones and a half tone; the CHROMATIC, with an augmented second (or extra long step) and two half tones; and the ENHARMONIC, utilizing a major third (or double step) and two quarter tones (see Example 19). Actually the interior intervals of these three tetrachords

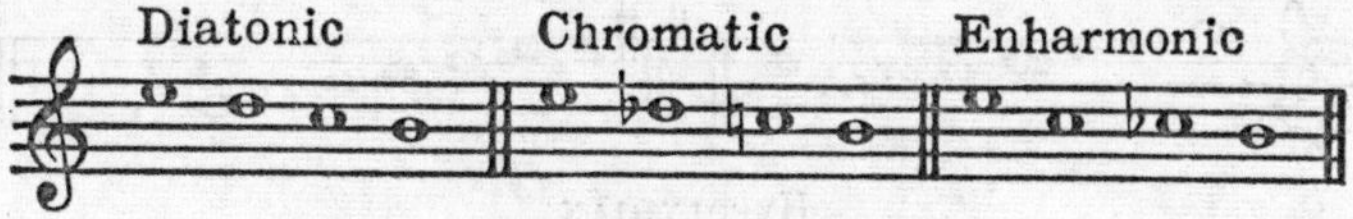

Example 19

have been spelled out in too concrete a fashion; they must be considered only as approximate pitches, for only the encompassing perfect fourth was absolute, and thus microtonal intervals did exist–tones foreign to scalar formations in Western theory. Eventually a two-octave scale–descending, as were all Greek scales–including all the basic notes (either theoretical or practical) necessary to Greek music was contrived by a conjunct and disjunct arrangement of four diatonic tetrachords plus an added note; this scale was known as the Greater Perfect System, and is shown in Example 20.

Example 20

Two theories predominate regarding the Greek modes. The first specifies seven different octave species of half- and whole-step arrangements, similar to the Church modes of the Middle Ages; this system can be found in the writings of many Greek theorists, beginning with Aristoxenus (4th century B.C.; his only extant work is a three-volume musical treatise, *Elements of Harmony*). The normal range of performance on a Greek lyre was about an octave, and, as far as it is possible to ascer-

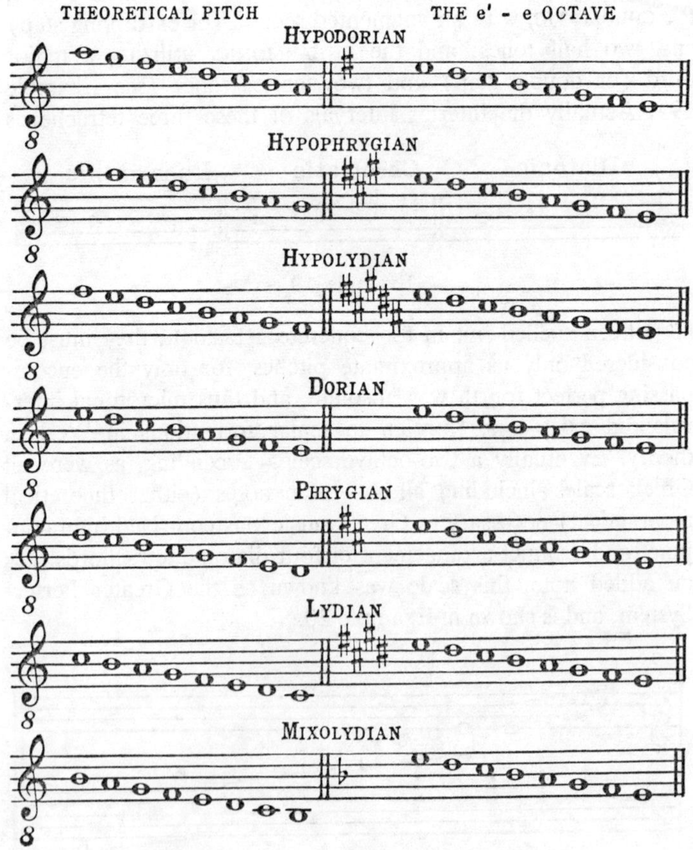

Example 21: The modes of Aristoxenus.

tain, the e′–e octave (the eight notes of the Dorian mode) was that range, one that was also the most suitable for the average male singing voice. The Greek modes, as exemplified in this theory, are shown in Example 21, along with the transpositions (except for the Dorian) to the characteristic e′–e octave. The ethos of a mode, in this case, is related to the tone-semitone (T-S) pattern of each individual mode.

A second theory regards each of the seven octave patterns

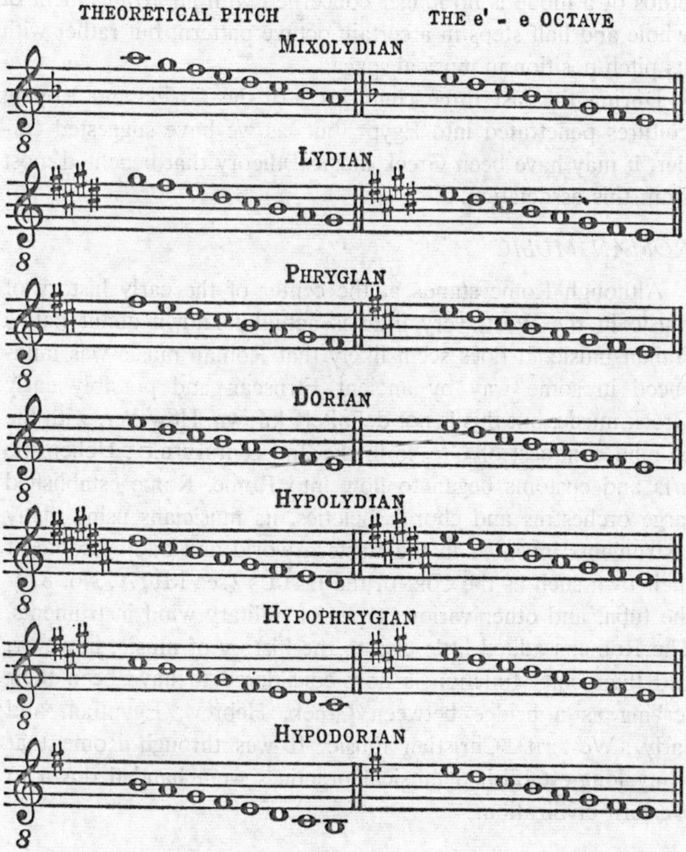

Example 22: The modes (keys) of Ptolemy.

as a Dorian T-T-S-T-T-T-S pattern, but with each beginning at a different pitch level; the mathematician and astronomer Ptolemy was one who held this viewpoint in his book, *Harmonica* (2nd century A.D.). Thus, in the light of the present-day concept of key, this theory would present a mode and a key as an identical phenomenon. Example 22 illustrates this second concept of mode and shows also how the notes of each of Ptolemy's keys would be arranged in the e′–e octave. Here the ethos of a mode is no longer concerned with an arrangement of whole and half steps in a certain octave pattern, but rather with its pitch position in musical space.

During the last three centuries B.C. the Greek and Roman cultures penetrated into Egypt, but, as we have suggested earlier, it may have been Greek musical theory that benefited most from this association.

ROMAN MUSIC

Although Rome stands at the center of the early history of music in the West, very little is actually known about native Italian music. It does seem likely that Roman music was influenced in some way by ancient Etruscan and possibly early Greek music, but this is not definitely known. However, with the Roman conquest of Greece in the 2nd century B.C., Hellenistic arts and customs began to flow into Rome. Rome established large orchestras and choral societies, its musicians using many instruments invented in the Eastern world and adding some of their own such as the CORNU, the LITUUS (see MITA, No. 87), the tuba, and other various types of military wind instruments. The Romans added little else to the history of music, however, and their chief function is now considered to have been their serving as a bridge between Greek, Hebrew, Egyptian, and early (Western) Christian music. It was through Rome that many long-established musical practices were handed down to Western civilization.

ORIENTAL MUSIC

While Oriental music, spanning some five thousand years of development, represents an art certainly comparable to Western music, it is strikingly different in that it concentrates primarily on the elements of melody and rhythm. Occidental music, on the other hand, since the 9th century A.D. has been most concerned with harmony and counterpoint, and even though Oriental musicians may occasionally use some minor polyphonic traits, these in no way approach the contrapuntal usage of Western music.

Eastern musicians excel in the intricacies of melodic formations, rhythmic subtleties, tonal shadings, and ornamental devices, and their melodies are generally conceived in a five-tone (pentatonic) scale, the basic scale of all Eastern music. Two special problems attend the present-day study of Oriental music, however: first, the vast reaches of time over which it has developed and of which we have little information; and, second, the lack of a satisfactory notational system because Oriental music, particularly Far Eastern, has been passed on aurally rather than written down. However, an exact notational system might have proved detrimental to this kind of music, for much of its charm rests in the wonderful nuances of the melodic line—a style that, if transmitted by a positive notation, would appear extremely cumbersome and not at all in keeping with the exotic sounds. Perhaps the only analogue to this style in Western art music is the Gregorian chant, where the Church has always maintained that the written notation represents only an *approximate* pitch. Still, Oriental music has tenaciously retained much of its historic traditions, and modern recording devices have been able to render the aural tradition virtually as stable and as accessible as if it were written down.

From the foregoing it is plain that Western and Oriental music have developed along separate lines and, until quite recently,
6 without much contact between the two traditions except pos-

sibly in the Near East. Therefore, as a study of Oriental music would involve learning essentially a new way of listening and a new set of things to listen for, we will confine ourselves in this book to tracing the development of music in the Western world.

CHAPTER 4

Music of the Middle Ages

MUSIC OF THE EARLY CHRISTIAN CHURCH

THE BEGINNINGS OF CHRISTIAN CHANT

HEBREW AND BYZANTINE INFLUENCE. The rites and the music of Christianity are both deeply rooted in the Jewish tradition. The first Christians were Jews, their ritual stemmed from Jewish practices, and they spoke Hebrew or Aramaic. Christianity, therefore, accepted many Jewish institutions but adapted them to suit its own needs.

One definite link between Jewish and early Christian music can be seen in the derivation of the post of precentor or cantor into the *psalmista* of the Church. Liturgical parallels can be found in the office hours of the Church, which are patterned after the prayer hours of the Jews, in a similar use of the Book of Psalms, in the alleluia and amen, which are of Jewish origin, and in the adaptation of the *"Sanctus, Sanctus, Sanctus"* from the Jewish Kedusha *"Kadosh, Kadosh, Kadosh."* Moreover, similarities of style between ancient Jewish melodies and early Christian chant may be observed in such traits as the absence of measured rhythms, identical practices in the singing of the psalms, the scalar formation of melodic lines, and the use of identical note patterns.

When Constantine the Great rebuilt Byzantium and made it the capital of the Roman Empire in A.D. 330, it became a flourishing center of Hellenistic and Oriental cultures, and also the fountainhead of the Byzantine Church. (The Hellenistic influence on Christian music can be seen in an early musical relic—a fragment of papyrus from the 3rd century A.D. found at the site of the old Egyptian city of Oxyrhynchos in 1896. The papyrus contains a Christian hymn with Greek text and vocal notation.) From Constantinople the Byzantine Church traditions influenced the West until the schism of the Eastern and Western churches in 1054. For a long time it was thought that Byzantine culture was merely a continuation–worse, a degeneration—of classical Greek culture, but continued research has cast doubt on the actual strength of the Greek influence on the Byzantine Church. While it is true that Byzantine culture had both classical and Oriental origins, the modern view is to see the Byzantine liturgy as a new art based primarily on Oriental (frequently Jewish) sources. For instance, the Byzantine system of modes (ECHOI) differs considerably from the Greek modes (TONOI) but is similar to those of the Western Church. Byzantine music is also more exclusively vocal than the Greek, but here it must be noted that Byzantine music was largely sacred music, and no secular music exists.

Byzantine melodies have many features in common with Western Christian chants, and among these are monophonic text, free rhythm, unaccompanied vocal performance, and smooth melodic lines. A major difference, however, lies in their textual make-up, for the Eastern Church makes use of free poetical creation, whereas the Western Church used only psalms as settings for chants. Therefore, some of the finest music of the Byzantine Church is found in its hymnody. The hymn, developed from the TROPARION, or "round," overshadowed the psalm itself, and it developed into two principal types: the *kontakia* and the *kanones*. The KONTAKION was a hymn of from eighteen to twenty-four stanzas, all in the same meter. A KANON had nine divisions called *odes* (theoretically there were nine, but often there were only eight), which referred to the nine canticles of the Old and New Testaments. It is possible here to see the influence of the Byzantine Church on the Western Church, for these canticles, with but one exception, are found today in the liturgy of the Roman Catholic Church, one of the most famous of them, musically speaking, being the Magnificat (Luke 1: 46–55).

THE WESTERN TRADITIONS OF LITURGY AND CHANT. As it was only in later times that Rome assumed authority over the Western churches, the early churches of the West remained quite independent of one another. Consequently, political and cultural differences in various parts of Europe produced four principal liturgies and styles of chant: MOZARABIC (Spain), GALLICAN (France), AMBROSIAN (Milan), and ROMAN or GREGORIAN (Rome). There was also a CELTIC liturgy (used in Great Britain, Ireland, and possibly Brittany), which was finally superseded in the 7th century by the Roman.

The early centuries A.D. were times of fierce warfare between the inhabitants of the Roman Empire and the members of barbarian tribes. By the end of the 5th century the kingdom of the Visigoths consisted of western France and Spain; farther to the north lived the Franks, who were soon to control all of Gaul. The Visigoths had been Christianized in the 4th century, and from their service, as developed in the 6th and 7th centuries in Spain, comes one of the oldest preserved liturgical Latin hymns with a refrain. The liturgy and music of the Visigothic Church was firmly established when the Arabs invaded Spain in 711, and it continued in practice after that time under the name "Mozarabic." This term does not mean that the service contained any Arabic elements; it did not. Rather, the word is derived from *musta'rib,* meaning a Christian living under Moorish domination. The Roman rite replaced it in 1071, but the Mozarabic tradition can still be heard today in a few churches in Spain.

The Gallican ritual was the shortest-lived of the four major Western practices, being in use in France only from about the 5th through the 8th centuries. Pepin, King of the Franks, introduced the Roman liturgy in the 8th century, and this rite was fully established in Gaul during the time of Charlemagne (Emperor of the West from 800 to 814). The Roman rite was to take over from the Gallican the *Improperia* ("The Reproaches" –see TEM, No. 2) of the Good Friday service, and also two hymns, *Crux fidelis* ("O Faithful Cross") and *Pange lingua* ("Sing, My Tongue").

Milan was one of the important cities of Europe at this time, its culture boasting close connections with Byzantium and the East, and it was also noted as a training center for bishops of the Church. St. Ambrose (A.D. 340–97), Archbishop of Milan from 374–97, is credited with the introduction of hymn and antiphonal psalm singing to the Western world. The Ambrosian liturgy (and its accompanying chants) has proved to be quite enduring, as it has survived to the present day in Milan despite a succession of efforts (Charlemagne's for one) to replace it with the Roman. The authorship of a number of hymns formerly attributed to St. Ambrose has been questioned, but a few at least have been attested to by St. Augustine (A.D. 354–430) in his *De Musica;* of these the *Aeterne rerum conditor* ("O eternal author of the universe") is given, set to three different melodies, in HAM I, No. 9a. The Roman Gradual finds its parallel in the Ambrosian *Psalmellus,* as can be seen from the *Redde Mihi* ("Restore unto me"), found in TEM, No. 1. The *Te Deum laudamus* ("We praise Thee, O Lord") is a great prose hymn that, according to legend, was composed on the spot by St. Ambrose and St. Augustine at the time of the latter's baptism.

THE GREGORIAN CHANT

The Edict of Milan (A.D. 313), by which Constantine granted freedom of worship to Christians, served to encourage the formation of Christian liturgy and song. Under Pope Celestine I (Pope 422–32) a *schola cantorum* was organized in Rome for the composition and study of chant and for the training of Church musicians. This school was later reorganized and expanded under Gregory the Great (Pope 590–604), and he also caused the great body of Christian chant that had grown up by that time to be carefully classified and organized; it was for these efforts by Pope Gregory that the Roman chant now bears the title Gregorian chant. In the 12th century the name *cantus planus* ("plain song" or "plain chant") was added to distinguish monophonic chant from *cantus figuralis* or *musica mensurata* ("figured"–that is, "part music"; or "measured song"). Thus Gregorian chant became the established type of liturgical song, and at present this literature consists of nearly three thousand melodies.

The rites of the Roman Catholic Church are based on a liturgical year that begins with the First Sunday of Advent–the first of four Sundays preceding Christmas–and that is comprised of the seasons Advent, Christmas, Epiphany, Lent, Easter, Ascension, and Pentecost. This ecclesiastical year, therefore, may be considered a master plan on which to plot the various teachings of the faith, accomplished through liturgy and music. The principal service of the early Church was called the EUCHARIST (Greek for "good grace"), a commemoration of the Last Supper; it later was called MISSA ("Mass"), the term derived from the service's closing portion: *Ite, missa est* ("Go, this is the dismissal"). The liturgical portions of the Mass were rather slow in developing, and it did not reach its completed form until the 11th century. We have presented a full outline of the Mass in Chapter 2.

A second important service, or rather series of services, is the *Divine Office* (*Canonic Hours* or *Office Hours*). These originated in and are now maintained by the monastic orders, and they are held throughout a twenty-four-hour span. The Hours developed from the "vigils," or the custom of keeping watch on the night before Easter, with the Eucharist following in the morning of the next day (a Sunday). Thus Sunday became, in the Christian Church, the Lord's Day. The Canonical Hours consist of MATINS, before sunrise; LAUDS, at sunrise; PRIME, at 6 A.M.; TERCE, at 9 A.M.; SEXT, at noon; NONE, at 3 P.M.; VESPERS, at sunset; and COMPLINE, before retiring. The service of Vespers includes the Magnificat, and is the only daily office that permits figured music; the Benedictus is a part of Lauds, and Compline makes use of the Nunc Dimittis.

The early chants of both Mass and Office were notated in a system called NEUMES. It has been suggested earlier (in the section on Jewish music) that their origin might have been the *ta'amin* as used to indicate melodic formulas in the music of the Jewish temple (see HAM I, No. 6), but another theory proposes that they were derived from the grammatical accents of Greek and Latin literature. These literary markings did not indicate actual accentuation, but rather a rising and falling of the voice. Whatever their origin, the neumes of the early Church did not indicate pitch or intervallic movement, but implied only a melodic outline. Evidently the chants were passed on in an oral tradition, and the neumes served only as broad guides for the singers, or perhaps they were notations to be interpreted by the choir director, who in turn conducted the singers through hand motions.

THE CHURCH MODES. Gregorian chant, with its Oriental and Near Eastern background, was foreordained to be founded on some sort of modal system. Thus, in the 8th century, and after the Gregorian organization, a system of eight ecclesiastical or Church modes was established and applied to the chants. The chant, of course, had a long period of development before the theory was established, and some chants even today do not confine themselves to any one of the octave modes. It seems certain, too, that many of the earlier melodies were rewritten to conform to the new modal system; nevertheless, a great many chants can be satisfactorily analyzed using the system of eight modes.

Four of the modes—Nos. 1, 3, 5, and 7—are called authentic; the other four, plagal. The AUTHENTIC MODES, like modern scales, are erected on the bottom note *finalis* ("final"), with the fifth note, called *confinalis* ("against the final"), serving as a secondary tonal center (dominant). The third mode, however, presents an exception to this structure, as it has the *confinalis,* or dominant, on the sixth step in order to avoid the note B (a note that produced melodic difficulties). The melodic skip of the tritone from the notes F to B (augmented fourth) was corrected in the chant by flatting B—the only accidental found in Gregorian chant. Some very early chants may have had other accidentals as well, but they were evidently eliminated later by transposition of these plain-song melodies.

The PLAGAL MODES bear a relationship with the authentic modes: 2 with 1, 4 with 3, 6 with 5, and 8 with 7. The plagal stands in range a fourth below its corresponding authentic mode, uses the same final, and has a dominant a third lower than the dominant of the related authentic (an exception being mode 8, which uses as a dominant the note C instead of B). Thus, the final in a plagal mode occurs in the middle, with the dominant a few steps above it; Example 23 illustrates the eight Church

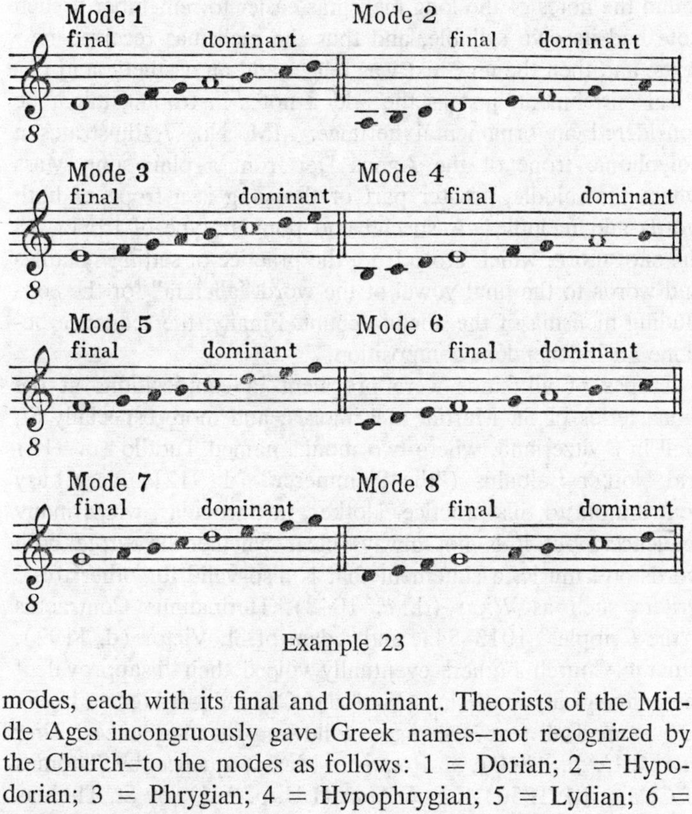

Example 23

modes, each with its final and dominant. Theorists of the Middle Ages incongruously gave Greek names–not recognized by the Church–to the modes as follows: 1 = Dorian; 2 = Hypodorian; 3 = Phrygian; 4 = Hypophrygian; 5 = Lydian; 6 = Hypolydian; 7 = Mixolydian; 8 = Hypomixolydian.

TROPING. Before the rise of the universities in the 12th and

13th centuries, the only seats of learning were the monasteries, and consequently the early music theorists and scholars were monks. In their hands the chants of the Church underwent a process called troping, or the interpolation of additional words to the authorized texts of Gregorian chants, with the new material either being set to the already existing music or having new music written for it. Also, the trope could be inserted anywhere in the chant. The practice arose about the 8th century, and one explanation for it might be the following: the monks found the notes of the long melismas easier to remember if each note had its own syllable, and thus the melismas received new texts, and then the new text was felt to add an aesthetic and poetical enrichment, just as the added notes in troping might be considered an ornamental heritage. MM, No. 7, illustrates a polyphonic trope of the Agnus Dei from a plain-song Mass where the middle, greater part of the song is a trope of both words and melodies. A special and popular type of trope was the SEQUENCE, which arose from the practice of setting syllables and words to the final vowel of the word "alleluia" for the concluding melisma of the alleluia chant. Finally, the sequence became an independent composition.

Tropes of all kinds were prevalent in compositions at the monasteries of St. Martial at Limoges, and more especially St. Gall in Switzerland, where two monks named Tuotilo (d. 915) and Notker Balbulus ("the Stammerer" [d. 912]) were busy contributors to this practice. Notker, in particular, wrote many sequences, but it is not always clear whether he wrote both words and music, a statement that is also valid for other trope writers such as Wipo (d. *c.* 1048), Hermannus Contractus ("the Cripple," 1013–54), and Adam of St. Victor (d. 1192). But the Church Fathers eventually voiced their disapproval of these liturgical tamperings, and the Council of Trent (1545–63) banned all tropes save the following four sequences: *Dies irae* (LU, p. 1810), a Requiem Mass sequence by Thomas of Celano (d. 1250); *Lauda Sion* (LU, p. 945), by St. Thomas Aquinas (d. 1274), composed for Corpus Christi; *Veni sancte Spiritus* (LU, p. 880), a 12th-century sequence for Whitsunday; and Wipo's *Victimae paschali* for Easter Sunday (LU, p. 780; see also MM, No. 3). A fifth sequence–the *Stabat Mater* (LU, p. 1634) as composed by Jacopone da Todi (d. 1306) for the Feast of the Seven Dolours–was authorized in 1727.

THE ROMANESQUE PERIOD (1000–1150)

SACRED MONOPHONIC MUSIC

The Mass reached its completed form in the 11th century with the inclusion of the *Gloria in excelsis* and the *Credo in unum Deum* sections. A century earlier the notation of the chant had emphasized a better definition of pitch. The hitherto vacillating movement of the melodic line was more clearly presented by the placing of the neumes at different heights above the text; these came to be called "heighted neumes." The next notational step forward occurred when lines were added in the scoring, a horizontal red line to show the pitch *f*, and a second, yellow line for *c′*; thus neumes grouped around these two lines offered much more in the way of definite pitch.

The 11th-century invention of the four-line staff (still used in Gregorian notation today) has been credited to a monk named Guido of Arezzo (*c.* 990–1050). Guido retained the earlier red *f*-line and the yellow *c′*-line and drew between and above them black lines representing *a* and *e′* respectively, and he wrote the plain-song notes on these lines and the ensuing spaces. Thus the 11th century saw not only the completed Ordinary of the Mass, but also a staff capable of expressing the complete octave range of a typical Gregorian chant from one of these Masses.

The greater part of Guido's fame, however, rests on another of his "inventions"–a system of solmization (the designation of the degrees of the scale by syllables instead of by letters) in which he set the symbols for the individual tones of the major hexachord (ut, re, mi, fa, sol, la) by borrowing the first syllable of each line of the *Hymn of St. John,* as shown in Example 24 (observe how the syllable and notes of the hexa-

Ut que-ant la - xis re-so-na-re fi-bris
Mi - rage-sto-rum Fa-mu-li tu-o - rum, Sol-
ve pol-lu-ti La-bi-i re - a-tum, San-cte Jo-an-nes.
Example 24

chord agree in the song: ut = C; re = d; mi = e; fa = f; sol = g; and la = a). Also credited to Guido is the "Guidonian hand," a pedagogical aid used to facilitate the singing of melodies with overlapping hexachords (there were seven such hexachords in the range G–e″). Guido taught his students to sing musical intervals by pointing with the index finger of his right hand to a position on his open left hand, and each of the notes in the G–e″ range was represented by a joint or position on the left hand.

The final notational development in Gregorian chant was reached in the 13th century with the establishment of square-shaped neumes. These are the note shapes found today in some liturgical books of the Roman Catholic Church.

After the 13th century Gregorian chant began to decline, prompted to some degree by the growing interest in part music. After many centuries of neglect the task of restoration was entrusted to the Benedictine monks of the Abbey of Solesmes. The results of their studies have appeared in the *Paléographie musicale,* a truly heroic collection of successive volumes which began publication in 1889; this version of restored chant was officially adopted by the Church in 1904 as the *Editio vaticana.* One major problem in any restoration of Gregorian chant concerns the rhythm. The Solesmes version treats all notes of a chant as if they all had one basic value, and next groups these notes in a free combination of binary and ternary patterns in an effort to produce a sense of order within variety, but all this is based on the natural rhythm of the Latin words, phrases, sections, and periods for which the music has been written.

SACRED PART MUSIC

In the first millennium of the Christian era the Christian Church was primarily concerned with the absorption of the music of the ancients. This means an essentially monophonic style of song which came to fruition in the Gregorian chant. Naturally, this would not exclude singing in octaves and heterophony, for this too was part of the inheritance from the East, but the actual practice of polyphony prospered particularly in the West and indeed became a specialty of Western composers. The practice of singing in parts developed with the continued growth of the Church, but whether it evolved out of early musical practices or came out of a separate tradition is hard to tell. Suffice it to say that in art evolution is not always the preferred method of development. The first mention of part music appears in a treatise dated near the end of the 9th century, but we can surmise that the practice had been underway for some time, although it began to flourish only in the Romanesque period.

The *Musica enchiriadis* ("Handbook of Music") and an accompanying commentary, the *Scholia enchiriadis* (notes on the handbook), were the first books (late 9th century) to describe singing in parts–a process called ORGANUM, which has already been discussed in Chapter 2. Two references to MM are added here: No. 6, which gives a sequence setting in parallel organum; and No. 8, a piece of melismatic organum from the school of St. Martial–located at the aforementioned Abbey of St. Martial in Southern France. The St. Martial style borrowed a part or the whole of an earlier chant and cast it in the tenor voice in extra-long (sustained) note values; above this tenor a second, solo voice sings freely composed melismatic passages. This style is variously known as "St. Martial organum," "melismatic organum," or "sustained-tone organum."

The school of St. Martial closed out the scholarly development of music in the Romanesque period. It is well to remember that in all organa of this period the consonant intervals are the unison, octave, fourth, and fifth; all other intervals that occur in the unfolding of the polyphony are treated as dissonances that require appropriate resolution. The rhythm is the free rhythm of plain song, the basis on which these compositions were formed.

EARLY AND MIDDLE GOTHIC PERIODS (1150–1300)

THE ARS ANTIQUA

The last half of the 12th century and the whole of the 13th constitute a period designated in musical art by the term *ars antiqua* ("old art"), a name that theoretical writers of the later Middle Ages gave to the music of this period to distinguish it from their own 14th-century style of music, called, understandably enough, *ars nova* ("new art"). The most impressive contribution by composers of the *ars antiqua* was made in the solution of rhythmical problems, brought about primarily by the increase in numbers and complexity of the voice parts. The first approach to rhythmical control was made shortly after 1200 with a system in which the over-all rhythmic pattern of a melody, called a RHYTHMIC MODE, was specified by certain combinations of notes and note groups. There were established six rhythmic modes identified by numbers as shown in Table XIV, these probably being derived from Greek poetic meters.

TABLE XIV

Greek Poetic Meter	*Rhythmic Mode Number*
Trochee	1. ♩ ♪
Iamb	2. ♪ ♩
Dactyl	3. ♩. ♪ ♩
Anapaest	4. ♪ ♩ ♩.
Spondee	5. ♩. ♩.
Tribrach	6. ♪ ♪ ♪

A second major breakthrough in the field of rhythm occurred around the middle of the 13th century, when the first attempts to introduce duple meter took place. The musician of the early *ars antiqua* knew only triple meter, which he considered *tempus perfectum* ("perfect time") mainly because it had a beginning, a middle, and an end, and because it bore a resemblance to the Trinity of the Godhead. But with the rise of more and more secular music in the late years of the *ars antiqua,* duple meter –known as *tempus imperfectum* ("imperfect time") largely because it was felt to have only a beginning and a middle and no end, and because it did not resemble the structure of the Godhead–was deemed to have an appropriate place. Shortly after 1300 triple and duple meters coexisted as equal partners in musical literature.

Léonin (fl. 1175). The focal point for the development of musical art in the *ars antiqua* was a school centered in Paris at the cathedral of Notre Dame, and its earliest master was Léonin. Léonin advanced the St. Martial style in his organa, and also composed pieces in which the rhythmic modes were utilized. As a practical point it should be noted that Léonin, although considered a member of the Notre Dame school, probably did at least some of his work in the earlier cathedral on the Île de la Cité, for the cornerstone of the Notre Dame Gothic edifice was not laid until 1163, and the choir, transepts, and bays were not completed until about 1183. According to the theorist Anonymous IV (an unknown Englishman who apparently had studied in France in the latter 13th century), Léonin compiled the *Magnus liber organi* ("Great Book of Organum"), which consisted of two-part liturgical settings for the entire church year. A sample of the musical style of his organa may be seen in a setting of the gradual *Haec dies* ("This is the day") from the Mass for Easter Sunday (HAM I, No. 29); here various rhythmic patterns appear in the top voice, and in the *clausulae* (sections written in discant style) both voices use rhythmic modes; there are also two lines in plain song for the chorus.

Pérotin (late 12th to early 13th centuries). Pérotin was Léonin's successor in the Notre Dame school. He expanded the writing of organa from two to three and even four parts. The voices, from the bottom up, are called tenor, *duplum, triplum,* and *quadruplum;* three-voiced organum, or ORGANUM TRIPLUM, became standard in Pérotin's era, and this number of parts in polyphonic writing was to remain in favor until late in the 15th century. In Pérotin's art the free passages of the older St. Martial organa were to give way to measured music, and triadic melodic patterns and incipient canonic traits began to appear. In this measured manner Pérotin himself worked over many of the organa in Léonin's *Magnus liber* (compare the Pérotin style of HAM I, No. 30 with that of Léonin in HAM I, No. 29); also another setting of the *Haec dies,* now in Pérotin style and in three parts, may be studied in HAM I, No. 31. The soloists' parts are now more evenly measured but still alternate with plain-song choruses, and all voice lines in the polyphonic sections use rhythmic modes. However, compositions with long-note tenors are still found in Pérotin's style (see MM, No. 9).

THE CONDUCTUS AND THE MOTET

With Pérotin and his contemporaries the composition of organa reached its highest development, and musicians began to turn their attention to the polyphonic conductus and the compositional type known as the 13th-century, or medieval, motet.

THE CONDUCTUS. The conductus, which is thought to have developed from rhymed tropes that accompanied processionals of priests in various religious rites, involved the setting of a metrical Latin poem that was nonliturgical in nature but was nevertheless sacred or at least serious and moral in tone. It had two distinguishing features: (1) it used freely composed melodies instead of pre-existing melodies from plain song or other sources; this is the first instance of polyphonic music in the West using original thematic material; and (2) all voices (up to three) used the same Latin text and the same rhythms as well, thus presenting a uniform movement in all parts, a note-against-note manner of composition which later came to be known as "conductus" or "familiar." This "conductus style" can be found in other compositions as well, and it is not uncommon to read about a "conductus motet." A two-voiced conductus, *De castitatis thalamo* ("That pure nuptial chamber"), is found in MM, No. 11; and *Haec in anni janua* ("At this beginning of the year"), a conductus in three parts, may be seen in HAM I, No. 39.

THE MOTET. The motet developed early in the 13th century, when a complete text was added to the upper voice (*duplum*) of the *clausulae*—the *clausulae,* or discant sections, of the motet being those where the *duplum* was cast (like the tenor) in a rhythmic mode as against other sections where this voice part was in a free and melismatic style. The motet eventually became the chief compositional form of the 13th century. Although the classical motet embodied a textless tenor derived from plain song and a *duplum* and *triplum* each with sacred Latin texts, French and Provençal texts soon found their way into the upper voices, and these words, in conjunction with the wordless tenor, produced a secular composition. The tenor, although borrowed from plain song, bore little resemblance to its source, for the former chant melodies were now fragmented and written for the motet tenor in a system of reiterated rhythmic patterns called ORDINES. This word is the plural for *ordo,* a medieval word meaning "phrase"; the *ordo* specified the number of times a rhythmic modal pattern was repeated before its interruption (usually by a rest), such as the first *ordo,* second *ordo,* third *ordo,* etc. The normal way of identifying a motet was to call it by the first few words of each voice part, from the top down; thus *En non Diu–Quant voi–Eius in Oriente* is the rather involved title of the motet in MM, No. 10.

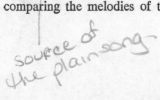

In the secularized motet just mentioned—in which the French texts of the *duplum* (*motetus*) and *triplum* speak of the love of Robin and Marion—the tenor is in the first *ordo* of rhythmic mode 1. The incipit, *Eius in oriente,* comprises the first words of the Gregorian chant phrase from which the tenor melody is taken. The interchange of melodies between voice parts—STIMMTAUSCH, a rather common 13th-century practice—may be observed by comparing the melodies of the *triplum* and *motetus*

in measures 1–4 with those of measures 21–24. Also the beginnings of the imitative procedure can be seen in the canon at the unison in the upper voices of measures 5–8.

Another technical aspect of 13th- and 14th-century part writing was the HOCKET (somewhat related to the practice of *Stimmtausch*), the interchange of melodies between voice parts. Whereas *Stimmtausch* interchanged melodies, hocketing involved the passing of fragments or even single notes of a melody from part to part, with the first voice resting while the second voice sang and then vice versa. Performing the hocket, it may be said, was the next thing to a self-induced case of hiccups. Use of this device can be found in the motet *Je cuidoie –Se j'ai–Solem,* perhaps by Petrus de Cruce (fl. 1270–1300); compare the two upper voices of this work (HAM I, No. 35) in measures 8–9, 17–18, 26–27, 34, and 39–40.

The mention of canon in the above motet *Eius in oriente* brings to mind one of the most successful of the early English polyphonic works–the ROTA ("round") "Sumer is icumen in," which dates from about the middle Gothic period. Its major tonality, its fullness of sound through the use of thirds in the harmonies, and its jocularity all mark it as of English origin. (HAM I, No. 42, pictures the four-voiced canon as it evolves into a polyphonic composition sung over a two-part PES, or foot–six parts in all.)

OTHER CHARACTERISTICS OF ARS ANTIQUA PART MUSIC. In the *ars antiqua* the fifth and the octave remained as the vertical consonant intervals in part music. The fourth now began to receive status as a dissonance, and the third was starting to be admitted to the final chord of principal closes. In the 13th century, cadence forms, as shown in Example 25, became standard formulas that were to remain in use for the following two centuries. The vocal ranges were exceedingly tight, remaining rather consistently within a two-octave span for all voices from the top to bottom of the musical score.

Musical notation took a long and seriously needed step forward at this time through the work of one Franco of Cologne, whose *Ars cantus mensurabilis* (written in the second half

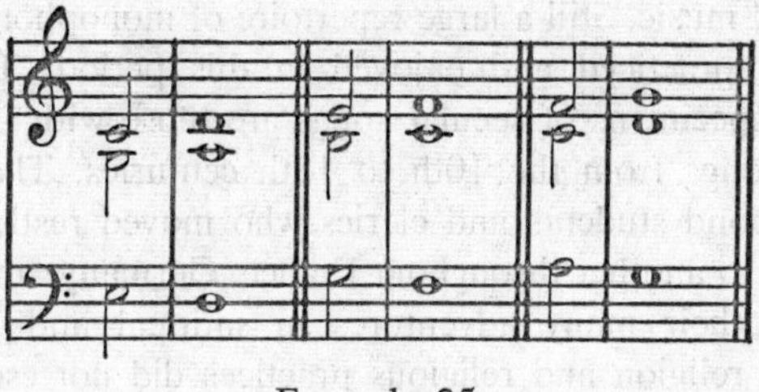

Example 25

of the 13th century) was one of the most famous and important works on music before the 15th century. In it Franco established rules for the time values of notes, ligatures (notes bound together), and rests, the notation being based on the rhythmic modes in the honored ternary division of the Middle Ages. Four types of notes were employed:

the double-long ▬
the long ■
the breve (the tempus or basic time unit) ■
the semibreve ◆

Also a new method of writing music on the page came into being. The early polyphonic works of the period had been written in score, but now compositions, such as the motet, had the upper voices singing different texts; the *duplum* and *triplum* came to be written on opposite pages of the music book or on separate vertical halves of the same page, with the tenor on its own staff horizontally across the bottom of the page or pages. This was called CHOIR-BOOK format, and continued in use well into the 16th century.

THE SECULAR FORMS OF THE ARS ANTIQUA

From what we have said so far it would seem that all music of the Romanesque and *ars antiqua* was preponderantly sacred, but this was not altogether true. However, the scholarly treatises of these periods all came from primarily church-supported research, and thus the greatest body of knowledge is concerned with sacred music. Still a large repertoire of monophonic secular music was practiced and enjoyed in this period. The oldest preserved specimens of secular songs are those with Latin texts —goliard songs from the 10th to 12th centuries. The goliards were vagabond students and clerics who moved restlessly from one school to another throughout France, Germany, and Britain, singing of their many adventures in satirical and humorous song; even religion and religious practices did not escape their pointed satire.

TROUBADOURS. Another type of secular song arose in the 12th century among the troubadours of Southern France, who wrote in the *langue d'oc* or Provençal, a language still spoken today in that region. The origins of this music, whose texts deal with the theme of courtly love—usually directed by the singer toward the wives of other men—are uncertain; the Gregorian chant, Arabian influence, and the Crusades have all been held liable in part for its inception. Troubadours were poet-musicians, both knights and commoners, who (as their name suggests) "found" or "invented" this new type of sophisticated art. Their art continued for about two centuries and embraced in the neighborhood of twenty-five hundred poems sung to some three hundred melodies. Prominent troubadours were Jofre Rudel; Raimbaut de Vaqueiras (d. 1207) of Orange; Bernart de Ventadour (d. 1195), from Hautefort; Folquet, who lived in Marseille, Arnault Daniel (fl. late 12th century), and Guilhem IX of Poitiers (d. 1127).

Although the singing of the troubadours is frequently pictured as accompanied by a stringed instrument, the melodic lines of the song were probably merely duplicated on the instrument or the instrument was used merely to furnish a prelude, interlude, or postlude to the song; accompaniment as known in the modern sense did not exist. The rhythms of these songs have long been in dispute, but the consensus today is that they held in performance to the rhythmic modes. As an example of a troubadour song the reader is referred to a *canso* of six stanzas by Bernart de Ventadour, printed in TEM, No. 6.

JONGLEURS. A special class of singers in the Middle Ages

was the jongleurs who sang the *chansons de geste* (such as the "Song of Roland," the national epic of France) and other secular songs. The jongleurs were professional musicians–men and women–who wandered from town to town as show people, gaining a meager living by singing, performing tricks, and presenting animal acts before audiences in the villages or castles. They were not creative poets and musicians, but sang and danced to the creative efforts of others.

TROUVÈRES. Gradually the art of the troubadour spread from Provence into Northern France, where it became the property of the trouvères who wrote in the *langue d'oïl,* the dialect of medieval France from which modern French developed. There the literature was augmented by some four thousand poems and fourteen hundred melodies. The trouvères were aristocratic poet-musicians, and included such famous personalities as King Richard the Lion-hearted (1157–99); Thibaut, King of Navarre (1201–53); Blondel de Nesle (1150–1200); and Adam de la Halle (*c.* 1240–87). The art of the trouvère was somewhat better organized than that of the troubadour, a favorite form being the PASTOURELLE. This was a dramatic ballad invariably concerned with the rather comical romantic affairs of a knight and a shepherdess, the story ornamented with monophonic songs of a folk nature and colored by appropriate musical instruments. A famous musical play of this type is the *Jeu de Robin et de Marion,* written by the last and perhaps greatest of the trouvères, Adam de la Halle. The score is written in the square-note notation of Gregorian chant (as was the music of the troubadours), and the first performance was said to have taken place in 1285 at the French court in Naples, where Adam died in 1287.

THE MINNESINGERS. A final development in this secular solo song of the Middle Ages came in a German school, where the knightly poet-musician was called a minnesinger. These minnesingers were the German counterpart of the French troubadours and trouvères, but the love songs of the minnesingers were on a higher plane; some of their songs were even capable of reference to the Virgin Mary. However, many (like the ode to spring by Neidhart von Reuenthal [13th century] in MM, No. 5) sang of the joys of earthly life. Other famous names among the minnesingers were Walther von der Vogelweide (*c.* 1170–*c.* 1230); Tannhäuser (*c.* 1205–70); and Heinrich von Meissen (d. 1318), called Frauenlob for his "praise of women." The music of the minnesinger, in general, is slower paced than the French solo song, and has some of its melodies in duple meter. More dignified in nature, the German songs show close ties with the ecclesiastical modes, whereas troubadour and trouvère melodies often look far ahead in their use of tonal attributes.

THE MEISTERSINGER. The successors of the minnesingers were the Meistersinger, who were tradesmen and craftsmen living in the German cities. Though their music did not flourish until the 15th and 16th centuries, a short discussion of their art is included here because it represents the culmination of this style of music. The Meistersinger were organized in guilds, the characteristic features of which were the pedantic rules that governed their meetings on Sundays after church, their competitions, complete with prizes, and the promotion of members into various advanced classes. This whole guild movement has been charmingly described by Richard Wagner in his 19th-century music drama *Die Meistersinger von Nürnberg,* the libretto based on Johann Wagenseil's book *De Sacri Rom. Imperii Libera Civitate Noribergensi Commentatio* (1697). The cobbler-poet Hans Sachs, the central figure of Wagner's opera, actually lived in the 16th century, and was a leading Meistersinger, composing over four thousand poems and many melodies. Most of the songs of the Meistersinger are written in the bar form of the minnesinger (AAB, in which AA represents the first two units of a stanza and the concluding portion, B, has new melodic material), as, for example, the *Gesangweise* of Hans Sachs in TEM, No. 22.

DEVOTIONAL HYMNS OF THE 13TH AND 14TH CENTURIES. The influence of French troubadour music can be seen in religious (although nonliturgical) songs of praise such as the Italian LAUDE and the Spanish CANTIGAS. The *laude* were conceived about the time of St. Francis of Assisi (1182–1226) and were sung as monophonic songs by groups of flagellants (penitents) in the 13th and 14th centuries. Similar in style to the *laude* and of the same historical period, the Spanish monophonic *cantigas* were mostly composed to honor the Virgin Mary.

LITURGICAL DRAMA

Liturgical drama probably began with the enactment of the dialogue trope *Quem quaeritis in sepulcro?* ("Whom seek ye in the sepulcher?"). This was sung before the Introit of the Easter Mass, and gradually the entire Easter season was used for subject material. Next the Christmas texts were presented in dramatic situations, and finally other texts from both Old and New Testaments were utilized. Some of the most popular of the stories included those of the raising of Lazarus from the dead, the conversion of St. Paul, Daniel in the lions' den, the legends dealing with St. Nicholas, and, of course, anything connected with the Last Judgment. The texts were in Latin, although from time to time vernacular phrases cropped up in the manuscripts. The music written for these plays formed a real part of the musical history of the Middle Ages, although in the earlier writings, and in some of the later ones, the musical settings were written with neumes, which now often make interpretation difficult.

The dramas grew greatly in length, calling at last for many participants and large spaces in which to be performed. They found a place in the great Gothic cathedrals of the period. The rubrics of the manuscripts called for costuming and cathedral properties of many kinds, showing that the productions must have been splendid spectacles. The first musical settings to these plays were probably unaccompanied monophonic songs, but with the growth of the drama instruments of many kinds were added.

Only a few manuscripts dealing with Old Testament subjects remain. Of these, two based on the Book of Daniel best reveal their original nature. Both are products of the middle of the 12th century, the first written by the Franco-German scholar Hilarius, and the second by a group of clerics at the cathedral school of Beauvais. The two manuscripts follow the biblical story closely, although both use the apocryphical scene where the prophet Habakkuk is taken by an angel to feed Daniel in the lions' den. Also, both end with the prophecy of the coming of Christ, which associates the drama with the Christmas season. Although Hilarius's version must have had music, it has not been preserved; however, as there is a clearly written musical setting on a four-line staff for the Beauvais play (Egerton 2615, Fol. 95–108, in the British Museum), and as the work has been recorded and performed recently, it would be well to discuss it further.

THE BEAUVAIS "DANIEL." This drama was probably written to be performed before the Te Deum of Matins or prior to the Magnificat of Vespers on the first day of January, but just where is open to question. The cathedral of Beauvais, built in honor of St. Peter and meant to be the largest of the Gothic cathedrals, was not begun until 1247. By 1272 only the choir and the radial chapels were completed, and as construction difficulties slowed the work, the addition of the transepts was not started until the 16th century; the nave was never attempted, leaving the cathedral unfinished. So it is highly improbable that the *Play of Daniel* was ever performed in what is known today (in its incomplete form) as Beauvais Cathedral. However, since Beauvais was the seat of an archbishop in the 12th century, there must have been a church there designated as the cathedral in which *Daniel* could have been performed. It might have been one (probably the latter) of the following: a small church known as "Basse Oeuvre," built around 997; or St. Stephen's, built about 1120–23 and rebuilt in 1180 after a fire.

The play must have been a thing of pomp and pageantry, for a dozen courtly processionals are written into it. Probably all the treasures of the church–vessels, vestments, crowns, and other properties–were brought out for use. Stage directions are meager, but there is one mention that leads to the belief that the angel who appeared to Daniel in the lions' den sang from the triforium–the tiny gallery that overlooks the nave and the choir. The play was probably performed in the nave crossing or on the steps of the choir in front of the choir screen. Every indication is that female roles would have been sung by boys or by men in falsetto. In the event of any liturgical drama being performed in the sanctuary, the singing and dancing would have been done only by monks.

Nearly fifty melodies are found in the Beauvais *Play of Daniel.* Most of the time a new speaker in the play means a different tune, but whenever King Belshazzar or King Darius is approached the salutation "*Rex, in aeternum vive*" ("Long live the king") rings forth, set always to the same melody. Most of the texts are set in the manner of the sequence–that is, in syllable style–and the choruses of the processionals and some other scenes derive much power from these syllabic settings. The quieter moments, however, reveal a more ornamented style. The original manuscript fails to indicate rhythm, instrumentation, tempi, or dynamics with any certainty, but the text of the drama itself does indicate some of the instruments to be used.

By the beginning of the 13th century these religious dramas could be called little else than church operas, and in 1207 Pope Innocent III (Pope 1198–1216) forbade their performance inside the church; yet dramatic presentations in churches were slow to die out, as seen from the fact that Innocent's proclamation had to be reaffirmed by Pope Gregory IX (Pope 1227–41), and it was not until the close of the 13th century that liturgical drama became professional, with its place of operations moved from the nave and choir to the outside steps of the cathedral and finally to the market place.

LATE GOTHIC PERIOD (1300–1400)

FRENCH ARS NOVA MUSIC

The Frenchman Johannes de Grocheo (fl. *c.* 1300) dared–he was the first musical theorist to do so–to discuss the *musica vulgaris,* or popular music, along with the solemn music of the

Church. Also he displayed a skeptical attitude toward the earlier justification of terrestrial music on the grounds of the prevalence of music among the angels and the stars; in short, he foreshadowed a new attitude that was to distinguish the whole period. Moreover, music both sacred and secular–and its notation–had reached such a state of complexity at this time that around 1325 the brilliant theorist and composer Philippe de Vitry (1291–1361) wrote a book entitled *Ars nova* ("New Art"), to explain the new developments. The title *Ars nova* was to be adopted by the future to designate the art and musical style of the entire 14th century.

Naturally, the new style did not take over without a struggle on the part of the earlier *ars antiqua*. But events in the 14th century like the Black Death, the Great Schism, and the Peasants' Revolt weakened the structure of the earlier Middle Ages and made the time ripe for striking out in new ways. There was the rise of vernacular literature in Dante, Boccaccio, and Chaucer, and also the growing rift between the Church and the temporal powers. With Giotto we can see the rise of the creative artist as an individual, for his paintings show a greater concern with realistically portraying the human condition than does the more stylized art of previous ages, and in this he represents the beginning of the transition from the Gothic to the Renaissance.

In music the battle raged over the 14th-century acceptance of the duple division of time values and the multiplicity of note values, as contrasted with the 13th century's insistence on triple division of time values and a more compact notational system. The Church, fearful for its authority, made its pronouncement on the question when Pope John XXII, from his papal seat in Avignon, wrote in a famous bull of 1324 his denouncement of the new meters, the rapid tempi, the notation, and the secular tunes of the modern school. Yet in spite of the anxieties of Pope John, the music of the Church was not in decline; it was only engaging new pathways.

Guillaume de Machaut or **Machault** (*c.* 1300–77). The most important French musician–and poet–of the 14th century was

Guillaume de Machaut. Born most probably in the province of Champagne, he studied theology and took holy orders, and was in the service of King John of Bohemia and the French court of Charles V. From 1337 he was a canon at Rheims Cathedral, residing in that city from 1340 until his death. From his pen we have one of the most famous musical works of the 14th century—the *Messe de Nostre Dame* ("Mass of Our Lady"), a four-part setting of the Ordinary of the Mass, to which is added a polyphonic setting of the dismissal formula, *Ite, missa est*. This Mass is of great historical importance, since it the first known attempt by a single composer to set the full Ordinary to music and thus achieve a sense of unity impossible to a setting by several composers. Only one polyphonic Ordinary setting—the *Mass of Tournai*—stems from an earlier time, and this is believed to be a compilation.

The Machaut Mass presents many fascinating features. Example 26 illustrates a melodic figure that appears time and again

Example 26

throughout the Mass, and it is altogether possible that Machaut used this to obtain melodic unification. Also, a connection with the Gregorian chant can be seen in the borrowing of chant melodies for use in the Kyrie, Sanctus, and Agnus Dei sections as tenor *cantus firmi*. In the Kyrie the melody is borrowed from the Kyrie of Mass IV (LU, p. 25); and in the Sanctus and Agnus Dei the melodies are from the corresponding sections of Mass XVII (LU, p. 61). These sections are either wholly or partly given an additional unification through a rhythmic and melodic principle called ISORHYTHM ("same rhythm").

The isorhythmic structure developed from the *ordines* of the 13th century. It consisted of one or more repetitions of a phrase made up of a rhythmic pattern called a TALEA (shades of the ancient Eastern world's rhythmic *ostinati*). Repetitions of the melody (COLOR) were also used, and these repetitions of *talea* ("rhythm") and *color* ("melody") could coincide, or they could overlap by occurring at different times; in the case of an overlap the melody would then receive a new rhythmical setting. This technique appeared early in the 14th century as an important feature of the tenors of the thirty-three motets of the *Roman de Fauvel,* a famous poem written by Gervais de Bus in 1310 and 1314 (see one of these motets in HAM I, No. 43). Incidentally, the *Roman de Fauvel* showed the trend of the times by its violent attack on the Church. Isorhythm became an important attribute of the motet style and will be further discussed and illustrated later in connection with the *ars nova* motet.

A textual examination of the setting of Machaut's Mass reveals a syllabic setting ("conductus style") of the Gloria and Credo—obviously chosen to expedite the performance of the extended text of these sections—and a more flowing style in the other parts of the Mass. The phrase *"Jesu Christe"* of the Gloria and the whole of the text from *"Et incarnatus est"* through *"et homo factus est"* in the Credo are set throughout all parts in long-note values to emphasize the gravity of the text.

Although this Mass has been discussed in some detail as an extremely important 14th-century work, it represents only a fraction of Machaut's work. The major body of his compositions consists of motets and secular forms; besides the Mass, his surviving works include only six other liturgical pieces, all motets. His secular works include numerous ballades, lais, rondeaus, virelais, and seventeen secular motets. Most of the motets use isorhythmic tenors, and the three-voiced secular motet *De bon espoir-Puisque la douce-Speravi* (EM, p. 88) amply demonstrates this use of isorhythm. Table XV lists the measure numbers of the *talea* based on twelve notes and the *color* of eighteen notes (with their respective repetitions) as they appear in the tenor voice of this motet; the Roman numerals represent the numbering of the *talea* and *color,* and the

Arabic numbers give the measure numbers of the music involved in each successive *talea* and *color*.

TABLE XV

Talea		*Color*	
I:	1–34	I:	1–53
II:	35–68	II:	54–102
III:	69–102		
IV:	103–19	III:	103–28
V:	120–36	IV:	129–52
VI:	137–52		

A close comparison of the measure numberings of the *taleae* and *colores* will show how Machaut has shortened the note values as the piece progressed in order to heighten the interest, a procedure frequently adopted by later composers, and also how *talea* IV and *color* III start afresh together again in measure 103 as the note values shorten. This rhythmic and melodic technique was to stand as the main structural device of the 14th-century motet. As later composers developed the idea of isorhythm, parts other than the tenor were treated in this way, and finally, around 1400, some motets were written that used isorhythm in the upper voices only, the tenor remaining in free rhythm.

Compared with the notable advances in rhythmical techniques in the *ars antiqua,* the outstanding achievements of composers of secular music in the *ars nova* lay in the further advancement in rhythmical procedures and in the greater sophistication and expressiveness they brought to the melodic element of 14th-century music. Borrowed melodies (*cantus firmi*) were abandoned in favor of freely composed tunes, and the new style brought forth concentration upon a single, flowing melody in the top voice, with the lower voices serving primarily as accompanying parts. In France these polyphonic works went under the names of *ballades, virelais,* and *rondeaux.* Machaut's ballade *Je puis trop bien* may be found in HAM I, No. 45; two virelays, the first monophonic, by the same composer can be seen in HAM I, No. 46; and a rondeau by Baude Cordier (fl. *c.* 1400) is printed in HAM I, No. 48. In the last quarter of the 14th century French music entered one of the most complex periods, with respect to rhythmic counterpoint, that the history of the art has ever known—as complex, in many ways, as the music of our present day. These rhythmical intricacies are found in extended syncopated passages, and in the simultaneous use of different meters and other cross rhythms produced by irregular note groupings between voices. These devices gave individual voice lines rhythmic independence to a marked degree, demonstrated in period music by the French composers Solage, Trebor, and Jacob de Senleches. Matheus de Perusio and Anthonello de Caserta were two Italian composers who also wrote in the French style, probably when they were with the popes at Avignon.

ITALIAN ARS NOVA MUSIC

Italian composers have always written music with a smooth melodic grace, and their 14th-century secular works prove no exception. These works were categorized by the generic names *madrigali, caccie,* and *ballate*. The *Squarcialupi Codex,* a 15th-century manuscript named for its onetime owner, the famous Florentine organist Antonio Squarcialupi, is a major source for these compositions. The Italian madrigal of this period shows the influence of the *formes fixes* of troubadour medieval poetry and music, and also of the conductus. The form comprises one to four stanzas all sung to the same music and concluded by a *ritornello* (not here a refrain) of two lines in a contrasting meter. The piece *Nel mezzo* (in HAM I, No. 50), by Giovanni da Firenze (fl. *c.* 1350) illustrates the madrigal very well. A colorful top voice—after all, the song is about a beautiful peacock—is placed against the firm lines of the bottom part. The *caccia* is a very special type—a "hunting song." The formal style paints the chase in a realistic manner, with the two upper voices in a canon at the unison over a slower-moving supporting bass. Most *caccie* have a second section (*ritornello*) in which the canon continues, but with a metrical change. No better illustration could be found than *Con brachi assai* ("With hounds aplenty"), also by Giovanni da Firenze as notated in TEM, No. 16. The *ballata* corresponds in style and structure to the French virelay.

Francesco Landini (1325–97) was the most outstanding composer of the Italian *ars nova.* He was proficient on the organ, lute, and flute and was renowned (like Machaut) as a poet and also as a philosopher. For many years he was organist at the Church of Lorenzo in Florence; a prolific composer, his works alone represent over a third of the extant Italian 14th-century musical manuscripts. He had a decided preference for the *ballata* form (writing over 140 of them), and here Landini sings forth with the charm and fluency known only to Italian vocal art. As an example of the *ballata* and of Landini's expressive style, we will discuss his *Chi più le vuol sapere* ("Who wishes to know them better"); the selection is preserved in the *Squarcialupi Codex* and may be seen in a modern edition in MM, No. 14. A cadential formula not heretofore mentioned is found in measures 18 and 19 in the MM print. It is identified by a stepwise descent in the bottom voice and the melodic scale-step formula 7-6-8 in the upper part. Example 27 re-

Example 27

produces this cadence in both its simple and, as it frequently appears, ornamental forms. The close has been called the "Landini-sixth cadence" after its supposed inventor, but it appears that the cadence was in use prior to Landini's day and that a more correct and more exacting name might be "under-third cadence."

NOTATION OF ARS NOVA MUSIC

The need for a way of transcribing 14th-century music which would indicate both duple and triple division of note values resulted in a new French system of notation which had developed out of the Franconian method and which involved a new technique called *mensuration:* the metrical relationship between one note value and the note of the next smaller value. Mensuration (note division) was concerned primarily with the breve and the semibreve; division of the breve was called TIME (*perfect* if triple and *imperfect* if duple) and that of the semibreve PROLATION (more often called *greater* if triple and *lesser* if duple). Table XVI illustrates the principal meter signs and the division of the breve and the semibreve under each, and the equivalent meter in modern notation.

TABLE XVI

Mensuration

⊙■ = ◆◆◆	(perfect time) =	♩♩♩ ♩♩♩ ♩♩♩	(greater prolation)	= 9/8 meter
⋹■ = ◆◆	(imperfect time) =	♩♩♩ ♩♩♩	(greater prolation)	= 6/8 meter
O■ = ◆◆◆	(perfect time) =	♩♩ ♩♩ ♩♩	(lesser prolation)	= 3/4 meter
C■ = ◆◆	(imperfect time) =	♩♩ ♩♩	(lesser prolation)	= 2/4 meter

It can be observed from Table XVI that a circle indicated perfect time and the broken circle imperfect time; a dot added to the meter sign was the indication of greater prolation. Two new note forms were added in this system:

the minim ♩
the semiminim ♪

In the middle of the 15th century a new system called "white mensural notation" was developed. This system prevailed through the 16th century, and two of the signs it introduced remain in present-day notation: C, now meaning 4/4 meter, and ₵ (*alla breve,* meaning the basic pulse is assigned to the breve), for 2/2. Both white notes and new black notes, the FUSA and SEMIFUSA, were used:

the long
the breve
the semibreve
the minim
the semiminim
the fusa
the semifusa

Composers of the Gothic period (and those of the Renaissance as well) did not always indicate all the accidentals in their scores. That additional sharps and flats were to be used, either by reason of necessity or of beauty, however, was well known, and the singers were supposed to include them at their discretion or where they were told to by the musical director. This practice was called *musica ficta* or *musica falsa.* The following melodic usages were understood without the accidentals being notated: F up to *B*♭ and down a semitone to A, and B down to F♯ and up a semitone to G (both of these to avoid the melodic tritone), and the neighboring-note formulas A-B♭-A; G-F♯-G; A-G♯-A; and D-C♯-D. Harmonically speaking, two basic rules prevailed: (1) Fifth, octave, and twelfth intervals in polyphonic passages should be made perfect if not already so, and (2) A third expanding stepwise into a fifth should be major, the same being true for a sixth moving thus into an octave; a third contracting stepwise into a unison should be minor. One rule at least–the calling for a major sixth leading into the octave–prophesied the development of the raised leading tone on the seventh step of later major and minor scales.

INSTRUMENTAL MUSIC OF THE ARS NOVA

Most of the instruments of the late Middle Ages came into Europe by way of Byzantium and Rome or through the Islamic cultures of Spain and North Africa. Reading the 14th-century illumination in MITA, No. 99 from left to right, a drum, flute, vielle, shawm, another vielle, psaltery, and bagpipes may be distinguished. Both the straight flute (recorder) and the transverse flute were known in the Middle Ages, and the bowed stringed instrument was called the VIELLE. A better illustration of the psaltery may be seen in MITA, No. 107.

The harp was perhaps the most characteristic instrument of the age, and angels are often pictured with this instrument in their hands (MITA, No. 97). The lute was played in the Gothic period, as demonstrated in the picture in MITA, No. 123, but it became better known in the Renaissance. Besides the very large and very stationary organ, two other, smaller types were known: the POSITIVE, movable in spite of its name (see MITA, No. 106); and the PORTATIVE (MITA, No. 126). Trumpets, horns, and percussion instruments of many types are seen in many situations (see again MITA, No. 126 and Nos. 100, 101, and 103). A rather peculiar instrument was the HURDY-GURDY or ORGANISTRUM; it had the shape of a lute or viol, but its strings were set in vibration by a rosined wheel operated by a crank at the lower end of the instrument; the hurdy-gurdy had several freely vibrating bass strings (drones) and two melody strings running across the fingerboard, the latter stopped by tangents connected to keys (two 18th-century hurdy-gurdies are shown in MITA, Nos. 311–12). The organ, which had lost its keyboard in the early Middle Ages, regained it in the 13th century, and in France and the Low Countries the 14th century saw organs with two manuals and a pedal clavier. The earliest clavichord- and harpsichord-type instruments were invented in the 14th century, but like the lute were to achieve their greatest use in the Renaissance.

Just how all these instruments were used—especially in ensembles with voices—and what music they played is not altogether known. The principle of contrasting timbre appears to have been well established, and this would permit ensembles of voices and instruments in various combinations. Some musicologists consider the Notre Dame school tenor parts—those parts without words—to be instrumental, but other authorities believe that they were vocalized–that is, sung on the first syllable of the plain-song *incipit* until a new section and a new syllable were introduced; illuminations from 13th-century manuscripts and books showing groups of singers and no instruments indicate that the latter idea may be the more correct. The Italian *caccia* is generally assumed to have an instrumental tenor; and some works, such as the polyphonic "instrumental motet," appear to be performed solely by bowed stringed instruments. It might not be at all unreasonable to say that the parts of a musical composition could be played or sung by any voice or instrument at hand capable of playing or singing the various melodic lines. Of course, certain instruments have been used for the dance since earliest times, and in Western music some of these instruments began to be used from at least as early as the 13th century to perform dance tunes as independent literature. Processionals, accompanied by instruments, were also known, probably in the conductus and liturgical drama productions.

PART THREE

The Renaissance and Baroque Periods

CHAPTER 5

Music in the Renaissance

INTRODUCTION

The rift between church and state mentioned in the previous chapter in the discussion of *ars nova* widened continuously throughout the 15th century and finally established in the 16th century a rather firm conception of the separation of church and state powers altogether. It is these two centuries (1400–1600) that are generally considered the period of the Renaissance, but such a specific limitation is, of course, largely arbitrary. The word "renaissance" signifies a new birth or revival, and in this context the Renaissance was a movement concerned with reviving the study of classical Greek and Latin cultures. Actually man rediscovered himself and his heritage from this study of the past; he opened his eyes to the nature of society and to the condition of human conduct. Throughout the Middle Ages the powerful influence of the Church had kept man's eyes heavenward, his thoughts on the life hereafter, but in the Renaissance the Church had to share its authority over the soul of man with his new desires for a life of happy pursuits during earthly existence. This is an extremely simplified statement of Renaissance ideals, but mostly the change can be seen in the use of the word HUMANISM, a term that showed the Renaissance's intense concern with human life and human nature.

Thus the Renaissance man with his new concerns turned to the classical spirit of antiquity. Manuscripts were carefully sought out, and long hours were spent in their transcription and comparison. Architects and sculptors began to take notice of the ruins of Rome, drawing new inspiration from their observations. From the Renaissance humanists came the foundation for studies in the "humanities"–philosophy, history, literature, and the fine arts; they created, through their emancipating efforts, the "liberal" arts.

The early humanistic pursuit of arts and letters, as it came out of the late Gothic period, was embodied in the works of Dante, Petrarch, Boccaccio, and Giotto. Since all these men were either born in or lived primarily in Florence, it is not surprising that the early flowering of the Renaissance occurred in Italy. Florence was to remain in the 15th century the cradle of the Renaissance, leading the way in painting, sculpture, and literature. But evidently Italy's concern at the time was primarily with letters and the visual arts, for the 15th century produced very little Italian musical art of lasting fame. It is rather in England, Burgundy, and the Netherlands that one must seek the early history of Renaissance music.

It is appropriate here to comment on one of the greatest aids that musical art has experienced–the advent of printing in the Western world. In the last quarter of the 15th century this newly discovered process was applied to monophonic music, and very early in the 16th century polyphonic music was printed on a large scale. Ottaviano dei Petrucci, of Venice, was the first great printer of part music. His first effort, the famous *Harmonice musices odhecaton A,* came forth on May 14, 1501, followed by *Canti B* and *Canti C* in 1502 and 1504, respectively. All these are in choir-book form (Petrucci's choir books were of small size, measuring only eight inches long by six and a quarter inches high), but for performances special part books were printed–one little volume for each voice or part.

By 1523 Petrucci's musical prints numbered fifty-nine volumes. He used the method of double impression, which meant one round of printing for the staves and a second round for the superimposed printing of the notes. For vocal music a third time through the press was necessary to add the text. The *Odhecaton*–the title has been translated both as "One-hundred Songs," although the book contains only ninety-six, and as "A Century of Songs," meaning the 15th century–established Petrucci's fame early in his printing career; the volume is an outstanding collection of three- and four-voiced chansons by Busnois, Ockeghem, Obrecht, Isaac, Des Prez, and others, and places Petrucci as a printer of music in a position comparable to that of Gutenberg as a printer of books.

EARLY ENGLISH AND BURGUNDIAN SCHOOLS

ENGLISH SCHOOL

Although English music had known a commendable literature in the early and middle Gothic, little progress was made in style and technique in the 14th century in that country.

John Dunstable (d. 1453). In the early 15th century the Englishman John Dunstable was to exert a strong leadership as canon of Hereford Cathedral, 1419–40, and also as the founder of the "Continental School" of English music. The political situation at the time–the Hundred Years' War was coming to a close and the English had large holdings on the Continent–made it quite natural for English music to become influential in France and Burgundy. Probably Dunstable himself was on the Continent in the service of the Duke of Bedford, who represented King Henry V as Regent of France, 1422–35.

English music showed one of the earliest tendencies toward the use of tonality (in opposition to modality), and also to a full and sonorous harmonic functional feeling. English music was the first to accept the third and sixth as consonances; and this use of the third and sixth (later given the name *gymel,* or "twin voices") produced English music as early as the 13th century with long passages of consecutive intervals of these two types. In the early 15th century this same feeling for the sixth and the desire for a full-sounding harmonic structure–another characteristic of English music–brought about a style of writing called ENGLISH DISCANT, in which a passage of music in, say, three voices began with the two upper voices at the intervals of a fifth and an octave above the opening note of the lowest part and moved forward in what amounted to a series of triads in the first inversion (chords of the sixth) until the close of said passage where the 1-5-8 chord was again used. Continental composers from about 1420 to 1450 were to refer to their similar constructions, undoubtedly influenced by the English practice, as *faux-bourdon* ("false bass").

Apart from this general style of English music of the time, Dunstable's art reflects also his liking for triadic motives, his free and fluid treatment of borrowed chant melodies, and the fact that nearly half of his total output of Masses and motets are freely composed (without any borrowing whatsoever of Gregorian chant melodies). He was also among the first, along with the English composer Lionel Power, to link two Mass movements together by using the same chant melody in each. It is very probable that it was at this time, and in the English school, that the idea of the *cantus firmus* Mass originated—that is, a Mass in which all movements are based on the *one* borrowed plain-song melody (the cyclic Mass).

Dunstable wrote in all the principal styles of his time, including sections of the Ordinary of the Mass, isorhythmic motets, three-part settings of various liturgical texts, and secular vocal pieces. In his motet *Veni Sancte Spiritus* ("Come Holy Ghost"), published in TEM, No. 18, something new in the way of dissonant treatment—the suspension—appears. The suspension involved a temporary suspending of the forward movement of one note of an interval or chord while the other note or notes moved to the next interval or chord; this idea began in early-15th-century music and is illustrated in Dunstable's motet between the second and third beats of measure 5.

HAM I, No. 62 (*Sancta Maria*), illustrates a Dunstable hymn setting in three voices, and HAM I, No. 61, is a setting of *O rosa bella* ("O beautiful rose") by the same composer. The secular text of *O rosa bella* is from the pen of the Italian poet Giustiniani. Both these compositions reveal the easy, flowing melodism of Dunstable, with the triadic pattern so noticeable at the beginning of the pieces. The modal cadences as established in the 13th century combine with the under-third melodic formula to close the sections, but with the frequent addition of a flat to the note E in *O rosa bella* it is not difficult to realize the tonal key of *g* minor in that particular piece. The texture of the "beautiful rose" setting is handled in a very progressive manner, one feature being the large number of imitative points, and a second that of the use of a faux-bourdon passage, measures 24–26. The hymn *Sancta Maria* further illustrates, in measures 43 and 44, the use of the suspension.

With the death of Dunstable in 1453 English musical influence declined on the Continent. Though turned inward and insular, severing its connections with developments on the Continent, English music did continue to flourish, putting considerable emphasis on the CAROL. The name probably came from the medieval French word "*carole*"—a term for a round dance. The earliest examples are from the first half of the 15th century and are three-voiced settings of religious poems, often on the subject of the Incarnation, possessing texts in a mixture of English and Latin. The form is strophic in the manner of a modern hymn, with a chorus before and after each stanza. The Incarnation carols were probably used as processional numbers during Christmastide.

BURGUNDIAN SCHOOL

The leading music school of the early Renaissance was known as the Burgundian school. It derived its name from association with the flourishing cultural activities of the kingdom of Burgundy, which had grown in the 15th century—through intermarriages, purchases, and conquests under the reigns of Dukes Philip the Good (1419–67) and Charles the Bold (1467–77)—to include what is today parts of Eastern France, the Netherlands, and Belgium. Its capital was the city of Dijon, which at this time set the cultural pace for all of Europe, and reflected as well a fairy-tale life where peaked shoes, cone-shaped hats with butterfly veils, and clothing in multicolored hues were all the vogue.

The English influence on the Burgundian school is substantiated by the French poet Martin le Franc when he wrote in a poem of the early 1440's how the great Burgundian composers Dufay and Binchois followed Dunstable and the English manner. The sacred compositions of the Burgundian school were formally like those of the English, but the secular chanson with French text was peculiar to the Burgundian region. The over-all range of these three-voiced compositions was close to the two-octave c–c″, just as were the similar-voiced works of the 14th century. However, as the mid-15th century was a time of spectacular change in music, we will discuss here the forms of the Mass, chanson, and motet as they began their Renaissance development in the Burgundian chapel and court.

Until the time of Guillaume Dufay (*c.* 1400–74) there had been little interest in the setting of the Ordinary of the Mass as a complete unit; in fact, until the 15th century the *Tournai Mass* and the Mass of Guillaume Machaut were the only complete contrapuntal settings of the Ordinary, and of these only the latter is a unified work–that is, with all sections written by the same composer. But around 1450 there was an upsurge of interest in the composition of polyphonic Mass settings.

Four main types of Mass composition existed in the 15th century, identified as follows:

(1) *Missa Choralis,* or Plain-song, Mass. This is a noncyclical Mass setting, with a different plain-song tune used in each movement and drawn from a corresponding section of a Gregorian monophonic Mass.

(2) *Cantus Firmus,* or Tenor, Mass. Here the same melody, usually found in the Mass tenor voice, is employed in all the movements of the Mass. It may appear exactly as borrowed; almost exactly; in augmentation or diminution; in retrograde movement or in contrary motion; or almost completely disguised in a florid presentation. The sources for *cantus firmi* were: (a) liturgical chant, except that the Proper chants of the

Mass, e.g., Introit, Gradual, were seldom used, since these melodies were already heard many times during the Mass itself (but the four Blessed Virgin Mary antiphons *were* often used), and (b) secular song–the French chanson, Italian madrigal, German lied, Dutch lied, Spanish canción, and English air.

Some *cantus firmi,* however, were not borrowed, but "invented." For example, a "hexachord Mass" was merely based on a six-note scale, and another type employed *soggetto cavato dalle vocali,* which is a musical subject derived by "carving out" vowels from a literary sentence and transforming these vowels into a melody by associating them with the solmization syllables of the Guidonian hexachord. Finally, there was the *quodlibet* Mass, in which a combination of two or more sacred or secular tunes or a mixture of both was used simultaneously in different voices of the Mass.

(3) Parody, or Transcription, Mass. The "parody" type of Mass made use of material from a pre-existent polyphonic model and included much more than the mere borrowing of a melody, employing, as well, borrowed voice entries, harmonic structures, imitative points, cadences, etc. Sometimes the entire structure was taken over in principle; when this was done and when the borrowed composition was given the new Mass text, this process of exchanging texts was called *contrafactum.*

(4) Freely Composed Mass. This meant *all* voices of the Mass newly composed, with no borrowed material of any kind. Actually this group of Masses was quite small.

Of course, it was possible for these four categories to blend together in one way or another; for example, it is quite possible to have parodied passages in a *cantus firmus* Mass.

The later Masses of Guillaume Dufay are among the earliest complete settings of the Ordinary of the Mass based on a *cantus firmus* and employing a MOTTO–a melodic motive, usually in the treble, occurring at the beginning of each Mass movement. The English cyclic Masses do not use the motto beginning until the latter half of the 15th century, probably picking up this device from the Franco-Flemings. Dufay must have been almost the first to use secular tenors (from French chansons) in the Mass. Thus, the Mass based throughout on a single *cantus firmus* derived from a sacred or secular source, and frequently using a motto at the beginning of the main sections of the Ordinary, was to constitute the typical cyclic Mass that came to dominate European musical composition of the second half of the 15th century.

The incipient use of secular thematic elements in sacred music around 1450 marks one of the most interesting aspects of Renaissance music. Although (as was mentioned above) Italian, German, Dutch, Spanish, and English tunes found their way into the Renaissance Mass, composers of the 15th century relied mainly on the French chanson for their borrowed secular melodies. Today one can only speculate as to how this practice got started, and the following three explanations are offered: (1) these tunes were so familiar they were considered folk songs and hence were not thought to be objectionable for religious thematic material; (2) the practice imitated the 13th- and 14th-century secular motet art; and (3) it may be noted that new harmonic means were made available to composers through the adoption of a fourth part, or a real bass, around the middle of the 15th century. Through the use of this four-part construction, Dufay had set up, in his later works, a feeling for tonality through the "dominant-tonic" cadence relationship. It would seem obvious that the secular chanson, the harmonic structure of which leaned more often in the direction of the major and minor modal system than did sacred music of the period, would provide a stimulating *cantus firmus* for composers looking for new vertical combinations, melodic elements, and rhythmic patterns.

The Burgundian chanson may well represent the earliest model of the chanson Mass. However, it is doubtful if the polyphonic settings that were used as Mass models were composed earlier than the second quarter of the 15th century. The chanson of the first half of the century was written for the most part in three voices, the principal melodic line (of a freely flowing diatonic nature) being found in the top voice. The two lower voices (particularly the contratenor part) were often unvocal, with leaps of all intervals, and usually contained notes of longer time values than the uppermost part. The musical form of these pieces was dominated by the literary form of the ballade, virelay, and rondeau. (In this discussion of French Renaissance music one term—"French chanson"—is used to cover all three of these literary forms. In fact, with Dufay and the composers who followed him, the title "French chanson" is applied to *all* works with a French text.) Dissonant treatment here developed more regulation, but it still had to await the 16th century for its final perfection. There were also two popular cadential formulas in use. One had the ornamental VII_6—that is, the ornamented first inversion of the triad on the seventh scale step—together with the "Landini sixth" (see Example 28;

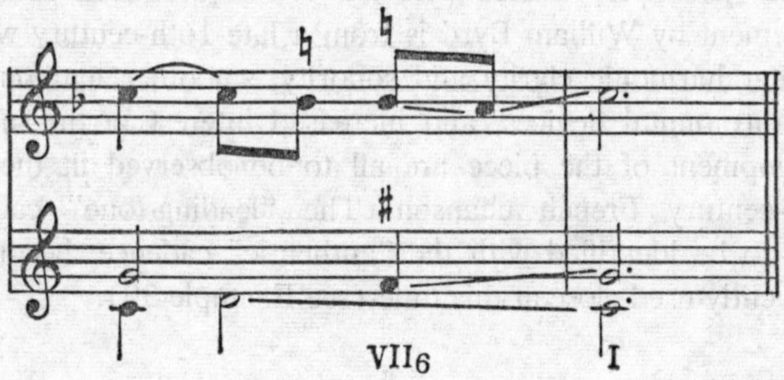

Example 28

note that this formula has two leading tones—one each to the fifth and to the octave of the final chord; this cadence is also now known as the "Burgundian cadence"). The other was the "dominant-tonic" close, with the upward resolution of an octave in the contratenor voice to "avoid" parallel fifths (Example 29).

A fourth part was added to the polyphonic chanson around the middle of the 15th century, and the voices tended to become more of a unified structure. In the latter half of the 15th century a greater effort was made to develop imitation as a true element of style. A particularly striking feature here is the

Example 29

use of a "point of imitation" at the outset of a piece; this usually consisted of an imitative pattern, employed in all the voice parts, and based on the opening notes of the chanson's principal melody. This procedure, as developed in the chanson, quickly became common usage in the opening of many Mass movements (Example 11 illustrates this technique, albeit this Mass movement by William Byrd is from a late-16th-century work). Greater harmonic clarity and sonority, smoother manipulation of contrapuntal devices, and increased interest in the musical development of the piece are all to be observed in the late-15th-century French chanson. The "leading-tone" cadence, later to be identified with the "authentic" cadence, becomes a frequently used close at this time (see Example 30).

Example 30

As we have seen, the motet originated in the 13th century as a French sacred work; however, in that and in the following century it literally "fell from grace" and took on a highly secular cast. In the 15th century it once again reversed its position and became a widely used form written in the new Renaissance style, using for a text any Latin sacred words except those of the Mass. And this is pretty much the way it is understood today.

Guillaume Dufay (*c.* 1400–74), the chief composer of the Burgundian school. It seems that he was born at Hainaut and received his early and valuable musical education as a choirboy at Cambrai Cathedral. Dufay apparently worked and lived in many places; in 1436 he received an appointment as canon of the cathedral in Cambrai, but evidently this did not prevent long absences from Cambrai. Actually these appointments were often pretexts or additional sources of income for church musicians, and they were not obliged to reside at the seat of the position. (This too must have been the situation concerning Dunstable's position as canon of Hereford Cathedral.) Martin le Franc's *Le Champion des dames* connects Dufay and a second composer, Gilles Binchois, with the Burgundian court at the time of Philip the Good, but the nature of this connection is not clear. Dufay's last days were spent in Cambrai.

The major works of Dufay, like those of most other 15th-century composers, were his Masses. Of some eight such compositions credited to him, five are *cantus firmus* Masses, each of which is based throughout on a single borrowed melody. From these five the *Missa Se la face ay pale,* composed after 1450 and probably close to 1460, will demonstrate the *cantus firmus* type of Mass in a four-voice setting. With four voices becoming the standard setting after 1450, the borrowed *cantus firmus* is now found in an inside voice; the three-voice designation of *superius* (*discantus*), *contratenor,* and *tenor* expanded into *superius, contratenor altus* (later just *altus*), *tenor, contratenor bassus* (later *bassus*); thus here is seen the derivation of the modern *alto* ("high") for a low female voice.

Dufay used as the *cantus firmus* of the *Missa Se la face ay pale* the tenor melody of his chanson of the same name (this chanson melody is given following Kyrie I in MM, No. 15; the Kyrie I shows how the melody is taken into the tenor voice). The chanson tenor melody is found in the Mass tenor throughout that work. A feature of the Mass is the treatment of the *cantus firmus* in long-note values, perhaps an effort to disguise the secular source, while at times, it is true, the chanson tune is heard in normal note values, many times it is used in double augmentation (one measure of tenor equivalent to two measures of the other parts) and in triple augmentation (where one measure of the tenor is now set against three measures in

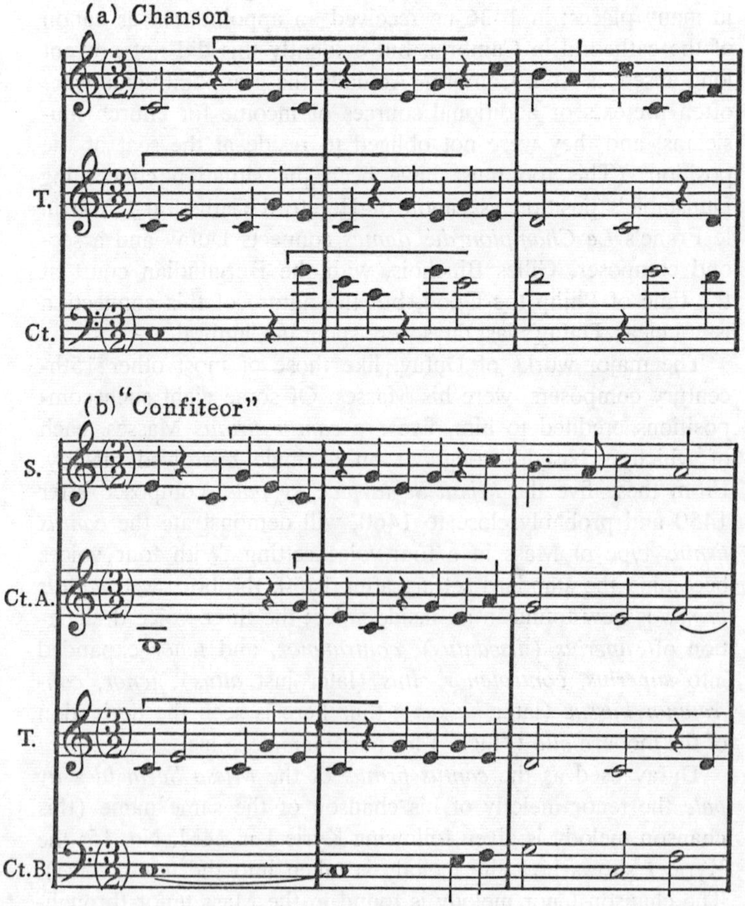

Example 31

the other three voices). MM, No. 15, shows the chanson melody in double augmentation in the Mass tenor.

Duets precede the entrance of the tenor in all the openings of main sections of the Mass except in the Kyrie. Dufay also unified the *Se la face ay pale* Mass with a short motive or motto, which appears as the opening notes of the *superius* voice in many sections. This motto, found altogether nearly twenty times in various rhythms and note formations, is an early use of the motto in a *cantus firmus* Mass, but it does not seem to be derived from the chanson as the *cantus firmus* is. However, there is another direct correlation between the chanson *Se la face* and the Mass. Bars 25–27 of the chanson appear to be part of a concluding instrumental postlude, without text—a sort of a fanfare ending. Dufay must have found all these voices interesting, as he incorporated them into the Mass in spots in the Kyrie II, the "*Cum sancto spirito*" of the Gloria, and in the "*Confiteor*" of the Credo (Example 31). This parody

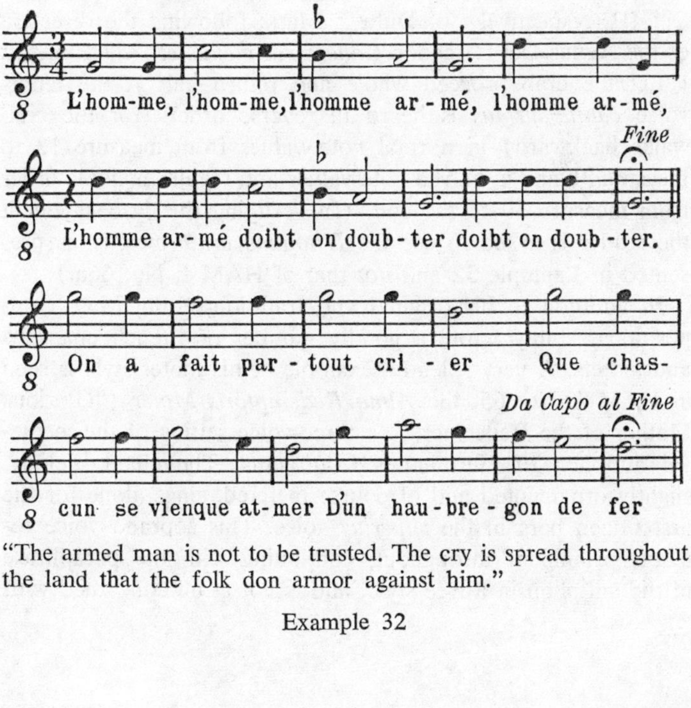

"The armed man is not to be trusted. The cry is spread throughout the land that the folk don armor against him."

Example 32

technique, present in the Mass to a limited degree during the time of Dufay, was to become a common procedure in the Mass of the 16th century.

A second Mass by Dufay, *L'homme armé,* will be given only a brief consideration here. This Mass gains in stature since the *L'homme armé* melody (see Example 32) is without doubt the most famous of all the French chanson tunes used as *cantus firmi* in the polyphonic settings of the Mass. The universal popularity of this melody is demonstrated by its use in the Masses of Burgundian, Flemish, Dutch, French, German, Spanish, and Italian composers. Strangely enough, considering its immense popularity, neither the origin of the tune nor its first polyphonic secular setting has been established with certainty. However, practically every composer of any importance in the Renaissance wrote one or two *L'homme armé* Masses, and it is very probable that Dufay was the first to compose a Mass around this melody. HAM I, Nos. 66b and 66c, presents "The Armed Man" tune in the tenor voice of the Kyrie I and Agnus Dei III, respectively, of Dufay's Mass; following the direction of the Agnus Dei III canon *Cancer eat plenus et redeat medius* ("Let the crab proceed whole and return half"), the tenor-voice *cantus firmus* is heard in reverse order (for the crab walks backward) in normal note values from measure 13 to measure 38 and in halved note values and regular melodic order from measure 39 to the end. (In verifying this last statement the reader is asked to use the *L'homme armé* melody as presented in Example 32 and *not* that of HAM I, No. 66a.)

In addition to his original and tradition-setting Mass compositions, Dufay wrote a goodly number of French chansons and motets. A very splendid example of his motet style is seen in HAM I, No. 65, the *Alma Redemptoris Mater* ("Glorious Mother of the Redeemer"), a three-voice setting of the medieval antiphon of Hermannus Contractus. The chant melody, slightly ornamented and of course metered, sings alone for the first fifteen bars in the *superius* voice. This soprano voice remains prominent throughout, continuing with the paraphrase of the antiphon in a free style, and is not at all concerned with certain regulating procedures (for example, isorhythm) sometimes imposed upon *cantus firmi* when they are placed in tenor voices. The closing portion of the motet is written in block chords, each with its own fermata marking (𝄐 = a lengthening or holding of the time duration of each chord beyond that of its notational value); this fine, full effect is further enhanced by a few bars in faux-bourdon-like style, and by the final three measures, which are in chords of four notes each with the very last cadence a "dominant-tonic" progression.

Other Burgundian Composers. Turning now from the chapel to the court in Burgundian musical art, the chanson is seen as the most popular type of entertainment music. Two famous composers of these 15th-century songs were Gilles Binchois (*c.* 1400–60), a member of the ducal court of Philip the Good, and Antoine Busnois (d. 1492), who served under both Charles the Bold and Mary of Burgundy. Many of their three-voice chansons have melody-dominated soprano voices, with the two lower parts providing an instrumental accompaniment. Though polyphonic, these works seem not to be overly concerned with imitative procedures. MM, No. 16, is a modern edition of *Adieu m'amour* ("Farewell, my love"), a composition by Binchois. This sad and rather dark-colored chanson closes quite a number of passages with the so-called Landini cadence, combining this melodic formula at times (as in the final two bars) with the "crossed-voices" cadence that became so popular in the Burgundian school.

THE EARLY FLEMISH SCHOOL (1450–1520)

During the one hundred years 1450–1550 most of the important musical positions in Europe were held by musicians from the Low Countries–the region that today is Northern France, Belgium, and Holland–and the profound and scholarly art of these Flemings dominated the music of all of Europe. These men were the great musical teachers of the Renaissance, and the fact that they chose to travel to all the major cultural centers of Europe (in France, Germany, Italy, England, and

Spain) made possible one of the most uniform period styles that the history of music has ever known. Flemish musicians even played a large part in the formation of the various "national" types such as the French chanson, the Italian madrigal (hence the English madrigal), and the German lied. Theirs was truly the "universal art."

Johannes Ockeghem (*c.* 1425–95). At the head of this Flemish school stands Johannes Ockeghem. His birthplace remains a mystery, but it was probably a city in Flanders. In the year 1443–44 he served as a boy chorister at Antwerp Cathedral. He probably studied music with Binchois, and he was a pupil of Dufay in 1449. From 1454 he served as court and chapel composer to three successive French kings—Charles VII, Louis XI, and Charles VIII—a position that could hardly fail to exert musical leadership.

Ockeghem evidently built his fame more on quality than on quantity, for his extant works include only sixteen Masses (eleven of which are complete), nine motets, and about twenty chansons. His Masses reveal his compositional talents and abilities best, and he is classed with the later composers Obrecht and Palestrina in this respect; but his style stands in rather sharp contrast to that of the preceding Burgundian school. For instance, Ockeghem has a tendency to renounce chromaticism in favor of modal diatonicism, and the extended range of his bass parts lends dignity, sonority, and a certain new dark coloring to his music. Furthermore, he makes use of a free-flowing phrase structure with overlapping cadences, as contrasted with the clearer-cut phrases and cadences of Dufay and Binchois. This continuous polyphonic style produced a maze of intertwining sounds that exemplified the wave of religious mysticism that the late Middle Ages had bequeathed the Netherlands. Thomas a Kempis's *Imitation of Christ,* written in a Netherlands monastery about 1420, is a literary expression of this same feeling.

The imitative process cannot be considered a foremost feature of Ockeghem's style, but he did cultivate rather extensively the use of canon (as did nearly all Netherlandish composers to one degree or another). His effective employment of canon is demonstrated in the *Missa Prolationum,* which, incidentally, is without either a *cantus firmus* or a motto. This Mass is unified by a cycle of double canons, in which the Kyrie begins with a double canon at the unison and the following sections build up in the same manner interval by interval to the octave. Two voices only are notated, the other two parts of the four-voice Mass being derived from the written pair, with the proper interval of response being indicated either by the position of the meter signatures on the staves or by the position of the clefs. MM, No. 17, prints a realization of the first part of the Sanctus of the *Missa Prolationum* and shows the double canon being introduced in the alto and bass voices, with the strict imitation at the interval of the sixth in the soprano and tenor voices, respectively, 13 bars later. This canonic cycle stands as a precedent to works like Bach's *Goldberg Variations* and is the first work of its kind. Two other of his Masses, *Missa Mi-Mi,* and *Missa Cuiusvis toni,* are similar to the *Missa Prolationum* in that they are freely composed.

The Mass setting of the "Armed Man" chanson melody permits a close look at Ockeghem's highly figured counterpoint —a technique found in so many of his compositions. This is clearly shown in the Agnus III (HAM I, No. 73b). The intertwining long lines and overlapping cadences move the music forward in sweeping melismas. A curious deterrent, however, is the redundant use many times of the "tonic" chord in an anticipatory fashion just before the strong and concluding V-I cadences. In his chansons Ockeghem followed much more closely the traditions of the Burgundian school; the three-voice structure, the modal cadences with the 2-1 intervallic melodic endings in the bass, and the rather narrow range are all stylistic inheritances. But the part writing of *Ma bouche rit* ("My mouth laughs") in HAM I, No. 75, nevertheless reveals the partiality of Ockeghem toward a fabric of continuous melody and the avoidance of strong interior cadences.

Later Developments. In the generation of musicians following Ockeghem, new harmonic and melodic combinations were explored, the motive became an important thematic consideration, and the development of imitation as a true element of style opened up new paths to the imaginative composer. The acknowledgment of imitative and motivic elements in the period 1475–1520 is seen in the beginning measures of both the French chanson and the Mass movements. The chanson openings fall into four general classifications:

(1) Imitative, in which all voices participate in a point of imitation on the first notes of the principal melody, which is usually found in the tenor or soprano.

(2) Polyphonic, in which not all voices participate in the imitation.

(3) Homophonic, in which the beginning notes of a single tune are announced simultaneously, but with different note values in the different voices.

(4) Homophonic, without imitation (quite rare).

Along with the tremendous growth in imitative techniques, and in motivic and thematic development, came the use of the *ostinato* and the melodic sequence. The control of dissonance in the harmonic structure and the smoothing out of the melodic line (foreshadowing the "Palestrina style" of the late 16th century), together with the continuous development of the "leading-tone" cadence ("dominant-tonic" relationship), are other important technical achievements of the period.

Jacob Obrecht (*c.* 1450–1505). One of the first men to be singled out in this change of direction is Jacob Obrecht. He was continuously moving about and changing his city of residence and also constantly composing, for, in contrast to Ockeghem, he was a prolific creator. His works number twenty-four Masses, nearly as many motets, and numerous chansons; several German sources credit Obrecht with the composition of the oldest known polyphonic setting of the Passion according to St. Matthew, but some earlier and probably more authoritative Italian sources show one Antoine de Longueval (fl. *c.* 1517 in France) to be the composer of this particular Passion. Striking points of Obrecht's music are to be found in the organization of his writings, in his use of short phrase lines and clear harmonies (at times of functional significance) with strongly defined cadences, and in the *ostinato* figures and repeated note-patterns and melodic sequences, which are such forceful unifying factors.

Obrecht's harmonic clarity and regularity of period structure are very pronounced in the four-voiced *Missa Malheur me bat,* based on the chanson by Ockeghem. Here Obrecht borrowed the chanson *superius* (principal melody) for use in the Mass *superius* in all four-voice movements. A single, different melodic fragment–there are nine such segments–is employed in each movement in augmented and normal note values; the *cantus firmus* is heard complete only in the Agnus III. Moreover, Mass sections in fewer than four voices adopt the tenor of the chanson as a *cantus firmus,* where it is heard at one time in the Mass in the tenor and at another in the bass. There is no motto, but imitation based on the opening notes of the chanson tune occurs at the start of several Mass movements. All in all, this is a lovely and mature work and may be considered one of Obrecht's finest; considerable use is made of *ostinato,* sequence, and imitation, and the composition reflects an advanced harmonic and melodic style.

Josquin des Prez (*c.* 1450–1521). With Josquin des Prez music began to make rapid strides toward the codification of a harmonic common practice that was to endure almost to the time of Debussy. Thus the compositions of Des Prez, as sung regularly by the best choral organizations of the present day, have the double appeal of familiarity and artistic genius. He is a rather rare example of an artist admired both by his contemporaries and by posterity. That he is one of the great musical talents of all time remains unquestioned.

Following a well-established practice, Des Prez began his musical career as a choirboy of the collegiate church at St. Quentin, where he later became canon and choirmaster. He may have studied with Ockeghem, for he admired him greatly and wrote a deploration on his death in 1495. Des Prez was active in Florence and Ferrara, finally settling in Burgundy. He died in 1521 at Condé-sur-l'Escaut. His musical works were sung in all parts of Europe, and he was lauded in particular for his expertness in fusing text and music. Both the contrasting styles of polyphony and homophony are present in his art, with the homophonic structures, perhaps, of Italian influence. Des Prez seems at his best in the motet form. This one may assume to be a direct result of the interplay of the two textures and his evident concern for the setting of the words; of course the motet offered freedom in textual thought and variety unobtainable in the Mass and was thus an added stimulation to his creative mind.

He also employed his compositional talents with splendid effectiveness in the chanson style, being considered one of the finest composers of his era in this form. His *Faulte d'argent* (HAM I, No. 91) is a magnificently proportioned five-voice chanson. This setting of the so very true text ("Lack of money is a great evil") reveals also a technique evidently close to the composer's heart, for he made use of it in many chansons and in others of his works as well: namely, his use of canonic imitation.

The reader should be aware of the variance in the definition of "canon" as used in discussing music today and in Des Prez's time. Currently it means a strict style of imitation, but this definition would have been applied in the Renaissance to the *fuga.* Canon in the 15th and 16th centuries meant an inscription appended to a puzzling score notation as a clue to its performance; imitation would have been a secondary factor, arising only if the solution of the canonic inscription brought it about. The canon *Cancer eat plenus et redeat medius* in the Agnus Dei III of Dufay's *L'homme armé* Mass has been previously discussed, and another type frequently found in the Renaissance was the mensuration canon. In this type a single written line serves for two or more of the parts, when the line is read according to different mensurations or meters. Such a canon and its solution are found in HAM I, No. 89, an Agnus Dei from Josquin des Prez's *Missa L'homme armé super voces musicales.*

A consideration of Des Prez's *Missa Hercules dux Ferrariae* will permit not only a look at the already-mentioned *soggetto cavato* technique, but also a discussion of why the technique was used. Example 33 illustrates the manner in which Des Prez

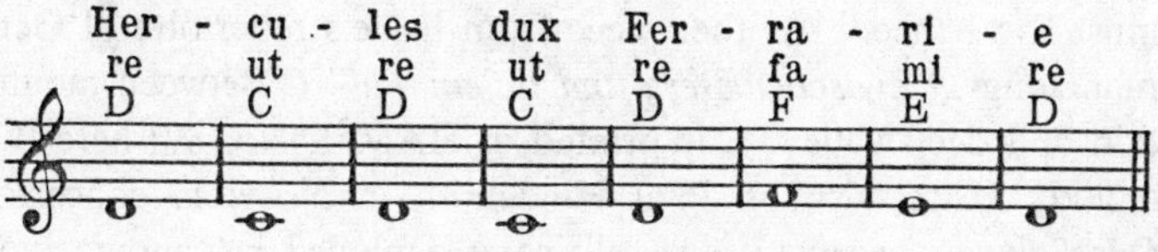

Example 33

derived the *cantus firmus* for the Mass by taking the vowels of his patron's name (Hercules was Duke of Ferrara from 1471 to 1505) and associating each with the corresponding vowel in a syllable of the natural hexachord. It was a secularization of the Mass comparable to the use of chanson and other secular tunes in the Mass, or perhaps it was even more comparable to a practice by painters (like Giotto, who in the 14th century painted his patron, Enrico Scrovegni, into a wall mural of the Arena Chapel in the act of presenting the chapel to a group of angels).

The *Hercules* Mass displays both the traditional past and the new ideas. It has a strict older style: for instance, the *cantus firmus* is rarely heard in any voice other than the tenor, and there it is found mostly in long notes; also the Landini-sixth cadence is still used. New departures are demonstrated in the imitative beginnings of all the larger sections, imitative passages involving only two voices, in the short patterns repeated sequentially or exactly, and in an extended sequential passage in Kyrie II. Moreover, and especially new in concept, the five major sections of the Mass end each with a complete triad–with the third in the final chord.

Henricus Isaac (*c.* 1450–1517). A well-known contemporary of Obrecht and Des Prez, Henricus Isaac, although a Fleming by birth, preferred to live much of his life in the sunny southern climes of Europe. His career was fashioned primarily out of service to Lorenzo the Magnificent at Florence and to the Emperor Maximilian I at Vienna and Innsbruck. It was upon his departure from Innsbruck that he wrote his famous

German part-song *"Innsbruck, ich muss dich lassen"* ("Innsbruck, I now must leave thee"); this melody was later given sacred words and sung as a funereal piece, "O world, I now must leave thee." Another piece from Isaac's repertoire of German songs, *"Zwischen Berg und tiefem Tal"* ("Between mountain and deep valley"), is printed in HAM I, No. 87; here the melody (used also by Paul Hindemith in his viola concerto, *Der Schwanendreher*) is a folk song deployed in canonic imitation between bass and tenor. But Isaac's crowning achievement is his cycle of motets, commissioned by the church at Constance (near Innsbruck), and known as the *Choralis Constantinus*. These motets are characterized by the then current Flemish style and are replete with passages of imitative counterpoint, repetitious patterns of notes, and melodic sequences.

THE MIDDLE FLEMISH SCHOOL (1520–50)

The chanson of the 16th century was written in a delicate manner, with its quick rhythms and imitative style resembling the contemporary motet. This meant a free imitative procedure that rarely made use of the somewhat inflexible and mechanical means of canon. Two styles are in evidence: (1) a work based on two or more motives that are continually passed from voice to voice in free imitative patterns, and (2) a chanson in which the melody is carried in the soprano and the other parts are subordinated to the melodic flow of this top voice.

Comparable styles are also seen in the Flemish Masses of the quarter century following the death of Des Prez. Perhaps the most important Mass style of the period is that employing the "through-imitative" technique (*durchimitierende Stil*). Here the phrase lines are short and the motives are developed in imitative passages between voices in a series of fugal expositions. Long rests are avoided in all the voice parts. A second style is found where a Mass borrows a pre-existent melody and stresses that melodic element. Usually the borrowed *cantus firmus* is taken directly into the *superius* of the Mass, where it may appear without change or may undergo rhythmic or melodic transformation combined with the insertion of original material.

Composers of the period seemed no longer concerned with a systematic augmentation or diminution of the borrowed tune (the reader may recall that when Dufay first used secular melodies in the Mass he placed these melodies in an inside, tenor voice in long-note values, probably as some sort of a scheme for disguising them); nor were the techniques of retrograde movement or contrary motion favored, except in compositions in which the composer appears to be giving a backward nod of approval to the technical prowess of the late years of the 15th century. Thus in the use of a secular tune in the melody-oriented style there is little effort made to disguise the borrowed element. On the other hand, the "through-imitative" technique, by its very nature, might well disguise a secular melodic source. Thus the Church, through the Council of Trent (1545–63), could have criticized the melodic style for its rather obvious portrayal of the secular inspiration and the "through-imitative" procedure for the distortion of the text of the Ordinary.

Masses and motets still borrowed from Gregorian chant as well, but these *cantus firmi* were now incorporated in a much freer style. Parody-type Masses gradually took the place of the older usage of a single *cantus firmus,* and composers of 16th-century polyphony began the expansion of four-part texture to five and even six voices.

Nicolas Gombert (*c.* 1490–1556). Probably the greatest composer of this period was Nicolas Gombert, an eminent pupil of Josquin des Prez. Gombert traveled extensively for many years with the court personnel of Charles V as that monarch visited Vienna, Brussels, and Madrid. The composer's sacred music made great use of the "through-imitative" style (or "pervading imitation," as it is sometimes called) and probably he was as influential as any other man in establishing the classical motet of the first half of the 16th century; and of course his travels spread this influence far and wide.

Of his 169 motets, the *Super flumina Babylonis* ("By the waters of Babylon" [HAM I, No. 114]) amply demonstrates

Gombert's use of many points of imitation throughout a composition. He achieves freedom of flow by studiously avoiding clear-cut cadential phrase terminations, and because of the many imitative points, motives deployed at close time-intervals become a feature of the style. Also in the *Super flumina* motet the transformation of rhythmic patterns combined with subtle syncopations–so characteristic of Gombert's technique–is in evidence.

Gombert was also a master of the parody Mass, as seen in his five-voice *Missa Sur tous regretz,* a parody of the four-voice chanson setting by Jean Richafort. The chanson is composed of a large number of dissimilar phrases, separated in the voice parts by rests. Points of imitation never extend throughout all voice parts; furthermore, these imitative sections, when used, are confined to the "head motive" of the phrase. In his Mass parody of this chanson Gombert likewise builds his phrase on the opening notes of the chanson phrase; chanson motives are rarely borrowed in the Mass in their exact form, until the employment of the chanson *superius* in the *superius* of the final Agnus Dei. However, in the Mass, free imitative points often are developed throughout the entire voice structure in a series of fugal expositions. This produces a rather thick and sonorous sound, since the development is continuous in all voices.

Jacobus Clemens (*c.* 1510–*c.* 1556). Recognized by music historians as one of the master musicians of his day, the Dutch composer Jacobus Clemens added materially to the development of the Mass, and particularly to the enlargement of the parody technique. Clemens, who also bore the name Clemens non Papa (perhaps to distinguish him from a poet named Jacobus Papa, who lived in Ypres, the birthplace of Clemens), wrote fifteen Masses. Save for the *Missa Pro defunctis,* which in normal fashion paraphrases the chant in such movements as are set polyphonically, all the Masses are parodies. Clemens, furthermore, acknowledges his parody technique by writing in his Mass titles "*ad imitationem moduli*" or "*cantilenae*" instead of "*Missa super.*" In these Masses the composer emphasizes the importance of the imitative technique by stressing the *durchimitierende Stil.*

Although the technique of pervading imitation may not be as consistently employed in such a motet as *Vox in Rama* ("In Rama was there a voice heard"), by Clemens (HAM I, No. 125), when this work is compared with Gombert's *Super flumina* (HAM I, No. 114) and Des Prez's *Ave Maria* (MM, No. 19), the analogy to the Gombert classical 16th-century motet style is–as it should be–strikingly apparent. The density of the works by Clemens and Gombert, obtained through sustained activity in all voice parts and the avoidance of rests, stands in strong contrast to the rather open structure of the Des Prez pieces of the earlier Flemish period.

Adrian Willaert (*c.* 1490–1562). A third great composer of this middle Flemish period is Adrian Willaert. The Flemish tradition had been passed down to him through his Parisian studies with Jean Mouton, who in turn had been one of the distinguished pupils of Josquin des Prez. After Paris, Willaert traveled to Italy, where in 1522 he entered the service of Duke Alfonso I d'Este at Ferrara. The year 1525 saw him working for Ippolito II d'Este, Archbishop of Milan. But 1527 was to be Willaert's year of destiny, for it was on December 12 of that year that he was appointed *maestro di cappella* at St. Mark's Cathedral, in Venice; this was undoubtedly the most important and the most sought after position of any in 16th-century musical circles. Willaert, through this position, was the founder of the Venetian school. He initiated the style of composing for two antiphonal choirs, a style no doubt prompted by the two choir galleries (each equipped with an organ) in St. Mark's. This polychoral practice, as continued in the hands of Willaert's great Italian pupil Andrea Gabrieli (*c.* 1520–86), was to provide one of the steppingstones to the Baroque musical art of the 17th century.

HAM I, No. 113, reveals a motet setting in six voices by Willaert of the Easter sequence *Victimae paschali laudes.* The first phrase only of the famous plain-song melody is heard in the *sextus* voice (the "sixth" voice part–the next-to-the-top part in the HAM print), followed by a complete statement of the chant in the *quintus* ("fifth" voice) part. The dense texture of the work demonstrates once again the prevailing style of the 16th-century Netherlandish motet. The double-chorus compositional technique can be illustrated by the motet *In ecclesiis* (HAM I, No. 157), from the pen of Giovanni Gabrieli (*c.* 1557–1612). This Gabrieli, a nephew and student of Willaert's pupil Andrea, represents in a grand manner the culmination of the Venetian school.

THE LATE FLEMISH SCHOOL (1550–1600)

The twilight of the Flemish tradition–but not by any means the least in value of Flemish composition–is found in some of the polyphonic works of the latter half of the 16th century. Two outstanding composers of the late Flemish period are Philippe de Monte and Orlandus Lassus. Both Monte and Lassus, like many of their contemporaries in the Low Countries, fashioned their real careers outside their homeland.

Philippe de Monte (1521–1603). From about 1541 to 1545 Monte was a tutor in the Pinelli family at Naples, where he knew Lassus. After spending some time in Rome and Antwerp he appeared in England as a singer in the choir of Philip II, husband of Queen Mary Tudor. Soon he became disenchanted with the prevalent number of Spanish singers in the choir, and in 1555 he left for Italy. In 1568 he secured the last position of his career, that of master of the chapel to Emperor Maximilian II of Vienna. His death occurred in 1603 while the court was in summer residence at Prague.

Monte published Masses and many books of motets and madrigals; he is perhaps best known for his Italian madrigals, products of his long sojourn in Italy, as he was a prolific composer in that field. However, the Sanctus of his *Missa Super Cara la vita* has been chosen for an example of his compositional style, as its presentation in HAM I, No. 146b, offers an excellent opportunity to compare the parody with the polyphonic madrigal upon which it is based, the madrigal being given in HAM I, No. 146a. The composer of the secular *Cara la vita*–Jacob van Werth–was a fellow Netherlander and, obviously, a writer of Italian madrigals. Note, in the Mass, Monte's tendency toward a free application of the parody technique, his liking for contrasting choral sections, his points of imitation within the piece, and his imitation in pairs of voices.

Orlandus Lassus (or **Orlando di Lasso**) (1532–94). Orlandus Lassus, or Orlando di Lasso, as he is sometimes known, represents the culmination of the entire century and a half of Flemish musical art. Born in Mons, he began his musical life there as a chorister in the church of St. Nicolas. Even as a boy soprano, he must have had few peers, for he was kidnaped and bodily transferred to other choirs no fewer than three times. He traveled the European continent rather extensively, but in 1556 he was offered a fine post at the court of Albert V of Bavaria and settled in Munich, where he remained more or less until his death thirty-eight years later.

Counterpoint is certainly the basis of Lassus's compositional style, and the rhythmic vitality and sensitive voice leadings of the individual lines suggest polyphonic treatment even in the obvious chordal passages. And yet in his polyphony the bass lines strongly support the harmony, with this harmonic strength further evidenced in the many chord roots that move by leaps of the fourth and fifth and in the fact that he notates the complete triad frequently, with the third of the chord clearly presented in the top voice. All this combines to add power and forward motion to the art of Lassus.

Lassus was an international composer of the first magnitude. His works, numbering about two thousand, include motets, Masses, Italian madrigals, French chansons, and German polyphonic lieder. Fifty-three Masses are extant. Most of them are parodies of chansons, motets, madrigals, and other Masses; two Masses even employ German sacred lieder. But the motets are said to reveal best his exceptional talents. The extensive nature of this literature is shown in Lassus's *Magnum opus musicum* (1604), a collection of 516 motets in from two to twelve parts.

A prominent factor in Lassus's composition–remarkable considering the many languages employed in his vocal music settings–is his masterful handling of the text. Some composers of the Renaissance (and of other historical periods as well) failed to observe such niceties as the matching of long syllables of the text with the longer note values of music; Lassus was not one of these. MM, No. 23 (*Tristis est anima mea*), demonstrates this and also his careful consideration of formal treatment in his sectional division of the motet into neatly balanced parts, again with due respect to the entire text. He, indeed, was master of the vocal setting.

FRENCH NATIONALISM

The early 16th century, in spite of the strong influence over the whole of Europe of the Netherlandish composers, was to witness the rise of national styles. In this age France, Italy, Spain, Germany, and England each began its quest for a stylistic independence, for a national music reflecting more accurately the salient characteristics of each country.

Masses by French composers were written with a hand lighter than that of Netherlanders, and have a simplicity and structural "emptiness" in their make-up. The imitative patterns are always clearly planned. This imitation is often paired between voices, and all Mass parts rarely move together for any great length of time. Most of these French sacred works reveal a mixture of polyphonic and homophonic writing, and in general display the lighter style of the contemporary French chanson. Thus the French Mass stands in sharp contrast to the 16th-century closely knit imitative Mass of the Flemings, which is characterized (as has been shown) by a heaviness of texture in a continuous musical discourse.

THE NEW CHANSON. The development of a new style in the chanson proved of interest to many French composers of the early 1500's. Chief among these were Clément Janequin (*c.* 1485–*c.* 1560), supposedly the founder of this school of writing, Claudin de Sermisy (*c.* 1490–1562), Thomas Crequillon (d. 1557), and Claude le Jeune (*c.* 1528–1600). The light, trim, highly maneuverable style, with its repetition of music for different lines of text, is revealed in Crequillon's charming *Pour ung plaisir* ("For a delight that was but fleeting"), in the print of MM, No. 20 (ignore for the moment the transcription for keyboard). The seemingly homophonic nature of the printed page belies the easy grace with which the song moves. Another composer of the group, Sermisy, cultivated a highly polished and graceful chanson in keeping with the court life of his employer, King Francis I, and Le Jeune specialized in the use of *vers mesuré* (see HAM I, No. 138) in a straightforward setting that heightened the declamation of the text by giving the strong syllables twice the duration of the weak ones.

Clément Janequin's forte in this new style was the program or descriptive chanson. His *L'Alouette* (HAM I, No. 107), which is full of nonsense words and much ado about nothing in how a man may treat his wife, pictures the characteristic employment of quickly moving patterns of notes and tight little groups of imitative passages. But perhaps better known is the same composer's *La Guerre*. In this "Battle" abrupt metrical changes, repeated notes, complex imitative procedures, and nonsense syllables combine to depict the sounds and action of the combat. A convincing and realistic portrayal of battle weapons, battle cries, battle songs, and the straining efforts of the horses is accomplished through the use of voices alone. Many of the chansons of Janequin and of other French and Flemish composers were published by Pierre Attaingnant (d. 1552), who was probably the earliest printer in France to employ movable type in printing musical scores. He issued a series of thirty-five chanson books, containing 927 polyphonic songs, during the decade 1539–49.

INFLUENCE OF CALVIN AND LUTHER. A great and lasting impact on music was made in the 16th century by the religious views of John Calvin and Martin Luther. Calvin's gradual conversion to Protestantism brought about his banishment from Paris in 1533. He took refuge in Basel, Switzerland, and there (in 1536) published his *Institution chrétienne* ("Institutes of the Christian Religion"); later, in Geneva, he was to establish a strict and highly moral theocratic government. Calvinism found acceptance in France in the Huguenot church in 1559, and a severe type of music, consisting of simple melodies set to metrical translations of psalms, became a part of the services in this new church. Clément Marot (*c.* 1495–1544), a poet in the service of Francis I, did the early translations of the psalms into the French language in the years 1533–39.

The first edition of Calvin's *Geneva Psalter* appeared in 1542 and contained thirty psalms by Marot. The melodies of the psalter had been adapted from various sources (some secular) by Louis Bourgeois (*c.* 1510–*c.* 1561). Continuing work on the psalter produced the enlarged *Geneva Psalter* of 1562; this work was to furnish tunes for the English Reformed Church and for the *Ainsworth Psalter,* the latter coming to America with the Pilgrims on the *Mayflower* in 1620. Harmonized versions of psalter melodies, intended only for private, home devotions, were made by Bourgeois (see HAM I, No. 132), and in more extensive polyphonic settings by Claude Goudimel (*c.* 1505–72) and Claude le Jeune, as may be seen in HAM I, No. 126.

GERMAN NATIONALISM

About the same time that a national type of French chanson and Mass was being developed, Germany was paying special attention to the polyphonic lied. An early beginning in the development of this type of lied is to be found in the *Locheimer Liederbuch,* written between 1455 and 1460. This collection represents the first use of German folk songs in polyphony, the settings using up to three voices. Another collection, from about fifteen years later, is known as the *Glogauer Liederbuch.* HAM I, No. 82, gives a three-voice *quodlibet* from the *Glogauer* book, a polyphonic *quodlibet* being a work in which different melodies (or bits of melodies) are simultaneously used in the various voice parts.

GERMAN POLYPHONIC LIED. Based as it is on the Flemish-styled polyphony of the late 15th century, these early beginnings of German part songs manifest slow-moving inner parts as *cantus firmi,* with the outer parts often moving in a more flowing style. Two German compositions of the Flemish composer Henricus Isaac have been briefly discussed earlier in this chapter, and more or less following in Isaac's footsteps were the later German composers Ludwig Senfl (*c.* 1490–1543) and Hans Leo Hassler (1564–1612). Senfl was a pupil of Isaac at Constance, and upon Isaac's death completed his teacher's *Choralis Constantinus.* A composer of both Catholic and Protestant music, Senfl wrote in a strong Germanic style.

Hassler, after early study with his father, became the first German composer of any particular note to journey to Italy for musical enlightenment. There he received valuable training under Andrea Gabrieli in Venice, also being influenced in his art through contact with the person and music of Giovanni Gabrieli. Upon his return to Germany, Hassler applied his training to the composition of strongly national German songs. One, a five-part secular song entitled *Mein Gmüth ist mir verwirret* ("My mind is confused [by a stubborn maid]"), had its melody become famous as a sacred piece, for shortly after Hassler's death the *superius* was supplied with the text *Herzlich thut mich verlangen* ("My heart is filled with longing"), and later it was used by Bach, with Paul Gerhardt's words *O Haupt voll Blut und Wunden* ("O sacred head now wounded"), in his *St. Matthew Passion.* Hassler's music is written in a predominantly homophonic style, and counterpoint and polyphonic practices are rarely developed in his compositions. Like Senfl, he wrote church music in both the Catholic and Protestant traditions. A Latin, polychoral motet *Laudate Dominum* (revealing his study in the Venetian school), printed in TEM, No. 28, demonstrates his direct and carefully organized homophonic concept of musical presentation.

PROTESTANT INFLUENCE ON GERMAN MUSIC. Martin Luther, the father of the Reformation in Germany, had an influence on German music which was felt from the 16th century on. He became disillusioned with Roman Catholicism after a trip to Rome in 1510/11, having been ordained a priest in the Church in 1507. He began to preach salvation by faith rather than by works, attacked the Church's sale of indulgences, and finally nailed to the church door at Wittenberg, in 1517, his famous ninety-five theses protesting many existing practices in the Church. Luther finally questioned the supremacy of the pope and was excommunicated by Pope Leo X in a bull issued June 15, 1520.

Martin Luther knew and appreciated the music of the best Flemish and German composers, and, of course, from his experience as a priest in the Catholic Church he was familiar with Gregorian chant. When music for his new church, the German Protestant Church, was being considered, Luther turned to the development of the chorale with German words. He wrote some thirty-six hymn texts, and probably a number of tunes as well; the melody for *Ein feste Burg* ("A Mighty Fortress") is generally credited to him. Chorale melodies were borrowed and adapted from plain song, German folk songs, and German popular songs, and taken into the service along with newly composed tunes. At first they were sung in unison by the congregation, but later harmonizations were made for choir performance with organ accompaniments. The chorale tunes of this new church were to inspire, through their adoption as *cantus firmi* into larger works, such magnificent music as the dramatic Baroque Passion-oratorios and chorale cantatas and organ chorale preludes by J. S. Bach in the 18th century.

Johann Walter (1496–1570). Luther's principal musical collaborator was Johann Walter, who brought out in 1524 the first polyphonic settings of chorale tunes in a collection entitled *Wittembergisch geistlich Gesangbuch* (see the setting of *Aus tiefer Not* in HAM I, No. 111a). All but one piece in this book used the chorale melody in the tenor, in a general motet stylistic setting of from three to six voices. As the flow of published collections followed into the last half of the century, there was a trend toward a standard simplified structure with the chorale melody in the soprano voice.

Henricus Glareanus (1488–1563). At this point an important theoretical treatise should be mentioned—the *Dodecachordon* ("Twelve Strings") written by Henricus Glareanus, a Swiss scholar born in Glarus. The work was published in 1547, and in it Glareanus advanced the theory of twelve modes against the commonly accepted theory of eight Church modes. Example 23 (see p. 113) illustrates the eight Church modes; Example 34 now adds four more. Mode 9 is called Aeolian;

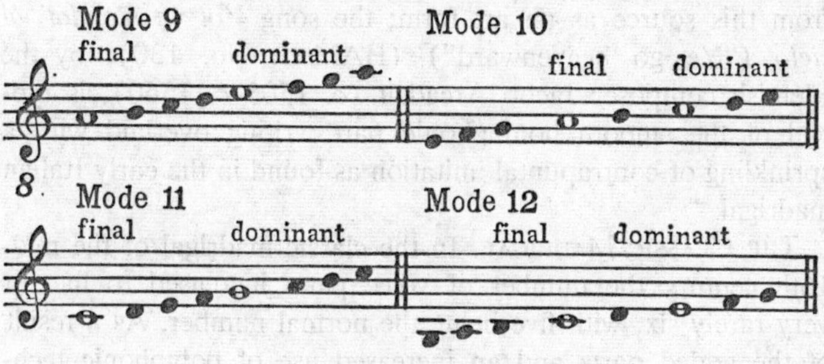

Example 34

10, Hypoaeolian; 11, Ionian; and 12, Hypoionian. In the third part of the *Dodecachordon,* Glareanus cites many works by composers of Des Prez's era as proof of the need for his new theoretical modes. Some later theorists speak even of fourteen modes, but Glareanus dismissed the pair of modes founded on the final note, B, since their scale notes would not break down (as in the case of the other twelve modes) into two groups within a perfect fifth and a perfect fourth (or the reverse).

ITALIAN NATIONALISM

THE EARLY MADRIGAL. The chief form of secular song developed in Italy was the madrigal; however, the initial impetus in its development came chiefly from the efforts of Flemish composers, and only some time later did Italian musicians assume leadership.

The madrigal appears to have developed from the *frottola,* a three- or four-part Italian secular song in chordal style (for two examples see HAM I, No. 95). When Flemish composers traveled to Italy in the early 16th century, they were much taken with this lively and entertaining form. As they began to write in this new (to them) style, the Flemings adopted the simple, chordal pattern of the *frottole,* producing hundreds of volumes of these little songs. Gradually the madrigal emerged from this source as an art form; the song *Voi ve n'andat' al cielo* ("Ye go heavenward") (HAM I, No. 130), by the Flemish composer Jacob Arcadelt (*c.* 1505–*c.* 1560), is typical of the smooth homophonic part writing overlaid with a sprinkling of contrapuntal imitation as found in the early Italian madrigal.

THE CLASSIC MADRIGAL. In the classic madrigal of the mid-16th century the number of voice parts increased to five or very rarely six, with five being the normal number. As a result of the added parts and an increased use of polyphonic techniques the texture began to thicken. Noticeable also is a more daring approach in harmonization and more chromaticism. The daring harmonics find their application in expressive renditions of certain textual passages. This classical style is exemplified in Cipriano de Rore's *Da le belle contrade* (HAM I, No. 131). Note the abrupt change in harmony at the words *"Ahi crud' amor"* ("Ah, cruel love"), an example of the expressive use of the harmonic element. Cipriano de Rore (1516–65) worked at St. Mark's Cathedral in Venice (also at Ferrara and Parma) and is one of the last of a long line of Flemish musicians to practice his art in Italy. The native-born Giovanni Palestrina also composed madrigals in the classic manner (see HAM I, No. 142), although his fame was established in the sacred music field and his secular madrigals (of which there are approximately eighty) are not well remembered. He will be discussed in greater detail later in the chapter.

From out of this middle period of madrigal development came the *Musica transalpina,* published in England in 1588. It contained fifty-seven Italian madrigals with their texts translated into English; among composers represented were Lassus, Monte, and Palestrina. *Musica transalpina,* augmented by a second volume in 1597, was to exert a tremendous effect upon English madrigal development in the late 16th century.

THE LATE MADRIGAL. The final development of the Italian madrigal occurred in the late 16th and early 17th centuries and foreshadowed the rise of the operatic solo tradition. The dramatic possibilities of the text were then more thoroughly explored than ever before. Declamatory passages and coloristic effects were sought through every possible means, and the extreme use of chromaticism tended to obscure the modal character of the works. Text painting occurred with great frequency; sometimes this procedure was clearly heard in the vocal performance, but at other times it was painted only in the notation–for example, tied notes in the manuscript at the point where the text spoke of "tying the knot" in the marriage ceremony, etc. The final trend in madrigal style inclined toward the Baroque ideal of a dominating solo line against a firm harmonic bass and chordal background, and turned away from a Renaissance ideal of equal voices in a polyphonic context.

Most madrigal texts were sentimental or erotic in subject matter, with borrowed scenes from and allusions to pastoral poetry, and this use of the pastoral scene was also to prevail in opera of the 17th century. While much of the poetry was of little literary value, some composers did use better texts for their settings–for instance, poems by Petrarch, Sannazaro (author of *Arcadia*), and Tasso. Cipriano de Rore had found Petrarch's verses especially attractive for musical settings.

The madrigal became established in the second half of the 16th century as the prime vocal medium of musical art, just as the motet and Mass had been earlier in the Renaissance. Three of the greatest names in late-16th-century Italian vocal literature worked with this form: Carlo Gesualdo (*c.* 1560–1613), Luca Marenzio (1553–99), and Claudio Monteverdi (1567–1643). Each of these three, and Gesualdo particularly, used chromatics in a mannered style, adapting them to passages written in a chordal pattern in order to accentuate the coloristic qualities of the chromatics. Twentieth-century writers in the areas of the fine arts and literature locate this "manneristic" style in certain of the creative works that existed in the transition period from the High Renaissance to the Baroque. "Mannerism" is broadly defined here as the over-prominent use of some distinctive but often affected style or technique. Thus Gesualdo, Marenzio, and Monteverdi, by their frequent use of advanced and detailed chromatic passages and by their highly expressive musical settings of the texts of their madrigals are sometimes classed as mannerists, and their musical works have been likened to the manneristic works of El Greco and Michelangelo (more especially Michelangelo's later work) and some of the later plays of Shakespeare.

In Marenzio's *S'io parto, i' moro* (MM, No. 27) tenderness of a sad farewell of one to his beloved is depicted. Marenzio was capable of painting visual objects, thoughts, and moods in musical sounds of exacting description, without, however, destroying the validity of these sounds as musical art; in his *S'io parto* it is the mood, the sad parting of the lovers, that is so effectively felt in the madrigal setting. *Moro lasso* (TEM, No. 33), by Gesualdo, has a text that also implies a severance between a couple, but now the words speak of unrequited love, and the grief of the poet is not shared by the loved one and is therefore the dregs of despair. Gesualdo's setting is extremely manneristic, with chromaticism in both melody and harmony, advanced dissonant treatment, and abrupt modal changes; again, the musical text painting found in *Moro lasso* projects the over-all mood rather than the heightening of individual words.

The last of the Italian madrigalists was Monteverdi, whose work with the madrigal was to lead him into the field of Baroque opera. He was a transitional figure of the late Renaissance and early Baroque. His earlier madrigals will be briefly mentioned here, and a more thorough examination of the art of this great composer will be found in the next chapter. Between the years 1587 and 1638 Monteverdi had published eight books of madrigals; of these only the first four (1587–1603) are in the Renaissance style of equality among voice parts. From his fourth book comes *Ohimè, se tanto amate* (HAM II, No. 188), which again in the text reveals the despair of a great love and the sorrow and mental unrest that it brings. The work demonstrates an advanced chromatic style of composition; the harmonic progressions forecast the functional approach of tonality (a feature found in late-16th-century madrigals by some other composers as well), and the dominant seventh and other dissonances are used without the preparation practiced in the "Palestrina style." Also characteristic of Monteverdi is the use of repeated notes for emphasis and for dramatic effect.

SACRED MUSIC. A look at Italian sacred music in the second half of the 16th century reveals the influence of the Council of Trent and the atmosphere of the Counter Reformation. By the beginning of the fourth decade of the 16th century the feeling for reform within the Catholic faith had reached a "do something" stage. The Society of Jesus, which was to play so important a role in the winning back of "lost souls" to the Roman faith, was founded in 1534 under the strong, guiding hand of Ignatius Loyola, and the papacy, along with these Jesuit priests, began once again to exert leadership in the realms of piety and reform.

Order within the Church was sought by the Council of Trent, convened by Pope Paul III, in a long series of meetings lasting from 1545 to 1563. Among the many problems aired, one concerned the music of the Church. Criticism had risen in many quarters regarding the use of secular melodies in the Mass, the overemployment of certain musical instruments in the churches (instruments of a type not considered conducive to meaningful worship), and the obliteration of passages of Latin texts by intricate musical settings in the polyphonic style. However, after due deliberation, a ruling handed down by the council in 1562 stated only that the music was to avoid anything detrimental to the divine atmosphere of the service.

Giovanni Pierluigi da Palestrina (*c.* 1525–94). At the head of the Counter Reformation, musically speaking, was Giovanni

Pierluigi da Palestrina. In his early years he was a chorister at the cathedral of his native town of Palestrina. He later received instruction in the choir school of the church of Santa Maria Maggiore in Rome. In 1544 he was appointed organist and choirmaster at the St. Agapit Cathedral in Palestrina. He also returned as maestro to Santa Maria Maggiore, in 1561. His last appointment (1571) was as maestro of the Cappella Giulia, a post he had held earlier under Pope Julius III.

Palestrina is the chief representative of the Roman school, and his works display a Renaissance vocal style of unsurpassed serenity and beauty. He was a busy composer, with his extant sacred compositions numbering several hundred motets, about one hundred Masses, and fifty-six sacred madrigals. Palestrina's sacred music, and particularly his Masses, best represents his somewhat reserved and controlled style. His works were uniquely treated, the "Palestrina style" being codified by Pietro Cerone's *El Melopeo y maestro* in 1613. The style was imitated, studied, and to a great extent revered by succeeding composers, even to its Romantic revival in the 19th century. The 20th century has based much of its theory of 16th-century contrapuntal practice on its study of the "Palestrina style."

Palestrina's musical style is based on the Flemish technique, but it possesses in addition a somewhat impersonal quality. Although it is true that he made use in his Masses of secular tunes such as *L'homme armé* (he based two Masses upon this popular tune: the first a *cantus firmus* type, and the second a transcription type published under the title *Missa Quarta*) and a few others, he demonstrated his strong religious bent through his use of some eighty Gregorian chant melodies as Mass material. In his melodic treatment Palestrina is about as close as one can get in polyphony to the free flow of plain song, and, like the chant, musical reflections of the text in an expressive manner do not play an important part. The melodic line of his works is constructed in a diatonic fashion, with few leaps, other than the octave, that exceed the interval of the fifth. Two basic rhythms control the music: the one called MACRO or greater rhythm, which measures the rhythm of the piece as a whole and defines the strong and weak beats; and the other, known as MICRO or partial rhythm, which indicates the rhythmic function of each voice part as it is derived through textual accentuation.

Perfect unisons, fifths, and octaves and major and minor thirds and sixths form the harmonic consonances. The fourth, generally, is treated as a consonance between upper parts, and as a dissonance between the lowest voice and any upper part. Harmonic dissonances were subject to careful handling and consisted of passing tones, suspensions, neighboring tones, and anticipations. A special dissonant formula was the *nota cambiata,* which in the 15th century was composed of three notes, and in the 16th century ("Palestrina style") was represented by a four-note figure. The 16th-century version may be explained as a passing-note figure with a change of direction, and it allowed a skip away from the dissonant (second) note of the pattern (see Example 35a). A second formula was the so-called "consonant fourth" passage, so named because the passage used a dissonant fourth, between the lowest part and an upper voice, which was supposedly rendered unobtrusive in this construction (Example 35b).

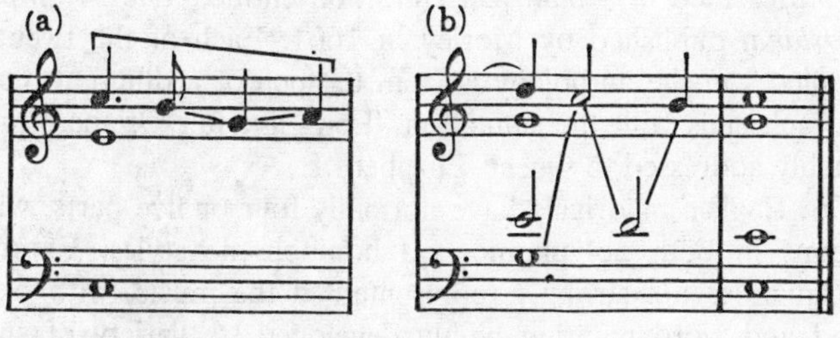

Example 35 (a and b)

An example of the *nota cambiata* can be found in measure 8 of Agnus Dei I from the famous *Missa Papae Marcelli* (HAM I, No. 140). This Mass, written in honor of Pope Marcellus II, who held the papacy briefly in the year 1555, stands as an excellent example of conformity to the reform movement in that its predominance of syllabic, note-against-note writing provides clear text declamation even though the work is in the polyphonic style. Palestrina's famous *Stabat Mater,* his *Improperia* ("Reproaches") for Good Friday, and his fine motet *Sicut cervus* ("Like as the hart desireth the water brooks"; HAM I, No. 141) also exhibit this clarity of stylistic presentation.

MUSIC IN ELIZABETHAN ENGLAND

THE MADRIGAL. The publication of the aforementioned *Musica transalpina* in England in 1588 spurred English composers to an indigenous expression in the madrigal form. The Elizabethan school, which ended around the year 1625, produced a host of madrigal writers who created one of the finest fusions of poetry and music in the whole history of music. Notable composers of the period were William Byrd (1543–1623), Thomas Morley (1557–1602), Thomas Weelkes (*c.* 1575–1623), John Wilbye (1574–1638), Orlando Gibbons (1583–1625), John Bennet (late 16th and early 17th centuries), and John Dowland (1562–1626), who is somewhat more prominent in the field of the lute song. Many of these artists are represented in a madrigal collection entitled *The Triumphs of Oriana,* published by Morley in 1601. Each of the twenty-five pieces in the anthology is from the pen of a different man, and each ends with the salutation "Long live fair Oriana," presumably addressed to Queen Elizabeth I.

The English madrigals have normally four or five parts, with sections in both polyphonic and homophonic styles. Expressive qualities are strongly represented in the music, with both mood and word painting highly developed. A variety of subjects is found in the texts; love themes and pastoral stories are predominant, but texts dealing with daily affairs and morality find their place as well. In general, these madrigals are closer in style to the Italian classic madrigal and make less effort to emulate the late Italian chromatic practice. However, chromaticism is frequently found in the madrigals of Weelkes and some others. Notice the chromatics in his *Hark, All Ye Lovely Saints*

(HAM I, No. 170) where the text reads "Ladies, why weep ye?" Observe also the nonsensical (and often danced) "Fa la la" refrains; the inclusion of this type of refrain in the madrigal style indicates a composition more properly called a *ballett,* of which another example is Thomas Morley's *My Bonny Lass* (HAM I, No. 159).

Another fine and interesting madrigal type is Dowland's *What if I Never Speed* (HAM I, No. 163). It appears in two guises, both by the same composer. The first is a lightly moving choral setting in four parts of a sorrowing love theme—a text so frequently chosen by the "doleful Dowland"; the second is a solo setting with lute accompaniment. Dowland's fame actually rests on his abilities as a lutanist song writer, for he served as one of the six lutanists to Charles I.

A more exacting illustration of the English madrigal is *Thyrsis, Sleepest Thou?* by John Bennet. A modern transcription is found in MM, No. 28. This nimble setting of a pastoral theme expresses the good humor of the majority of these English songs. Bennet's madrigal is replete with textual paintings: the questioning attitude at the beginning; the shouts on the word "Holla"; the call of the cuckoo (the cuckoo bird always sings the falling minor third); the broadening out in joyous good feeling on the words "this fair April morning"; the manner in which all singers stop and take a deep breath at bar 43 before the word "sighed"; and the bustling activity on the phrase "and drive him back to London." This is the madrigal style that leads one to believe that happy times abounded in Elizabethan England.

Church Music. A splendid era in English church music developed during the reigns of the Tudor kings, beginning sometime earlier than the madrigal period. This music had to make its way under rather difficult conditions, as England was much of this time in a vacillating position between the Catholic and Protestant faiths. These Tudor rulers and their reigns are summarized as follows: Henry VII (1485–1509); Henry VIII (1509–47); Edward VI (1547–53); Mary I (1553–58); and Elizabeth I (1558–1603). It was Henry VIII who sought and obtained from Parliament the Act of Supremacy (1534), which created a national church separate from the Roman Catholic Church and which made the king the head of the church and the clergy of England. But a more active step toward Protestantism occurred during the reign of his young son, Edward VI, under a regency, when the Act of Uniformity (1549) decreed that the liturgy of the English Book of Common Prayer be strictly adhered to *in toto.* The reign of Queen Mary ("Bloody Mary") was to restore Catholicism for a brief span, but with Elizabeth I the Church of England was firmly established. The last part of this period—so fruitful in music and letters—was to take place under the reign of James I (1603–25), the first of the Jacobean rulers.

The first notable musician of the period was John Taverner (*c.* 1495–1545), who gave up composing Catholic music and music of any description in 1530, when he joined the Reformation movement. Next was John Merbecke (*c.* 1510–*c.* 1585), to whom fell the task of providing the first musical setting of the English liturgy of 1549. This he did in his *Booke of Common Praier Noted* (1550). With Christopher Tye (*c.* 1500–*c.* 1572) and Thomas Tallis (*c.* 1505–85) began the composition of anthems and Services for the English church. Service settings were made for Morning Prayer, Evening Prayer, and Holy Communion, and were either "Great" or "Short." The Great Service used elaborate contrapuntal music, whereas the Short Service was in a simple syllabic style.

The 16th-century English anthem followed very closely the style of the Latin motet of the period, except that it had English words. Like the motet, it was sectionalized and used overlapping cadence points; on the other hand, it was usually more syllabic and in a simpler rhythmical structure. The anthem had a nonliturgical place in the Anglican liturgy (again like the motet in the Catholic service) and was originally sung at the close of Morning or Evening Prayer. An example of a quite early English anthem is *Heare the Voyce and Prayer,* by Thomas Tallis (in TEM, No. 27). With William Byrd, who, though he was a Catholic, wrote a great deal of music for the

Anglican church, came the verse anthem in which passages for solo voices alternated with sections for full choir, all accompanied by strings or organ. HAM I, No. 151, is such an anthem; here Byrd begins the piece *Christ Rising Again* with a duet for two solo voices, the soloists being joined in two later sections by a four-voice chorus.

William Byrd (1543–1623). William Byrd is considered the finest of the Elizabethan composers, and indeed one of England's all-time greats. Born at Lincolnshire, probably, he is believed to have studied music under Thomas Tallis. Byrd was appointed organist of Lincoln Cathedral in 1563, and was elected a member of the Chapel Royal in 1570, assuming his court duties, together with Tallis, as organist in 1572. He engaged in printing and publishing music with Tallis until the latter's death in 1585.

It was not unusual for composers of this period to write both Protestant and Catholic sacred music. Some of Byrd's finest music is found in his three Masses: one for three voices, another for four voices, and a third for five voices. But his motets, too, are models of late-16th-century polyphonic writing, and of such caliber that he may be called (with some reservations in stylistic considerations) the "English Palestrina." What has been said concerning the style of Palestrina, and thus the vocal style of the High Renaissance, can be applied, in general, to Byrd. But in such a composition as his motet *Ego sum panis vivus* (MM, No. 25) some of those stylistic reservations just mentioned can be seen. In this motet Byrd vacillates sharply between modality and tonality; he leans frequently to sequential passages in a true tonal manner and often uses the chordal melodic patterns and harmonic formulas of the tonal keys. With relation to the Palestrina style, there is more freedom in rhythm, vocal line (angular skips, etc.), and harmonic writing. Somewhat more peculiar to the Elizabethans than to the composers of the Roman school is the cross-relation, an example of which may be found in measure 28 of this motet (see Example 35c).

(Measure 28 of Byrd's *Ego sum panis vivus,* No. 25 in *Masterpieces of Music Before 1750,* New York, Norton, 1951)

Example 35c

Orlando Gibbons (1583–1625). A final name to be mentioned in Elizabethan sacred music is that of Orlando Gibbons, the last great composer of the English High Renaissance. His sacred music—hymn tunes, Services, anthems—was all composed for the Anglican church. His masterful handling of both contrapuntal and homophonic techniques can be seen in his *O Lord, Increase My Faith* and the verse anthem *This Is the Record of John,* HAM I, Nos. 171 and 172, respectively.

INSTRUMENTS AND INSTRUMENTAL MUSIC IN THE RENAISSANCE

LUTE MUSIC. Although vocal music predominated in Renaissance composition, the period also manifested the first real interest in an independent development of instrumental music. The lute became the popular household instrument, and every educated gentleman was required to demonstrate his ability to perform on it in addition to being able to read from a vocal part book. Lutes in various shapes and sizes are everywhere pictured in the Renaissance (see MITA, Nos. 129, 132, 134, 136, 137, 138, 140, 144). All lutes had at least one thing in common: a rounded back shaped much like a halved pear. The extant solo lute literature covers a span of time ranging from a collection printed in 1507, by Petrucci, to about 1770. The 16th-century pieces were in the form of dances, fantasias, variations, *ricercari,* free preludes, and transcriptions of vocal compositions. A few notable lute composers and performers of the period include the Spaniard Luis Milan (*c.* 1500–*c.* 1562), who really wrote for the *vihuela de mano,* a Spanish "lute" with a body like the guitar; the Italian Felice Anerio (*c.* 1560–1614); and John Dowland, of the English Elizabethan period. Several examples, all transcriptions from the original tablatures (the notational systems used for the writing down of lute music during the 16th, 17th, and 18th centuries), can be found in: (1) a fantasia by Milan in HAM I, No. 121, (2) Anerio's piece patterned after a three-voice vocal composition, *Al suon,* in HAM I, No. 160, and (3) a pair of dances by an anonymous musician in MM, No. 22.

WIND INSTRUMENTS. Wind instruments received much more attention than formerly. They were illustrated and discussed in Sebastian Virdung's *Musica getutscht und ausgezogen* ("Music in Germany") of 1511 and in Volume II of *Syntagma musicum* ("Musical Treatise") by Michael Praetorius, published in 1618. Perhaps the most important, and surely the best known today, of Renaissance wind instruments was the recorder. It was a fipple, or end-blown, flute with a "whistle" mouthpiece; its tone color was soft and just slightly reedy. The 16th century knew a whole family of such instruments, from treble to bass. Double-reed winds were known under the generic name of SHAWMS; the German name was *Pommer.* The CROMORNES were a special type of double reed with the reeds covered by a pierced wind cap, so that the player's lips did not touch the reeds and thus the reeds were set in vibration by wind pressure as in a reed organ pipe. The Renaissance trumpet was associated with heraldry, and the wooden CORNETT was used in chamber ensembles.

STRINGED INSTRUMENTS. An important group of bowed stringed instruments was the viols. These instruments, grouped in a set ("consort" or "chest") that included two basses, two tenors, and two trebles, were derived from medieval fiddles and were in turn superseded by the violin family in the 17th century. Their tuning followed that of the 16th-century lute—that is, in fourths with a third in the middle. When played, these instruments rested on the knees or were held between the legs of the performer; the back, wooden part of the bow was of a convex shape that permitted the playing of chords. The tone color was soft and quite delicate in timbre. An outstanding era of viol playing in "whole" or "broken" consorts arose in England in the Elizabethan age. Popular compositional types were the fantasia ("fancy") and the *in nomine*. The latter used a *cantus firmus* taken from the Benedictus of a Mass by Taverner. At the words of the Mass *"Benedictus qui venit in nomine Domini"* Taverner had used the antiphon *Gloria tibi Trinitas* (LU, p. 914). Thence up to the time of Henry Purcell, composers made use of this melody (as adapted by Taverner) in works for viols and for keyboard. HAM I, No. 176, is an *in nomine* setting by Thomas Tomkins (1572–1656) for treble viol, discant viol, and bass viol; the *cantus firmus* appears in the bass in long-note values.

KEYBOARD INSTRUMENTS. Throughout the Renaissance, and even as late as 1750, music for keyboard instruments—harpsichord, clavichord, and organ—was often merely designated by the term "clavier," with no special distinctions being made among these instruments. This literature flourished in Germany and Holland, Italy, Spain, France, and England; the instruments as used in the various countries—save for the organ—were a standard level of construction; however, the harpsichord existed in 16th-century Europe under several names: *clavicembalo* or *cembalo* in Italy; *clavecin* in France; and in England as the virginal or, in the small size, spinet. The music of the period for keyboard, and for lute and viols as well, makes considerable use of such forms as the *ricercare* and *canzona,* toccata, and theme and variations. A brief discussion of the *ricercare* and *canzoni,* showing their derivation from vocal models, has been given earlier in this book, in Chapter One. The toccata, the name meaning "touch piece" or a piece of "fast notes" (although some pieces labeled "toccata" are in a slow tempo), received special development in the 16th century in the hands of composers of the Venetian school. HAM I, No. 153, illustrates a toccata by Claudio Merulo (1533–

1604) of this school. Sections of brilliant passage work alternate with sections in the imitative, or *ricercare,* style.

The theme-and-variations form, which was to endure as one of the most popular of musical forms, evidently got its start in the early 16th century in Spanish lute and keyboard music, and was assiduously cultivated in the same century in the Elizabethan school. The great blind Spanish organist Antonio de Cabezón (1510–66) wrote an interesting and still frequently played set of variations on a cavalier's song (*Diferencias cavallero,* HAM I, No. 134), and William Byrd illustrated the Renaissance interest in daily affairs by composing an imposing set of variations for keyboard entitled *The Carman's Whistle.* Byrd is said to have heard the melody whistled by a London carman, a deliveryman of the market place. The English Virginal School (1560–1620), of which Byrd was the foremost member, was probably the most important instrumental school of the Renaissance; the keyboard music of this group is certainly the most entertaining of the period. The more than six hundred extant pieces include madrigal transcriptions, descriptive pieces, fantasias, dance groups, preludes, variations (often using ground basses) on melodies drawn from all walks of life, and liturgical organ works. The *King's Hunt,* by John Bull (*c.* 1562–1628), represents the descriptive genre and most graphically depicts the activities of this popular English sport. *The Fitzwilliam Virginal Book* (*c.* 1620) is a representative collection of 297 compositions, illustrating most of the types mentioned above. The style is replete with dashing scale passages, divisions (the "division" of longer-note values into shorter-note patterns), repeated chords, and ornaments. Imitation is little used, and the employment of 32nd- and 16th-note passages in the right hand is set (generally but not always) against harmonies in slower-note values in the left hand.

The portative organ was little used after the 15th century, although the positive was played to a later date. The large church organ attained solo stops and a more homogeneous sound in the 16th century, and at least in Germany and the Low Countries it developed into an instrument with several manuals and pedal clavier much as it is known today. Germany made important strides in the field of organ literature; Conrad Paumann (*c.* 1410–73) and Arnold Schlick (*c.* 1460–*c.* 1518) both contributed to the literature of the organist, and Schlick's book on organ builders and players, *Spiegel der Orgelmacher und Organisten,* 1511, remains an early source reference on such matters in German Renaissance music.

The use of voices and instruments in concert remained in the Renaissance in much the same flux as in the late Gothic period. Outside of the specified instrumental literature there was little distinction between polyphonic vocal and instrumental styles; music was performed by either voices or instruments or various combinations of both without any special grouping or designation of singers and players. For example, many compositions of the Elizabethan school were marked "apt for voices or viols." The late Venetian school made the first move toward a concrete distinction. Giovanni Gabrieli, in his *Sonata pian' e forte* (HAM I, No. 173), was the earliest known composer to indicate "*piano*" and "*forte*" and to give the exact instrumentation. He asked for two instrumental choirs: a grouping of a *cornetto* and three trombones pitted against a second choir, consisting of a violino and three trombones. This work pointed the way clearly toward the approaching Baroque age.

CHAPTER 6

Music in the Baroque Period

INTRODUCTION

The word "baroque" means irregular in form; it was originally applied to a pearl of distorted shape. When the term was applied to the art, architecture, and music of the period extending roughly from 1600 to 1750, it was done so in a derogatory sense, for many believed—at least in the initial phase of the period—that its creative efforts were grotesque and in corrupt taste. Today that attitude is no longer prevalent; Baroque art is now considered aesthetically satisfying, and its music is becoming more and more popular.

The 17th century saw Europe bitterly divided between Catholic and Protestant, and this division necessitated a change of direction among church-sponsored artists. While the painter Peter Paul Rubens in his *Elevation of the Cross* and the sculptor Giovanni Bernini with his impressive *Ecstasy of Santa Teresa* could carry on the Catholic tradition and treat secular subjects as well, certain sects of Protestantism, eschewing the attractions of art for religious purposes, forced many artists to turn only to contemporary secular themes for their inspiration. Thus, when the Netherlands fought for independence from Spain and against the rule of Philip II (reigned 1556–98), the Protestantism that lay behind the revolt was steeped in iconoclasm—the smashing and breaking of images and relics that had formed a part of the interiors of the Roman Catholic churches. The Netherlandish Reformed Church insisted on such strictness in its décor that religious art had little place in the works of the great Dutch painter Rembrandt van Rijn. He and his contemporaries among Dutch artists most often turned to scenes of everyday life in Holland, with particular emphasis on portraits and self-portraits as a popular means of artistic expression. However, unlike the Renaissance portrait (which gloried in man—his discovery of himself), the 17th-century portrait sought to portray the feelings of man, his happiness and his torments.

As for music, Protestantism in the Netherlands and in north and central Germany created a strong sacred organ and vocal literature based on the chorale melodies, beginning with the works of the Dutch composer Jan Pieterszoon Sweelinck and terminating in the great Lutheran organ and choral music of Johann Sebastian Bach. The Protestant courts in Germany were also offering a new direction in secular efforts by providing the facilities for productions of opera and chamber music. The Roman Catholic Church was not to be shunted aside so easily, however, and the Baroque was to see a continuation of the Counter Reformation (the inception of this movement was discussed in the previous chapter) in which many ex-Catholics were won back into the fold by the efforts of the Order of St. Dominic and the Society of Jesus. Of course, the arts were called upon to aid in this vast reconversion, and Baroque Catholic musicians responded with works of great scope and elaborate conception.

THE TWO PRACTICES. As with the Renaissance movement, Italy led the way into the era of Baroque music and remained the fountainhead of continuing changes as the period progressed. This is not to deny national strength elsewhere, for Baroque musical art had its day in France, Germany, and England, although these countries' respective phases of development followed similar ones in Italy. Seventeenth-century Italian musicians wrote in two practices (*stile antico,* or *prima prattica,* and *stile moderno,* or *seconda prattica*) and three styles (church, home, and theater). Of the two practices the *prima prattica* perpetuated the Palestrina style of the High

Renaissance and was cultivated in Rome and other religious centers concerned primarily with sacred music, while the *seconda prattica* relaxed the rules of strict counterpoint and permitted a freer use of dissonances–without special efforts at preparation or resolution–and concerned itself more with dramatic effects. The *stile moderno* (second practice) was the style of the new madrigals and other secular pieces performed in the drawing rooms of the upper class and the nobility, and the style as well in which the operas of the 17th century were conceived. Closely bound in with the new dramatic effects inherent in the *stile moderno* were the FIGURES OF AFFECTIONS. The doctrine of the affections involved the depiction in musical sound of states of emotion, i.e., sadness, gladness, anger, passion, and so on. But these states were not the emotions of the Romantics which are familiar to us; rather they were highly stylized "affections" or states of feeling. Musical figures of different types were then classified as representing one or another of these stylized affections or feelings; eventually it came to pass that where the writing of these musical figures became so stereotyped it threatened the originality of the composer.

New trends in melodic and harmonic procedures also played a part in the second practice. The melodies covered a greater range and seemed to "get there" more quickly, as diatonicism gave way to a more liberal use of intervallic leaps within the diatonic framework; augmented and diminished intervals became more common in melodic phrases, especially those written for instruments. In the chordal harmony, dissonant notes appeared without preparation and with resolutions either upward or downward; these unprepared harmonies were mostly of the seventh-chord variety, and altered notes were often found within these structures. These melodies and harmonic elements were presented in the widest of rhythmic possibilities, ranging all the way from a completely free, unmeasured style –Monteverdi's *senza battuta* ("without measure")–to a strictly barred metrical pulse.

OTHER NEW DEVELOPMENTS. Idiomatic writing–that is, musical composition that distinguishes between vocal and instrumental styles and that uses specific styles for specific instruments—became much more pronounced in the Baroque age, yet it cannot be denied that some of the old unconcern for particular idiom (as seen in late Gothic and Renaissance composition) remained. Along with idiomatic writing (such as that demanded for the new violin family), the rise of the opera, the oratorio, and the cantata created such stylistic innovations as recitative (*stile recitativo*), *concertato* style (*stile concertato*), and *basso continuo* ("thorough bass" or "figured bass").

The RECITATIVE was a vocal technique utilizing a sort of "sung speech" in which a line of text was recited to the accompaniment of chords on the harpsichord; with the addition of orchestral accompaniment the ARIOSO developed; and when the recitation assumed a more melodious character cast in distinct phrasings and a specific form, the ARIA came into being. The large secular and sacred vocal forms of the Baroque were to make use of all three of these sung types.

The emotional grandeur and the dramatic sweep of Baroque art are especially found in the music of the Counter Reformation, in the sacred literature of the Lutheran and Anglican churches, and in the secular field of opera. Important to this dramatic and emotional side of Baroque music was the CONCERTATO style. This involved a contrasting of the vocal and instrumental media, or it might have used only the contrast within a vocal or instrumental group. The *concertato* style is heightened in performance through the echo effect (that is, the terraced dynamic: *forte-piano*) and by abrupt rhythmical changes. The *stile concertato* first appeared in the polychoral works of the Venetian school, and Giovanni Gabrieli's *Sonata pian' e forte* (mentioned in the previous chapter) is an early usage of contrasting instrumental choirs.

The stylistic concept of the *basso continuo* is so important to Baroque art that the entire 150 years has sometimes been known as the era of thorough bass ("thorough" is the old spelling for "through"), and no ensemble music of the period fails to make use of it. The CONTINUO is a bass line that runs, as the name implies, continuously throughout the composition. Two players perform from this part; the one "realizes" a completed score for either a lute, guitar, harpsichord, or organ from figures written by the composer beneath the bass part (occasionally basses were unfigured and the harmonization was then left to the imagination of the performer), while the other player merely duplicates the line on a stringed instrument such as the violone or cello, or else in wind combinations on a bassoon. Thus the *continuo* line served both as a horizontal unifying element and in its realization as a vertical, harmonic stabilizing force. Improvisation entered into Baroque music in considerable measure through the realization of *continuo* parts, and all members of the ensemble were free to add ornaments and graces of all types to the often skeletally notated scores.

This new emphasis on the bass line was to have far-reaching effects. The Baroque age had inherited, of course, the polyphonic style of the Renaissance, but with this addition of a bass part with figures that dictated the harmonic structure of the upper voices, a new blend of horizontal and vertical associations was established, and it was called HARMONIC COUNTERPOINT. Whereas Renaissance polyphonic theory was based on intervallic considerations of the individual lines with only some regulation of vertical dissonant structures, the Baroque contrapuntal practice involved consideration both for the individual line and for the correct function of each chord of the harmonic structure in a given passage. The melody of the top part and the bass line became all important, with the inner parts of the score frequently improvised or else left by the composer for his students to complete. Today it is the custom, when editing music of the 17th and early 18th centuries, to add notes to the score, but only when informed study and good sense have deemed them advisable. This polarity of voices—the dominance of the soprano and bass lines—is uniquely Baroque and accounts for the improvisational character of the music; as only the outermost voices structurally defined a work, the inner voices could then be safely left to improvisation.

With the establishment of harmonic counterpoint came a drawing away from the modal system of the 16th century. The early Baroque served as the transitional period from modality to tonality, and music written during this time can be analyzed now in the modal system and again according to the tonal system as composers boldly ventured into the *seconda prattica.* But when these early-17th-century musicians did make use of the tonal chords, they at first had no knowledge of functional procedure, and as a result their compositions were either of short duration or consisted of a grouping of brief movements. Extended composition was not possible until the functional use of chord progressions and modulations to near-related keys was thoroughly established, which occurred around the year 1680.

EARLY BAROQUE: ITALY

THE BEGINNING OF OPERA

In the late 16th century many humanists displayed an interest in reviving the classical Greek drama, and a number of academies were founded to further this end. One such society, the Florentine Camerata, was composed of a group of intellectuals including the noblemen Count Bardi (whose palace was the first meeting place) and Jacopo Corsi; the singer-composers Giulio Caccini and Jacopo Peri; the poets Ottavio Rinuccini and Torquato Tasso; the theorist Girolamo Mei; the composer Emilio del Cavalieri; and Vincenzo Galilei, lutanist, madrigal composer, and father of the astronomer Galileo Galilei. It was Vincenzo Galilei who published, in 1581, the *Dialogo della musica antica e della moderna* ("Dialogue Concerning Old and New Music"), in which he denounced the Renaissance polyphonic style as incapable of rendering the text either clearly or expressively, and advocated instead a solo style that would follow closely the natural rhythms and inflections of the words, to be supported by a simple chordal accompaniment so designed as never to intrude upon the vocal line with its all-important text. This all led to a solo song in recitative style called MONODY, a Greek name for a supposed rediscovery of Greek solo singing; it was a style that supposedly represented the true sentiment or feeling of the text (*stile rappresentativo*).

Monodies quickly appeared in many collections and in operas, cantatas, and oratorios. Some early extant works in the Florentine monodic style are found in *Le Nuove musiche* by Caccini (*c.* 1546–1618), published in 1602. This "New Music" volume is a collection of twenty-two solo songs—twelve through-composed "madrigals" and ten songs in strophic style, the melodies to be accompanied by chordings on the *chitarrone* (a large lute; see MITA, Nos. 194 and 195).

The first usage of the monodic style in a dramatic situation of large scope—later to be called opera—was *Dafne* (*c.* 1597) with music by Jacopo Peri (1561–1633) and libretto by Ottavio Rinuccini (1562–1621); its score, save for a few short pieces, has been lost. The first complete opera, *Euridice,* dates from the year 1600, and is a joint effort by Peri and Caccini, with the libretto again by Rinuccini; the text is the well-known myth of Orpheus and Eurydice, but with a happy ending and a stressing of the pastoral element. It was first performed in 1600 at the marriage of Henry IV of France and Marie de Médicis; the next year each composer published his version of the opera, these being the actual surviving copies. These operas by Peri and Caccini are among the earliest works having *basso continuo* with figures. HAM II, No. 182, illustrates the recitative *Funeste piaggi* ("Sad shores") from Peri's *Euridice;* in his preface to this opera the composer stated how he had observed the speech habits of people and how he had reproduced them in his work. *Funeste piaggi* shows Peri's plan of keeping the vocal part at the same pitch until the text demanded a change, at which time the supporting chord also changed.

Claudio Monteverdi (1567–1643). Claudio Monteverdi was the greatest Italian musician of the first half of the 17th century, and in fact he is one of the finest composers in the history of the art of music. Monteverdi began his contacts with music as a chorister at the cathedral in Cremona, where he studied with Marc' Antonio Ingegneri (1545–92). About 1590 he entered the service of Vincenzo Gonzaga, Duke of Mantua; he lost this position upon the death of his patron in 1612, but in the following year he was appointed *maestro di cappella* at St. Mark's Church, Venice, where he remained until his death in 1643. As Monteverdi was a transitional figure, some of his earlier works are discussed in the previous chapter.

It was in Mantua, in 1607, that Monteverdi's initial opera, *Orfeo,* was first performed, and it scored an immediate success. Though perhaps the work may be said to be based on Florentine monody, it is a vastly expanded version of that style. The long, dreary stretches of recitative in the Peri and Caccini settings are now broken up by solos, duets, madrigal choruses (Monteverdi had thoroughly prepared himself for opera by the earlier writing of dramatic madrigals), and dances. The musical content is also more arresting, with a greater emotional impact through more expressive harmonies and melodies. Even Monteverdi's plot is a little different from the earlier works, for Rinuccini had imposed no conditions as to whether Orpheus could look behind him as he left Hades, thus securing a happy reunion of the principal characters (as do most later operas on this subject), while Monteverdi's source, a poem by Alessandro Striggio, retains the tragic atmosphere, with Eurydice finally being lost to Orpheus. Thus Monteverdi ventured, not only into opera, but into drama as well.

Orfeo is an opera in five acts; the first two are set in a pastoral scene, the next two are cast in the infernal regions, and the last portrays the rise of Orpheus to heaven on the merciful wings of Apollo. A number of "firsts" occur in the opera: (1) the use of *castrati* singers; (2) the approach to the arioso (accompanied recitative–parts written out, or realized, by the composer); and (3) a fanfare-type overture. Although the composer infrequently specifies particular instruments at any given spot, he lists around forty instruments in the score, dividing them into chord-playing and melodic-type categories. Of the former there were two harpsichords, two organs with wood pipes, a regal (a small, portable organ with reed pipes), and lutes, citharas, and bass gambas; the melody types included treble and bass strings, two *cornettos* (or zinks, of wood; see MITA, Nos. 145 and 177), one flute, trumpets, and trombones.

It was left to the music director, for the most part, to deploy these instruments for accompaniment as he saw fit. However, the composer did specify a few instrumental colors, such as in the infernal scenes of Act III. There he wanted the sounds of the regal, wood organ, bass strings, and trombones; the trombones thus began their traditional association with the *ombrae,* or ghostly scenes, of opera. *Orfeo* has twenty-six pieces for instruments alone.

The two musical peaks in the opera are Orpheus's song in Act II, when he is informed of the death of Eurydice, and his song in Act III, when he attempts to charm Charon into ferrying him across the river Styx. The first, *Tu se' morta* ("Thou art dead"), can be found in MM, No. 31; this song, in a recitative style accompanied by a wood organ and a *chitarrone,* attains its deep pathos through a subtle handling of repeated tones, chromatics, and word and mood painting. Orpheus's solo from Act III, *Possente spirto* ("Thou powerful spirit"), is the opposite of *Tu se' morta.* Four of its five stanzas have the same but rhythmically varied bass over which are written different and highly ornamented vocal melodies; moreover each stanza has a different instrumental accompaniment, in *stile concertato.*

Monteverdi's *Orfeo* has been discussed at some length because it is the first real masterpiece in the field of opera, but unfortunately his full development in this medium cannot be traced, as only two further complete operas, from his last years, are extant. An opera, *Arianna,* dates from the year 1608, but only one piece, the "Lament," is extant. It is, however, well worth having, for it is a famous song and was greatly admired in the 17th century. Even though Monteverdi assumed the post of chapel master at St. Mark's Church in 1613 he did not forget about opera, and after the first public opera house, Teatro San Cassiano, was opened in Venice in 1637 (two other houses followed in 1639), Monteverdi was one of the first to write opera for public enjoyment. In 1641 he produced *Il Ritorno d'Ulisse* ("The Return of Ulysses") and in 1642 *L'Incoronazione di Poppea* ("The Coronation of Poppea"), his last opera and one of the masterpieces of all operatic literature.

Both *Poppea* and *Orfeo* have had successful 20th-century revivals, but the former is perhaps the more easily appreciated by modern audiences. The libretto, by Francesco Busenello, deals with the Roman emperor Nero and his love for Poppea, who is the wife of Ottone, a general in Nero's army. The general is forthwith banished, Nero's wife, Ottavia, is divorced, and Poppea is crowned empress. The opera is not one of display, for few dramatic ensembles other than duets were written, but rather it is remarkable for its deep insight into human character. This is largely made possible by an extremely perceptive and sensitive libretto, and the timely arrival of the new Baroque concepts of dramatic, melodic, and harmonic expression. The love scenes between Nero and Poppea have been compared to the emotional feelings of Tristan and Isolde, and also to the masterful setting of the love duet of Otello and Desdemona at the end of Act I of Verdi's *Otello*. Technical features in *Poppea* include both through-composed and strophic songs, recitatives, full-blown arias, *ostinato* basses, and a closing duet in *da capo* form over a chaconne or passacaglia bass (the last named may be found in GMB, No. 178).

Before leaving Monteverdi comment should be made on his last four books of madrigals (his first four volumes were discussed in the previous chapter). These last four publications are considered Baroque works because they use the accompanying *continuo* part and because of the increased complexity of their dramatic element. They may also be considered the gateway to Monteverdi's operatic art. Of especial renown is his *Combat of Tancred and Clorinda,* included in Book VIII, entitled *Madrigali guerrieri et amorosi* ("Madrigals of War and Love"), published in 1638, although the *Combat* was earlier performed in Venice in 1624. The text is a passage from Tasso's *Gerusalemme liberata,* written in 1575. A Norman officer, Tancred, has fallen in love with an infidel maiden named Clorinda. One evening he chances upon her, but as she is armor-clad, he fails to recognize her. Thinking Clorinda another soldier, Tancred challenges her to a duel to the death, and after an all-night fight, in which Clorinda does remarkably well, he fatally wounds her. Tancred is, naturally, heartbroken when he lifts the metal visor of her helmet, and he does what he can for her by administering the baptismal rite before she dies. In the preface to this composition Monteverdi wrote how he had devised an agitated or excited compositional style (*stile concitato*) to set the action of the combat. This was accomplished through the dramatic usage of string tremolo and string pizzicato combined with a liberal number of quickly played repeated-note patterns. *Morendo,* the gradual diminishing of tone and tempo, was also employed, and the characters sang their parts in *stile rappresentativo,* affective solo melodies with a chordally conceived accompaniment. The dramatic madrigal used as well a narrator, and we can find in HAM II, No. 189, how this *testo* describes a portion of the combat. The accompanying instruments supply the agitation and sounds of the fight with irregular dotted rhythms intermingled with brief rests in the music and with tremolos by the strings.

SACRED MUSIC

Italian composers of the early Baroque made use of both *stile antico* and *stile moderno* practices in the composition of sacred music. The modern style embraced monody, a grand display type called "colossal," and the *stile concertato,* involving either a few or quite a number of performers. Surely the best example of the "colossal" Baroque style is the *Festival Mass* by the Roman Orazio Benevoli (1605–72), written for the dedication in 1628 of the Salzburg Cathedral. This massive work for fifty-three voices involved two eight-part choruses, soloists, and a *continuo* part for lute, harpsichord, two organs, and harps. What a magnificent sound it must have made in the open spaces of the cathedral at Salzburg.

An Italian, Lodovico Viadana (1564–1645), is credited with being the first composer to write sacred "concertos," in which the word "concerto" implies a contrast between a singer or group of singers and a required instrumental accompaniment. He published a collection of such works in 1602, called *Cento concerti ecclesiastici.* HAM II, No. 185, offers his *Exaudi me, Domine* from this volume, in which a solo voice sings to an organ accompaniment. Monteverdi's sacred compositions include two Masses with organ *continuo* and a considerable number of other religious settings. His later works use the *concertato* style, and while at St. Mark's he employed the agitated manner of writing exclusively.

INSTRUMENTAL MUSIC

Italy also led the way in the development of Baroque instrumental art. While it is true that the instrumentation of the opera orchestra laid the foundation for the establishment of the orchestra as a separate medium in the 18th century, of more immediate concern here is the early Baroque literature for organ and for string ensemble. A great number of the early instrumental works were conceived in connection with bass formulas, showing once again the importance of this line in Baroque music. Some of these became quite stereotyped, receiving such names as *romanesca, passamezzo antico, folia* (for these three see Example 36a, b, c; the circled notes are those basic to the pattern named, with the other notes of the bass line serving as ornamental or "filler" tones), and *passamezzo moderno* and *ruggiero.* The passacaglia and chaconne (see

(a) Frescobaldi: ***Romanesca***

Example 36

(b) Anonymous (16th century): *Passamezzo antico*

(c) Corelli: *Folia*

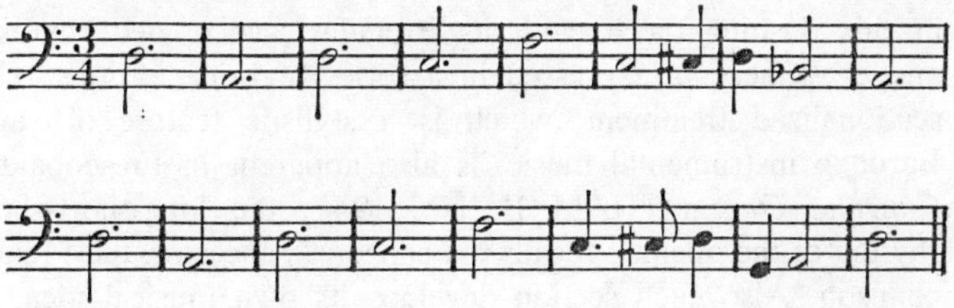

(d) Bach: *Passacaglia*

(e) Bach: *Chaconne*

Example 36 (cont.)

Example 36d, e) appeared as ground basses about the year 1600 in vocal and instrumental compositions (see Chapter 2 for a discussion of these types).

Girolamo Frescobaldi (1583–1643). An important name in

early Baroque Italian organ music was that of Girolamo Frescobaldi. After study in Ferrara, he took up residence for the year 1607 and part of 1608 in Brussels; at this time there may have been some exchange of musical influence between Frescobaldi and the Jan Sweelinck of Amsterdam (who was to be called the "maker" of German Baroque organists), for when Frescobaldi assumed the organist post at St. Peter's, Rome, in 1608 he was already so famous that a massive congregation of thirty thousand persons attended his first performance.

The toccata, canzona, and ricercare musical forms, established during the 16th century, received extensive development in the Baroque age. Frescobaldi's compositions illustrate early Baroque usage of these types. HAM II, No. 193, is a print of his Toccata 9. The excitement of this form of music is shown in this dashing piece, with its irregular, syncopated rhythms and cross accents expressed in a series of brief sections. The sectionalized treatment, which is a stylistic feature of early Baroque instrumental music, is also apparent in Frescobaldi's *Canzona Quarta* (HAM II, No. 194); the long-short-short rhythm of the opening recalls the canzona's ancestor, the French chanson. Also each section develops its own musical idea, in a contrasting manner. By way of a special comment, the dotted figures in this piece should be played in an active, well-marked style to conform with 17th-century performance practice.

Frescobaldi's *Ricercar dopo il Credo* (MM, No. 34), a monothematic *ricercare,* serves well as a direct predecessor of the fugue. The chromatic theme, typical of Frescobaldi's writing, begins on the tonic (*g* minor) and moves to the dominant of the scale; the bass entry in measure 5 shows the tonal answer moving from dominant to tonic, with the downward leap of a fourth in the subject compensated for by a skip downward of the fifth in the answer. Dissonant treatment is freely handled throughout the composition. The work is divided into two parts, the first ending in measure 24 with a *tierce de Picardie* (B♮) in the soprano; this shows the reluctance of Baroque composers to close any composition or principal section in a minor mode. The second section makes use of the subject in augmentation (measures 24–41). At measure 41, Frescobaldi begins an ending in free style, again a typical procedure, that is anchored by an inverted, dominant pedal point in the alto voice.

EARLY AND MIDDLE BAROQUE: THE NETHERLANDS AND GERMANY

THE NETHERLANDS

Jan Pieterszoon Sweelinck (1562–1621). Musical history has recorded Jan Pieterszoon Sweelinck as one of the greatest of Dutch musicians. He served as organist of the Old Church in Amsterdam for about forty years; his keyboard music is the most important part of his compositions, perhaps because the northern part of the Netherlands was Calvinist and the zeal with which this belief was practiced limited church music to the strict style of the Huguenot Psalter. Possibly Sweelinck and Frescobaldi knew each other's music, but Sweelinck certainly *was* influenced by the style of such English virginalists as Bull and Philips (for some of his pieces in that style are to be found in the *Fitzwilliam Virginal Book*), and the Dutch musician was in turn celebrated for his teaching and playing; nearly all of the leading North German organists of the next generation were his pupils.

Frescobaldi and Sweelinck were alike in that they both had a hand in developing the fugue form. Each composer often used a single, chromatic subject, Frescobaldi in the *ricercare* and Sweelinck in the fantasia. Also each had about the same approach to compositions of this type: chromatic subject, answers either real or tonal, figurative accompaniments to the theme which might pass for countersubjects, augmentation and diminution of the theme, the use of *stretto,* and a final flourish at the end usually combined with a pedal point. But Sweelinck made certain additional steps forward in organ literature, on the basis of an advanced construction of the instrument in the Netherlands. Since the organs of the Low Countries had a pedal clavier, he was among the first to assign a fugal line or theme to it and to develop organ contrapuntal writing on this new basis.

GMB, No. 158, is a *Fantasia cromatica* by Sweelinck, showing the advanced fugal stylistic features developed by this composer within the rhapsodic structure of the fantasy. All the way through, and especially in the second part, the scholarly movement of the fugal type vies with freely moving lines in fantasia style, the one complementing the other. Incidentally, it is the use of rhapsodic passages in Sweelinck's fantasias that distinguishes most markedly his form of fugal development from a similar one in Frescobaldi's more sober *ricercare*.

Sweelinck's keyboard variations on chorale tunes and on psalm tunes signal the beginning of the organ chorale literature. Protestant church melodies are set as *cantus firmi* by him in a musical framework that clearly shows its origin to be the style of the Elizabethan virginal school.

GERMAN VOCAL MUSIC

Germany at this time offers the sad picture of a land devastated by the Thirty Years' War (1618–48), and divided culturally and spiritually by a Protestant north and a Catholic south. Musically speaking, 17th-century German composers were concerned primarily with the writing of choral and organ music. In Protestant Germany two principal types of vocal religious settings developed which involved an important role for chorale melodies: (1) the chorale motet, written in the *prima prattica* and using the chorale tune either in fugal expositions or as a *cantus firmus,* and with an optional *continuo* part; or (2) the chorale *concertato,* in which the chorale appeared either as *cantus firmus* or in motivic fragments combined with the grandiose *concertato* style of the Venetian school, this time always with a *basso continuo.* To these two chorale types was added a third expression in dramatic *concertato* style, with biblical texts in Latin and German but not using chorale melodies.

The three great German "S's" of the period were Johann

Schein, Samuel Scheidt, and Heinrich Schütz. Scheidt will be discussed later in the chapter. It was Schein, along with Schütz, who introduced the Italian monodic and *concertato* styles into German art.

Johann Schein (1586–1630). Johann Schein became cantor at St. Thomas, Leipzig, in 1616, thus becoming one of Bach's predecessors in that position. One of his important publications while in Leipzig was the *Opella nova* or *Geistliche Konzerte* ("New Work" or "Sacred Concertos") (I, 1618; II, 1626). This work, in both parts, used German and a few Latin texts, chorale words and melodies, various instruments and *continuo.*

Heinrich Schütz (1585–1672). Heinrich Schütz wrote no independent instrumental works, but on the strength of his choral music he is considered the greatest German composer of the 17th century. Bowing to his parents' wishes, he entered Marburg University in 1609 to study law, but the call of music was too great, and he soon left for Italy to study with Giovanni Gabrieli. In 1617 he was appointed *Kapellmeister* to the Elector of Saxony at Dresden; another visit to Italy, in 1628/29, brought fruitful study with Monteverdi. Later he served at various times as court conductor at Copenhagen.

Schütz's Italian heritage is evident in his *Symphoniae sacrae* ("Sacred Symphonies") published in 1629, 1647, and 1650. Although raised in a Calvinistic environment, Schütz later accepted the orthodox Lutheran faith, but evidently his Lutheranism was subjugated to his Venetian training, or he felt cramped by the adoption of chorale tunes into his music, for little use is made of the chorale in his composition. However, the motets found in *Symphoniae sacrae* are especially representative of the vigor of Schütz's harmonic, melodic, and rhythmic invention, and his religious belief is strongly stated in a motet like *O Herr, hilf* ("O Lord, help"), represented in MM, No. 33. This piece has a firm rhythmical organization, together with an interesting rhythmic variant called hemiolia; the HEMIOLIA, meaning "three in the time of two," occurs in passages in triple meter in which the notation of two measures is so arranged as to give the feeling of three strong and slower pulses instead of the six quicker beats. Such a feeling occurs in *O Herr, hilf* in measures 38–39, 42–43, 56–57, and 59–60; the practice is not entirely new, but is highly developed throughout the Baroque period within the new concept of strict, metrical rhythm. Imitative points based on steady dotted rhythms occur here and there in the first section of the motet, and the music of the "Hosanna in the highest" text is effectively organized through the detailed use of the melodic and harmonic sequence.

Also from the *Symphoniae sacrae,* another motet, *Saul, was verfolgst du mich* ("Saul, why persecutest thou me?") HAM II, No. 202, reverts somewhat to an earlier polychoral practice, but with the assurance of maturity. The work is in a large *concertato* ensemble of six soloists, two choruses of four parts each, two obbligato violins, and an organ *continuo.* Schütz's dramatic abilities and deft handling of the German language and the musical setting are prevalent throughout, but they are especially notable in the opening calls (and elsewhere) to Saul and also in the parallel, dissonant seconds on the word "persecutest" (a technique he must have learned from Monteverdi). Still more graphic effects are found at the pictorial phrase "it is hard for thee to kick against the pricks."

Other prominent collections of Schütz's choral music include the *Psalmen Davids* (1619), written in the polychoral style of the Venetian school; the *Cantiones sacrae* (1625), in *concertato* style; and the *Geistliche Chormusik* (1648), which has works sometimes written with instrumental accompaniment and sometimes for voices alone, and is always reminiscent of the *stile antico.*

The first masterful settings of German Baroque oratorio and Passion music came from the pen of Schütz. *The Resurrection Story, The Seven Words of Christ on the Cross, The Christmas Story,* and the Passions according to St. Matthew, St. Luke, and St. John rank among the finest of the century.

A curious mixture of the old and the new, of modality and tonality, makes them somewhat strange to 20th-century singers on first reading, but they are definitely within the scope of good modern choirs and are of such beauty and profound religious inspiration that they could well be performed by Protestant church choirs today (samples from the *Seven Last Words* are given in GMB, No. 191, and HAM II, No. 201). The Passions are devoid of chorales and are in *a cappella* style; the words of Jesus and other soloists have plain-song settings; also another striking feature of the *Seven Last Words,* and some others of his works, is the "string halo" that accompanies the words of Christ.

Other Vocal Music Composers. To some the charming *continuo* lieder of the 17th century mark the beginning of German lieder. Outstanding among composers of the *continuo* lieder were Heinrich Albert (1604–51) and Adam Krieger (1634–66). Albert's style can be seen in *Auf, mein Geist* ("Rise, my soul"), printed in HAM II, No. 205, for solo voice, *continuo,* and an instrumental sinfonia (*ritornello*); it is vigorous, forthright, and expressive.

Adam Krieger's publication *Arien* (1656–66), for solo voice or small vocal ensembles with instrumental *ritornelli,* reaches a high level of perfection in the *continuo* lied. His songs combine the strong, strict rhythms of German dances with the beautiful, clear lines of Italian *bel canto,* and these secular works received performance in the homes of the middle class and by students at the universities. The duet *Frisch, fröhlich, frei* illustrates the rhythmic drive of a drinking song and is somewhat prophetic of a style coming later in the music of Bach and Handel. Another example is the solo lied *Aurora und Stell,* one of Krieger's most graceful songs. Written in praise of a beautiful Leipzig lady, it contains a lovely melody floating above an *ostinato* bass consisting of a falling and rising *D*-major octave scale. Here we see the Baroque moving toward the acceptance of the new tonal system and further illustrating the concept of polarity of voice lines.

GERMAN INSTRUMENTAL MUSIC

German keyboard music was concerned early in the Baroque with the organ, and only later with idiomatic writing for the clavichord and harpsichord. Composition and performance of this organ music divided Germany into three sectors: the northern, central, and southern schools. The northern and central schools developed the prelude and fugue, variations, and types using the chorale tune; the Catholic south specialized in the verset (a type of short prelude or interlude), *canzona, ricercare,* and toccata.

Especially prominent in organ music of the North German school were Delphin Strungk (1601–94), Heinrich Scheidemann (*c.* 1596–*c.* 1663), Franz Tunder (1614–67), and Jan Adams Reinken (1623–1722). This school was almost wholly derived from Sweelinck, his many German pupils furthering his style and passing on his influence to the High Baroque, where it directly affected the music of the great master, Bach. Scheidemann succeeded his father, upon the latter's death in 1625, as organist at St. Catherine's, Hamburg. It is said that Heinrich Scheidemann's playing and composition (see his two preludes in HAM II, No. 195) were like himself—popular, agreeable, cheerful, with no effort at pretense or showiness. Tunder became organist at the Marienkirche in Lübeck in 1641. His prelude and fugue in HAM II, No. 215, is a continuation and development of the early Baroque fugal style; the rhapsodic style of the prelude contrasts nicely with the tight little fugue based on a tight little subject, and the fugue culminates in the traditional flourish over a tonic pedal point. Probably the best known of the group is Reinken, a pupil of Scheidemann, who succeeded his teacher at St. Catherine's Church. Though this position placed a large four-manual organ at his disposal and gained him honor and fame, few of Reinkin's compositions are extant; however, a set of his variations for keyboard can be seen in GMB, No. 207.

Samuel Scheidt (1587–1654). Another distinguished Sweelinck pupil, Samuel Scheidt, formed the focal point of the Central German school. His work at Halle, both as organist of the Moritzkirche and as *Kapellmeister* to the Margrave of Brandenburg, was so widely appreciated that many young organists who were unable to come to Halle made provisions to study with him by correspondence! His famous *Tabulatura nova* (1624) revolutionized German notation, for it adopted Italian keyboard score in place of the old German tablature; that is, Scheidt wrote the compositions in this book on staves of five lines with a separate staff for each voice part. Other interesting features in his musical scores are passages for double pedal, phrase markings called *imitatio violistica,* rapid reiteration of a single note by a finger of each hand alternately (called tremolo by Scheidt), and directions for the use of stops and pedal clavier.

Johann Jacob Froberger (1616–67). As with Scheidt in the central school, the South German school may be said to be based on the works of a single outstanding musician, Johann Jacob Froberger. Toward the middle of his career he enjoyed five years of study with Frescobaldi, and he carried this association into his compositional style, especially in his keyboard *ricercari, canzone,* and toccatas. However, he also toured widely and knew the English and French styles, and was especially influenced by the latter.

Froberger is usually credited with the origin of the suite form. He used the allemande, courante, and sarabande stylized dances as the basic components of his suite, with the gigue (when used) as an interior dance movement. However, later editions tend to place the gigue as a final, climactic offering, as in the *Suite in e minor* (MM, No. 35). The allemande, which originated about 1550 as a German dance, is in duple meter with an up-beat, in a pace that is steady and not slow. The courante is of French origin (from the 16th century) and is in a running motion as the name suggests; although the meter is triple, the pulse is felt either as 1 2 3 4 5 6 or again occasionally as 1 2 3 4 5 6. The sarabande appeared in France and England about 1600, and earlier in Spain; it is performed in triple meter in a stately manner. The French-type gigue developed from the 16th-century Irish or English jig, and is in a lively 6/8 meter.

From his Italian years Froberger learned the prevailing, rhapsodic toccata style, with its short sections and discontinuous manner. The ornamental character, varied rhythms, and frequent metrical changes are apparent in his *Toccata 2*, found in HAM II, No. 217. Froberger is remembered as the first important composer for the harpsichord on the Continent.

Other Important Composers of the South German school. Christian Erbach (1573–1635), organist at Augsburg Cathedral from 1625 until his death; J. U. Steigleder (1593–1635), organist at Lindau and later at Stuttgart; and Johann Kindermann (1616–55), who accepted a church position in Nürnberg in 1636, were all important keyboard artists in South Germany. Since the time of Hans Leo Hassler these artists had been under the stylistic influence of Italian composers, which accounts for their preference for the toccata, ricercare, canzona, and verset forms. Also, some musicians in this group were Catholics and held Catholic Church positions; naturally, they did not use Protestant chorale melodies and verses in their sacred music.

THE STADTPFEIFER. The *Stadtpfeifer* were mostly brass players employed by the municipal councils of the cities of the Low Countries and of Germany. They played an interesting role in the development of the ensemble suite. Their duties included playing chorales three times daily from the tower on the city hall (*Turmsonaten*) and providing music for weddings and civic celebrations, and for these occasions dance suites were widely used. Representative composers include Johann Schein (see his *Intrada* in HAM II, No. 197) and Johann Pezel (1639–94). The latter's *Adagio* from a Leipzig *Turmsonate* of 1670 is printed in GMB, No. 221.

MIDDLE BAROQUE: ITALY

OPERA

The years 1630 to 1680 witnessed, in Italy, the continued development of opera and instrumental music and the establishment of the cantata, the oratorio, and the beginnings of comic opera (probably instigated by Stefano Landi, *c.* 1590–*c.* 1655, by his use of comic scenes in *opera seria*). In connection with the vocal forms here mentioned came an emphasis on the *bel canto* style of singing and a more positive concept of the function of the recitative, arioso, and aria. The *secco* ("dry") recitative (accompanied by a simple chording in the *continuo* part) gradually developed into a technique of quickly explicating the longer passages of narrative text; the arioso made less use of the smooth line and provided a vehicle for dramatic and often dissonant expression, and the aria became the real solo medium for lyrical song. The aria, more and more now distinguished from the recitative, began to make greater use of the *da capo* form (ABA), which was to reach its culmination in the hands of Bach and Handel.

The *bel canto* style–one of the great beauties of Italian song–transformed the aria into a lyrical piece with only an occasional ornamental passage here and there, in contrast to the early Baroque tendency toward exaggerated dramatics. The vocal line, written over a simple harmonic structure, was at first cast in short phrases, but as the period moved onward the "long line" evolved.

After Monteverdi, Venetian opera passed largely into the hands of Francesco Cavalli and Marc' Antonio Cesti.

Francesco Cavalli (1602–76). Francesco Cavalli studied under Monteverdi, sang in the latter's choir at St. Mark's Church, was appointed second organist at that cathedral in 1640 and first organist in 1655, and finally chapel master of St. Mark's in 1668. Of some forty operas, three achieved much success: *Giasone* (1649), *Serse* (1654, also performed at the wedding festivities of Louis XIV of France in 1660), and *Ercole amante* (1662). By the time of the writing of *Giasone,* Cavalli's use of the *bel canto* aria was well established, but a persistent trait of Cavalli lies in the alternation of aria and recitative sections in the operatic solo song. This practice can be seen in Medea's calling up of the furies in *Giasone* (GMB, No. 201), and again in the "letter scene" from *Serse* (HAM II, No. 206). Another of his traits is the constant use of 3/4 meter in the aria; Cavalli also firmly established the chaconne chromatic bass as a prominent device for the writing of laments in Baroque opera.

Marc' Antonio Cesti (1623–69). Marc' Antonio Cesti probably studied music with Giacomo Carissimi (who will be discussed below) at Rome. For a time Cesti was *maestro di cappella* to Ferdinand II de' Medici at Florence, and his masterpiece *La Dori* was performed in 1661 in that city. Although holding minor orders in the Church, Cesti's moral conduct was none too good, and he traveled to Vienna, where, while he was assistant chapel master (1666–68) to the Emperor Leopold I, his personal life was held in less disdain. His opera *Il Pomo d'oro* ("The Golden Apple") is yet another work written for the celebration of a marriage, this time that of Leopold I with the Infanta Margherita of Spain and first produced in Vienna in 1667. A gigantic spectacle, *Il Pomo d'oro* was set in five acts, sixty-seven scenes, forty-eight male roles, with a chorus and many instruments: strings of all types, flutes, trumpets, cornetts, trombones, a bassoon, and keyboard instruments. Outside of their normal accompanying functions, these instruments also provided introductions to all acts and *ritornelli* and sinfonias. Typical of the period, the work was elaborately staged with machines capable of performing feats of the wildest description. The overture, printed in GMB, No. 202, is in the French style with an ending retardation due to the notational values at the close rather than through the use of "retard" or "*rit.*"

CHAMBER CANTATA AND ORATORIO

The chamber cantata and the oratorio developed around the same time, toward the middle of the 17th century. The cantata (from *cantare,* meaning "to sing") was a conglomerate of recitatives, ariosos, and strophic arias, and its texts were of either a pastoral or dramatic nature, with a setting often in the *bel canto* tradition. Luigi Rossi (1597–1653) was one of the most noted composers of chamber cantatas; about 250 of his works are extant. Rossi utilized the two-part form that was so favored in the *bel canto* aria, but he also was very nearly the first to introduce the brief *da capo* aria (in ternary form) as manifested in his *Io lo vedo* (found in HAM II, No. 203). Also, both Carissimi and Cesti, although, respectively, best remembered for their oratorios and operas, wrote numerous chamber cantatas.

The oratorio derives its name from the place where works of the type were performed, the *oratorio,* or "prayer hall," of the Congregazione dell' Oratorio, in Rome. The English writer Charles Burney designated a very early-17th-century composition–the chief work of Emilio del Cavalieri, called *La Rappresentazione di anima e di corpo,* 1600–as the "first" oratorio, but this work bears only a passing resemblance to the oratorio type as later established, being actually something of a cross between the oratorio and "sacred opera"–that is, a work with a sacred libretto but staged in the same manner as an opera with a secular text.

Giacomo Carissimi (*c.* 1605–74). Giacomo Carissimi lived most of his life in Rome, where he was *maestro di cappella* in the church of St. Apollinaris from 1628 until his death. Of his oratorios sixteen are extant; among these are the impressive *Jephte, Judicium Salomonis, Balthazar,* and *Jonas.*

Carissimi renounced the deep-seated Roman "Palestrina style" and turned his efforts toward composition in the chordal manner. Solo lines with strong chordal leanings are coupled with simple chordal accompaniments, as evidenced in the "*Afferte gladium*" scene from *Judicium Salomonis* (MM, No. 32). But *Jephte* is considered his masterpiece.

The story of *Jephte* comes from the Book of Judges, 11:29–40. Jephte, about to lead the Israelites against the Ammonite army, implores the aid of the Lord and rashly vows to offer as a sacrifice the first member of his household he sees upon his return. When this person is his daughter, Jephte repents of his rashness, but the daughter is prepared to submit to the vow of her father. The vocal score of the oratorio is handled by a chorus of up to six parts, with solo parts for Jephte, his daughter, and the narrator, or *historicus*. The Baroque feeling for the dramatic is exemplified in the noise of battle, the shouts of joy in victory, the sad and drooping lines depicting Jephte's sorrow on first seeing his daughter on his return, his daughter's song of sacrifice filled with chromatics and repeated notes, and her later *agitato* in her song of sorrow (see GMB, No. 198).

The text is in Latin (as are most of Carissimi's oratorios), in contradistinction to a second type of *oratorio volgare* (in Italian), and the chorus parts are written in a chordal style. Carissimi's chordal passages, based as they are on the simplest of harmonies, become almost sterile at times, but monotony is avoided by the rhythmic devices he employs. An interesting point here is the harmonic usage of the so-called Neapolitan-sixth chord, usually introduced, however, by melodic voice leading. This chord is often connected with the "affection" of a single word, and again is often found in cadential passages in the *bel canto* style. Almost every composer of the middle Baroque period writing in this style used the Neapolitan-sixth chord. Example 37 clearly depicts the notation of this chord as found in the last three measures of the GMB, No. 198, selection. The use of this chordal structure proves the growing recognition of tonality in the minds of mid-17th-cen-

Example 37

tury composers, as it is a direct result of the integration of the flat second of the Phrygian mode into the major or minor key. (Incidentally, as with the "Landini sixth" cadence structure, the Neapolitan sixth is also a misnomer initiated by early musical research, which discovered it supposedly for the first time in music of the Neapolitan school of late Baroque opera.)

INSTRUMENTAL MUSIC

Following the pinnacle of fame attained by Frescobaldi, Italian keyboard music saw little development until the late Baroque. But chamber music prospered in Northern Italy; Modena, Venice, and Bologna enjoyed string ensemble music of the highest quality. A trend toward more virtuosity in an idiomatic string style can be found in the compositions of the Modenese school, as exemplified in the sinfonia for violin, cello, and *continuo* (GMB, No. 229), by Alessandro Stradella (1642–82).

Before 1650 the term "sonata" (from *sonare,* "to sound") meant a multisectional, single-movement work to be played by instruments. In Venice at this period the sections themselves were extended into separate movements, set in no order, but with the first and last movements cast in a quick duple meter, fugal manner, and encompassing slower movements of which one would be in triple meter. Giovanni Legrenzi (1626–90) was the most important writer of this style in Venice, and his *La Buscha* sonata (HAM II, No. 220) follows the pattern just described. As in a great deal of the early Baroque chamber ensemble music, the score permits several possibilities in instrumentation; the work may be performed by two (wooden) cornettos or string viols, a bassoon or violon, two violins, a viola, and *continuo.*

Giovanni Battista Vitali (1644–92). The leading light of the Bologna string school was Giovanni Battista Vitali. A pupil of Maurizio Cazzati, the founder of this school, Vitali is especially noted for sharpening the distinction between the chamber sonata (*sonata da camera,* composed of a series of dance movements in bipartite form) and the church sonata (*sonata da* *chiesa,* of a more dignified mien). His works manifest a tendency to return to contrapuntal practices, and his sonatas have movement contrasts of style and tempo. His trio sonata *La Graziani* for two violins and *continuo* (HAM II, No. 245) approaches the standard Baroque type as established in this form.

EARLY AND MIDDLE BAROQUE: FRANCE AND IBERIA

FRENCH VOCAL MUSIC

Musical entertainment in the Italian manner became a part of French court life during the time of Henry IV (reigned 1589–1610), but true French Baroque art was established under the patronage of Louis XIII (reigned 1610–43) and Louis XIV (reigned 1643–1715). The Italian vigor and the German grandeur of the Baroque never quite found a place in French music, for there was a restraint present–at least in vocal music–in the presence of the still-prevalent *vers mesuré* technique, as developed by the members of the Académie de Poésie et de Musique (founded in 1571). Marin Mersenne, in his *Harmonie universelle* (1636–37), objected to this trait in French music and criticized his colleagues for their emphasis on pleasing the ear without regard for the more emotional side of the art. Even the early *ballet de cour* was a reserved though popular entertainment, consisting of mimed entrees, dances, choruses, and a few solo songs; later an overture and a *grand ballet* were added, the dancing now often involving the royal household.

Italian opera was performed in Paris during the years 1645–62, and although the marriage of Louis XIV was celebrated in 1660 with the aforementioned Cavalli's *Serse* (a fantastic spectacle lasting several hours) the French never really found it in their hearts to enjoy Italian opera with its *castrati* singers. The French made an effort to develop a national opera, and the poet Perrin collaborated with the musician Robert Cambert (*c.* 1628–77) in this respect. Their *Pomone* (1671) is the first work worthy of the name "French opera." It was successfully received when produced as the opening endeavor of the newly created Académie Royale de Musique. The only remains of the opera today are several large fragments from the first two acts. HAM II, No. 223, prints the overture, and here the French-type overture, with a slow and pompous opening in dotted rhythms followed by a fugal allegro can be seen in the process of formulation. In performance all parts move together in a somewhat jerky manner, with all dotted rhythms adjusted to fit the shortest pattern in the music.

Jean Baptiste Lully (1632–87). Jean Baptiste Lully left Florence at the age of fourteen to seek a career in France. In 1652 he entered the service of Louis XIV and soon became involved in the composition of court ballets. But Lully was eventually to find his real place in the field of operatic writing, and in fact he is credited with establishing French tragic opera with his *Cadmus et Hermione,* produced in 1673. This work was followed closely by other masterpieces such as *Alceste* (1674) and *Armide et Renaud* (1686). Typical features of the operas were the French overtures, the prominent use of the chorus, the accompanied recitatives, the ariosos, the short arias, and the ballets.

Lully wrote in a conservative and diatonic harmonic fashion, using chromaticism only "affectively" in the lament, in imitation of the Italian style. Thickly scored strings form his basic instrumentation, to which winds are added from time to time for coloristic effects. The outer voices constitute the best music of Lully's part writing, a fact that has promoted the belief that he often left to his students the job of filling in the inner parts. The harmonies substantiate the major and minor modes only in the cadences, and there is an obvious lack of functional chordal procedure within the phrases. The overtures to *Alceste* (HAM II, No. 224) and *Armide et Renaud* (MM, No. 36) reveal Lully's compositional manner and further demonstrate the final evolution of the French overture. Although not considered altogether typical of his style, both these overtures make use of a slow coda-like ending in imitation of the opening passages. Finally, his procedure in the use of the recitative and aria may be examined in *"Le Ciel protège les héros"* ("Heaven protects the heros"), from *Alceste* (HAM II, No. 225).

FRENCH SACRED MUSIC

Church music held only a little importance in France at this time. Motets were written in the *concertato* style by Lully and by Marc-Antoine Charpentier (1634–1704), but Charpentier was more famous for his introduction of the oratorio (in Italian style) into French sacred music. A sample of his expressive compositional style may be seen in the *"Dialogue entre Madeleine et Jésus"* (HAM II, No. 226) from his *Le Reniement de St. Pierre* ("The Denial of St. Peter").

FRENCH INSTRUMENTAL MUSIC

String music was an important element of the French Baroque. A group called *Les Vingt-Quatre Violons du Roi* ("The Twenty-Four Violins of the King": six first violins, four second violins, four third violins, four violas, and six basses) was organized during the reign of Louis XIII and existed in principle until the year 1761. Not to be outdone, Lully petitioned Louis XIV for an orchestra of his own, and upon receiving the king's consent he organized a group of seventeen players (later expanded to twenty-one), becoming the conductor in 1655. These string orchestras became the finest in all of Europe. But Lully's ambition as a conductor proved to be his undoing, for the story goes that while conducting by beating time with a heavy cane upon the floor the stick struck his foot, gangrene set in, and he died of blood poisoning.

LUTE MUSIC. Of the nonbowed string types the lute reigned supreme, chiefly due to the famous Gaultier family of lute players of whom Denis Gaultier (*c.* 1600–72) was the outstanding member. *La Rhétorique des dieux* ("Language of the Gods") represents a collection of compositions extant, from the year 1652, in a handsome manuscript (HAM II, No. 211, is from this collection). His *Tombeau de Mademoiselle Gaultier* (*tombeau,* "tomb," a composition in honor of a dead person) is also from *La Rhétorique;* this piece, in TEM, No. 39, shows both the original tablature notation and its transcription into modern notation. With Gaultier's death began the decline of French lute music.

CLAVECIN MUSIC. From the "broken style" texture, ornamental figures, and pictorial patterns of lute music developed the idiomatic style of French clavecin (harpsichord) music. Jacques Champion de Chambonnières (*c.* 1600–72) was the first of a line of middle Baroque French clavecinists. His works were similar in style to Gaultier's lute dance suites; as yet these suites had no set order of dances established, but retained a uniformity of key between the movements. Chambonnières composed as well in the other instrumental forms of the period, such as the chaconne found in HAM II, No. 212 (the original source is his *Pièces de clavessin,* written about 1640 and printed in 1670). This chaconne is not in the continuous variation style, but rather the rondeau type of the French clavecinists and with each new couplet using the same key as that of the theme. Chambonnières was first chamber musician to Louis XIV, and his position and fame were such that he influenced not only his French contemporaries and followers but also, through Froberger (who visited Paris in 1652), German keyboard composers of the period.

Chambonnières's tradition was directly maintained in France by his pupil Louis Couperin (1625–61), the first distinguished composer of the famous Couperin family of musicians. He became organist of St. Gervais, Paris, about 1650, a post that members and descendants of the Couperin family held from that time until 1826 without interruption. Louis was much interested in key structure, and in his suites he used all the key relationships possible in the meantone system of tuning (see discussion on Bach's clavier compositions further on in this chapter). His *Menuet de Poitou* for harpsichord (HAM II, No. 229) is an early example of this dance type that was to play such an important role in musical history; the three-measure phrases are typical of the early minuet. Another member of this group of keyboard composers was Jean d'Anglebert (*c.* 1628–91). He was also a student of Jacques Champion de Chambonnières, whom he succeeded in 1664 as clavecinist to Louis XIV. Among d'Anglebert's works are to be found a *Tombeau,* in memory of his teacher, and a set of twenty-two variations on *Folies d'Espagne* (the tune later used by Corelli for his *Folia* variations).

ORGAN MUSIC. The French organs of the 17th century were of large size, some having as many as five manuals, and were well supplied with foundation, mutation, and mixture ranks. The French have always been great colorists in their music, but in this period of organ playing it is even more in evidence in their use of unusual color effects obtained through a variety of stop combinations. The pedal organs, however, had only a few stops, this clavier being used principally for the playing of *cantus firmi.* Of course the organists of Catholic France made no use of chorale melodies, but chose their *cantus firmi* from the ritual music of the Roman Church. Thus it can be assumed that the *Pange lingua* chant from the Vespers service of Corpus Christi, as used by Jean Titelouze–organist at Rouen Cathedral from 1588 until his death in 1633–in the bass voice of his organ hymn (HAM I, No. 180), would be assigned to the pedal keyboard (for the chant tune itself see LU, p. 957). Another great musician of the period, Nicolas de Grigny (1671–1703), served as organist of Rheims Cathedral. The great Bach, who learned to compose chiefly through studying the works of others, thought enough of Grigny's *Livre d'orgue* (printed posthumously in 1711) that he laboriously copied the entire book.

IBERIAN MUSIC

Spanish and Portuguese music of the 17th century for organ, harpsichord, and vihuela was well known over most of the Continent. Juan Cabanilles (1644–1712) played at the cathedral at Valencia in Spain and was the publisher of several hundred organ works. He had a firm grasp of stylistic and formalistic problems, as may be seen in the adroit workmanship of his *Paseos* (HAM II, No. 239), a set of continuous variations of the chaconne type, based on the four-measure harmonic scheme I-I-IV-V. The Portuguese composer Manoel Coelho (*c.* 1580–1623) gained fame as the composer of the collection *Flores de musica* ("Flowers of Music," 1620). He was organist of the cathedrals of Elvas and Lisbon, and his *Flores* includes versets for the Psalms and the Magnificat; although such versets were usually written for organ alone, Coelho added a part for voice, as in HAM II, No. 200.

Spanish choral music in the church style remained conservative, following the style of the Renaissance Spaniard Tomás Victoria, until the late Baroque. It is exemplified in the Introit by Juan Pujol (*c.* 1573–1626), found in GMB, No. 179, and again in the half-sacred, half-secular *Villancico* by Joan Cererols (d. 1676) of HAM II, No. 227. More of the typical Spanish flavor is apparent in the folklike syncopated rhythms of the *villancicos, tonadas,* and *ensaladas.*

EARLY AND MIDDLE BAROQUE: ENGLAND

OPERA

Court entertainment in England during the reigns of James I and Charles I (reigned 1603–25 and 1625–49, respectively) followed very largely the lead of the French court of the same period. The English court masque was much like the *ballet de cour,* with dancers, choruses, songs, and instrumental music. English writers of renown such as John Milton (1608–74) and Ben Jonson (*c.* 1573–1637) included in their literary efforts a number of masques. One of the most successful of these, the *Masque of Comus* (1634) combined the talents of Milton and the musician Henry Lawes (1596–1662). The song "Sweet Echo" from *Comus* is published in HAM II, No. 204.

John Blow (1649–1708). John Blow is well remembered today for his position in English chapel and court music of the

17th century. He served two terms as organist at Westminster Abbey, the first 1668–79 and again 1695–1708; he was also organist and composer of the Chapel Royal. Blow's outstanding stage composition for the English court was *Venus and Adonis* (*c.* 1682), which though entitled a masque can also be classed as a short pastoral opera, since its three acts are sung throughout. The overture is in the French style, followed by a prologue embodying jolly string music, a lovely chorus "In these sweet groves," and a dance by a shepherd and shepherdess. Each act is preceded by its "act tune." The second act is notable for the dance of the Graces, performed to a gavotte, saraband, and a ground of eight measures in 3/4 meter. Act III reveals the tragedy. When Adonis's friends appeared in Act I to take him on a hunt, Adonis had been reluctant to leave the side of Venus, but she had sent him away; now he returns mortally wounded by a wild boar. The lamenting chorus from the final act, built in traditional Baroque fashion on a chromatic ground (see HAM II, No. 243), is one of the finest things from the opera.

Henry Purcell (1659–95). The compositions of Henry Purcell represent the peak of Baroque musical art in England; he stands as the last great composer of that country until the 20th century. His teachers were Cooke, Pelham Humphrey (who had studied with Lully and in Italy), and John Blow. It was Purcell who served as organist of Westminster Abbey during the years between Blow's two appointments, and Purcell too worked in the Chapel Royal as an organist and composer. A third post of Purcell's bore the title "Composer in Ordinary for the Violins." Following in Blow's footsteps, Purcell wrote some outstanding works for the stage; chief among these is his *Dido and Aeneas* (*c.* 1689), written for performance at a girls' school near London. Scored for a four-part string orchestra and harpsichord, the opera reveals many traces of French and Italian stylistic qualities coupled with Purcell's individual style involving dotted rhythms, advanced dissonant treatment including clashing cross-relations, and a very expressive and pictorial handling of the text.

Dido and Aeneas, in three acts, as was Blow's *Venus and Adonis,* and with a libretto by Nahum Tate, tells the story somewhat differently from Virgil's account. The Trojan prince Aeneas is enamoured of Dido, Queen of Carthage, who secretly reciprocates the feeling. They are finally brought together by Dido's confidante Belinda, and in great bliss the two lovers depart on a hunting trip. However, their happiness is short-lived, due to the enmity of witches and sorcerers who send a false spirit, supposedly from Jove, instructing Aeneas to set sail at once for Italy. Dido is infuriated when she discovers his plans to leave, and Aeneas announces his willingness to defy what he believes to be the will of gods and remain with her. Dido, however, feels that she has been scorned and haughtily sends him away, preparing herself to die of a broken heart, which she soon does.

In this opera recitatives and arias are clearly differentiated, and the chorus assumes the same function as in the Greek drama—that is, a commentator on the action. The overture is in the best Lullian style, and three arias and the concluding dance of the first scene are all erected over ground basses. The sailors' chorus and dance near the opening of Act III is completely English, almost a foreshadowing of the later Gilbert and Sullivan style. Dido's lament from the last act ("When I am laid in earth," HAM II, No. 255)—a lovely melody over a descending chromatic ground—is unquestionably one of the finest vocal solos of the 17th century and a definite precursor of the tragic operatic arias of the 19th century. Finally, the drooping lines and intense feeling of the closing chorus seem in direct imitation of the last chorus in Blow's *Venus and Adonis.*

Purcell's stage works following *Dido and Aeneas* are all incidental music to plays and spectacles. They include *The Fairy Queen* (1692) and *The Tempest* (*c.* 1695), based on Shakespeare's *Midsummer Night's Dream* and *The Tempest,* respectively, and two with librettos by John Dryden—*King Arthur* (1691) and *The Indian Queen* (1695). Each of these four dramatic presentations makes great use of instrumental dances and *ritornelli,* the chorus, spoken dialogue, and fanciful stage settings. But, strangely enough, not one of the principal characters is required to sing.

Although Blow and Purcell are today considered the outstanding English composers for the stage in the 17th century, the first English opera is generally said to be a libretto entitled *The Siege of Rhodes,* written by Sir William Davenant or D'Avenant (1606–68), with music by Henry Lawes (1596–1662), Henry Cooke (d. 1672), and Matthew Locke (*c.* 1632–77). But this music (first presented in 1656) is not extant, and Locke's masque *Orpheus and Euridice* (1673) remains as the first true example of English operatic composition. As a matter of fact, Locke's name follows that of Purcell and Blow as the third great name of 17th-century English writers of stage music. He is especially noted for his music to James Shirley's *Cupid and Death* (1653) and to Thomas Shadwell's *Psyche* (1673), a revamping of Molière's work of the same name. But after 1700 English opera did not endure, and the field was lost to Italian opera as brought to London by the German Handel.

INSTRUMENTAL AND CHURCH MUSIC

On the instrumental side of 17th-century English music there is little to say about organ music, perhaps due to the slow development of the instrument, for the English organ still lacked a pedal clavier. Virginal music did not continue to develop following the death of the Elizabethan musicians; however, music for viols reached new heights in the middle Baroque, although members of the violin family also here found a place in ensemble and solo music after the Commonwealth (1649–60). The principal form of viol composition was the "fancy," or ensemble fantasia. Contrapuntal and harmonic techniques shared almost equal ground in these works, their outstanding creators being John Jenkins (1592–1678), Matthew Locke, and Henry Purcell.

English church music continued to flourish in the 17th century. The verse anthem, introduced by William Byrd, was the favored type. Restoration composers wrote into these anthems alto, tenor, and bass solo trios, instrumental sinfonias and *ritornelli,* conventional dotted rhythms, and concluding alleluia passages, and their works have become known as the cathedral style of English sacred composition.

In the more advanced settings of psalms and canticles for singing by trained choirs, composers such as Blow and Purcell seemed to prefer chordal settings, with some use of counterpoint, to an involved contrapuntal style. The former is illustrated in Blow's setting of the Jubilate Deo in TEM, No. 43, from his *Service in G;* both words and music of the concluding "*Gloria patri*" are inscribed on Blow's monument in Westminster Abbey.

LATE BAROQUE: ITALY

THE STRING ENSEMBLE

In the Italian late Baroque the musical scene was dominated by instrumental compositions, and especially those using stringed instruments. Surely the art of the instrument makers in Cremona was at least partly responsible for this upsurge in string playing, for no finer violins, violas, and cellos have been made than those by Niccolò Amati (1596–1684), Antonio Stradivari (1644–1737), and Giuseppe Guarnieri (1698–1744), often called "Giuseppe del Gesù" from his habit of inscribing the letters IHS on his labels.

The *concerto grosso,* which has been discussed in Chapter II, was the principal large-ensemble form of Baroque instrumental music. It was basically a string group in Italy, with the *concertino* nearly always two violins and a cello (with *continuo*) and the *ripieno* composed of a string orchestra. Stylistically these late Baroque *concerti grossi* (and the solo concertos, as well, in which the *concertino* as described directly above is replaced by a solo violin) maintain a steady, marked pace, the forward motion being enhanced by repeated notes, repeated patterns, antiphonal passages between instruments, rapid change of harmonies, and bustling themes and scale passages that often outline the major or minor modal background of the compositions.

Undoubtedly the most famous of Italian concerto composers were Arcangelo Corelli, Giuseppe Torelli, and Antonio Vivaldi.

Arcangelo Corelli (1653–1713). Little is known of Arcangelo Corelli's early life, but from 1671 until his death Rome was his city of residence. There he enjoyed honor and fame, achieving a distinction as a virtuoso on the violin and founding many modern violin techniques in the way of bowing, double stops, and chordings.

The *concerto grosso* was established by Corelli with the twelve works of *Concerti grossi, Op. 6,* which the composer may have begun creating as early as 1682; the collection was first published in 1714, the year after his death. The first eight of these were intended for church use (*concerti da chiesa*) and the last four for playing in the home (*concerti da camera*). The *concertino* here is the basic group of two violins and cello, and the works are in five or more short movements, as in the early multimovement *canzone*. Some of the movements (indicated by tempo markings) make better musical sense when grouped together, as shown below in an outline of the famous "Christmas" concerto (Op. 6, No. 8):

(1) *Vivace–Grave*. A very short introductory *Vivace* is followed by a slowly moving line-and-a-half of score with one suspension following another.

(2) *Allegro*. This movement, in AB form, can stand pretty much alone. The *concertino* carries the angular lines briskly along with reinforcing utterances by the *ripieno*. The entire ensemble indulges in a terraced dynamic *forte-piano* in the second half of the B part of the form.

(3) *Adagio–Allegro–Adagio*. These three movements together create an attractive three-part section in the middle of the composition. The opening measures of the *concertino* show antiphonal interplay between the two violins and then the cello.

The *ripieno* supplies a steady movement with repeated notes. The *Allegro* is a charming piece built around very rapid reiterations of notes and note patterns. The concluding *Adagio* returns to the gravity of the opening.

(4) *Vivace*. This minuet-styled movement, again in binary form, offers the relief of a dance type although part of a *concerto da chiesa.*

(5) *Allegro*. This is the longest of the regular movements and is in two-part form. It is also the most forceful section of the *concerto grosso* and shows the greatest contrast between *concertino* and *ripieno,* and between *forte* and *piano.*

(6) *Largo*. This final movement is a pastorale in 12/8 meter which may be played ad libitum—at the whim of the performers. The composition draws its "Christmas" name from this movement and from the fact that it was written for the night of the Nativity.

Corelli's compositions reveal the final acceptance of the tonal system through the use of such techniques as the following: (1) sequences through the circle of fifths, (2) modulations to near-related keys only, (3) functional chord progressions within a specific key, (4) cadences solidly stated in the major or minor mode, and (5) thematic statements formed either on chordal patterns or on scales linked to the one or the other mode. This full acceptance of the tonal system came about the year 1680, at approximately the same time that Corelli began the composition of the *concerti grossi* of Op. 6. (The Greek modes were presented in Example 21 as the theoretical basis of Western music; next the Church modes used in Western music of the Middle Ages and Renaissance were given in Examples 23 and 34; now the major keys and their relative minors—the tonal system—are listed in Example 38.) Along with this new harmonic system, harmonic counterpoint —to reach its final peak in the music of Johann Sebastian Bach —becomes an established fact; and harmonic resources are expanded to permit the use of a seventh chord on any degree of the scale. Yet, in spite of this new and forward-looking spirit,

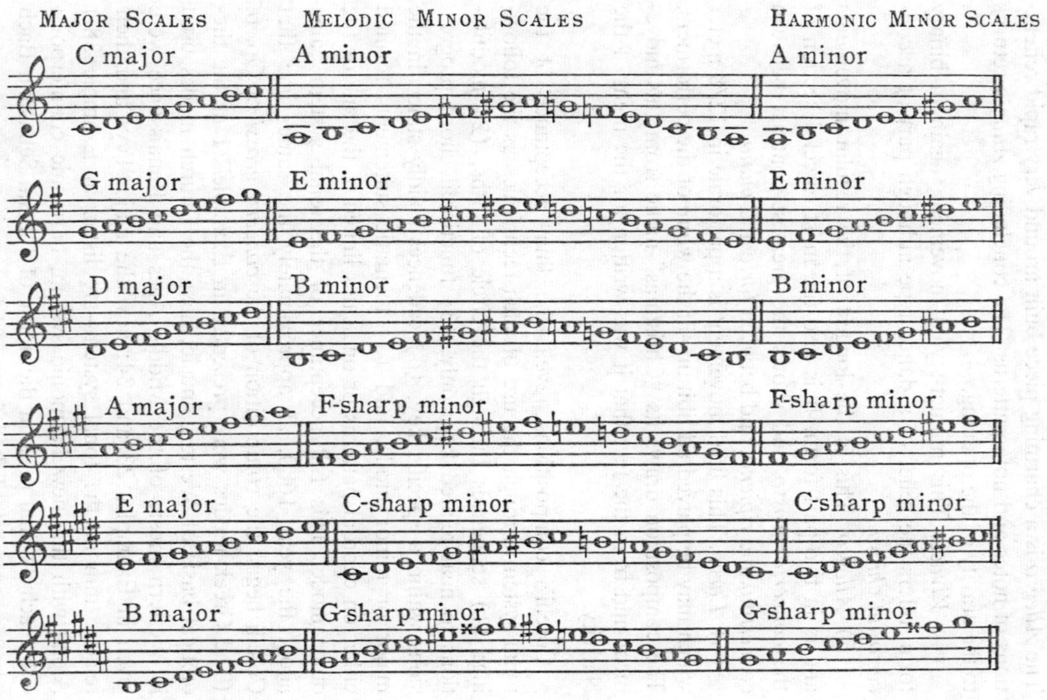

Major Scales
Melodic Minor Scales
Harmonic Minor Scales
C major
A minor
A minor
G major
E minor
E minor
D major
B minor
B minor
A major
F-sharp minor
F-sharp minor
E major
C-sharp minor
C-sharp minor
B major
G-sharp minor
G-sharp minor

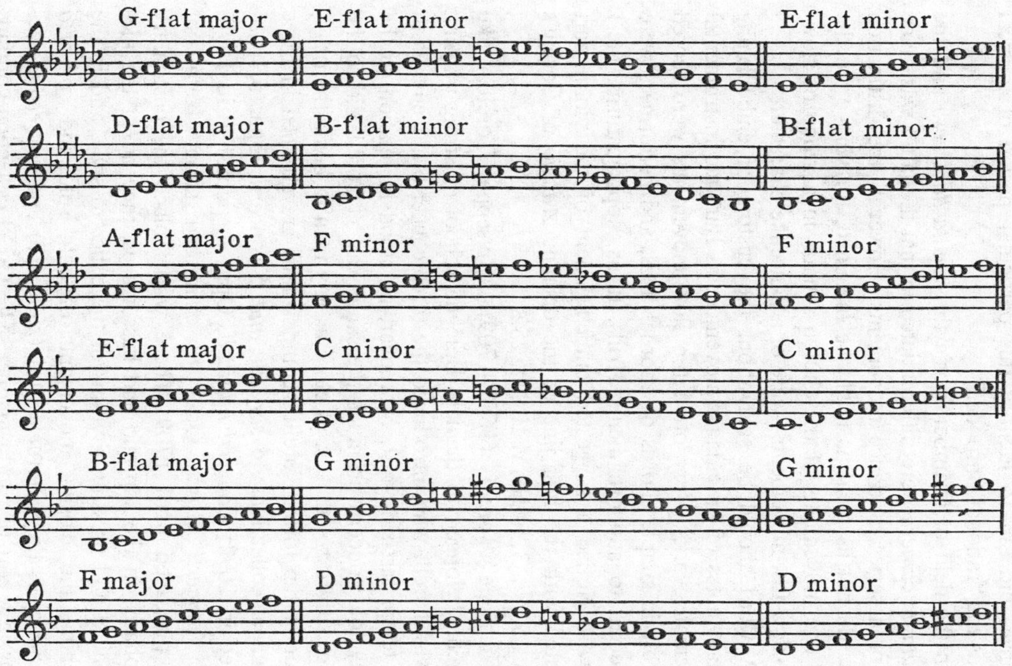
G-flat major
E-flat minor
E-flat minor
D-flat major
B-flat minor
B-flat minor
A-flat major
F minor
F minor
E-flat major
C minor
C minor
B-flat major
G minor
G minor
F major
D minor
D minor

Example 38

the over-all balance and correct proportions and other organizational controls in the music of Corelli and his Italian contemporaries bid fair to identify this particular period of musical art as the "rational Baroque."

In the field of chamber music the *sonata da chiesa* and the *sonata da camera* were differentiated in that the latter was made up of a series of dance movements. However, the distinction was still not as great as might be imagined, for very often the last two movements of the church sonata–in a group of slow-fast-slow-fast movements–were of a dancelike character.

A word should be said about the custom of embellishing certain notes of the adagio movement in Baroque instrumental ensemble works. Very often the slow movements were scored merely in simple chords or chordal lines, and performers were expected to add ornaments (trills, turns, appoggiaturas, etc.) at will. Notice a suggested embellishment of the violin part printed with the first line of the opening *Adagio* of Corelli's Opus 5, No. 3, in HAM II, No. 252.

Giuseppe Torelli (1658–1709). Giuseppe Torelli, like Corelli, belonged to the late Bologna school of string players. It was Torelli who introduced the three concerto movements in the tempi fast-slow-fast. Moreover, he stood in relation to the early solo concerto in much the same way as Corelli did to the *concerto grosso*–that is, as close as any man to being the originator of the form. Torelli's compositions are grouped in three principal collections: *6 sinfonie and 6 concerti,* Opus 5, published in 1692; *Concerti musicali,* Opus 6, published in 1698; and *Concerti grossi,* Opus 8, composed about 1690 but not published until 1709. These works place the customary emphasis on the soprano and bass voices, they adopt the mechanical and pressing rhythms of the concerto style, and in the opening and closing movements of both solo and *concerto grosso* types they alternate tutti (*ritornelli*) and *concertino* sections in a sort of rondo manner. The Op. 8 collection contains six *concerti grossi* and six solo concertos written in *concerto grosso* style but in which a single violin serves as the *concertino.*

An illustration of one of these solo concertos is printed complete in GMB, No. 257.

Antonio Vivaldi (1678–1741). Antonio Vivaldi was the son and pupil of the violinist Giovanni Battista Vivaldi. He later studied with the well-known Italian composer Giovanni Legrenzi. Vivaldi took holy orders in the Church and because of his red hair was called the Red Priest. His career took him on many travels, but a number of years were given to teaching and conducting at the Hospital of the Pietà in Venice. In 1740 he went to Vienna, hoping to attach himself to the court of Charles VI, but he was unsuccessful and died there in abject poverty.

Vivaldi fully established the three-movement concerto form initiated by Torelli. His themes for these movements are clear-cut and simple, and as the first and last movements lengthen, the number of alternations of tutti and solo passages increase; in the various tuttis we find the late Baroque principle of continuous expansion on a single theme. Two famous Vivaldi collections of concertos are the *L'Estro armonico,* Op. 3 ("Harmonious Whim"), published in 1715 and *Il Cimento dell' armonia e dell' inventione* ("The Trial Between Harmony and Invention"), Op. 8, printed in 1725. Bach was a great student of Vivaldi's music and evidently spent a great deal of time with Op. 3, for there are many Bach transcriptions from this volume of twelve concertos. These transcriptions include three concertos for harpsichord alone (Vivaldi's No. 3 = Bach's BWV978; No. 9 = BWV972; No. 12 = BWV976); one concerto for four harpsichords with the accompaniment of two violins, viola, and *continuo* (No. 10 = BWV1065); and two concertos for organ alone (No. 8 = BWV593; No. 11 = BWV596).

The first movement of Vivaldi's Op. 3, No. 8 (No. 6 in some editions), is found in HAM II, No. 270. (The identification as Op. 3, No. 6, in HAM is from the London edition.) Three strong chordal thrusts, outlining the tonic key, open the piece and the first tutti; next there is a sequence based on the circle of fifths in measures 6–9; lastly, the three measures driving toward the final cadence of the opening tutti begins with the Neapolitan-sixth chord (first beat of measure 14), and this passage with this chord is seen again several times in the course of the movement. The tutti alternates with solo passages by the string *concertino,* the tutti returning, as first stated, in measures 52 and 68 and in various guises at other points. The use of keys near related to the tonic *a* minor is preserved through modulations to *C* major and *d* minor.

Vivaldi's Op. 8 is a second set of twelve concertos, a number that appears to be rather common for these collections. The Red Priest here indulges in some flights of programmatic fantasy, coming up with some colorful titles for his pieces (e.g., "The Hunt," "The Tempest"). The first four concertos are a group called *Le Stagione* ("The Seasons"): No. 1, Spring; No. 2, Summer; No. 3, Autumn; and No. 4, Winter. Each has its proper programmatic implications, and each is supplied with a descriptive sonnet. TEM, No. 47, has the first movement of the "Spring" concerto, with a translation of the accompanying sonnet. Vivaldi wrote many more concertos in addition to these mentioned, in all about 450, and a considerable number of them make use of wind instruments in the *concertino.*

Other String Composers of the Period. Another composer's name should be added in the area of chamber music–that of Giuseppe Tartini (1692–1770). He had great fame as a violinist and in particular improved the techniques of bowing to the extent that his ideas still serve as models in present-day performance. Examples of his composition for solo violin may be found in HAM II, No. 275, and in GMB, No. 295.

Also active as writers of string music in concerto and chamber music forms, though perhaps of lesser stature than those just mentioned above, were the Corelli pupils Francesco Geminiani (*c.* 1687–1762) and Pietro Locatelli (1695–1764). Both these men were concert violinists known throughout all of Europe. In addition, Geminiani is remembered as the author of the earliest known violin instruction book–*The Art of Playing on the Violin,* published without bearing his name in London in 1730. In it Geminiani sets forth the performance principles stipulated by his teacher, Corelli.

VOCAL AND KEYBOARD MUSIC

Naples at this time was the main center of activity in opera. *Opera seria* developed there in a style that became known as Neapolitan opera–a style destined to penetrate all of the Continent (save France) and England. The prima donna held the center of the stage, and audiences demanded and received in these operas a great number of *bel canto* and *da capo* arias. Choruses were rare and the orchestra was relegated to overtures, *ritornelli,* and an occasional aria accompaniment. *Castrati* singers, with their powerful yet tremendously flexible voices, sang both male and female roles during the period 1650–1750, which may be one reason that these operas are little heard today.

Alessandro Scarlatti (1660–1725). Alessandro Scarlatti is the most important early name in Neapolitan opera. He established the Italian overture, in imitation of the concerto, using the tempi fast-slow-fast; but as yet the overture stood apart from the opera and made no use of the themes of the opera itself (see A. Scarlatti's overture to *La Caduta de Decem Viri,* TEM, No. 44). It was from its use in the operatic works of this school that the Neapolitan-sixth chord drew its name; it can be seen at the beginning of measure 41 (with the *g*-minor cadence established at measure 45) in the Act II, Scene 4 duet between Griselda and Ottone in Scarlatti's opera *La Griselda* (GMB, No. 259).

Also in the field of vocal music are to be found over six hundred cantatas by A. Scarlatti; an entire solo cantata for soprano by this composer is given in GMB, No. 260. The Neapolitan composers established the cantata as four-movement form recitative-aria-recitative-aria, frequently with a slow introduction; the arias are differentiated one from the other and are in *da capo* form.

Giovanni Pergolesi (1710–36). Comic episodes, which had their start as intermezzi between the acts of serious opera, now found expression in the full-length work called *opera buffa,* made famous by Giovanni Pergolesi. The most popular of these early two-act comic operas was *La Serva padrona* ("The Maid Mistress") by Pergolesi. This work, which involved only three characters (one a mute), using only a string orchestra, with neither chorus nor dancing, became quite well known on the Continent. The *opera buffa* style can be clearly discerned in the recitative and aria in TEM, No. 50, from the comic opera *Livietta e Tracollo,* by Pergolesi. When the opera houses closed down for Lent, it became the fashion to sing oratorios written in operatic style. Pergolesi is also known for his oratorio *Stabat Mater,* from which an aria is printed in GMB, No. 275.

Domenico Scarlatti (1685–1757). Son of Alessandro, Domenico Scarlatti was the foremost composer of keyboard music in the late Italian Baroque. More than five hundred of his harpsichord sonatas were edited and catalogued by Alessandro Longo (complete edition, 1906–10), but the "L." numbers do not indicate chronological order of composition. The "K." numbers of the harpsichordist Ralph Kirkpatrick now arrange the sonatas in a probable chronological order; both the Longo and the Kirkpatrick catalogues appear in Kirkpatrick's *Domenico Scarlatti* (1953). The sonatas follow the binary form with the triad, seventh, ninth, and altered chords forming the basis of the harmony; modulations often make use of a chord common to both the old and the new key. His keyboard technique employed octaves, arpeggios, leaps, trills; rapid runs in unisons, in thirds, and in sixths; the crossing of hands; and tremolos and glissandos. It is evident from this that Scarlatti's style did much to point the way to modern keyboard performance. His *Sonata in c minor* (L. 352 and K. 11) is illustrated in MM, No. 42.

THE ROCOCO: FRANCE

After the death of Lully in 1687, French music began to turn away from the expressive grandeur generally associated with the Baroque age to seek a more delicate, highly ornamented, and entertaining style known as the ROCOCO. This name, derived from the French word *rocaille* (a kind of artificial rockwork), denotes in the visual arts a style rich in the curving forms of eroded rocks, of shells, and of plants; and in other graceful and picturesque motifs playfully imitating nature. Rococo was also called *style galant* ("gallant style"), and this hints at its origins in the aristocratic manners of the time. Echoing the grace and genteel playfulness of the visual arts, Rococo music appeared in the late years of court life under Louis XIV (reigned 1643–1715), but had its full flowering under Louis XV (reigned 1715–74). The style is almost entirely French, but its influence was felt in Germany and Italy and can be detected in some works of Telemann and Domenico Scarlatti.

François Couperin (1668–1733). The first important representative of the French Rococo was Couperin le Grand, so called to distinguish him from his uncle François Couperin (*c.* 1631–*c.* 1701). Le Grand was the most illustrious member of the Couperin family of musicians. From 1685 until his death he held the post of organist at St. Gervais, and also became, in 1693, organist of the Chapelle Royale. He had various titles as chamber musician in connection with his service to the French kings Louis XIV and Louis XV.

It was Couperin who introduced the trio sonata into French chamber music. His *Concerts royaux* ("Royal Concerts") of 1714–15 are written in suite form and contain the usual stylized dances with added preludes, airs, and echoes. The notation is for a melody instrument and figured bass, with a third part sometimes sketched in; the instrumentation indicated strings (violin and viol) and such winds as oboe, bassoon, and flute, and the clavier. These works were first performed for the royal court of Louis XIV during Sunday-afternoon musicales in the Versailles palace apartments. They are still popular today, with a "realized" third part. Another set of ensemble sonatas appeared in 1726 under the title *Les Nations, Sonatas et suites de symphonies en trio;* the four sonatas of this publication–*La Françoise, L'Espagnole, L'Impériale,* and *La Piémontoise*–were as fully developed as anything Couperin wrote in this form, and yet the composer himself designated them as preludes to the four suites also found in *Les Nations.*

The argument concerning the merits of French versus Italian musical style flourished mightily during the opening quarter of the 18th century, but Couperin strove to use the good in both. His *Les Goûts réunis* ("The United Tastes"), an attempt to show the benefits of uniting French and Italian styles, was published in 1724. The work contains ten trio "concerts," for various instruments and *continuo;* it ends with a grand trio sonata entitled *Le Parnasse ou l'apothéose de Corelli*–the glorification of Corelli as seen in his warm reception by the gods on Mount Parnassus. In the following year (1725) Couperin again attempted a union of French and Italian tastes in the *Apothéose de Lully.*

Probably the greatest achievements–stylistically, at least–of the French rococo were the clavecin (harpsichord) pieces. They are short, loosely constructed works often in binary form bearing pictorial titles. Almost the entire concept is melodic, but the melodies are so richly endowed with ornaments that the line is practically obscured. Couperin is again the foremost master in this medium and in the years 1713, 1716, 1722, and 1730 he published the four volumes of his *Pièces de clavecin.* The individual pieces are descriptive only in what the listener imagines he hears due to the promptings of each work's title.

Also from Couperin's hand remains an enduring pedagogical work entitled *L'Art de toucher le clavecin* ("The Art of Playing the Clavecin," published in 1716), which explains the manner of performing the ornaments and offers a new fingering system. In his capacity as a church organist Couperin was inspired to write also for the organ, publishing the *Livre d'orgue* in 1690. Thus his compositional output may be categorized in three respects: (1) for the court, (2) for the general public, and (3) for the Church.

Other Keyboard Composers of the Period. A few lesser composers of French clavecin and organ music during this period were Louis Marchand (1669–1732), organist of the Chapelle Royale at Paris from 1708 to 1714; Louis Nicolas Clérambault

(1676–1749), who not only wrote much organ music but also composed stage works for the French court theater; and Marchand's pupil Louis-Claude Daquin (1694–1772), whose published works include *Pièces de clavecin* (1735) and *Noëls pour l'orgue ou le clavecin.* Selections from Daquin's *Noëls* often appear on recital programs by present-day organists and on recordings.

Jean Philippe Rameau (1683–1764). Although his compositions are rarely heard today, one of the great names of the late French Baroque and Rococo was Jean Philippe Rameau. He received his formal schooling (until the age of fourteen) at the Jesuit College at Dijon; his musical training followed, culminating in a trip to Italy. Rameau received lessons in organ and violin playing, and became in his lifetime one of the foremost organists in France, holding a number of outstanding cathedral positions. Perhaps his most lasting contribution to music was in the theoretical field, for his *Traité de l'harmonie* (1722) laid the foundation for the common practice of harmony. He advocated the building of chords through a series of superimposed thirds, and classified a chord and all its inversions as the one and the same entity. Rameau set up the theory of chord function by designating the tonic, dominant, and subdominant as primary tonal centers, relating all other possible chords within a key to these three. Moreover, he visualized within the functional chordal progression a *basse-fondamentale* ("fundamental bass"), which consisted of a line of real or imaginary "root tones." Modulation from the prevailing key to a new key took place at a point where a single chord was able to assume a correct function in the old key and another, equally correct function in the new key; temporarily such a harmony was "two-faced," and today is called a "pivot chord."

Rameau published his *Pièces de clavecin* during the years 1706–31, of which one selection is the attractive *Le Rappel des oiseaux* ("Bird Calls"), but he was to become best known in his day as an opera composer, the foremost French writer in this medium in the 18th century. Rameau waited until he was fifty years old to produce his first opera *Hippolyte et Aricie*

(1733) with a libretto by the popular Abbé Pellegrin, but reaction to the work was not altogether favorable, since the "battle" over French and Italian styles was still on and advocates of the French style thought *Hippolyte* much too "Italian." *Castor et Pollux* followed in 1737. Some connection between overture and opera is found here through the use of a theme in the overture from the opera finale; and MM, No. 41, prints the music from a scene in *Castor et Pollux* illustrating the basically serious Rameau style as overlaid with the light graces typical of the period. In the broad outline Rameau's operas follow the Lullian model. His short airs interspersed with recitative are reminiscent of Lully, but the longer arias look forward toward Gluck. As one would expect from a theorist, the harmonic basis is more clearly and richly revealed in Rameau's works, but Rameau surpasses Lully as well in expressive melodic content, in brilliant choral writing, and in the coloristic quality of his instrumental scoring. However, in spite of the virtues of Rameau's operas as music, two factors militate against a modern revival of them: (1) their generally poor librettos, and (2) their fidelity to the theatrical conventions of their own time, which makes them appear quaint and foreign to today's audience.

French composers after Lully had begun to introduce arias more explicitly in the Italian style (*ariettes*) and to continue to enlarge and to render more spectacular the *divertissement* scenes involving choruses and ballets. Soon the opera-ballet evolved, *L'Europe galante* (1697), of André Campra (1660–1744), being an early example, which he followed with *Les Fêtes vénitiennes* in 1710. Rameau produced a successful opera-ballet entitled *Les Indes galantes* in 1735 (in the preface of which he tried to counteract unfavorable public opinion of his works by expressing appreciation of Lully's French-styled works). Rameau's operatic compositions remained primarily of a serious nature until his appointment as court composer to Louis XV in 1745, and after that time his operas became lighter in style and more in the Rococo manner. As a matter of fact, of the twenty-six stage works composed by Rameau after 1744, only three may reasonably be called operas; the others, written in a more frivolous style, are ballets.

LATE BAROQUE: GERMANY

Almost all types of music of the late German Baroque were influenced in one way or another by earlier Italian models. In the latter part of the 17th century Italian composers had brought Italian opera to the German courts of Dresden, Munich, and Hanover, where its reception had been most favorable. Girolamo Frescobaldi must have brought some influence to bear on the Catholic organists of Southern Germany and perhaps, through Sweelinck, on the North and Central schools of German organ players. Orchestra and chamber music of this German period was in great debt to the Italian works of Vivaldi and Corelli. And church music, whether it was Protestant north or Catholic south, was composed (at least in part) in the *concertato* style, which had originated in Italy. But to all these influences, German composers added their solid harmonic and contrapuntal treatment and knowledge of the skillful use of musical form.

VOCAL MUSIC

Agostino Steffani (1654–1728). Agostino Steffani was perhaps the finest Italian opera composer who chose to present his art in Germany. Steffani was active in Munich and Hanover, and his music illustrates the transition from middle to late Baroque style; the Italian aria techniques, the French overture style, and the German contrapuntal borrowings all unite to form his operatic style, which had considerable influence on the 18th-century Germans Keiser and Handel (Steffani's successor at Hanover). HAM II, No. 244, is an early aria by Steffani; the title is *Un Balen d'incerta speme* ("A flash of uncertain hope"), from the opera *Henrico Leone* (Hanover, 1689). Notable features of this *da capo* aria include the motto beginning, which was common to late-17th- and early-18th-century arias (where the voice part begins with a single phrase followed by a rest, the phrase being then repeated and developed) and the typical affection through the use of chromatics on the word *dolor* ("pain").

Reinhard Keiser (1674–1739). The greatest impetus in founding a German opera came about the turn of the 18th century with Reinhard Keiser. In his years of writing for the stage in Hamburg (between 1696 and 1734) he composed over one hundred operas, of which twenty-five are extant. To the *bel canto* style of the Italian aria and to the French overture Keiser added a depth of orchestration and harmonic writing that was to characterize native German opera at this time. But in place of the word "opera," perhaps the German term *Singspiel* should be used, for many of these "operas" replaced recitative with the spoken word. Keiser's aria *Hoffe noch* ("Hope yet"), in TEM, No. 46, is from his *Croesus,* produced in 1710 at Hamburg. In this *da capo* aria the motto sounds three times in a sequential pattern, and in the original score the *da capo* repeat is written out. The piece demonstrates Keiser's happy facility for expressive textual setting and his considerable compositional skill.

Georg Philipp Telemann (1681–1767). The Hamburg opera was short-lived, lack of public support forcing it to close in 1738. One of the last of the Hamburg school of opera writers was Georg Philipp Telemann. He was perhaps the most prolific composer of his age, writing in all media, and he was in his lifetime better known than Bach; he wrote about forty operas, among a total of over four thousand works. It may have been Telemann's lighter style of writing that made his music of such immediate appeal, for the French "gallant" manner is reflected in much of his music. This "reflection" may seem rather pale, as the German *empfindsamer Stil* was actually quite different from its French counterpart. Where the French Rococo sought an elegant, restrained, formal touch, the German *Empfindsamkeit* was more sentimental, more concerned with creating a mood or feeling. This style can be immediately detected in Telemann's *da capo* aria *Liebe! Was ist schöner als die Liebe* ("Love! What is more beautiful than love"), found in GMB,

No. 266. Telemann's music went into eclipse after his death, but his chamber works especially are being heard again today.

INSTRUMENTAL MUSIC

In writing their concertos and trio sonatas and other chamber works German musicians accepted the classical style of the late Italian Baroque and added to that the depth of German musical art and feeling. The songs with *continuo* and string *ritornelli* by Philipp Erlebach (1657–1714) reveal just this special quality, as may be seen in *Himmel, du weisst meine Plagen* ("Heaven, thou knowest my sorrows"), HAM II, No. 254. Even the refinement of Georg Telemann's compositions does not conceal the solid workmanship of such as the first movement of his *Sonata for Flute, Violin, Violoncello, and Harpsichord* (HAM II, No. 271), and the German predilection for polyphony and double-stopping in the small but important literature for violin without accompaniment is evident in that composer's *Fantasie* in TEM, No. 48.

From the opening years of the 18th century comes some very interesting German harpsichord and clavichord music. Johann Kuhnau (1660–1722), Bach's immediate predecessor at St. Thomas's, Leipzig, became the musical director of the University of Leipzig in 1700 and cantor at St. Thomas's in the following year. In 1700 Kuhnau published some of the earliest keyboard programmatic sonatas, called *Biblische Historien*. The six sonatas of this collection are all based on biblical stories; two of the best known are *David and Goliath* and *Hezekiah: Mortally Ill and Then Restored to Health*.

The *Ariadne Musica* (1715), of J. K. F. Fischer (*c.* 1665–1746), is an impressive set of preludes and fugues using nineteen different tonal keys; it is important in its own right and also as the model for Bach's *Well-Tempered Clavier*. From Fischer's *Ariadne* is taken the *Prelude and Fugue in E Major* in HAM II, No. 247. This composer also published an earlier collection of suites in the style of Couperin–*Musikalisches Blumenbüschlein* (1696)–of which HAM II, No. 248, is one example.

ORGAN MUSIC

One of the most glorious phases of organ literature is that of the late German Baroque. This extensive literature was made possible by an instrument of goodly proportions, with three or four manuals and an independent pedal keyboard capable both of providing a solid foundation to the hand keyboards and of soloistic playing by the feet (especially in the sounding forth of chorale melodies). The principal builder of organs for the North German school was Arp Schnitger (1648–1719); his instruments could manage both colorful melodic presentations or full ensembles of a brilliant nature. In the 18th century the outstanding builder was Gottfried Silbermann (1683–1753), whose work was much respected by Bach.

Members of the North and Central German schools were of course Lutheran organists, and these men made great use of the chorale in their compositions and service playing. In many instances these chorale preludes were written to be performed before the congregation sang the chorale itself. Other forms used with considerable virtuosity were the prelude and fugue, passacaglia, and toccata.

Dietrich Buxtehude (1637–1707). A foremost name of the North German school was that of Dietrich Buxtehude, a musician second only to the great Bach. A son-in-law of Franz Tunder, Buxtehude, who was born in Denmark, followed Tunder at the Marienkirche in Lübeck in 1668. (The acquiring of a coveted position at this time often hinged on the marrying of a daughter of the incumbent.) There Buxtehude developed the *Abendmusiken*–evening musicales following the afternoon service on the five Sundays preceding Christmas. These provided the last displays of the "colossal Baroque" and in fact became quite famous all over Germany. A high point in these musicales was Buxtehude's organ playing; his instrument contained fifty-three ranks of pipes, one of the finest organs then in the world, and it provided him a wealth of opportunity to display his talents. As a composer, Buxtehude was at his best in the forms of the prelude and fugue. Written in a decisive instrumental style, the fugue subjects have a variety of expression, and the preludes and fugues alike are often written in several sections that are welded together with an easy facility (for an example see HAM II, No. 234).

Johann Pachelbel (1653–1706). One of the most celebrated of 17th-century Nürnberg organists was Johann Pachelbel. After a period of training under Caspar Kerll at St. Stephen's in Vienna he eventually settled at Nürnberg as organist at St. Sebald's, where he became the teacher of Vetter, Johann H. Buttstedt, and Johann Christoph Bach, brother of J. S. Bach. A member of the Central German school, Pachelbel not only developed a certain chorale prelude type that today bears his name, but he was also instrumental in transferring the Austrian virtuoso style of keyboard playing to Germany. An example of this Austrian style, featuring manual virtuosity over extended bass pedal points, can be seen in his *Toccata in e minor* (MM, No. 37). HAM II, No. 251, is a *Magnificat Fuga* from the composer's famous collection of ninety-four such pieces written for service performance at St. Sebald's, where they were played in place of the even-numbered verses of the Magnificat.

Other Organists of the Period. Georg Böhm (1661–1733) was another famous composer and organist of North Germany. Organ works, replete with ornaments in the French style, flowed from his pen during his long service at the Johanneskirche in Lüneburg (1698–1733)—compositions that ranked with the best of this period. His works were influential in forming the compositional style of J. S. Bach.

A second well-known musician of the Central German school was Johann Krieger (1651–1735), municipal organist at Zittau for the last fifty-four years of his life and noted in one respect for his excellent chorale partitas. He is occasionally confused with his elder brother, called Johann Philipp Krieger (1649–1725), a court musician at Halle from 1677 until his death.

This section on German organ music closes with Georg Muffat (1653–1704), an organist of the South German school; he was the last of the southern school of Roman Catholic organists to hold a position of any importance in the art of music. Although he is perhaps best known as a composer for the twelve toccatas from his *Apparatus Musico-organisticus* (1690), we will call attention here to his *Passacaglia in g minor* (HAM II, No. 240), also from the *Apparatus.* It is somewhat unusual in that it combines variation and rondeau forms and consists of twenty-four variations *without* a ground bass. His son, Gottlieb Muffat (1690–1770), followed in his father's musical footsteps, serving the Vienna court as musical director and organist from about 1714 until his retirement in 1763.

THE WORKS OF BACH

Johann Sebastian Bach (1685–1750). Johann Sebastian Bach was born in Eisenach, Germany, on March 21, 1685, the son of the town musician Johann Ambrosius Bach. After the death of both of his parents, young Bach, in his tenth year, went to live with his elder brother Johann Christoph at Ohrdruf, who gave him instruction on keyboard instruments (J. S. Bach's father had previously instructed him in playing the violin). In 1700 he became a chorister at St. Michael's, Lüneberg, and there he received his education. Bach secured his first organ position in Arnstadt at the church of St. Boniface. During this time he visited Lübeck to hear Buxtehude's *Abendmusiken.* In 1707 he was at Mühlhausen as organist at St. Blasius', but he stayed there only one year. The next nine years were spent first as court organist and then, after 1714, as concertmaster of the chamber orchestra to the duke in Weimar. In 1717 Bach was appointed *Kapellmeister* and director of chamber music to Prince Leopold of Anhalt, at Köthen. Finally, in 1723, he went to Leipzig as cantor at St. Thomas's School (where he taught Latin as well as music) and became director of music at the churches of St. Thomas and St. Nicholas. Bach worked twenty-seven years in Leipzig, right up to his death on July 28, 1750.

Although Bach as a composer was evidently little appreciated by his contemporaries (he was renowned as a performer), he is today regarded as highly as any other composer in the history of music. His works fell into an eclipse shortly after his death, but since the *St. Matthew Passion* was revived by Felix Mendelssohn in 1829, Bach's compositions have been continually before the general public and have proved of inestimable value to all students of music. He wrote in all the Baroque forms save that of opera, and in a style that shows a complete mastery of the art of harmonic counterpoint. By copying the scores and hearing the music of his fellow workers, Bach was able to assimilate the prevailing German, French, and Italian styles and turn them toward his own masterful ends.

ORGAN WORKS

During his Weimar years Bach became renowned as an organ virtuoso and was hired to inspect many new organ installations (inspection in Bach's time must have been somewhat analogous to the dedicatory organ recital of the present day). His court position and concert tours provided an opportunity to compose new organ works, and the Weimar period is noted for its new compositions of a virtuoso nature. Those still frequently played today include the *Prelude and Fugue in D Major* (BWV532), *Prelude and Fugue in a minor* (BWV543), *Toccata, Adagio, and Fugue in C Major* (BWV564), and the *Toccata and Fugue in d minor* (BWV565); all these were probably written about the year 1709. At the close of his stay at Weimar came forth the grand *Passacaglia and Fugue in c minor* (BWV582); for a short comment on the *Passacaglia,* for which Bach borrowed the first four bars of the eight-measure theme from the French organist André Raison, see Chapter 2; the double fugue written here used Raison's theme as the first subject, with the second subject (which begins immediately) consisting of a single measure repeated in sequence.

Bach may have written the *Fantasia and Fugue in g minor* (BWV542) and the *Orgelbüchlein* ("Little Organ Book") during his stay in Köthen. He is reputed to have impressed the old German organist Johann Adam Reinken with his playing of the former composition in Hamburg. (The powerful and rhapsodic fantasy is printed in GMB, No. 283.) The *Orgelbüchlein* was evidently planned as a set of 164 organ chorales of which only forty-five were composed. These are extremely useful for instructional purposes, and that, indeed, was their original purpose; the text of the chorale with which each instrumental work is associated is important to the understanding of the organ piece, for Bach often used pictorial painting in these compositions.

Some products of his years in Leipzig are: the *Six Trio Sonatas* (BWV525–30) written for the instruction of Bach's son Wilhelm Friedemann and representing the transference of the Italian trio sonata style to the organ; the *Eighteen Chorale Preludes* (BWV651–68) representing revision of earlier works and newly composed pieces of Bach's last years; large-scale chorale preludes of all types, some in the form of the chorale fantasy and the chorale fugue; the *Clavierübung III* (BWV-669–89), a collection of twenty-one preludes on the Catechism and other hymns, sometimes called an "Organ Mass," whose concluding fugue has acquired the title "St. Anne," for its subject bears a resemblance to William Croft's hymn tune of that name; the *Schübler Chorales* (BWV645–50), six organ arrangements from cantatas, of which *Wachet auf, ruft uns die Stimme* ("Sleepers, wake, a voice is calling"), from *Cantata No. 140,* is the best known.

CLAVIER COMPOSITIONS

Of Bach's clavier (harpsichord and clavichord) music, the earliest work to be of interest is the programmatic *Capriccio on the Departure of His Beloved Brother* (BWV992), which Bach wrote in Arnstadt in 1704 on the occasion of the leaving of his brother Johann Jacob to play the oboe in the military band of the Swedish King Karl XII.

The composer's Köthen period gave fruition to many clavier and chamber music works, with a large number of the clavier pieces written for instructional purposes. Of these Part I of the *Well-Tempered Clavier* (BWV846–69), containing twenty-four preludes and fugues, one for each major and minor key (*C* major, *c* minor, *C*♯ major, *c*♯ minor, etc.), and the *Inventions* (BWV772–801) are just as valuable for piano students of today as they were for the clavier players of the 18th century. The former work suggests by its title the period's interest in a new tuning system for keyboard instruments.

Tuning systems in music began with Pythagoras in the 6th century B.C., when he arranged a series of five successive pure upper fifths and one pure lower fifth in order in the same octave to produce the octave scale. The Renaissance development of polyphonic music in the Western world was concerned with two tunings: just intonation and the meantone system. In JUST INTONATION all intervals are calculated from the pure fifth and pure third; this provides for an excellent sound in the three fundamental triads, or "natural triads," of the key, but other harmonies suffer. MEANTONE tuning was in use in the early 16th century, as in Arnold Schlick's *Spiegel der Orgelmacher und Organisten* (1511). The system is based on a slightly flat fifth, so that a series of four such fifths (c-g-d′-a′-e″) produces a pure third between the fundamental and e″. In keys having up to two accidentals the sound was very good both melodically and harmonically, but when composers began to use keys with from three to six sharps or flats, equal temperament became necessary.

EQUAL TEMPERAMENT tuning divides the octave into twelve equal semitones. Only the octave is pure; the discrepancy of the fifth interval is so slight that the ear usually cannot notice the difference; the tempered third is considerably larger than the pure third, but modern ears find no difficulty in accepting this, and thus there evolved a system capable of supporting all music in all keys. Bach anticipated equal temperament in writing the *Well-Tempered Clavier* (which finally achieved printed publication in 1799), but final acceptance of this tuning occurred in Germany only about the beginning of the 19th century and in England and France in the middle of that century. Of course all keyboard instruments of the present day are tuned in equal temperament.

Bach wrote two sets of keyboard suites–six in each set–identified as "French" and "English" (the names were not Bach's, nor do they indicate the true styles of the music). The standard Bach suite sets the dance forms in the order of allemande-courante-sarabande-gigue, each in binary form; optional dances are also included. The *French Suites* (BWV812–17) represent the fusion of German, French, and Italian styles, but the *English Suites* (BWV806–11) have preludes in the Italian style–save for *No. 1*–and other movements mostly in the French manner. The last work to be mentioned from the Köthen residency is the *Chromatic Fantasy and Fugue in d minor* (BWV903); a popular work then and now, the fantasy is in much the same rhapsodic style as the aforementioned *g*-minor fantasy for organ.

The Leipzig years produced the first of Bach's harpsichord works to be published in his lifetime. *Six Partitas* (BWV825–30) were printed in the *Clavierübung I* in 1731. The important *Italian Concerto* (BWV971), representing the Italian orchestral concerto form transferred to the keyboard, came out in 1735 in the *Clavierübung II*. The *Aria with 30 Variations* (BWV988)–the *Goldberg Variations*–is found in the *Clavierübung IV*, of 1742. Part II of the *Well-Tempered Clavier* (BWV870–93) was compiled in 1744 but not printed, as noted above, until 1799.

CHAMBER AND INSTRUMENTAL MUSIC

Chief among Bach's chamber music output are the *Six Solo Violin Sonatas and Partitas* (BWV1001–06); the *Six Solo Violoncello Suites* (BWV1007–12); the *Six Sonatas for Violin and Harpsichord* (BWV1014–19); the *Three Sonatas for Viola da Gamba and Harpsichord* (BWV1027–29), which are mostly performed today on the cello, although gambas (see MITA, No. 230) are back in use; and two sets of *Three Sonatas for Flute and Harpsichord* (BWV1030–35). The solo violin and cello works offer considerable difficulties for the performer in their use of multiple stops and divided voice lines; and the violin sonatas, the gamba sonatas, and some of the flute sonatas depart from tradition in that each has a written out (not figured) harpsichord part. All of these works are from Bach's Köthen period.

The concertos and orchestra suites were composed in Köthen and Leipzig. This literature includes seven solo harpsichord concertos (BWV1052–58); three for two harpsichords, two for three harpsichords, and one for four harpsichords (see BWV1060–65); the last named is an arrangement of a Vivaldi concerto for four violins. Bach wrote two solo violin concertos —one in *E* major (BWV1042) and a second in *a* minor (BWV1041)—and a *Concerto for Two Violins in d minor* (BWV1043). *The Harpsichord, Flute, and Violin Concerto in a minor* (BWV1044) he arranged from earlier works.

In 1721, while at Köthen, Bach sent the Margrave of Brandenburg six concertos; these are now known as the *Brandenburg Concertos* (BWV1046–51). Each has a distinctive combination of instruments, with the trumpet featured in the second, the violin in the fourth, and the harpsichord in the fifth; however these three are not solo concertos, they are actually *concerto grosso* types with three or four solo instruments. The four orchestral suites (BWV1066–69) were called *"ouvertures"* by Bach. The first two, perhaps written in Köthen, are for woodwinds and strings, whereas the latter two, probably written by Bach for the *collegium musicum* he conducted at the University of Leipzig, add trumpets and timpani. Each of the four opens with a French overture, the following movements being dance types.

The *Musical Offering* (BWV1079) and *The Art of Fugue* (BWV1080) stand in a special class and complete the listing of the principal instrumental works of J. S. Bach. In 1740 Bach's son Carl Philipp Emanuel had entered the service of Frederick II of Prussia, and in 1747 Bach paid his son and the king a visit at Potsdam. While there he tried the Silbermann pianos and the principal organs of the city, improvising upon a theme handed to him by the king. Upon his return to Leipzig he wrote out a ricercare in three parts and another in six parts and ten canons and a trio for flute, violin, and *continuo,* all on the king's theme; he sent the completed work to Frederick as a "musical offering."

The Art of Fugue represents a summing up of all the technique of fugal writing. It is the last great work by Bach, and in fact was left incomplete at his death, breaking off just as Bach had introduced for the first time the theme on the letters B-A-C-H, which in the German nomenclature signify the notes B♭-A-C-B♮.

VOCAL MUSIC

Of Bach's large-scale vocal compositions only about a dozen are well known and rather frequently performed today. They would include a number of the cantatas, the *Christmas Oratorio,* the *St. John Passion* and the *St. Matthew Passion,* a couple of the motets, the *Magnificat in D major,* and the great *Mass in b minor.* Between the years 1704 and 1745 the master wrote some three hundred cantatas of which about two hundred are extant. They were written, of course, for the Lutheran service and were performed after the Creed on Sundays and holy days, except during the penitential seasons of Lent and the last three Sundays of Advent; the cantatas in two parts had the second half sung after the sermon. The scoring of most of these works is for a combination of solo voices, vocal ensembles, choruses, and orchestral accompaniments with organ *continuo;* many of the cantatas make use of chorale melodies. Some of these compositions are for solo voices alone, and in all the cantatas the various instruments enjoy considerable independence in their accompanying parts. The numbering of the cantatas, such as *Cantata No. 140,* for "Sleepers, wake," follows their numbering in the famous *Bach-Gesellschaft* publication and does not represent the chronological order of composition.

The best known of the cantatas are probably (at least in their final form) all from the Leipzig days. These would include *Cantata No. 4* ("Christ lay in death's dark tomb," BWV4), *Cantata No. 80* ("A mighty fortress is our God," BWV80), and *Cantata No. 140* ("Sleepers, wake," BWV140). There are a number of secular cantatas by Bach also—as close as he got to the writing of opera—and the *Cantata No. 211* ("Coffee Cantata," BWV211) and *Cantata No. 212* ("Peasant Cantata," BWV212) occasionally receive performance today.

The above-mentioned *Cantata No. 4* was written (or rewritten) for Easter Day of 1724. The sinfonia and each of the seven movements are based on the *Christ lag in Todesbanden* chorale melody (in turn derived from the 12th-century *Christ ist erstanden* song), and each vocal setting uses one stanza of Martin Luther's chorale text. The final movement of this work —a simple harmonization of the chorale—and one of the large choruses are printed in MM, Nos. 46 and 48, respectively.

The Reformation Festival of 1730 in Leipzig prompted Bach to rework a previous Weimar cantata as set to a paraphrase by Salomon Franck of Luther's mighty text *Ein feste Burg.* The chorale melody used is probably Luther's also. The musical strength of this *Cantata No. 80* is tremendous, as would be necessary to match the text. Two massive choruses, one polyphonic and one with unison voices, stand out in the composition. Perhaps the loveliest of all the cantatas is *No. 140,* written for the twenty-seventh Sunday after Trinity (in November), 1731. The chorale text and tune that Bach employed are by Philipp Nicolai and were first published in the latter's *Frewden-Spiegel des ewigen Lebens,* of 1599. The story begins with the parable of the wise and foolish virgins and ends with a description of the bliss involved in the marriage of the Christian soul to Christ, the bridegroom. Many portions of the text are given pictorial and symbolic representation in this Bach piece—another illustration of the Baroque affection. Baroque composers made very little if any differentiation in stylistic practices in their secular and sacred vocal forms, with the result that "operatic" styles and the *stile concertato* are found in both. So it is not surprising to find the heavenly love of the *Wachet auf* cantata expressed at times in very earthly terms.

The *Christmas Oratorio* (BWV248) is a string of six cantatas to be performed during the Christmas festival that opens on Christmas Day and closes on Epiphany. The oratorio, with a text from St. Luke and St. Matthew and with eleven of the sixty-four numbers borrowed directly from secular cantatas and set to new sacred words, is from the year 1734. The work opens and closes with the Passion chorale "O Sacred Head now wounded."

The *Passion According to St. John* (BWV245) was composed in Köthen, 1722–23, and was probably first performed in St. Thomas's, Leipzig, on Good Friday of 1723. The biblical text is from St. John 18 and 19, with the account of the earthquake and St. Peter's sorrow added from St. Matthew. Bach also used words borrowed from (or based on) a Passion text by Barthold Brockes of Hamburg in a number of the arias and ariosos and in the final chorus (the last being a musical highlight of the *St. John Passion*). The basic instrumentation is strings, two flutes, two oboes, organ, and *continuo;* the *oboe d'amore, oboe da caccia* (see the "hunting" oboe in MITA, No. 154), lute, viola d'amore (MITA, No. 239), and a viola da gamba are introduced at various places in the *Passion.*

Although the *Passion According to St. Matthew* (BWV244) was given its first performance in Leipzig on Good Friday of 1729, Bach later revised the work and copied out a complete score about 1740 in which all quotations from the Holy Scriptures are interestingly presented in red ink. In its final form the *St. Matthew Passion* is a huge work of seventy-eight parts, requiring two full choruses, soloists, strings, organ, and *continuo,* plus the following winds in pairs: transverse flute, recorder, oboe, *oboe d'amore,* and *oboe da caccia.* The biblical text is from St. Matthew 26 and 27, with other texts in the nature of commentary on the Gospel message by Christian Friedrich Henrici, of Leipzig, who wrote under the pseudonym of Picander.

Compared with the *St. John Passion,* the *St. Matthew* is somewhat more lyric and contemplative, yet it does not lack dramatic elements when they are required. Text symbolisms and pictorialisms are deeply painted into the music in many spots. Bach reached back into historical precedent in providing a "string halo" for the words of Christ, and a neat touch is added when he abandons the strings at Christ's words "My

God, why hast Thou forsaken me!" Intense picture painting is done in the organ part at the point where the temple veil is rent in twain and the earthquake takes place (this is the borrowed passage found in the *St. John Passion*), and the alto setting of "Ah Golgotha" in MM, No. 49, is another example of the same thing. As in the *St. John* there is a considerable use of harmonized chorales (probably for participation by the congregation), with the Passion chorale employed five times with different texts and varied harmonizations.

Of smaller scope but still of great beauty are the six motets Bach set to German texts. In all probability they were composed at Leipzig. *Singet dem Herrn* ("Sing to the Lord," BWV225) is for double chorus and was probably intended for a New Year's performance. The final movement contains a stunning fugue for four-part chorus. *Jesu, meine Freude* ("Jesu, priceless treasure," BWV227) has many lovely parts. A chorale text of 1653 by Johann Franck is used in the odd-numbered sections, the other divisions using a biblical text from Romans 8.

Ever since the time of the Cult of the Virgin in the Middle Ages, the Magnificat ("Mary's Song of Thanksgiving," Luke 1:46–55) had been well known to the laity. Its use in Vespers, where figured music was permitted, had led to many contrapuntal settings. Bach's setting of 1723 (revised in 1730) was another in the long historical line (see BWV243), but what a magnificent *Magnificat* is Bach's musical creation. The work in *D* major is set for a five-part chorus, soloists, and an orchestra with trumpets (clarino types, as in MITA, Nos. 167–70) and timpani in addition to the usual flutes, oboes, bassoon, strings, and *continuo.* In many movements a rhythmic motive is introduced at the outset, to be manipulated and varied in typical Baroque fashion throughout that movement. Instrumental openings are often repeated at ends of movements, and several sections are joined by instrumental *ritornelli.* Also, Bach uses the plain song *Tonus peregrinus* (see LU, p. 117) in the oboes in movement No. 10.

This discussion of Bach's work will conclude with his great

Mass in b minor (BWV232). He had sent the Kyrie and Gloria to Augustus II, Elector of Saxony, in 1733 along with the request for a court title (which he did receive three years later); the Credo, Sanctus, and Agnus Dei settings were probably completed by 1738. The entire work takes nearly three hours for performance, too long of course for liturgical usage, although separate movements can be used (and were and are used) in the church service. This Mass might be called "The Best of Bach," for in organizing its numbers Bach borrowed heavily in material and ideas from his earlier cantatas, as Table XVII illustrates.

TABLE XVII

B Minor Mass	borrows from	*Cantata Number–Movement*	
Gloria		191	1
* Gratias agimus		29	2
Domine Deus		191	2
Qui tollis		46	1
Cum Sancto		191	3
Patrem		171	1
Crucifixus		12	2
Et exspecto		120	2
Osanna		215	1
Agnus Dei		11	4
* Dona nobis		29	2

* same music throughout

The chromatic chaconne bass in the Crucifixus sounds the everlasting song of sorrow of the Baroque age, and the marching quarter notes of the *Credo in unum Deum* setting symbolizes the strength of the Christian through his belief in one God.

The instrumentation of the Mass calls for two flutes, three oboes, two *oboi d'amore,* two bassoons (MITA, No. 173), three trumpets, *corno da caccia* (MITA, No. 174), timpani, strings, and *continuo;* Bach does not spare the voices, often assigning to them parts in a pseudoinstrumental style. The Credo (No. 12) opens with a plain-song *incipit* (see beginning of Credo II, LU, p. 66), and another line of plain song is introduced by the bass part (in canon with the alto) at measure

73 of the Confiteor, thence to the tenor voice in whole-note values until measure 118 (compare with the same text of the chant in Credo II, LU, p. 68). Thus Bach, the Lutheran, speaks in this Mass for the universal Christian church.

THE WORKS OF HANDEL

George Frederick Handel (1685–1759). George Frederick Handel (in German Georg Friedrich Händel) was born in Halle on February 23, 1685. His family line, contrary to that of Bach's, was not musical. Although the boy's father hoped that his son would study law, young Handel was permitted to undertake lessons on the harpsichord, oboe, and organ and in counterpoint and fugue with Friedrich Wilhelm Zachau, organist of the cathedral at Halle. Handel duly entered the University of Halle, in 1702, as a law student, but his heart was not in it and the next year found him following a musical career at Hamburg. There he worked with Reinhard Keiser and Johann Mattheson.

From 1706–10 Handel was in Italy learning the Italian style of composition in general and the *bel canto* aria style in particular; during this Italian visit he made the acquaintance, among others, of the two Scarlattis and Corelli. In 1710 Handel returned to Germany as *Kapellmeister* to the Elector of Hanover, gaining that post through a recommendation by his predecessor, Steffani. Handel made a brief trip to London for an operatic production in 1711, returning again in 1712 to make London his home; he became an English citizen in 1727 and upon his death on April 14, 1759, was buried with great honor in Westminster Abbey.

OPERA

Handel wrote his first opera in 1705 and his last in 1741, and it is strange that such a famous musician is so little known by the medium that occupied so much of his creative endeavors. *Almira* (1705) is the only one of three operas written in Hamburg to have survived. *Agrippina,* his first important opera, was successfully produced in Venice in 1709. The year 1711 saw a production of *Rinaldo* in London, and after Handel took up permanent residency in London one successful opera after another followed: *Ottone* (1723), *Giulio Cesare* (1724), *Tamerlano* (1724), *Rodelinda* (1725), *Admeto* (1727), and *Orlando* (1733). But all these were set to Italian librettos, and the English eventually tired of the foreign tongue–if they had ever really approved of it in the first place. This, plus the competition of a rival grand opera house in London and the further competition of English ballad opera in the form of Gay's and Pepusch's popular *Beggar's Opera* (for illustrations see GMB, No. 281, and HAM II, No. 264), finally led to the decline and neglect of Handelian opera. Modern revivals of these works have not been very successful, for Handel's operas were written in the conventions of their time, which make present-day performances cumbersome and unrealistic. However, a number of them are recorded, and there the music makes them wonderfully enjoyable.

ORATORIO AND OTHER VOCAL WORKS

When Handel forsook operatic writing, he turned with considerable zeal to the oratorio form, which in itself was little more than sacred opera presented in concert form without staging. However, the oratorios composed by Handel had English texts, which immediately strengthened their appeal and the scope of this appeal. Today in England, Germany, and the United States the genius of Handel in vocal and choral writing is known through his oratorios.

Not all the oratorios can actually be classed as sacred. For instance, *Alexander's Feast* (on a text by Dryden) was written in 1736 to an allegorical subject, and Congreve's text for *Semele* (1744) is based on mythology. On the other hand, perhaps the greatest and surely the best known of the oratorios do have biblical texts: *Israel in Egypt* (1739), *Saul* (1739), *Judas Maccabaeus* (1747), *Solomon* (1749), and the *Messiah* (1742).

The *Messiah,* of course, is the work that brought Handel his greatest renown and most enduring fame. Written in the white heat of inspiration in twenty-four days, it was given its first full-fledged public performance in Dublin on April 13, 1742. The text, selected by Charles Jennens from the Bible, is set in three large sections: (1) the prophecy of the coming and the birth of Christ; (2) His sacrifice on the cross; and (3) His triumph over death. It seems incredible that such a large work as the *Messiah,* comprising, as it does, some fifty numbers, could have been written in such a short span of time. Of course, some of this music had been previously composed, and Handel, a notorious borrower from many sources, including his own earlier works, only adapted these portions to the new text; for example, the choruses "And He shall purify the sons of Levi," "For unto us a child is born," "His yoke is easy," and "All we like sheep have gone astray" are all simply new settings of Italian love duets written by Handel.

Today audiences frequently hear the large-scale choral works of Handel done by somewhat overwhelming numbers of performers. (This is to some extent true also of similarly large works by Bach, but the openness of the Handelian scores allows them to maintain better their clarity in this type of presentation than do the more involved harmonic-contrapuntal textures of Bach.) It is interesting to note that Handel's original performance in Dublin was done with five soloists, a chorus of thirty-eight voices, and an orchestra of four oboes, four bassoons, two trumpets, two horns, and a string group numbering about twenty-eight members. Handel conducted this relatively compact ensemble from the keyboard, placing himself now at the harpsichord and again at the organ. An interesting, and still-existing, tradition stems from the first London performance, at which King George II was so deeply moved by the opening chords of the "Hallelujah Chorus" that he rose to his feet; the audience followed suit, and all remained standing throughout the chorus.

It has been suggested that there is little stylistic difference, musically speaking, between the operas and oratorios of Handel, and this is true. To each Handel brought the *bel canto, da capo* aria style (the "*Cara sposa*" from *Rinaldo* is an example –see MM, No. 44), coupled with *recitativo secco* and *recitativo accompagnato.* Baroque affections are expressed through word paintings and through musical figures, but of greater moment is the use of musical symbolism. However, there is a marked difference in the use of the chorus in the two forms. Handel's operas, in the Italian tradition, feature the aria, with the chorus appearing only occasionally, usually at the end of an act; on the other hand, the chorus is more apt to be the focal point of attention in the oratorios. Handel is one of the greatest composers for chorus in the history of musical art. His technique is to alternate a spacious fugal texture with chordal sections–in contrast to Bach's consistently rich contrapuntal web –in order to achieve a grandiose effect within the bounds of relative simplicity (see the chorus "Draw the Tear from Hopeless Love," from the oratorio *Solomon* in MM, No. 45).

A few of Handel's small-scaled sacred works are still sung by choral societies today. Best known among these are the *Utrecht Te Deum and Jubilate* (1713), written to celebrate the Peace of Utrecht; *Zadok the Priest,* the first of four texts set by Handel for the coronation of George II in 1727; and the *Dettingen Te Deum* (1743), composed in celebration of the English victory over the French at Dettingen.

INSTRUMENTAL MUSIC

In comparison with his output in the large vocal forms, Handel's purely instrumental works are few in number. Three sets of suites for keyboard stem from the years 1720, 1733, and 1742. The group of famous variations now called "The Harmonious Blacksmith" is from the fifth suite of the first collection, and Brahms took his theme for his *Handel Variations* from the first suite of the 1733 book. The *Six Fugues or Voluntarys* (1735) are for organ or harpsichord. Handel's principal chamber compositions, showing the influence of Corelli, include sonatas playable by a flute, by an oboe, or by a violin, plus a *continuo* instrument (Op. 1) and two collections of trio sonatas (Opp. 2 and 5).

Handel's orchestral concertos are important contributions to instrumental literature. These comprise: six works from the year 1729 for woodwinds and strings called collectively "oboe concertos" (Op. 3); twelve for strings alone (Op. 6, dated 1739); and three sets of six each of organ concertos, 1738 (Op. 4), 1740 (without opus number), and 1760 (Op. 7). Particularly significant among his orchestral suites are the *Water Music* and *Royal Fireworks Music.*

On July 17, 1717, a festival took place on the Thames River, at which King George I and his royal court was entertained by some fifty musicians on a nearby barge playing music composed by Handel. How much of the music of this concert was actually a part of the later published score called *Water Musick* is difficult to say. The *Royal Fireworks Music* was the result of a commission Handel received in 1749 to compose music that would accompany a display of fireworks in Green Park in celebration of the Treaty of Aix-la-Chapelle, signed in 1748; the score was published in 1749 by John Walsh (see below).

The organ concertos were written for Handel's personal use; he played them between the acts of his oratorios. The organ parts consist of a melodic line and a figured bass (accompanied by an "orchestra" of two oboes and strings), actually only a skeleton score with a great deal left to the imagination and improvisatory skill of the performer. Many of these organ concertos, like the harpsichord concertos of Bach, are arrangements of other instrumental compositions. Of all the organ concertos only No. 1 of Op. 7 has a pedal part written into the original score; this can be explained by the fact that few English organs of the time had a pedal clavier; the organ in St. Paul's (after 1724) was an exception, which leads to the speculation that Handel wrote Op. 7, No. 1, for performance by him at that cathedral. As a matter of fact, these three sets of concertos were printed at the time of the above dates of each by the London publishing house of John Walsh as "Concertos for the Harpsichord or Organ." All told, as works involving keyboard instruments, these concertos have much more of the

Italian fire and virtuosity and much less of the German contrapuntal depth and severity.

With the deaths of Bach and Handel the Baroque age is brought to a close, and it is hard to visualize another period of musical history that ends with such a prodigious display of musical talent. Actually there was nothing left to say in the Baroque style after Bach and Handel had had their turns; all was completely summed up. It was just as well, however, for the inevitable cycle of change in art presented itself in the middle of the 18th century, and the Age of Reason was to turn the minds of men in their approach to the arts toward the rational and the formal, as it was doing in other walks of life, and the Classical style was to be music's new pathway.

PART FOUR

The Classical and Romantic Periods

CHAPTER 7

The Classical Period

INTRODUCTION

"Classical" is an extremely overworked term in musical criticism. Many people call "classical" all music of a more serious nature than "The Indian Love Call," but, strictly speaking, Classical refers to the dominant style of composition from, roughly, 1750 to 1800. To complete the confusion of these terms, the latter half of the 18th century is often known as the "Neoclassic Era," to distinguish it from antiquity, and the ideals of its art, literature, and music are termed neoclassic ones.

The neoclassic concept of life and art in the 18th century was in many ways linked to that of the Renaissance. The latter part of the 15th and most of the 16th centuries were very similar to the 18th in that both eras produced men with questioning attitudes; everything in the life of these times was suspect: religion, politics, science, literature, art, and music. The skeptical mind turned to reason as a tool for examining the world, and as the Renaissance humanists had attacked abuses in the Church and revived ancient learning, so the 18th century saw satires on human conduct–*Candide,* by Voltaire, and *Gulliver's Travels,* by Jonathan Swift–and a renewed study of the world as science gained new perspectives from experiments of Isaac Newton in physics and optics and from the inquisitive studies of Benjamin Franklin in electricity. In England the desire for something resembling Greek order and balance is reflected in the couplets and odes of John Dryden, and later in those of

Alexander Pope and Thomas Gray. The French in turn produced the polished comedies of Molière and the tragedies of Corneille and Racine, all of which represent the fullest expression of French Classical theater.

Consequently, in England the period of Queen Anne (reigned 1702–14) acquired the name "Augustan Age," for English artists and architects attempted to reproduce the splendors of the days of the Roman Emperor Augustus. But perhaps the greatest interest in Classical revival was stimulated by the German archaeologist Johann Joachim Winckelmann (1717–68) when he published, in 1764, his monumental *Geschichte der Kunst des Altertums* ("The History of Ancient Art"). Winckelmann's influence can be seen in the works of the great Classical painters Jacques Louis David and Jean Auguste Dominique Ingres in France.

The desire for a return to Greek and Roman ideals was due, of course, to the basic philosophy of the 18th century–the keen feeling for order and conformity which gave the century the titles "Age of Reason" and the "Enlightenment." Put in its simplest form, this belief postulated that good common sense and good reasoning could solve all problems of mankind which needed attention. To this was added the "back to nature" philosophy of Jean Jacques Rousseau, which taught that nature embodied the simple life and the good life. Perhaps living close to nature and recalling the manner of life of olden times would not solve all the problems (and it surely did not), but the order and simplicity of ancient times were ideals that the artists and thinkers of the 18th century felt eminently worth striving for.

When the large-scale PATHOS art of the musical Baroque–that is, art where the personal or subjective emotions of the creator seem to dominate the work–had nearly run its course, the 18th century witnessed a rise in the ETHOS quality of its music–an artistic quality where universal or objective elements outside the personality of the artist exercise control upon his efforts.

Classical music and its attendant characteristics (order, refinement, structure, balance, and restraint) reached the height of their expression in the works of C. P. E. Bach, J. C. Bach, Gluck, Haydn, Mozart, and Beethoven. Although masterpieces were created in vocal forms, it was instrumental music that advanced most radically in this era; the string quartet and the symphony orchestra were standardized, and the literature of all chamber music media was greatly augmented. The increased length of, and emphasis on, pure instrumental types in a new style required new musical forms and concepts to preserve their order and clarity. (A number of the Classical forms–sonata, sonata form, minuet and trio, rondo, sonata-rondo, and the Classical solo concerto–have previously been discussed in Chapter 2.) Many other forms introduced into the art in previous historical periods, such as the binary, ternary, and theme-and-variations forms, were retained and adapted to the needs of the Classical style, but the sonata and sonata form have remained the basic core of instrumental music form to the present day.

In contrast to the Baroque plan of spinning out an opening musical figure of a distinctive melodic and rhythmical pattern, Classical composers worked on the idea of contrasts between sections and within sections of their forms (for example, the two keys and the two themes within the exposition of the sonata form), and carried out their contrasts even within the melodic themes themselves (seen in the differentiated antecedent- and consequent-phrase structures of many of their themes). Some of these melodic elements, constructed in a simple two- or four-measure phrase often subjected to immediate repetition, followed a chordal pattern; others were in a bold and free style; and still others carried the name SINGING ALLEGRO (themes or tunes fashioned perhaps after the style of Neapolitan *opera seria* melodies–themes that gained their "singing" quality through a lyricism obtained by casting notes of comparatively longer time values in a passage of otherwise rapid progression). Abrupt melodic shifts from major to minor mode or vice versa were common, but melodic decorations (especially in the slow movements) recall a similar usage in Baroque and Rococo styles.

There was little change in harmonic material from the Baroque style, although harmonic rhythm in the Classical age was considerably retarded. Nevertheless, a great deal of activity does occur, especially in transitional and developmental sections of the sonata form, over and above the traditional harmonies in the slower harmonic rhythm. The driving motion of the music of the high Baroque and the rational Baroque is still found to some extent in the Classical style; the drive to the cadence is evidenced at the close of some principal sections of the fast movements, accomplished through regular patterns of notes and by an insistence on the dominant and tonic chords of the key.

PRE-CLASSICAL STYLE: INSTRUMENTAL MUSIC

The period of formulation of the Classical style–that is, the first half of the 18th century–is often designated as the pre-Classical era; the development of the Classical style is found, of course, in the works of Haydn, Mozart, and Beethoven. Keyboard and orchestral music in the early 18th century was patterned after the Italian opera sinfonia or overture, adopting the fast-slow-fast sectionalized structure of this form, and soon orchestral symphonies of three movements began to appear, following the above arrangement of movement tempi. The works by Giovanni Battista Sammartini (1701–75) were some of the first of these (the opening, *Allegro* movement of his *Symphony in D Major* may be seen in HAM II, No. 283). This Italian beginning was imitated by composers of many other Continental nations, and thus the symphony–one of the most important contributions of the Classical era–was born.

THE MANNHEIM SCHOOL. German composers played a particularly important role in the development of the symphony after 1740, with the prominent centers of activity located at Mannheim, Vienna, and Berlin. Duke Carl Theodor (1724–99) set out to make Mannheim a cultural center and collected musicians from Austria, Bohemia, and Italy into his service. The court orchestra was expanded in instruments and personnel up to as many as forty-five players; the instrumentation included the usual strings and flutes, oboes, bassoons, horns, a harpsichord, and sometimes the trumpet and timpani. The clarinet, introduced into orchestral groups by Rameau and Vivaldi, was also used by the leader of the Mannheim group, Johann Stamitz (1717–57), after he had heard it in Paris. This was a rather large orchestra for the period, and later directors such as Haydn often worked with smaller groups of some thirty to thirty-five players.

Stamitz introduced a fourth movement in his symphonic compositions for this group, being one of the first symphonic composers to do so. His *Symphony in D Major,* Op. 5, No. 2, is such a four-movement work, with the movements marked *Presto-Andantino-Menuetto-Prestissimo;* the *Presto* movement is given in HAM II, No. 294, and demonstrates a number of the techniques employed in the Mannheim school. The string orchestra is the basis of his ensemble (as, indeed, it continues to be throughout the Classical period) with the winds relegated to a background position of doubling or holding parts for strengthening both the structure and color of the composition. This Mannheim orchestra became quite famous for its meticulous ensemble playing, which was obtained through uniform bowings, phrasings, and careful observance of dynamic shadings. Its graduated dynamics of the *crescendo* and *diminuendo* were a performance feature that never failed to move its audience.

THE PRE-CLASSICAL VIENNA SCHOOL. The pre-Classical Vienna school stands as the direct predecessor of the Viennese school of the masters Haydn, Mozart, and Beethoven. Its important composers were Georg Matthias Monn (1717–50) and Georg Wagenseil (1715–77), both of whom favored a light, melodious style–a somewhat traditional Viennese manner of composition. They also promoted a dualistic principle of the first and second themes in the sonata form, a technique that may be found as well in the works of the Mannheim school. The last movement of Monn's *Symphony in D Major* (HAM II, No. 295) is a short but complete sonata form; this entire composition, in four movements, has been called the first complete symphony.

THE BERLIN SCHOOL. The composers associated with the court of Frederick the Great at Berlin and Potsdam were a rather conservative lot, holding to a serious style in a three-movement form. The principal composers of this group were the brothers Johann Gottlieb Graun (1703–71) and Karl Heinrich Graun (1704–59), and C. P. E. Bach (discussed below). These composers followed the three-movement plan as developed from the Italian overture, but they contributed formal strength and interest to the opening sonata form; for example, although holding to the monothematic principle in the exposition of the form, they instigated the idea of expository thematic involvement in the digression or development section.

Carl Philipp Emanuel Bach (1714–88). In addition to his symphonies (some of which are now available on records) Carl Philipp Emanuel Bach, the second surviving son of Johann Sebastian Bach, was an important figure in the development of 18th-century keyboard music. Young Bach studied law and philosophy, but his artistic interests drew him into a musical career, which led him to Berlin in 1738; two years later he entered the service of Frederick the Great as court harpsichordist and chamber musician, remaining in this post for twenty-seven years. From 1767 until his death in 1788 he held a church position of importance at Hamburg. His *Essay on the True Art of Playing Keyboard Instruments* (1753–62) was a pedagogical contribution of considerable value; Haydn, Mozart, and Beethoven all based their teaching methods on this book. This text, along with a treatise on violin playing by Leopold Mozart (1719–87) and one on flute playing by Johann Joachim Quantz (1697–1773) provide invaluable information on 18th-century musical practices.

Two distinct styles are evident in C. P. E. Bach's compositions in the keyboard medium: the one in the *empfindsamer Stil* and the other a more emotional utterance related to the

Sturm und Drang of German literature of the 1770's. Two devices especially are typical of his *empfindsamer Stil;* these are the melodic "sigh," an appoggiatura-like figure in which a note is introduced on a strong beat to be immediately resolved downward (*portamento*) on the next weak beat, and the use of a chromatic line, the latter found oftener in a slow-moving notation. Two illustrations of Bach's manipulation of these devices in the *empfindsamer* style can be cited: *Les Langueurs tendres* (GMB, No. 304); and the second movement of the *Sonata No. 3* of the *Sechs Klavier-sonaten für Kenner und Liebhaber* ("Six Clavier Sonatas for the Connoisseur and the Amateur," published in 1779), printed in HAM II, No. 297.

The *Sturm und Drang* style of writing began toward the latter part of the 18th century, when a group of younger German writers led something of a revolt against the rationalism and classicism that predominated in the arts at the time. This revolt was influential to some extent in the works of Classical artists, but certainly it was more important in preparing the way for the Romantic movement. The school drew its name from the play *Sturm und Drang* ("Storm and Stress," 1776) by Friedrich Maximilian von Klinger (1752–1831). The philosophy of this group is found in Klinger's passionate utterance to the effect that he at times felt like destroying the entire human race and himself with it; in short, the group favored a more emotional and personal approach to art than the practices of Classicism were used to. Two important literary geniuses of the *Sturm und Drang* were Goethe and Schiller; both will be mentioned later in connection with Romanticism.

The emotional, *Sturm und Drang* style of C. P. E. Bach is displayed in his keyboard music in the abrupt, contrasting notational writing and dynamic markings of his *Fantasia,* published in HAM II, No. 296. It can also be found in the opening theme and, later, in the startling divergencies within the development section of the first movement of his *Sonata in f minor* from the *Sechs Klavier-sonaten* of 1779. It was this *Sturm und Drang* style of dramatic intensity that influenced

Beethoven's piano sonata music and indeed was carried through into Romantic keyboard style.

Bach's favorite keyboard instrument was the clavichord, but both this instrument and the harpsichord were to be superseded by the piano, the first practical instrument of this type (made by Bartolommeo Cristofori) dating from the year 1711. The sonatas of 1780–87 of C. P. E. Bach were written for the piano.

Also the desire of 18th-century musicians for a keyboard tone that could be gradually swelled or diminished can be seen in organ building when Faustino Carvalho enclosed thirteen stops and eighteen ranks in a "swell box" in a Spanish organ of 1703; this technique was developed more extensively in later English organs, and finally in nearly all such instruments.

Johann Christian Bach (1735–82). Johann Sebastian Bach's youngest son, Johann Christian Bach, fashioned his career (after 1762) in London. His symphonies and keyboard music bear the stamp of the *style galant*–music that was to influence the early compositions of Mozart. Christian Bach's light, pleasant style is reflected in the first movement of his *Sonata for Pianoforte,* Op. 17, No. 4 (HAM II, No. 303). Example 39 from this sonata shows a type of bass pattern, called the *Alberti bass,* used in many keyboard works of the 18th century; it was named for the Italian composer Domenico Alberti (*c.* 1710–*c.* 1740), and promotes forward drive in the music by breaking up left-hand chords into more quickly moving chordal patterns.

Together with Karl Friedrich Abel, J. C. Bach gave a series of public concerts in London in 1764; the fine reception of these concerts demonstrated the interest of the 18th-century middle class in attending musical functions. Christian's elder brother, C. P. E. Bach, had also been aware of this new interest in music by all classes when he indicated that his sonatas of 1779 were for connoisseur and amateur.

Other Composers of the Period. Shortly before J. C. Bach's arrival in London the musical scene there had been dominated by the Englishman William Boyce (1710–79). His contribution to 18th-century symphonic writing includes an enter-

Example 39

taining set of eight symphonies published in London in 1750. However, Boyce's greatest work was probably the completion of the three volumes of *Cathedral Music,* in which are found artistic creations of the greatest English cathedral musicians of all periods up to his time.

Another figure of importance in pre-Classical instrumental music was the eminent Italian cellist and composer Luigi Boccherini (1743–1805). He was a prolific composer, with the bulk of his works being written for chamber ensembles in a style that blended Italian lyricism and the French *style galant* with the solidity of Franz Joseph Haydn's music, which Boccherini admired so very much.

PRE-CLASSICAL STYLE: OPERA AND LIEDER

REFORM OPERA

The Age of Reason could make little sense of the string of arias that constituted early-18th-century Neapolitan *opera seria,* and by the 1750's reform was in the air. It was evident that the will of the prima donna would have to bow to the exigencies of the libretto or else all reason would depart from the plot. This did not mean forsaking the *da capo* aria entirely; rather, it meant placing it in its proper perspective. The chorus reappeared, and the orchestra assumed more importance in instrumental numbers and in accompanying recitatives and choruses. Two names of importance in early reform of *opera seria* were Niccolò Jommelli (1714–74) and Tommaso Traetta (1727–79), but Christoph Willibald Gluck was the real champion of this reform.

Christoph Willibald Gluck (1714–87). Born at Erasbach, Bavaria, Germany, Gluck was the son of a Bohemian forester. He completed the last of his formal education at Prague, earning his living at the time by playing violin and cello for country dances and by singing in church choirs. In 1737 Gluck journeyed to Milan, where he learned the Italian style of composition while studying with Giovanni Sammartini. Later he met the Italian poet and dramatist Metastasio (1698–1782) in Vienna; the lyric dramas of this poet made a deep impression on Gluck and furnished him with material for a number of his operas. But the Metastasian librettos did not feature in Gluck's operatic reforms, and, even more, the traditionalism of Metastasio found Gluck's ideas increasingly hard to take, a fact that can be seen from his opinion of Gluck's later operas—an opinion that held them to be fiery but mad.

Gluck left Milan in 1745 for London, where he came into contact with Handel. Next there followed a series of operatic productions in various European cities, and in 1750 he married a Viennese lady and settled in Vienna. Gluck's outstanding work of this period was *Orfeo ed Euridice* (1762), on the oldest plot in opera history. The libretto was in Italian, and the part of Orpheus was sung by the famous castrato Gaetano Guadagni. (See the song *Chiamo il mio ben* for Orpheus in HAM II, No. 292.) The libretto was by the Italian Raniero da Calzabigi (1714–95). *Orfeo* stands as Gluck's first reform opera; in it he curtailed the *da capo* aria and made the orchestral music of greater moment, including several instrumental interludes. Next followed *Alceste* (1767), also to an Italian text by Calzabigi. In the preface to this opera Gluck expressed his opinion that music should serve the libretto in heightening the dramatic situations without impeding or interrupting the action in any way–another step in his reform of the concept of opera.

In 1773 Gluck was persuaded to continue his career in Paris. In the French capital he produced *Iphigénie en Aulide* ("Iphigenia in Aulis," 1774), with a libretto in the French language adapted from Racine's tragedy by François du Roulet. The outstanding success of this venture provoked a revision of both *Orfeo* and *Alceste* (both now with French texts) for performance in 1774 and 1776, respectively; the revision of *Orfeo* entailed a rewriting of Orpheus's part for a tenor voice.

However, the fires of conflict over French and Italian styles still burned brightly in Paris, and Gluck, with his unique French opera, soon found himself pitted against the popular Neapolitan composer Niccolò Piccini (1728–1800), although the personal relations between the two composers were friendly. Neither composer appeared to suffer from the debate, and Gluck's *Armide* gained public approval upon its production in 1777. The styles of Gluck and Piccini can be compared by examining Renaud's aria from *Armide* (GMB, No. 313) and that of La Fleur from Piccini's *Le Faux Lord* (HAM II, No. 300), produced at Paris in the year 1783. The finest of Gluck's operas, *Iphigénie en Tauride* ("Iphigenia in Tauris"), came out in 1779. Here the vocal soloists, chorus, orchestra, and ballet are found in a compatible balance with the dramatic plot.

COMIC OPERA

Constant interest in Italian *opera buffa* was demonstrated by successful works in this genre by Piccini and Giovanni Paisiello (1740–1816). The consummate mastery of this style, of course, was to appear in Mozart's *Don Giovanni* and *The Marriage of Figaro*. A revival of Pergolesi's *La Serva padrona* (with an Italian cast of comedians) in Paris in 1752 brought on the so-called *Guerre des Bouffons* ("War of the Comedians"); this quarrel split Paris and the royal court right down the middle. Louis XV, Madame de Pompadour, and the plutocracy backed the national French serious opera in the style of Lully and Rameau; the queen, Rousseau, Denis Diderot (1713–84), editor of the French *Encyclopédie* (a monumental addition to the Enlightenment, which in 1780 came to a grand total of thirty-six volumes), and some others favored *opera buffa*. The latter faction based its stand on the supposed superiority of Italian melody, emotional feeling, and natural expression.

The "War" did not succeed in settling the old debate concerning the superiority of the one style over the other, but it did precipitate increased activity in France's own brand of comic opera–the *opéra comique*. Gluck tried his hand at a number of these. And Rousseau, in spite of his Italian leanings, wrote in 1752 a clever little work in this style called *Le Devin du village* ("The Village Soothsayer"). Mozart was later to set the same plot with the title *Bastien und Bastienne*. In 1784 the Belgian-born André Ernest Modeste Grétry (1741–1813) produced *Richard Coeur de Lion* ("Richard the Lion-Hearted"), initiating a type known as "rescue" opera, in which the long-suffering hero is finally saved through the devoted efforts of a loved one. The romantic "rescue" plot was to become quite popular; even Beethoven used it in his *Fidelio* (1805).

GERMAN OPERA

Eighteenth-century German *Singspiel* prospered in the hands of Johann Adam Hiller (1728–1804) of Leipzig; his song of Lisuart's servant Derwin (*"Bald die Blonde, bald die Braune,"* from *Lisuart und Dariolett;* HAM II, No. 301) is comparable to Leporello's "Catalogue Aria" from Mozart's *Don Giovanni.* A notable contribution to German comic opera was also made by the composer Carl Ditters von Dittersdorf (1739–99). His combination of light Viennese humor and Italian fire provided the springboard for the Mozart operatic style (see the song by Sturmwald from Dittersdorf's *Doktor und Apotheker* in HAM II, No. 305). It should be remembered that all these national forms of light (comic) opera, save *opera buffa,* used spoken dialogue instead of recitative.

LIEDER

The foremost center of 18th-century Lieder composition was Berlin. The style of writing was quite simple, one note to a syllable in strophic form and with keyboard accompaniments of little or no pretense. Principal composers of Lieder around the middle of the century were C. P. E. Bach, J. J. Quantz, and Karl Heinrich Graun. The names Johann Friedrich Reichardt (1752–1814) and Carl Friedrich Zelter (1758–1832) appear later in the century; both of these men wrote a great many songs on texts by the German poet Johann Wolfgang von Goethe (1749–1832). Goethe himself spoke most highly of the musical settings of his poems by Zelter, and the admiration of these two artists for one another was to develop into a fast friendship.

THE WORKS OF HAYDN

Franz Joseph Haydn (1732–1809). Franz Joseph Haydn was born in the small town of Rohrau, Austria, on March 31, 1732. His parents were not professional musicians, but they both took part in the music of the village church and the making of music was encouraged in the Haydn home. When he was eight years old he was sent to Vienna and became a chorister under the tutelage of Georg Reutter at St. Stephen's. Unfortunately his musical instruction at that cathedral choir school left much to be desired, and upon leaving the school he felt compelled to embark upon a period of self-education in theory and keyboard playing, using as a source for the latter the sonatas by C. P. E. Bach. Sometime later he did manage some composition lessons with the noted Italian composer Nicola Porpora (1686–1768). Through him he made the acquaintance of Wagenseil, Dittersdorf, and Gluck. In his twenty-ninth year Haydn entered the service of Prince Paul Anton Esterházy at Eisenstadt, not far from Vienna; the following year (1762)

Prince Nikolaus, the "great" Esterházy, succeeded his deceased brother Paul. Prince Nikolaus built a magnificent summer palace, which he called Esterháza, on a remote country estate at one end of Lake Neusiedler, where he proceeded to fashion a cultural center comparable to that of the French Versailles palace. Haydn's duties at Esterháza were considerable, for he was required to stage two operas and direct two concerts each week, in addition to the daily musical activities. But the fact that an orchestra of some twenty-five members was in residence at Esterháza (plus singers for the operas as needed) gave Haydn an ever-ready workshop for his musical ideas, and soon he obtained distinction and honor throughout Europe.

When Prince Nikolaus died in 1790, his son, Anton, reduced Haydn's musical duties, but at the same time increased his salary. Now Haydn was famous, and his time was virtually his own. The impresario Johann Salomon induced the composer to come to London in 1791 and again in 1794 for a series of concerts; it was for these concerts that Haydn wrote the "Salomon" symphonies, which were received with all due acclaim. After London, Haydn took up residence in Vienna, and upon his death in 1809 he was buried there, but a later reinterment made Eisenstadt his final resting place.

The full extent of Haydn's compositions will probably never be known. Today's accounting of his principal works tabulates one hundred four symphonies, eighty-three string quartets, fifty-two piano sonatas, twenty-three operas, four oratorios, and a number of Masses. Of special historical interest is the group of chamber compositions involving the *viola di bordone,* or baryton, for this was the instrument played by Prince Nikolaus.

The early works of both Haydn and Mozart reflect much of the Rococo spirit of the 18th century, but as they move through the second half of the century both become true Classicists. Thus it is quite natural that the musical public of today appreciates more the later music of Haydn and Mozart, with the consequence that their earlier works in the *empfindsamer Stil* are little heard today. In like manner, the operas of Haydn, though undoubtedly of interest in their day, are no longer a part

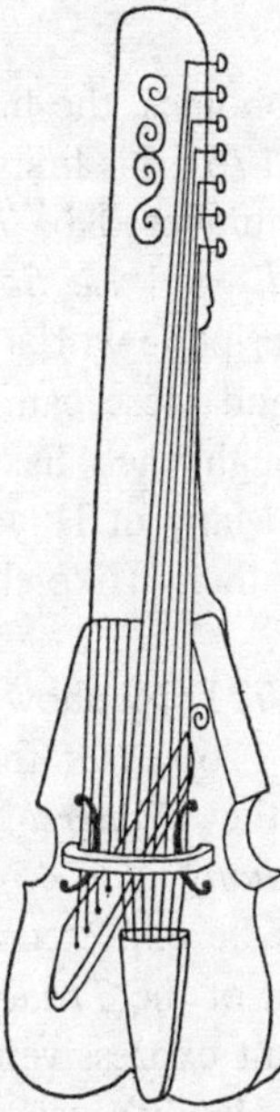

Fig. 13: Viola di bordone.

of the present stage offerings (although his comic opera *The Apothecary* has been revived by small groups). Of his works for keyboard the *Andante con variazioni in f minor* (1793) is perhaps his most famous and most beautiful piano composition; a number of the piano sonatas are played today, *No. 35* in *C* major and *No. 37* in *D* major having achieved a measure of popularity and the last three (Nos. 50–52), written for Thérèse Jansen, showing Haydn at his best. *No. 51* in *D* major points the way toward Beethoven's piano art, and *No. 52* in *E♭* major ranks in stature with the Haydn late quartets and symphonies. Nevertheless, his piano works as a whole have been relegated to a secondary position, with the principal interest in Haydn's music focused on the symphonies, the string quartets, the Masses, and the oratorios.

SYMPHONIES

In discussing the symphonies, the first mention will be of the triptych Haydn wrote in 1761, his first year with the Esterházys. The three symphonies, numbered 6, 7, and 8 and bearing the titles *Le Matin, Le Midi,* and *Le Soir* ("Morning," "Noon," and "Evening"), are descriptive works portraying nature studies in a day at Eisenstadt, and these can be best described as entertainment music, although each has the four movements of the Classical symphony. Many of Haydn's works have pictorial titles, but only a few of them (like the three just mentioned) come from the composer.

The symphonies of 1771–74 show growth in breadth and depth over those of the 1760's. Of the former *Symphony No. 44 in e minor,* called the *Trauersinfonie* ("Mourning Symphony"), and the *Symphony No. 45* (*Farewell*) are of particular interest. As might be expected from the tempo and the name, the slow movement of the *Trauersinfonie* achieves a profound measure of poignant expressiveness, and the entire work stands as a document of Haydn's use at this time of the *Sturm und Drang* style. The *Farewell* symphony gains its title from a story associated with a long *Adagio* passage appended to the final *Presto* movement. It seems that Prince Nikolaus had stayed overlong one summer at Esterháza, and the musicians (who, with the exception of Haydn, were not allowed to have their families with them) wished to return home. As a gentle hint to Prince Esterházy, the closing *Adagio* had the performers depart one by one until at the last only two violinists remained. The tale is concluded happily, with the entire court leaving for home on the next day.

The six "Paris" symphonies of 1785–86 and Nos. 88–92 of 1787–88 reveal the arrival of Haydn's consummate powers as a symphonist. They show also full entrance into the Classical style, with the last vestiges of the *style galant* gone. The "Paris" symphonies were commissioned works, written for a Parisian organization called *Les Concerts de la Loge Olympique;* they were played during the 1787 season of the *Concert Spirituel.* The *Symphony No. 85* of this group *"La Reine,"* said to have been a favorite of Queen Marie Antoinette) is a piece of particularly happy inspiration. The second movement, in theme-and-variations form, has already been discussed (in Chapter 2 under the heading "The Forms of Music"). Haydn acknowledges the Paris audience in the second movement through the use, as a theme, of the French chanson *La Gentile et jeune Lisette* ("The gentle and young Lisette").

Early in 1785 Haydn was invited by Mozart to hear the six quartets that the latter had dedicated to him. Haydn was much impressed by Mozart's artistic abilities, and his own works begin now to show more extensively the influences of the younger Mozart; these influences are manifested in particular in Haydn's adoption of a more singing melodic style and in a greater profundity of expression, especially in the slow movements. From the years 1787–88 stem the symphonies *No. 88* and *No. 92* ("Oxford"), both of which have found a place in the repertoire of modern symphony orchestras. In *No. 88* Haydn follows pretty much the four-movement structure of *La Reine* symphony: sonata form, theme and variations, minuet and trio, and a modified sonata-rondo design. The final movement introduces canonic procedure, a contrapuntal feature found with greater frequency in this period of composition. *Symphony No. 92* (1788) received its "Oxford" title through its subsequent performance in 1791, when Oxford University conferred upon Haydn the honorary title Doctor of Music.

The music required for the London concerts of 1791–92 and 1794–95 spurred Haydn to supreme efforts in his symphonic composition. The symphonies numbering 93–104, written for the two series, are considered his finest works in this medium. Of these *Symphony No. 94* ("Surprise"), *No. 100* ("Military"), *No. 101* ("Clock"), *No. 103* ("Drum Roll"), and *No. 104* ("London") have become the best known. Although *No. 104* bears the specific title "London," the entire group of twelve also is collectively designated as the "London" symphonies; and, again, they are often called the "Salomon" symphonies, as mentioned before. The "Surprise" derives its name from the fortissimo chord (complete with kettledrums and known in Germany as *"mit dem Paukenschlag"*) following a soft passage in the *Andante* movement. It has jokingly been said that Haydn inserted the loud chord in the music to awaken the sleeping ladies at the English concerts, but Haydn is also quoted as saying that it was intended as a device to draw attention to his concerts, which were at the time being given in direct competition with a series by his pupil Ignaz Pleyel. The "Clock" symphony is so named because of the "ticking" sounds in the second movement, and *Symphony No. 103* draws its nickname from the timpani solo opening the work.

Since the "London" symphonies mark the peak of Haydn's contribution to the history of this form, a few general comments are perhaps in order. The orchestration is fully developed and the result is a deep, rich sound; clarinets, trumpets, and timpani regularly appear, and all woodwind and brass parts assume a greater independence. Like the orchestration, the harmonic structures have achieved the ultimate in Classical presentation; the music is capable of abrupt change in both mode and key, with the quick introduction of remote keys not unusual. Chromatic writing as a stylistic element may be heard in the last works. Melodies in folk-song style are heard in all periods of Haydn's composition, but the Balkan folk tunes of the "London" symphonies have been especially easy to trace. Probably they represent another facet of the composer's desire to make these symphonies overwhelmingly attractive to the general listening public. In a considerable number of his works in sonata form Haydn adopted the monothematic principle in which the same or very similar themes serve as the melodic material of both key centers of the exposition, but in the "London" symphonies a greater use of two (principal and subordinate) themes can be seen. Finally, the opening sonata forms of a large number of the symphonies from the "Paris" group through the "London" set are written with a slow introduction.

STRING QUARTETS

Whereas such titles as "Father of the Symphony" and "Father of the String Quartet" were at one time assigned to Haydn, only to be withdrawn when the contributions of the Mannheim, the Berlin, and the early Viennese schools were made known, the fact remains that the establishment of the Classical tradition in these forms rests largely with Haydn. The growth of this style in Haydn's symphonies has been briefly shown, and the development of his string quartets followed much the same pattern as that of his symphonies. Of early importance are the quartets of Op. 20, written in the year 1772; they are known as the "Sun" quartets, since an early title page showed a picture of a rising sun. Form, musical content, and the independence of the four string instruments within a balanced group attain a high level of masterful creation. The next set is Op. 33, called "Russian" (from a dedication to a grand duke of Russia who later became Tsar Paul I). These six quartets, composed in 1781, have also received the title *Gli scherzi* ("The Jokes"), since the composer had labeled the minuet movements either *scherzo* or *scherzando,* desiring a faster performance tempo than in previous minuets. The third of this set, in C major, got its name of "Bird" from the light ornaments of the first movement and the trills of the second (*Scherzando*). The first and third movements are in sonata form; the final movement is a rondo, and the second is a minuet and trio marked for a slightly faster-than-usual playing. A feature of the trio is its performance by only the two violins.

The quartets of the late 1780's are in quality on the same high plane as the symphonies Nos. 82–92. The constructional features and forms (the sonata is the four-movement form of both symphony and string quartet) are very similar, as well they might be, being composed in the same period, but the quartets make no use of the slow introduction. The opus numbers of these quartets are 42 (a single quartet from 1785), 50 (another set of six, composed during the years 1784–87; they are called "Prussian" because of their dedication to Frederick

William II, King of Prussia 1786–97, who played the cello), 54 (three quartets from 1789), 55 (three more written in 1789), and 64 (again a set of six, composed in 1790). The *String Quartet in D major,* Op. 64, No. 5 ("Lark") is perhaps the most performed of all Haydn's quartets. Opp. 54, 55, and 64 were all dedicated to Johann Tost, a wealthy merchant who may have been a professional violinist before becoming a businessman. These "Tost" quartets do give a special prominence to the first violin, which at times almost overrides the position of the second violin, viola, and cello in the complete ensemble. Thus in Op. 64, No. 5, the beautiful singing and soaring of the lark in the first movement is the property of the first violinist.

The ten years 1793–1803 brought forth Haydn's last string quartets. The opus numbers are 71, 74 (three in both Opp. 71 and 74), 76 (six quartets), and 77 (two of Haydn's finest works in this form), and 103 (one work in only two movements). Op. 76, collectively speaking, is performed more than any other set of Haydn's, and, as a group of masterpieces, can be rivaled only by Beethoven's six quartets of Op. 18. Haydn's Op. 74, No. 3, written in Vienna after his return from the first series of London concerts, draws the name "Horseman" from the jogging themes of the first and last movements (see one of these, the opening theme of the quartet, in Example 40). It

Haydn: "Horseman" Quartet

Example 40

seems that a prerequisite for the success of any Haydn work is that it be assigned a nickname. However, this does not always follow, for the two masterworks of Op. 77 do not seem to have gained this doubtful distinction. Other quartets that do have titles are Op. 76, No. 2 ("Quartet of the Fifths" or "Quinten," from the falling fifths of the first movement, also called "The Bell" or "The Donkey"), Op. 76, No. 3 ("Emperor," because of the use of Haydn's Austrian national anthem in the slow movement), and Op. 76, No. 4 ("Sunrise," after the rising violin line in the first movement). These names do make identification easier, and suggest in a small way the thematic or some other condition inherent in the composition.

In 1797 Haydn wrote the inspiring hymn *Gott erhalte Franz den Kaiser* ("God save the Emperor Francis") as a birthday present for the young Francis II, last of the Holy Roman Emperors (1792–1806), who was to serve also (1804–35) as the first Emperor of Austria under the name Francis I. This song was to become the Austrian national anthem, and no doubt the "Emperor" string quartet draws its renown from the fine set of variations in the second movement written on the tune. (The melody can be found today, not only in each string part of the slow movement of Op. 76, No. 3, but also in a number of present-day church hymnals.) But the other movements of this quartet need not be discounted, for they are equally splendid.

VOCAL WORKS

Of Haydn's choral works in the large forms, those considered most important today are his last six Masses and his two oratorios, *The Creation* and *The Seasons*. Haydn was deeply impressed by a performance of Handel's *Messiah* which he attended in London in 1791, and these late works (all written between the years 1796 and 1802) show influences of the English choral style. The six Masses were composed for Prince Nikolaus II (Anton, son of Nikolaus I) of Esterházy. The best known of this group is the *Missa Solemnis* (1798), listed also under such titles as *Lord Nelson, Coronation,* and *Imperial.* During the time of composition of this Mass Admiral Nelson defeated the French fleet in the Bay of Aboukir, and the admiral's name became associated with the Mass. Others, of equal value, are the *Missa in Tempore Belli* ("Mass in Wartime"), also called "Kettledrum" Mass; *Missa Sancti Bernardi de Offida* or *Heiligmesse* ("Holy" Mass, so named from the hymn tune *Heilig, heilig* used in the Sanctus); *Theresienmesse* ("Theresa" Mass); and the *Harmoniemesse* ("Wind Band" Mass). All are festival-type works, with a full complement of four soloists, chorus, and orchestra. Operatic elements are not excluded from these Haydn Masses (nor were they from Mozart works in the same genre), and the Church has seen fit to frown on the liturgical aspect of some of them. But Haydn did not agree with those who implied that he was not a pious Catholic, for to him religion was an expression of gladness.

The Creation is Haydn's most famous choral work. The German text was a translation by Baron Gottfried van Swieten of an English work compounded from Milton's *Paradise Lost* and the Book of Genesis. Again Haydn has come under some criticism for his novel setting of the text in a work of religious import, but it must be remembered that he composed during the Enlightenment and that pictorial settings of nature subjects were in reality a worship of God. *The Creation* is cast in three parts: (1) order from chaos, (2) the creation of nature, and (3) the story of Adam and Eve, the third part being rarely performed in modern church productions. The opening, "Depiction of Chaos," is a direct forecast of Romanticism and the programmatic character of its music; Gabriel's solo with chorus "The Marv'lous work" and his air "With verdure clad" along with Raphael's "Rolling in foaming billows" and the chorus "The heavens are telling the glory of God"–all from the first part–are unforgettable in their impact, while the chorus "Achieved is the glorious work" is the most spectacular feature of Part 2.

The text of *The Seasons* is based on the poem of the same name by James Thomson. Like the Masses and *The Creation* it uses soloists, choruses, and orchestra. Though the basic concept of *The Seasons* is religious, it can also revel in the portrayal of nature scenes and simple life.

For some time Haydn has stood somewhat in the shadow of Mozart and Handel, yet he is now coming into his own as more and more of his music is performed.

THE WORKS OF MOZART

Wolfgang Amadeus Mozart (1756–91). Wolfgang Amadeus Mozart was born in the city of Salzburg, Austria. His father, Leopold, was a very capable composer, violinist, teacher, and author (his book *Versuch einer gründlichen Violinschule,* or "A Treatise on the Fundamental Principles of Violin Playing," was published in the year of Wolfgang's birth). Leopold was in the musical service of various archbishops of Salzburg. Mozart's father observed at a very early stage the genius of his son, and thereafter devoted much time to the training and furthering of his career in music. This devotion particularly manifested itself in a number of short and extended European family trips for the express purpose of learning and concertizing, both for young Mozart and his elder sister Maria Anna ("Nannerl"), also a musical prodigy.

Mozart prepared himself as a performer on the clavier, violin, and organ, and composed music from a very early age. Journeys with his father to Munich, Vienna, Paris, London, Mantua, and Rome (to name only a few of the cities visited) made the young Mozart's talents well known by the time he was fifteen, and he had also received invaluable aid and inspiration through contacts with such artistic masters as J. C. Bach, Handel, Hasse, and Metastasio.

When only fourteen years of age he received an appointment as concertmaster to the Archbishop of Salzburg; upon that archbishop's death in 1772, Hieronymus, Count of Colloredo, assumed the archbishopric. From the outset Mozart's relationship with this employer was never what one might call favorable, and it steadily declined. In 1777 he secured a leave of absence, which he used to search for a better position, but trips to Munich, Augsburg, Mannheim, and Paris availed him nothing toward this purpose. Finally, in the summer of 1781, he left the service of the archbishop and repaired to Vienna, where he spent the remaining years of his life. For a time things went well for him there, but gradually his financial position worsened and he died a pauper and rests today in an unmarked, unknown grave.

Studying Mozart's compositional techniques reveals little of his genius. Considered in terms of the barest elements of music —melody, rhythm, and harmony—there is nothing startlingly new or different about his art. The rhythmic elements seldom leave the traditional Classical approach; the span of harmonic resources is much tighter than the very next (Romantic) historical period; and the harmonic rhythm is not nearly as fast as the preceding Baroque. Formally Mozart adheres closely to the sonata form, rondo, minuet and trio, and theme and variations, the four basic Classical forms. Mozart's music is never "flashy," as technique is not used for technique's sake, and he is equally at home with either homophonic or polyphonic textures; fugal writing, as such, was a minor consideration of the master, although canonic passages are not foreign to his works and indeed are featured in some of the most famous compositions. His music is even at times astonishingly plain and simple. But soon the analyst abandons his pursuit of the Mozart genius in the musical score, realizing that somewhere beyond his vision—either in the mind or in the heart—is the stuff of which Mozart's art is made.

PIANO SONATAS AND STRING QUARTETS

From the year 1778, which Mozart spent in Paris, come some of his best-known piano sonatas, identified by the Köchel or "K." numbers 310, 330–33. These numbers were assigned by Ludwig von Köchel, the first man to catalogue Mozart's works. It was customary for composers of the Classical period to write their music on commission or for their own use. Mozart probably wrote the piano sonatas for his own repertoire, as he undoubtedly did for most of his piano concertos, too. The Paris sonata K. 331 (in *A* major) has made a great many friends through its splendid set of opening variations and the *Alla turca* march of the finale. The *Sonata in C Major* (K. 545), composed in Vienna in 1788, has become almost too well known through its association with the field of popular music;

two other piano works from the Vienna period—a fantasia (K. 475) and a sonata (K. 457), both in *c* minor and published together in 1785—are respected for their forward-looking treatment of harmonic and melodic resources. Of the sonatas for violin and piano, the one in *e* minor, K. 304 (again composed in Paris in 1778) and those in *B*♭ major, K. 454 and *A* major, K. 526 (Vienna, 1784 and 1787, respectively) are favored by present-day performers of such Mozart sonatas.

Mozart wrote nowhere near the number of string quartets produced by Haydn (approximately twenty-six compared to eighty-three), yet what Mozart did accomplish found a welcome place in the literature for this medium. In his "Russian" quartets of 1781 Haydn had advanced a technique of thematic development involving all four instruments of the ensemble; this new method was adopted and furthered by Mozart in his six quartets published as a group in 1785, which he promptly dedicated to Haydn. Although the "Haydn" quartets were not Mozart's first venture in this medium, he had written nothing better before them, nor was he ever to surpass them in later quartets. They are all fine works, but perhaps two may be singled out for special attention—"The Hunt" (K. 458) and "Dissonant" (K. 465). Both take their nicknames from their opening passages; the violin theme of K. 458 sounds the nature of a hunting call (but is far from the best range or horn timbre for a real hunting call, and surely the rest of the quartet has little to do with the sport); and the entire ensemble of K. 465 indulges in some close harmony involving tight, dissonant intervals and cross-relations (see Example 41).

From the good-humored fun of the first movement, the "Hunt" quartet moves into a smooth-gliding, melodious minuet, contrasted in turn by a puckish trio. The first violin and cello share themes in a lovely slow third movement. A bouncing finale may lead some to imagine the excitement of a chase only because the quartet is labeled the "Hunt." In K. 465 the emotional intensity of the opening *Adagio* prevails throughout the entire work. The first movement as a whole is tightly drawn; the second is quite dark in both key and context. The dance

(a) "Hunt," K 458

(b) "Dissonant," K 465

Example 41

movement is a solid, forthright statement, and the quick tempo and lively spirit of the last movement cannot quite hide its serious undertones.

Other string quartets of the Vienna years are the "Hoffmeister" (K. 499) and the three of a projected set of six (K. 575 in *D* major; K. 589 in *B*♭ major; and K. 590 in *F* major) dedicated to Frederick William II, the same gentleman to whom Haydn dedicated his Op. 50. Perhaps Mozart was overzealous in the writing of melodious cello parts (to the detriment of the "King of Prussia" quartets as a whole) to please this cellist-king. The last ten of Mozart's quartets–K. numbers 387, 421, 428, 458, 464, 465, 499, 575, 589, and 590–are called the "Ten Celebrated Quartets." From this period comes also some of Mozart's finest string writing in the quintets (two violins, two violas, and cello) in *C* (K. 515), *g* (K. 516), *D* (K. 593), and *E*♭ major (K. 614). Also the masterful *Quintet in A for Clarinet and Strings* (K. 581) should not be forgotten; the exposition of the sonata form of the first movement contains three themes in place of the usual two, and a second trio is added in the dance movement. Further discussion of Mozart's abundant chamber music must be forgone because of space limitations, with only a mention possible of the *Piano Quartet in E*♭ (K. 493), the *Trio in E*♭ *for Clarinet, Viola, and Piano* (K. 498), the *Piano Trio in B*♭ (K. 502) –all composed in 1786–and the beautiful serenade *Eine kleine Nachtmusik* (K. 525, "A Little Night Music") written for two violins, viola, cello, and contrabass in 1787.

THE SYMPHONIES

The symphonies for which Mozart is remembered today were composed during the years 1782–88. These are the "Haffner" (*No. 35,* K. 385), the "Linz" (*No. 36,* K. 425), the "Prague" (*No. 38,* K. 504), and especially his last three: *Symphony in E*♭ *Major* (*No. 39,* K. 543), *Symphony in g minor* (*No. 40,* K. 550), and the *Symphony in C Major,* "Jupiter" (*No. 41,* K. 551). All were written in Vienna save the "Linz," which was composed in Linz for a concert in that city during a stopover on a return trip from Salzburg to Vienna. It will always remain a marvel that Mozart composed the last three symphonies within the space of six weeks in the summer of 1788.

The *Symphony No. 39* opens with a stately introduction in

which appear passages involving downward-moving scales–a figure to be used later in other sections of the movement. Then the sonata form is developed in a craftsmanlike manner, with full expression within the essence of Classicism. The second movement, intertwining variation and abbreviated sonata forms, approaches the Romantic expressiveness of a later age; this is followed by a rather perfunctory minuet with a trio embodying a delightful use of a flute and two clarinets. The symphony ends with a finale in which the sustained rhythmic drive is completely captivating–a movement very comparable to the finale of Beethoven's *Symphony No. 7.*

The "Jupiter" symphony opens with a combination of melodic themes with Jupiter-like thrusts in a wonderfully moving context. The second movement is another of Mozart's incomparable slow-moving wonders, and the dance movement is a happy, lilting thing remarkably out of place considering Mozart's emotional condition in 1788. The final movement displays the contrapuntal skill of a master, not so much in the canonic treatment of thematic elements (although the usage is very clever), but in that it is all done so skillfully that one still hears and feels only the emotional impact intended in a true Classical finale.

CONCERTOS

Although Haydn may have been the guiding light toward the establishment of the Classical symphony and string quartet, to Mozart must go first place as the master of the solo concerto. His works outstrip all others in number in that form, and a great many remain in the modern repertoire. Mozart's concertos were a result of his commissions and the needs of his friends, his pupils, and himself. For example, his friendship with Joseph Leutgeb and Anton Stadler, virtuosos on the horn and clarinet, respectively, accounts for the four horn concertos (K. 412, 417, 447, and 495) and the *Concerto in A Major for Clarinet* (K. 622). The *Clarinet Quintet* (K. 581), of an earlier date, had also been composed for Stadler. The bassoon concerto (K. 191) was produced on commission from Baron Thaddäus von Dürnitz, who took great stock in that instrument, and in like manner a commission by the Dutch flutist De Jean was responsible for the two flute concertos K. 313 and K. 314. Mozart's personal relations with the flute-playing Duc de Guines and his daughter (Mozart wrote to his father that on the harp she was "*magnifique*") induced him to compose the delightful *Concerto in C Major for Flute and Harp* (K. 299).

The first important piano concerto (K. 271) was written in Salzburg in 1777; he wrote this one for a French virtuoso named Mademoiselle Jeunehomme, who was visiting Salzburg at the time. Early in 1779, he wrote, for himself and his sister, the two-piano *Concerto in E♭ Major* (K. 365). The years 1784–86 were especially fruitful for the composition of piano concertos, probably written for personal performance in Vienna. The year 1784 saw those in *B♭* (K. 450), *D* (K. 451), and *G* (K. 453). The last named was composed for his Viennese pupil Barbara Ployer, evidently a gifted player (the first movement of this concerto is outlined along with the study of the modified sonata form as used in the solo concerto, in Chapter 2.) The years 1784–85 produced the *Concerto in F* (K. 459); a masterpiece in *d* minor (K. 466), perhaps his most outstanding work in this form; and one in *C* major (K. 467). Products of 1785–86 are the queenly *E♭* major (K. 482), the tuneful *A* major (K. 488), and the symphonic *c* minor (K. 491), containing the largest instrumentation of any of the concertos. The popular "Coronation" concerto (K. 537) Mozart played at the coronation festivities for Leopold II (Frankfurt, 1790). And the *Concerto in B♭ Major* (K. 595) is from the last year of the composer's life.

The three violin concertos that most of our present-day violinists play are all from the year 1775. These are in *G* (K. 216), *D* (K. 218), and *A* (K. 219). Mozart himself played the violin well enough to appear in public as a soloist, and the viola with enough competence to play that instrument's part in the string quartet. It is known that the composer did perform these violin works in Salzburg with himself as soloist, and that he also made them available, with some movements rewritten, for performance with Gaetano Brunetti (concertmaster in the Salzburg court orchestra) as soloist. These concertos are more intimate than those for piano, but they bear the mark of a master and meet the highest standards of the Classical period.

VOCAL MUSIC

Although Mozart held positions connected with the Church in Salzburg, his sacred vocal music has something of a secondary role in his over-all production. Nevertheless, his motet *Ave verum corpus* (K. 618), written in Baden in 1791, still receives concert performances, and the *Mass in c minor* (K. 427) is recognized as a great work and indeed is called "The Great," not for its size (the Credo and Agnus Dei movements were never finished), but for its intrinsic musical value. Also, a fine *Requiem* (K. 626) was left unfinished at the time of his death, to be completed by his pupil Süssmayr.

He was adept, too, at the song form, some of his most popular works in this medium being *"Das Veilchen," "Der Zauberer,"* and *"An Chloe."*

OPERA

In the field of Classical operatic composition Mozart had no peer. Of course, it is not surprising that even this master's early operatic works are little known today, since they were the products of his youth. These include *La Finta semplice,* K. 51 ("The Pretended Simpleton"; Salzburg, 1769), and *La Finta giardiniera,* K. 196 ("The Pretended Gardener"; Munich, 1775), in the Italian *opera buffa* style; the *opera seria* types *Mitridate, re di Ponto,* K. 87 ("Mithridates, King of Pontus"; Milan, 1770), and *Lucio Silla,* K. 135 (Milan, 1772); two "serenatas," or pieces for special occasions, called *Ascanio in Alba,* K. 111 (Milan, 1771), and *Il Sogno di Scipione,* K. 126 ("The Dream of Scipione"; Salzburg, 1772); a festival opera *Il Re pastore,* K. 208 ("The Shepherd King"; Salzburg, 1775); and a German *Singspiel* entitled *Bastien und Bastienne,* K. 50 (Vienna, 1768), on the same plot as Rousseau's earlier *Le Devin du village.*

Of Mozart's mature operas, only two are *opera seria.* Of

these, *Idomeneo, re di Creta,* K. 366 ("Idomeneus, King of Crete"; Munich, 1781), was completed just before the composer moved his residence to Vienna. Having a libretto written by the Salzburg court chaplain Abbé G. B. Varesco, it is Mozart's finest work in this style. The last *opera seria, La Clemenza di Tito,* K. 621 ("The Clemency of Titus"; Prague, 1791), was a failure. The first Vienna opera was *Die Entführung aus dem Serail* ("The Abduction from the Seraglio," K. 384), a German comic opera written in 1782 at the command of Emperor Joseph II, who had high hopes of formulating a national German opera. (The Turkish theme so popular in the late 18th century is reflected here in the use of the "Turkish" instruments in the overture, in a duet, and in two choruses involving Janizaries.) But the emperor's hope did not materialize, and Mozart turned again to Italian *opera buffa.*

When Mozart secured the services of the Viennese court poet Lorenzo da Ponte (1749–1838) as his librettist, three of his greatest operas were the happy result. From this union of musician and poet came *The Marriage of Figaro* (K. 492; 1786), *Don Giovanni* (K. 527; 1787), and *Così fan tutte* (K. 588; 1790).

Figaro is given first rank in the field of 18th-century *opera buffa* for many reasons. First of all, the overture, arias, small ensembles, and the second- and fourth-act finales contain music of the highest quality. Secondly, the opera moves beautifully, with the arias and ensembles so constructed that they enhance rather than impede the action. Mozart's musical characterization is almost unsurpassable here, and Da Ponte's skill can be seen by the manner in which he adapted Beaumarchais's *Le Mariage de Figaro* (a satire on the aristocracy) so that it was both a fitting plot for a musical setting and, as the original had been censored, acceptable to the authorities. An interesting operatic convention is seen in the musical score in the use of the horn to depict the cuckold husband (as in Figaro's aria *"Bravo, signor padrone,"* of Act I).

Many words have been spoken and written concerning the place of *Don Giovanni* as a comic opera or as a serious opera.

Certainly it is a little of both. Some of the predicaments of Don Juan brought about by his loose love affairs are hilarious, but the scenes embodying Don Juan and the Commandant's statue (in which Mozart utilizes trombones in the best operatic tradition of *ombra* scenes) must also be recognized as drama. The opera deals essentially with the concept of sensual love (expressed through the escapades of the "hero"), the aspect of divine retribution, and the conflict projected by these conflicting ideas. Thus, despite the fact that the work is set in *opera buffa* style, it ends with a moral justifying the condemnation of the "wicked" Don Juan. But Mozart does attempt to lighten the dramatic scenes by including happier material such as Leporello's "Catalogue Aria," *"Madamina"*; Don Giovanni's "Champagne Aria," *"Finch' han dal vino"*; and his serenade *"Deh! vieni alla finestra"*; Don Ottavio's *"Dalla sua pace"*; and Zerlina's *"Batti, batti, o bel Masetto."*

Così fan tutte ("Women Are Like That") is a real *opera buffa,* enjoyable all the way through in both libretto and musical setting. With an absolute minimum of chorus, the opera depends upon six soloists alone to reveal the complicated plot in a series of gemlike arias connected by lilting recitative.

The Magic Flute (*Die Zauberflöte*) is Mozart's last opera; he died ten weeks after its first performance. The libretto, by Emanuel Schikaneder, is a strange mixture of a fairy tale and the lofty ideals of Freemasonry. The musical setting is actually a reversion to *Singspiel,* with spoken dialogue instead of recitative, but the music speaks with such authority that it must be considered the first modern German opera. What Schikaneder and Mozart, both members of the order of Freemasonry, meant to express in *The Magic Flute* has never been clearly understood by the average operagoer. (Goethe, also a Mason, as were Voltaire, Frederick the Great, and Haydn, pronounced the opera good theater and maintained that it would be understood by the initiated.) The supposedly Masonic connotations of the three opening chords of the overture and the symbolism employed in the second act suggest the striving of the brotherhood of men of good intentions against the forces of darkness and evil. The musical score, with its simple strophic folk songs, on the one hand, ornate arias, on the other, and elaborate ensembles and choruses, is in all respects as diversified as the labyrinths of the plot, but somehow it all proves successful in the end. Although the Church condemned Freemasonry, the Catholic Mozart was endeared to the craft, for besides the music of *The Magic Flute* he wrote a number of other works for Masonic occasions, and these were always in a serious mood and key. (*Die Zauberflöte* is K. 620.)

THE WORKS OF BEETHOVEN

Ludwig van Beethoven (1770–1827). The initial steps in the musical education of Ludwig van Beethoven were taken by his father, as in the case of Wolfgang Mozart. But the circumstances were somewhat different, for Beethoven's father seemed to be devoted less to the boy's talents than to the opportunity for financial profit from his exhibition. Bonn was the city of Beethoven's birth, and there he learned to play the clavier, organ, violin, and viola. During the year 1787 he visited Vienna and while there favorably impressed Mozart with his playing of the piano. Beethoven's mother died in 1787, and his father's intemperate ways gradually brought about a deterioration in his home life.

In 1792 Beethoven took up residency in Vienna and from that year his musical career began to blossom. The next few years were spent in study with such well-known names as Haydn (with whom Beethoven was little pleased as a teacher), Schenk, Albrechtsberger, Salieri, and Förster. His first public performance in Vienna constituted the playing of one of his piano concertos in the Burgtheater, in 1795. Thereafter followed many recitals and concerts. About 1800 Beethoven began to experience difficulty with his hearing, an unfortunate happening for any person and an outright calamity for a musician. Although the ensuing twenty years finally brought about a total loss of hearing, Beethoven was not to be prevented from producing some of the world's greatest musical literature.

Beethoven was the first musician able to meet members of the aristocracy on his own terms. He knew socially and was respected by Princes Lichnowsky, Lobkowitz, and Kinsky; he was familiar to Counts Lichnowsky, Waldstein, Rasumovsky, and Brunswick; and was known to Baron von Gleichenstein and Archduke Rudolf of Austria. Beethoven also had more financial sense than most musicians; he profited through carefully calculated dealings with his music publishers, and this income plus the annuities bestowed upon him by admiring members of the aristocracy made the late years of his life free of financial distress.

Beethoven appeared on the musical scene equipped with the knowledge and personality that his historical time seemed to demand. He had inherited a Classical style fully formulated and accepted, and moreover he had the ability and depth of purpose to develop further what he had inherited. His was a revolutionary age—a fact reflected in his personal musical style. Without giving the appearance of instability, Beethoven's music was capable of violent contrasts—passages of almost demonic fury quickly followed by stretches of tender emotion. However, composition for Beethoven never held the spontaneous ease that it did for Mozart. Beethoven's sketchbooks are filled with themes subjected to workings and reworkings, and he rewrote many completed compositions as well, but when he was finally satisfied with a piece, it was generally satisfying to all. In general, Beethoven's compositional career demonstrates a movement from Classical objectivism to the abstractions of Romanticism. His music shows a tendency in his later life to blur the lines of demarcation and to extend and otherwise complicate the musical material of the Classical forms; cadences become evasive and the musical passages tend to proceed in long arcs in a quasi-improvisational style. And without adding materially to Classical orchestration, his symphonic works take on an added heaviness in texture and sonority. Thus in emotional fervor, depth, and expansion of formal construction, and in the concept of orchestration, Beethoven closes out the Classical period and moves forward into Romanticism.

Outstanding in a catalogue of Beethoven's compositions are the nine symphonies, eleven overtures, a violin concerto, five piano concertos, one opera, *Fidelio,* two Masses, thirty-two piano sonatas with opus numbers, twenty sets of piano variations, sixteen string quartets, ten sonatas for piano and violin, and five sonatas for piano and cello. Other works include an oratorio *Christ on the Mount of Olives,* incidental music to plays, and many other fine chamber music compositions. These will be discussed under the three periods of Beethoven's life, for his style of composition showed definite changes as he matured from the early Classical works to his later Romantic style.

EARLY PERIOD

Piano Sonatas. Beethoven's musical life up to about 1802 was spent in formulating his compositional style and in public performance. This has been called his imitation period, and most particularly represents the Classical strains of his art. The piano sonatas of this time include the three works of Op. 2, which are dedicated to Beethoven's teacher Joseph Haydn and which show that master's influence, and the "Pathétique" (Op. 13).

Concertos. For piano and orchestra he composed the *Concertos Nos. 1, 2,* and *3. Concerto No. 2* (Op. 19, 1795) was actually composed earlier than that now called the first (Op. 15) which reached completed form in 1798; Op. 5 constitutes two sonatas for piano and cello and bears yet another dedication to King Frederick William II. The six string quartets of Op. 18 were completed in 1800 and are perhaps the most outstanding works of this first period of composition. Although these are early works and stick pretty close to the Mozartean form and do incorporate Rococo elements, they also have Beethoven's depth and style and new ideas. The *Scherzo* of the last quartet of this group (in *B*♭ major) is crammed with wit and delightful, catchy rhythms.

Symphonies. *Symphony No. 1 in C Major* (Op. 21, 1799) has been called "Mozartean" and is without doubt the most Classical of Beethoven's symphonies; it is dedicated to Baron van Swieten, that ardent lover of Bach and Handel who made known this admiration to Haydn, Mozart, and Beethoven.

MIDDLE PERIOD

PIANO SONATAS. Beethoven's second period—to about 1816—brought about a close musical contact with his listeners. The works from these fourteen years are favorites of present-day audiences and were of the greatest influence on composers following Beethoven. Most of the famous piano sonatas with nicknames are products of this time of composition. First is the so-called "Moonlight" (Op. 27, No. 2), written in 1801; during 1803–04 Beethoven worked on the "Waldstein" sonata (Op. 53), named for its dedication to Count Waldstein; and 1804–05 brought forth the appropriately titled "Appassionata" (Op. 57), in the key of *f* minor. In 1809 Beethoven composed the programmatic *Sonata in E♭ Major,* Op. 81a (*"Les Adieux"*), with three movements entitled *Das Lebewohl* ("The Farewell"), *Abwesenheit* ("The Absence"), and *Das Wiedersehen* ("The Return"); this all came about when Archduke Rudolf of Austria, Beethoven's pupil and patron, was forced to flee Vienna when that city was under siege by the French army led by Napoleon.

CHAMBER MUSIC. In the field of chamber music, a trio for piano, violin, and cello (Op. 97, 1811) also bears a dedication to Archduke Rudolf and is now universally known as the "Archduke Trio"; it is particularly famed for the *Andante cantabile* movement. In the years 1802–03 Beethoven wrote the *Sonata for Violin and Piano,* Op. 47, dedicating the work to the famous violinist Rodolphe Kreutzer; it is said that that gentleman refused to play the now famous "Kreutzer" sonata, with the remark that it was too difficult—Mr. Kreutzer's personal loss, to be sure. The fine sonata for piano and cello (Op. 69, dedicated to Baron von Gleichenstein) also stems from this second period.

STRING QUARTETS. The three string quartets of Op. 59 (1805–06) show a poetic and personal side of the composer that begins to override the formal aspect so common in his earlier works. Without making use of virtuosity for its own sake, Beethoven here runs the gamut from intense emotion to relaxed tranquillity in a sort of personal *Sturm und Drang.* These quartets are in the famous group called "Rasumovsky." They were commissioned by Count Andreas Rasumovsky, the Russian ambassador to Austria, whose interest in string music was so compelling that he maintained a string quartet as a part of his household, with he himself as the second violinist of the group. In the final movement of the dramatic quartet of Op. 59, No. 1, Beethoven utilizes the same Russian melody that Moussorgsky has the chorus sing in the coronation scene of his opera *Boris Godunov.* Another Russian tune shows up in the *Allegretto* movement of the second quartet of this group. Op. 59, No. 3 sometimes is known as the "Hero" quartet; this title, for whatever reason it was bestowed, clearly demonstrates the philosophical thoughts of these years of Beethoven's life as expressed in his music, and may be compared with other such titles as the "Eroica" symphony, of 1803, and the opera *Fidelio,* of 1805. Two further quartets from these years should be mentioned–the "Harp" (Op. 74, 1809), so named from the participation by all four instruments in the pizzicato playing of the principal theme in the first movement; and the *Quartet in f minor* (Op. 95), of 1810, which expresses the composer's most intimate feelings in a concise, compact language–giving rise to the nickname "Serious."

OPERA. Beethoven's one excursion into the field of opera–*Fidelio,* Op. 72–was first performed in 1805 in Vienna. The original French libretto, with the title *Léonore, ou l'amour conjugal,* was written by Jean Nicolas Bouilly; Joseph Ferdinand Sonnleithner did the German version for Beethoven. Following a rather cool reception, Beethoven withdrew the opera, and after rewriting and condensing it into two acts he presented it again, in the spring of 1806. The overture *Leonore No. 2* opened the production of 1805, but with the revision of 1806 Beethoven introduced a new overture, *Leonore No. 3.* Next Beethoven had a falling out with his co-workers and again withdrew the opera. In 1814 the libretto was completely done over by Friedrich

Treitschke, the score again rewritten (Beethoven was having a particularly difficult time with the opera), and the work presented for a third time, now with the *Fidelio* overture.

The overture *Leonore No. 1* (Op. 138) perhaps was intended for a presentation of the opera in Prague which never came about, or it may have been rejected for *Leonore No. 2* in the first-night performance of 1805. But the 1814 showing in Vienna was to establish *Fidelio* as a successful opera. Beethoven's obvious concern for this work is shown through the four overtures and the many, many rewritings within the opera itself. Today's performances use the *Fidelio* overture at the outset, but the *Leonore No. 3* (the finest of the four but somewhat unsuited as an opera overture) is often interpolated between the first and second scenes of Act II. Beethoven's two other particularly famous overtures are *Coriolan* (Op. 62, 1807), written for the tragedy by H. J. von Collins, and *Egmont* (Op. 84, 1810), composed along with other incidental music for the play by Goethe. In the field of vocal music Beethoven is also noted for his songs, particularly the cycle *An die ferne Geliebte*.

SYMPHONIES. The symphonies numbering two through eight were composed during the years 1801–12; they represent some of the finest literature in the symphonic form. Beethoven has been described herein as a man of rather violent contrasts, both in his personal traits and in his artistic endeavors. This is illustrated even in the chronology of his symphonies, for Nos. 2, 4, 6, and 8 contrast in their less demonstrative nature to the large scope and dramatic expression of Nos. 3, 5, 7, and 9; for no really good reason therefore (other than the association just drawn), Nos. 3, 5, 7, and 9 are declared the greatest of the Beethoven symphonies.

The *Symphony No. 2 in D major* (Op. 36, completed in 1802) begins to exhibit the enlargement of content and form brought into symphonic composition by Beethoven. The slow introduction of the opening movement is the longest such passage to date in this literature, and the finale has a coda of greater length than its development section, and uses completely new thematic material. Beethoven was to develop a habit of expanding the coda in such a way as to create a virtual second development section in the sonata form.

The *Symphony No. 3 in E♭ major* (Op. 55) is one of the most important works of the composer's middle period. The legend exists that Beethoven originally dedicated the symphony to Napoleon Bonaparte, but angrily destroyed the title page when Napoleon proclaimed himself emperor; thereafter the subtitle was merely "Eroica" ("Heroic Symphony"). The principal theme of the first movement is of the simplest nature, built around the tonic triad of *E♭* major. A second subject, in the *B♭* tonal center, is comprised of a group of themes. The long development section works over a number of the themes and manages to introduce an entirely new one; a masterful coda underlines the second development idea, and the new theme of the regular development section is used again. Rhythmical elements are forcefully presented in the opening movement, the basic ternary meter being converted into a duple pulse in several passages through the introduction of the hemiolia. The second movement is a dignified funeral march, and the third a rollicking *Scherzo.* The variation form is the basis for the finale —a study in contrasts. The principal theme of this movement must have had a special attraction for Beethoven, for he had used it previously in the *15 Variations for Piano* (Op. 35, 1802), in the *Prometheus* ballet music (Op. 43, 1800–01), and in one of a group of twelve *contredanses* for orchestra, composed in 1800–01.

The *Symphony No. 4 in B♭ major* (Op. 60, 1806) contains one of the most lyrical slow movements of the early Romantic symphonic literature. But these even-numbered symphonies are not entirely without fire and energy, and the fourth has its vigorous moments.

Symphony No. 5 in c minor (Op. 67, completed in 1808) qualifies in present-day musical circles as perhaps the most frequently performed of the nine symphonies and certainly as the most recorded one of the set. Beethoven himself described the opening theme of the first movement as Fate knocking at the door; thus this symphony may have been written in the composer's defiance of the trials besetting his life and career, particularly in respect to his hearing affliction. After the opening movement has manipulated this four-note "Fate" motive in every conceivable fashion, a second movement presents two themes instead of one in a theme-and-variations form. The trio of the *Scherzo* movement offers an energetic theme that is subjected to fugal treatment, and allows the double basses more of a display part than had ever previously been written for them in a symphony. The *Scherzo* ties into the last movement with a gradual build-up that finally erupts into a finale opening with a marchlike subject for full orchestra, evoking a feeling of high spirits that holds to the end of the composition. The trombones in the score appear for the first time in any symphony.

The *Sixth Symphony in F major* (Op. 68) introduces the nature theme into his symphonic music. This "Pastorale" symphony, as it is known, has the notation "Cheerful feelings upon arrival in the country" penned to the first movement; the second is called "A scene by the brook" and imitates in musical sounds flowing water and the calls of the nightingale and the cuckoo; the third movement is a dance at a "Merry gathering of the peasants," whereas the fourth movement introduces the "Storm" and a finale (fifth movement) the "Shepherds' song–joy and gratitude following the storm." This work, composed in the summer of 1808 at Heiligenstadt, bears ample testimony to the master's deep and abiding love for nature and the countryside.

The year 1812 gave to the world *Symphony No. 7* (Op. 92) and *Symphony No. 8* (Op. 93). The seventh symphony, in *A* major, ranks with Nos. 3 and 9 as the "giants" of the symphonies. It begins with a slow, sustained section involving several key centers and two themes; next follows a marvelously constructed sonata form with an underlying "general motive" expressed in a dotted rhythmic figure of driving force. The second, *Allegretto* movement was encored at the first performance and has remained popular with audiences ever since. Through written-out section repetitions Beethoven turned the traditional ABA *Scherzo and Trio* third movement into a five-part form

(ABABA); as a matter of fact, the composer wrote four bars of a third B section, only to break off as if tired of it all, bringing the movement to a close with five crashing down-beat chords. The last movement is marked *Allegro con brio*–"quick with brilliancy"–and is the type of music that grabs hold of the listener and refuses to let go until the last note has died away. *Symphony No. 7* had its première performance at the University of Vienna on December 8, 1813, with Beethoven as conductor of the orchestra.

The *Symphony No. 8 in F Major,* in direct contrast to *Symphony No. 7* and in a strong comparison with the string quartet Op. 95 of 1810, speaks in a sparse, concise language, achieving full symphonic size only through the lengthy coda constructions of the first and last movements.

CONCERTOS. Beethoven's *Piano Concerto No. 4* (Op. 58) was completed in 1806. Dedicated to Archduke Rudolf, the work received its first performance in March of 1807 at a concert in the palace of Prince Lobkowitz. This concerto broke with tradition by having the work open with a piano solo espousing the principal theme; only then was the orchestra allowed to enter and help express and develop the thematic material of the first movement. The second movement is a dialogue between piano and orchestra, and the last a bit of good-natured fun.

The *Concerto No. 5* (Op. 73, 1809) is the last and most impressive of the piano concertos; its grand scale and majesty are responsible for the nickname "Emperor." Following the opening hammer stroke by the full orchestra, a short piano cadenza announces the orchestral presentation of two principal themes. The first movement then continues with the expansion of this thematic material along true symphonic lines. The second movement is in the nature of a set of variations on an imposing theme announced by the strings, and the work is terminated by a gay rondo movement. The first Vienna performance of the "Emperor" concerto was given in 1812 by Beethoven's pupil Carl Czerny (1791–1857), a famous pianist and teacher.

Beethoven, Mendelssohn, Brahms, and Tchaikovsky are

alike in at least one respect—in that each contributed a single masterwork in concerto form to 19th-century violin literature. Beethoven's *Violin Concerto in D major* (Op. 61) follows the general trend of his concerto composition: a first movement of symphonic proportions involving extensive thematic development; a relaxing second movement (in this case the violin embellishes the orchestral melody with light arabesques); and a concluding rondo in a bright, quick style. The *Violin Concerto* was written within a short period of time in 1806, for a performance in Vienna on December 23 of that year by the Austrian violinist Franz Clement (1780–1842); it is reported that the soloist had to read his score from sight, as Beethoven was busy writing the part up to the last possible moment.

FINAL PERIOD

The final period of Beethoven's creative efforts—from about 1816 until his death in 1827—is one of profound thought and deep reflection. Now the compositions approach the abstract, formal lines of demarcation are blurred, as are phrase and tonal movements, new sonorities are attempted, themes and motives receive the full measure of development techniques, and contrapuntal practices frequently appear (as in the late works of Haydn and Mozart, but utilized in greater depth by Beethoven). Most of the opus numbers over 100 had to wait at least fifty years for full acceptance in the musical circles and even today offer considerable challenge to the listening audience.

VOCAL MUSIC. The *Missa solemnis in D Major* (Op. 123) and the *Symphony No. 9 in d minor* (Op. 125) are the two works of largest scope from the last period. The *Mass* is too long and musically too involved for liturgical use, and like Bach's *Mass in b minor* it finds its place in the concert repertory. Unlike Bach's *Mass,* which consists of a series of independent numbers, Beethoven's work is a vocal and instrumental symphony in five movements following the five broad sections of the Ordinary of the Mass. Beethoven followed the text quite closely, utilizing all opportunities for effective word and mood painting; thus music of high emotional content is found contrasted by sections of a sublime and contemplative nature. The composer worked for several years on the *Mass in D;* it was ready for performance by 1824.

SYMPHONIES. During most of his creative life Beethoven had meditated on a musical setting for Schiller's *Ode to Joy.* This desire finally reached fruition in 1823, when he incorporated a number of stanzas of that poem into the finale of his *Symphony No. 9.* But in spite of the use of vocal soloists and a chorus in the tremendous concluding movement (which imparts to this composition the name "Choral"), it remains basically instrumental in concept and the voices become part of the instrumentation. The most extensive and profound by far of all the symphonies, *No. 9* was first performed along with an overture by Beethoven and the Kyrie, Credo, and Agnus Dei of his *Missa solemnis in D Major* at a Vienna concert of May 7, 1824.

PIANO SONATAS. Beethoven's last five piano sonatas (Opp. 101, 106, 109, 110, 111) were composed during the span of years 1816–22. Since their inception they have remained the property of the highly gifted pianist. The conventions of Classical form no longer apply; even the traditional four-movement plan is abandoned in three of these sonatas. These works are the "giants" of the piano sonatas, but are not heard as often in performance or recordings as some from the second period. The master had wanted these pieces known as having been composed for the *Hammerklavier,* but this name is remembered today only in connection with Op. 106.

Beethoven made considerable use of the variation form in his sonatas and symphonies, and in independent works as well. One of his interests consisted of writing compositions in this form using themes from operas. Such themes included airs from Mozart's *Don Giovanni, The Marriage of Figaro,* and *The Magic Flute;* Grétry's *Richard the Lion-Hearted; La Molinara,* by Giovanni Paisiello; and from Dittersdorf's *Rotkäppchen* (a *Singspiel*). But themes came also from other sources. For example, the Austrian composer Antonio Diabelli handed to Beethoven a little waltz tune of no particular consequence, upon which Beethoven proceeded to write one of the most imposing sets of keyboard variations of all musical history. This work, the finest of its kind since Bach's *Goldberg Variations,* received publication in 1823 under the title *Thirty-three Variations on a Waltz by Diabelli,* Op. 120.

STRING QUARTETS. Without doubt the late string quartets of Beethoven require more performer and listener concentration than almost any other of the works from that master's pen. They are composed in such deep seriousness and are of such length that close attention is necessary to comprehend their full impact. The last quartets were composed in 1825 and 1826 and have the high opus numbers 127, 130, 131, 132, and 135. Opp. 127, 130, and 132 all have slow introductions, as if to forecast the weighty messages that lie ahead. Music's most scholarly form, the fugue, begins the Op. 131, and Beethoven had originally intended Op. 130 to close with a movement in this procedure. However, Op. 130 had accumulated six movements before the contemplated fugal close, and upon the advice of his publisher Beethoven withdrew this final movement and published it separately as the *Grosse Fugue in B♭,* Op. 133, for string quartet. But Op. 131 did reach, in published form, a grand total of seven movements. Little now remains inherent in these compositions to illustrate the Classical ideal as established by Haydn and Mozart. The new Romantic era has arrived.

CHAPTER 8

The Romantic Period

INTRODUCTION

Romanticism as expressed in the art and music of the 19th century had its origin in a philosophical and literary movement that developed out of the 18th century. Rousseau's concept of the essential beneficence of "nature" had made a deep impression on the 18th-century mind if for no other reason than that it made clear the failures of contemporary society. The seeds of dissatisfaction thus sown, even by those children of the Enlightenment the Encyclopedists themselves, eventually ripened into the American and French revolutions, the curtain closers of the absolutistic, rationalistic, and Classically oriented 18th century.

If the Romantic spirit was ushered in by political revolutions, it did not stop there in its search for newness. Once liberated from the patronage of the aristocratic classes and from the church, both institutions being virtually the sole sponsors of music until the 19th century, Romantic music discarded also the restraint and order imposed by these earlier patrons. Imagination became the key word for the Romantics, and whatever lent color and flight to this imagination they eagerly sought. Thus literary works of the Middle Ages and the Renaissance were avidly devoured and inspiration from Greek and Roman sources was sought, not, however, to be used as the Classicists used them, to provide order in art, but rather to furnish material with which to escape from the everyday world of reality.

The Romantic artist, then, engaged as he was in exploring the depths of his own soul and the mysteries of life and the universe, often presented a strange and lonely figure frequently beset by spells of morbid despondency. This Romanticism reached the height of its development in the first third of the 19th century, but its influence on music prevailed for approximately another fifty years.

The pictorial arts manifested the Romantic spirit in the nature paintings of Joseph Turner; in the troubled insights of Francisco Goya as seen in his *The Third of May, 1808;* in Théodore Géricault, especially his emotional *Raft of the "Medusa";* and in the revolutionary temperament portrayed in *Liberty on the Barricade* by Eugène Delacroix.

In literature Rousseau and Goethe largely influenced the later Romantic writers like Schiller, Novalis, and Ludwig Tieck. Followers in the footsteps of these men were William Wordsworth, Samuel Taylor Coleridge, John Keats, Percy Bysshe Shelley, George Byron, and Victor Hugo. The power of Goethe's works over the minds of the Romantic musicians is legendary, and the other writers here mentioned exercised a great influence on musical composition as well.

Of course, the immediate past was not completely forgotten; composers like Felix Mendelssohn and Johannes Brahms, for instance, are frequently cited as Romantic-Classicists, and Franz Schubert also bears a close tie with Classical aims and ideals. However, there are definite characteristics that identify Romantic music; and to a large extent they apply to the post-Wagnerian or post-Romantic period as well. This last period is discussed fully in the next chapter.

RHYTHM. The rise of subjective thought in musical composition led to a degree of rhythmical imbalance that vastly upset the standardized metrical rhythmic schemes that had been so prevalent at the beginning of the 19th century. Naturally, metrical schemes that featured 2/4, 3/4, 4/4, or 6/8 meter with regularly recurring accents on the first beat of each measure were certainly not abandoned in the 19th century, but deviations from this schematic regularity were introduced through a pronounced use of syncopated formulas, and of hemiolia patterns in which two successive measures of a passage in 6/4 meter were notated in such a manner as to imply a 3/2 pulse within the combined two measures. (The hemiolia is not new to the Romantic period; this rhythmical device can be found in music history as early as the 15th-century Burgundian chanson.)

Complicated cross-rhythms were also widely employed, with composers using such devices as the celebrated "three against four" and "two against three" arrangements of notes which have caused so much consternation among youthful pianists, and triplet patterns in strange and irregular groupings were also used. Beethoven pointed the way in the use of such devices, and they were further developed in the works of Schumann, Chopin, and Brahms. Later in the century the nationalistic movement (discussed fully in the next chapter) was to draw heavily on the irregular rhythms of folk song and dance.

MELODY. The melodic line in Romantic music took on a marked plasticity. The Classical composer, accustomed as he was to logical repetitions of phrases and of structural sections, had created his melodies for the symmetrical rhythmic patterns of his period. The Romantic composer, concerned more with expressing his personal feelings directly, spun out his melodies in an asymmetrical manner that resulted in phrases of different lengths, and he also used a less emphatic repetition of thematic material. Moreover, cadential formulas and musical punctuation in general become veiled and less obtrusive in Romantic music. Such a change in melodic style is immediately evident in the emotional outpouring of early- and mid-19th-century Lieder, and especially in the through-composed song types of Schubert, Schumann, and Brahms. As far as instrumental music is concerned, the listener need only hear Berlioz's *Symphonie fantastique* (published in 1830) to appreciate how the emotional background of this work newly colored the melodic element of the music.

HARMONY. This expansion of rhythmical and melodic conceptions may be further traced with regard to the harmonic basis of Romantic music. Harmonic color is often advanced for its own sake, and harmonic direction becomes less important; in fact, it sometimes appears that the Romantic creative mind considers the chord as "all-important." The triadic system, the theoretical basis of music from about 1600 to 1900, is exploited to its fullest potential in the 19th century; modulation into distant and not merely near-related keys occurs freely. An extensive use of the chromatic alteration of chords during this period produced a complicated chromatic harmony, and this plus a dissonant treatment of unprepared and unresolved non-chord tones contributed to the breakdown of the major-minor system. The compositions of Chopin and Liszt frequently demonstrate this new harmonic technique, and the "endless melody" of Wagner largely results from pronounced chromaticism, vagaries of harmonic center, and lack of definite cadential resolutions. Schubert, among others, made a practice of freely mixing the major and minor modes by using chords related to one mode in the other, and the later nationalist Russian and Bohemian composers further confused the tonal picture by introducing numerous modal degrees of the scale into harmonizations of folk and pseudo-folk melodies. These added harmonic resources brought a concurrent thickening in musical texture, and this density of texture came to its peak in the music dramas of Wagner. It was continued in the post-Wagnerian era by the symphonic masters Anton Bruckner, Gustav Mahler, and Richard Strauss.

In the Romantic era the musician's concern with literary associations, with nature scenes, with evil, and with the supernatural led to a descriptive style known as PROGRAM MUSIC —that is, music inspired by a mood, an idea, a story, a scene, or a dramatic play. Berlioz was one of the first Romantics interested in descriptive music, and a little later Liszt established a descriptive genre called the SYMPHONIC POEM or TONE POEM. The symphonic poem intrigued composers for the remainder of the century, and it was developed to a high degree of realism in the late-Romantic tone poems of Richard Strauss (discussed in the next chapter). In the tone poem Classical forms are no longer needed, nor indeed desired, for here the form is dictated by the "idea" or "program." Even in absolute–nonprogrammatic–music (save in the works of Mendelssohn and especially Brahms, who both showed a definite favoritism for Classical formal ideas), the emotional content of Romantic music overwhelmed the basic outline of the sonata form, ternary form, scherzo and trio, and theme and variations. These forms are not discarded; they still serve as the keystone of sonata and symphonic writing, but they showed a new pliability, a new capacity for almost infinite expansion by the Romantic composer's subjective approach to composition. Occasionally the new descriptive feeling is combined with an old formal concept. Tchaikovsky's overture-fantasy *Romeo and Juliet* amply demonstrates this, for, while Shakespeare's play provides the program, the whole work is cast in the Classical sonata form.

The remarkably close association of music and language in Romanticism can be seen, not only in the large-scale operatic works of Verdi and Wagner and in the symphonic poems for orchestra by Liszt, but also in the miniatures of Lieder by Schubert, Schumann, and Brahms, in the miniatures for piano with descriptive titles by Schumann, and in a yet more subtle sense in the *Songs Without Words* for piano by Mendelssohn. The association of literature and music is further demonstrated in the literary abilities of famous musicians such as Schumann, Berlioz, Liszt, and Wagner. And perhaps the prime example is found in the works of that most Romantic novelist and composer E. T. A. Hoffmann (1776–1822).

It is the virtuoso performer who finds his true place in Romantic music. The rise of the recital, the concert tour, a public audience, and instruments capable of expressing the emotional content of 19th-century music opened the door for composers like Paganini, Liszt, and to a lesser extent Brahms. Some works for violin and for piano were written with special regard for the virtuoso performer, and many symphonies and operas were abandoned in their first rehearsal attempts on the expressed opinion of the players that they were too difficult for performance. Paganini, who played mostly his own compositions, was said to be in league with the devil, and Liszt wrote and performed in a manner copying that of Paganini; it has even been said that Brahms's violin concerto is written *against* and not *for* that instrument.

Niccolò Paganini (1782–1840) was the first great 19th-century virtuoso. Shortly after the turn of the century he undertook a series of concert tours that made him the performing idol of Europe and a wealthy man. The pyrotechnics of his style—double and triple stops, brilliant pizzicato passages, elaborate use of arpeggioed figures and octaves and harmonics, and the tremolo and the trill—all are to be found in his twenty-four *Capricci per violino solo,* Op. 1. Of the three concertos for violin, the *Concerto in D Major* is still played today. The impact of the *Capricci* on other musicians of Paganini's century may be seen in the fact that Schumann and Liszt transcribed several of them for the piano, and that "Caprice No. 24" furnished the theme for Brahms's *Variations on a Theme of Paganini* and Rachmaninov's *Rhapsody on a Theme of Paganini.*

Through the combined efforts of composers, performers, and instrument makers the orchestra grew in personnel, instruments, range, variety, and brilliance of sound. From the some thirty-odd players of the Mozart orchestra the ensemble grew during this period to the hundred musicians needed to perform the huge scores of Gustav Mahler. This orchestral expansion is briefly depicted in Table XVIII.

When composers like Berlioz, Liszt, and César Franck wrote for this new orchestra, they worked not so much on the development of themes as on the presentation of melodies in repetitions of varied orchestral colorings. The theme itself became a unifying device in this mass of sound and color, and thus Berlioz used the *idée fixe,* Liszt thematic transformation, and Franck the cyclical treatment of themes. Bruckner and Mahler, moreover, used much repetition and variation in thematic material in their long and extensive symphonic works. When Wagner developed his music drama, he turned to the leitmotif, or leading motive, as a unifying device, assigning

TABLE XVIII

Mozart, *Symphony No. 40*, K. 550 (1788)	Berlioz, *Symphonie fantastique* (1830)	Mahler, *Symphony No. 5* (1902)
Flute	Piccolo	4 Flutes
2 Oboes	2 Flutes	3 Oboes
2 Clarinets	2 Oboes	English Horn
2 Bassoons	English Horn	3 Clarinets
2 Horns	2 Clarinets	2 Bassoons
Violins	4 Bassoons	Contrabassoon
Violas	4 Horns	6 Horns
Cellos	2 Cornets	4 Trumpets
Double Basses	2 Trumpets	3 Trombones
	3 Trombones	Tuba
	2 Tubas	Timpani
	Timpani	Glockenspiel
	Cymbals	Cymbals
	Bass Drum	Large Military Drum
	Violins	Small Military Drum
	Violas	Triangle
	Cellos	Gong
	Double Basses	Harp
		Violins
		Violas
		Cellos
		Double Basses

them equally to the orchestra and to the singers. Carl Maria von Weber, Berlioz, and Verdi often brought back, in later sections of their operas, previously stated themes as a sort of REMEMBRANCE MOTIVE.

These are some of the criteria of Romantic style and techniques. We will turn now to the different musical forms that most intrigued the Romantic composer.

FORMS OF ROMANTIC MUSIC

SOLO KEYBOARD MUSIC. The piano was the solo instrument par excellence of the 19th century, and the piano virtuoso was to the 19th century what the orchestral conductor is to the 20th. Some contemporaries of Beethoven, famous in their day as pianists, teachers, and composers, were Jan Dussek (1760–1812); Johann Nepomuk Hummel (1778–1837); Muzio Clementi (1752–1832); Clementi's illustrious pupils John Field (1782–1837) and Johann Cramer (1771–1858); Ignaz Moscheles (1794–1870); and Carl Czerny (1791–1857), who studied with Beethoven and received advice from Hummel and Clementi, and who in turn taught Liszt. These names, artistically speaking, are a part of the past; some studies by Clementi (and his sonatinas), a few pieces by Cramer, Moscheles, and especially Czerny are played by piano students today, but very few other compositions of these men are now heard. Schubert, Mendelssohn, Schumann, Chopin, Liszt, Franck (chiefly for the organ), and Brahms are the most notable of Romantic composers for keyboard instruments.

SYMPHONIC WORKS. At one end of size and emotional creativity in 19th-century musical Romanticism were the art songs and the piano miniatures; at the other end stood the symphonic works and the operas. The Romantic symphonic works (and we include the concertos in this category) actually move in two directions. There is still the use of the forms of the Classical symphony, while at the same time the new program symphony or symphonic poem is being created. However, if a 19th-century composer did elect to use the musical forms of Classicism, his Romanticism manifested itself in his use of rich (often chromatic) harmonies, in his flowing breadth of melodic line, in the full-bodied colors of his orchestration, in his density of sound, and in the rhythmic cross-currents and variety of tempos and moods within his movements. Most notable among the Romantic composers of symphonic works are Schubert, Mendelssohn, Schumann, Chopin, Berlioz, Liszt, and Brahms.

CHAMBER MUSIC AND NONOPERATIC VOCAL WORKS. In moving from Classicism to Romanticism, the Lieder and piano miniatures lean toward Romanticism (where the opera also throws its weight), while the larger piano compositions (especially the sonata) and the chamber music works tend to look back to Classicism. Thus the best composers of chamber music among the Romantics were those who obviously retained rather strong ties with the Classical tradition. Foremost among these were Schubert and Brahms, with Brahms considered to be the successor of Beethoven in both chamber music and symphonic works. On the other hand, Berlioz, Liszt, and Wagner showed no interest in chamber music whatever.

The Lied, the form most connected with the Romantic spirit, actually was formulated in the 18th century by the composers Carl Zelter and Johann Reichardt of the "second Berlin school." (These composers followed in the wake of Quantz, the Graun brothers, and C. P. E. Bach, the "first Berlin school." See Chapter 7.) Another important song composer of the last years of the 18th century was Johann Rudolf Zumsteeg (1760–1802). His dramatic ballads for solo voice and piano—settings of works by Schiller, Goethe, and others—established a standard for the full Romantic development of this type by Schubert and by Carl Loewe (1796–1869). Loewe still retains a place in music history through outstanding ballads like his *Edward*. Schubert, Schumann, and Brahms are the most famous of the Romantic Lied composers.

Romantic sacred choral music was greatly influenced by the Cecilian reform movement of the Catholic Church. This movement, named after St. Cecilia, music's patron saint, turned the thoughts of practicing Catholic Church musicians of the 19th century back to the music of Palestrina by its insistence that that was the most appropriate kind of music for liturgical service. It was not that the Romantics lacked the ability to write fine sacred music in the liturgical forms—Schubert, Berlioz, Verdi, and Bruckner all did so—but the Church could not countenance a style in religious art which from the time of the late Classical masters had made free use of operatic and theatrical elements, and in the famous *motu proprio* (1903) of Pope Pius X a formula was definitely stated that banned the

Masses of Haydn, Mozart, Beethoven, Schubert, Berlioz, Liszt, Verdi, and Bruckner from the Divine Service. Today these works are relegated to the concert hall, or else they are heard in some Protestant churches.

OPERA. In the early part of the 19th century Paris became the focal point of operatic production. There a trend in opera writing developed in which the Gluckian "heroic" was combined with the type known as "rescue opera," *La Vestale* (1807), of Gasparo Spontini (1774–1851), being an important example. Based on a libretto by Étienne Jouy (1764–1846), which set the rescue theme of sacrifice for the beloved in a touching story within the framework of the French tragedy, Spontini's *La Vestale* remains one of the most effective operatic works, from a theatrical viewpoint, of all time.

Next in line of development was "grand opera," a species that in true Romantic fashion was devised to develop each scene and situation (often of a pseudohistorical nature) for its full emotional and spectacular value; to this end the ballet, chorus, and mob scenes were directed, and a new and rising group of middle-class theatergoers responded enthusiastically. *Opéra comique* continued to thrive alongside grand opera in a sort of peaceful coexistence. However, it followed two paths: one, a true *opéra bouffe* that leaned toward satire, and a second, which led to a style called "lyric opera," with Romantic drama and situations as its basis. Gioacchino Rossini excelled in writing the grand opera, and Charles Gounod's *Faust* is a prime example of the lyric opera. Other composers who contributed greatly to the development of Romantic opera are: Meyerbeer, Berlioz, Bellini, Donizetti, Weber, Verdi, and Wagner.

THE WORKS OF SCHUBERT

Franz Schubert (1797–1828). Franz Schubert was born in Lichtenthal (then a suburb of Vienna), where his father was a schoolteacher and an amateur cellist. Thus he grew up in a musical atmosphere, heightened by a position as chorister in the Vienna court choir and through a musical education in the court-connected *"Konvict"* school, where he had instruction in violin, piano, singing, and music theory. When his voice broke, young Schubert taught for a few years in his father's school, but gave up teaching for a free-lance musical career in Vienna. Schubert had many friends–one in particular, a baritone named Vogl, did everything he could to further the popularity of Schubert's songs–but life for Schubert was a continuous struggle, and he died poor and without distinction in his time.

SOLO KEYBOARD MUSIC

Schubert's piano compositions include eleven sonatas, the six *Moments musicaux* (D. 780, 1823–28), eight *Impromptus* in two sets of four (D. 899, 935, 1827?, 1827), and the *Fantasia in C* (D. 760, 1822). The "D." numbers are from a chronological listing in a catalogue of Schubert's works prepared by Otto Deutsch (see p. xv). The last three sonatas (1828) follow Beethoven; one of these three, the *Sonata in B♭ major* (D. 960), is Schubert's finest work for piano. Schubert's melodic gift so evident in his songs is transplanted to the piano through the *Moments musicaux* and *Impromptus;* these little pieces vary in mood from the poetic and pensive to the bright and sparkling; the shortest and most popular of the *Moments musicaux,* in *f* minor, takes only a minute and a half to perform. The *Fantasia in C Major* is called the "Wanderer" fantasia, because Schubert used the melody of his song *Der Wanderer* (D. 493) as an important theme in the slow movement. This fantasia is the most played of Schubert's larger piano pieces; the opening motive (see Example 42a) is also heard in various forms in each of the three other movements, and a lovely first-movement melody reappears in a modified shape in the trio of the *Scherzo* (Example 42b); these unifying techniques anticipate the principle of thematic transformation as developed later by Liszt. In the writing of piano duets Schubert has had no peer in the history of music.

(a) Opening motive

(b) First-movement melody

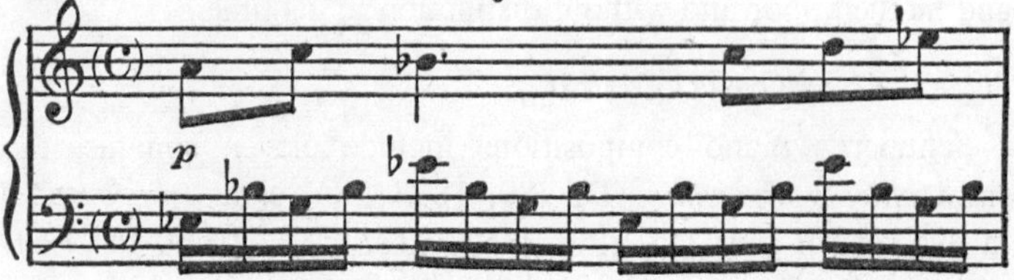

Trio

Example 42

LIEDER AND OTHER VOCAL WORKS

Schubert stands as the master of German Lied. In fact he brought such a new and fresh approach to solo song that many have called him the creator of the Lied. Schubert's songs (over six hundred) follow several different formal types: (1) strophic form; (2) modified strophic form; (3) *Durchkomponiert* or "through-composed" form; and (4) declamatory song.

Strophic form can best be described as the form and style of a hymn tune; Schubert's *Heidenröslein* ("Heath Rose") (D. 257, 1815) is a perfect example. The sparkling song *Die*

Forelle ("The Trout") (D. 550, 1817) exemplifies the modified strophic form—where one or two stanzas deviate from the regular musical repetition and take on new and different settings. The "through-composed" manner is essentially the form of the ballad; here exact musical repetition is avoided and an attempt is made to compose music of special significance for each line of the poem. Schubert's brilliant song *Der Erlkönig* ("The Erlking") (D. 328, 1815) is a ballad. The declamatory style, where the voice declaims the text in something of a recitative style, while the piano part provides support and continuity, is clearly demonstrated in *Der Doppelgänger* ("The Phantom Double") (D. 957, No. 13, 1828).

Schubert's melodies are so natural as almost to defy description. They represent an outpouring of the soul of such beauty that the equally inspired and important harmonic piano part is sometimes passed over too lightly. The real secret of the art song lies in its complete union of verse, voice, and accompaniment. Schubert often paints details of the poem in the piano part—the wild ride on horseback of the father and sick child in *Der Erlkönig;* the whirring of the spinning wheel in *Gretchen am Spinnrade* ("Gretchen at the Spinning Wheel") (D. 118, 1814); the tolling of the chapel bell in *Die Junge Nonne* ("The Young Nun") (D. 828, 1825); the sounds of the guitar in *Ständchen* ("Serenade") (D. 889, 1826); and many others.

For his texts Schubert leaned heavily on the poems of Goethe and Schiller; also he used those by Wilhelm Müller (1794–1827), and six of his songs he based on the poems of Heinrich Heine (1797–1856). Some of the finest and best known of Schubert's Lieder are from the song cycles called *Die schöne Müllerin* ("The Beautiful Miller's Daughter") (D. 795, 1823) and *Die Winterreise* ("The Winter Journey") (D. 911, 1827), which are composed of twenty and twenty-four songs, respectively, set to poems by Müller. Though the basic theme of *Die Winterreise* is a "winter journey," each song maintains an individual character and represents one scene in the journey of the rejected lover. The *Schwanengesang* ("Swan Song") (D. 957, 1828), composed of fourteen songs including six on poems by Heine, was not intended as a song cycle but was published posthumously as such.

As mentioned earlier, the sacred music of the Romantic and Classical composers was deemed inappropriate for liturgical use by the Church. Schubert wrote seven Masses in all, two of which, the *A*♭ (D. 678, 1819–22) and the *E*♭ (D. 950, 1828), are inspired creations, and they are deeply and subjectively Romantic.

SYMPHONIC WORKS

Schubert wrote eight symphonies (with a ninth completely sketched); they are constructed formally along Classical lines, but the breath of Romanticism is felt in the warmth of the melody, harmony, and orchestral tone color. Two of his symphonies rank with the best: the *"Unfinished" in b minor* (D. 759, 1822), and the *Symphony in C Major* (D. 944, called the "Great") of 1828. The title "Unfinished" for the *Symphony in b minor* is justified only in the sense that the *Scherzo* is left undone and the traditional fourth movement was never begun. This symphony opens with an important theme (later to form the basis of the development section) in the low strings; it is soon to be joined by a songlike melody played by the clarinet and oboe; the second theme proper is one of the most divine themes ever given to a cello section, the lyrical Schubert at his best. After a fresh and spontaneous development the exposition material is recapitulated in a quite normal manner. The second, and last, movement provides the listener with some of the most profound writing in symphonic literature in a setting of almost childlike simplicity. Yet all is not so simple, for some first-rate contrapuntal writing is to be found here.

The "Great" *Symphony in C Major* is perhaps most noted for its second and fourth movements; the second movement may be stated in a sectional scheme such as the following: March –Song in *F*–March–Song in *A*–March. The last movement of the symphony is one of constant drive and motion–motion that is not so much "forced" as it is "perpetual."

In 1823 Schubert wrote incidental music for Wilhelmine de

Chézy's play *Rosamunde,* of which the overture, the ballet music, and the third entr'acte are extant. The ballet music, written in a charming Viennese style, is still popular, and the third entr'acte has that beautiful melody used also by Schubert in the slow movement of his *String Quartet in a minor* and in his piano *Impromptu in B♭ Major.*

CHAMBER MUSIC

Listed among Schubert's outstanding chamber works are the three string quartets in *a* minor (D. 804, 1824), *d* minor (D. 810, 1824–26), and *G* major (D. 887, 1826); the *Piano Quintet in A* (D. 667, 1819) and the *String Quintet in C* (D. 956, 1828); the *Trio in B♭ Major* (D. 898, 1827?); and the *Octet in F for Clarinet, Horn, Bassoon, and String Quintet* (D. 803, 1824). The earliest work of the group, the *Piano Quintet,* was written in imitation of Hummel's *Piano Quintet* scoring, which used the violin, viola, cello, double bass, and piano. In the fourth of five movements Schubert borrows the melody of his song *Die Forelle* ("The Trout") (D. 550) for a theme and six variations, and thus gives this quintet the name "Trout." The *Octet* was commissioned by the amateur clarinetist Count Ferdinand Troyer, a resident at the court of Archduke Rudolf of Austria; it is said that he had in mind something on the order of Beethoven's *Septet,* and resemblances between the completed *Octet* and the Beethoven *Septet* are remarkable. The year 1827 has been questioned as the time of composition for the utterly delightful and happy *Trio in B♭*, for this was a period when Schubert was known to have been in the throes of despair.

Of the three string quartets mentioned above, only the one in *a* minor was published during Schubert's lifetime. He borrowed the placid tune of the second movement of this quartet from his earlier incidental music to *Rosamunde,* and he was to use the melody again in *Impromptu No. 3,* Op. 142 (D. 935). The *Quartet in d minor* is known as "Death and the Maiden" since the five variations of the slow movement are based on the melody of Schubert's song *Der Tod und das Mädchen* (D.

531, 1817). The last quartet, in *G* major, keeps the listener somewhat undecided as to a stable tonal center, as the variances between the major and minor modes, together with the deliberate and spontaneous harmonic surprises, are designed to accomplish just this purpose. However, the energetic concluding rondo, with its final statement in the bright *G*-major key, brings the whole to a satisfying and exhilarating close. Of all Schubert's chamber music, however, nothing can rival the beauties of the *String Quintet in C* (D. 956) for two violins, viola, and two cellos. It is his masterwork in the chamber music field and bids fair to stand alongside his *Piano Sonata in B♭* and the great *Symphony in C Major.*

THE WORKS OF MENDELSSOHN

Felix Mendelssohn (1809–1847). In contrast to Schubert, Felix Mendelssohn lived a life of ease and fame. He was born in Hamburg, but when he was three years old the family moved to Berlin, where he grew to maturity. His parents were wealthy, and music played a major role in their family life. In Berlin, Mendelssohn sang in the Berliner Singakademie under Carl Zelter, and he was able to pursue his musical education at home, where a small orchestra was maintained for his disposal. Mendelssohn quickly became famous as a pianist, but he also gained honors as a conductor and later was responsible for a revival of interest in the music of Johann Sebastian Bach through a performance of the *St. Matthew Passion* in the Singakademie on March 11, 1829. During his lifetime he made a number of successful concert appearances in London and on the Continent. Important posts included the conductorship of the famous Gewandhaus Orchestra in Leipzig; in that city also, Mendelssohn founded the Leipzig Conservatory of Music in 1843.

SOLO KEYBOARD MUSIC

Probably the best known and most popular of Mendelssohn's piano pieces are the *Songs Without Words,* many of which use the simple ternary form. They were published in eight volumes during the years 1830–45, and, as their name implies, the piano sings forth in lyrical fashion. The most enduring piano work, and perhaps Mendelssohn's finest effort in this medium is his *Variations sérieuses* (Op. 54, 1841), in which thoughtful, slow variations vie with others in a virtuoso style. Also, in a period when there was not much composition of organ pieces, Mendelssohn's three preludes and fugues (Op. 37, 1837) and his *Six Sonatas* (Op. 65, 1844–45) represent an outstanding and a welcome addition to the organ repertoire. Present-day recitalists on the instrument still use these works.

SYMPHONIC WORKS

In Mendelssohn's symphonic music we find a great deal of mood-and-picture-painting, but he is never guilty of overdoing it. A trip to Scotland in 1829 produced the inspiration for *The Hebrides* overture (Op. 26, 1832; also called *Fingal's Cave*) and the *Scotch Symphony* (Op. 56, completed in 1842).

The *Italian Symphony* (Op. 90) was composed in 1833 as a result of a trip to Italy made two years earlier. While nothing is literally depicted in the music based on the Scotland trip, the *Italian* symphony does make use of an Italian carnival dance–a saltarello–in the final movement. Altogether Mendelssohn wrote five symphonies.

The famous overtures to Shakespeare's *Midsummer Night's Dream* and Victor Hugo's *Ruy Blas,* composed in 1826 and 1839 respectively, are of course literary-inspired music; however, in his overtures, as in the movements of his symphonies, all of Mendelssohn's Romantic and programmatic associations are controlled by Classical forms. Yet, even in his *Violin Concerto* (Op. 64, 1844), one of the finest pieces in the whole violin repertoire, and a form most connected with the Classical teachings, one can recognize the Romantic mood of his overtures. Neither of his two piano concertos can measure up to his violin concerto, but the *Piano Concerto No. 1 in g minor*

(Op. 25, 1831) is still popular and has had many performances.

CHAMBER MUSIC

Although Mendelssohn published well over a dozen chamber works (including six string quartets), he was not at his best in the medium, chiefly because his flair for pictorial composition has no place here. Still, two works in particular have become popular and are heard from time to time: the youthful *Octet in E♭ for Strings* (Op. 20, 1825) and the *Piano Trio in d minor* (Op. 49, 1839). A second piano trio (Op. 66, in *c* minor) is also rather frequently heard. The *Octet* is for double string quartet, although it is treated as a group of eight; considerable doubling of parts, except in the contrapuntal last movement, occurs as an expected result of the instrumentation.

VOCAL WORKS

As a composer of oratorio, Mendelssohn stands in a direct line of descent from Handel and Haydn. His *St. Paul* (Op. 36, 1836) and *Elijah* (Op. 70, 1846) retain much of the Baroque and Classical approach, yet manage to add also a touch of the Romantic spirit. The first performance of *St. Paul* was held at the Lower-Rhine Festival in Düsseldorf in 1836, and Mendelssohn conducted the work the next year at the English Birmingham Festival; *Elijah* was first heard at Birmingham in 1846. Thus, as with Handel and Haydn, the choral-loving English people were extremely receptive to the music of Mendelssohn; however, the "Help, Lord," "Baal," "Thanks be to God," and "He watching over Israel" choruses, along with a number of fine solos, have made the *Elijah* popular in all corners of the earth where choral music is appreciated. Mendelssohn also felt the Romantic desire for expansion of musical materials in his settings of *Psalms 115* (Op. 31) and *95* (Op. 46) for soli, mixed chorus, and orchestra; *Psalms 114* (Op. 51) and *98* (Op. 91) for male chorus and orchestra; and *Lauda Sion* (Op. 73) for chorus and orchestra. Goethe's influence on Mendelssohn can be seen in the composer's *Die erste Walpurgisnacht* ("The

First Walpurgis Night," Op. 60; composed in 1832 and rewritten in 1843) for soli, chorus, and orchestra and called by Mendelssohn a "ballade."

THE WORKS OF SCHUMANN

Robert Schumann (1810–56). Born at Zwickau, Saxony, Robert Schumann was the son of a bookseller, which perhaps accounts for his great and lifelong love of literature. After an unsuccessful attempt at the study of law, he became a piano pupil of Friedrich Wieck. (Schumann later married Wieck's daughter Clara. She is perhaps the most gifted and famous woman pianist of all time, and her courtship with Schumann is one of the great romances in the history of music.) Schumann founded the periodical *Neue Zeitschrift für Musik* ("New Journal for Music") in 1834, and up to the time when he resigned the editorship in 1845 his writings were of the greatest musical influence. For a while Schumann taught at the Leipzig Conservatory; later he held conductorships in Dresden and Düsseldorf, but mental illness finally forced an end to his career.

SOLO KEYBOARD MUSIC

Schumann introduced the first piano masterworks in the true Romantic style. Collections of pieces are often grouped under such picturesque titles as *Papillons, Davidsbündlertänze, Carnaval, Phantasiestücke*–those of Op. 12 being probably the most popular of the piano pieces–*Kreisleriana,* and *Nachtstücke*. Splendid teaching material for children is to be found in the *Album for the Young* (*43 Piano Pieces for the Young,* Op. 68, published in 1848) and in a set of *Piano Duets for Small and Large Children,* Op. 85. The most outstanding of the larger works are the *Symphonic Etudes* (Op. 13, 1834) and the *Fantasia in C Major* (Op. 17, 1836).

In typically Romantic fashion Schumann gave pictorial titles to many of his works, although most of the names were affixed after the compositions had been written. He also created a wholly imaginative private society, the *Davidsbund,* or "League of David," the object of this society being to espouse the principles of the modern style against the die-hards of the old school, whom Schumann grouped under the name "Philistines." As a proponent of the new style of Romanticism, the composer used the fictitious names of *Davidsbund* members Florestan, Eusebius, and Raro (or their initials) in his compositions and as signatures to his articles in the *Neue Zeitschrift für Musik* as an indication of his personal feelings. These names represented the side of his personality that he felt he was expressing at that time: Florestan was the impulsive type, Eusebius signified the dreamer, and Raro exemplified a middle ground.

Schumann was another of the Romantics who tended toward specialization; at least he specialized in certain media in certain periods; for example, Opp. 1–23 are all for the piano, and 1840 is known as his Lied year. Stylistically, in a way unlike that of Schubert, Schumann's piano idiom is quite novel. He gave up the generally accepted patterns of scale passages and Alberti basses and developed a fundamentally chordal concept. He used especially interesting rhythmic procedures, making prominent use of dotted rhythms, cross-accents, and syncopations.

LIEDER AND OTHER VOCAL MUSIC

Schumann's great gift to the Lied form was the virtual amalgamation of the vocal line and the piano part. His happiest medium was the piano, and even in the song accompaniments the piano strives to point up moods through little introductions, interludes, and endings. Some songs reach such an equality of voice and piano parts as to make the term "piano accompaniment" scarcely applicable. Schumann, too, had a hand in the development of the ballad; *Die beiden Grenadiere* ("The Two Grenadiers," 1840), using for text Heinrich Heine's poem concerning the return of two French soldiers from captivity in Russia and ending with the music of *La Marseillaise,* is written in ballad style. Some of Schumann's finest Lieder are his love songs of 1840, the year of his marriage to Clara Wieck. From this year come 138 of his nearly two hundred songs, including the two song cycles *Dichterliebe* ("A Poet's Love," Op. 48), on poems by Heine, and *Frauenliebe und Leben* ("A Woman's Love and Life," Op. 42), the poetry of which was the best-known verse of Adelbert von Chamisso (1781–1838). Schumann also came under the influence of Goethe, as can be seen in his *Scenes from Goethe's Faust* (1853), in which characteristically enough the Romantic Schumann set *first* the redemption of Faust, although this occurred in the *last part* of the drama. The redemption theme is strong in Schumann's religious music, too, as can be seen in his *Paradise and the Peri* (Op. 50, 1843) and *The Pilgrimage of the Rose* (Op. 112, 1851). Actually these works are not true "religious music," but rather secular oratorios combining morality, allegory, fantasy, and even exoticism.

CHAMBER MUSIC AND SYMPHONIC WORKS

After the song year of 1840 Schumann turned his attention to the symphony orchestra and to the chamber music forms. In 1842 he brought out his three string quartets, the *Piano Quintet* (Op. 44) and the *Piano Quartet* (Op. 47). The following years produced other chamber music, including several piano trios. The *Piano Quintet* is the first work ever written for string quartet and piano, and is Schumann's most inspired chamber music work; the themes are alive and flashing and their developments are masterfully handled; a particularly fine moment is reached in the coda of the finale, where the main theme of the first movement returns in augmentation as the subject of a *fugato,* with the original theme of the last movement as the countersubject–an example of the best of Schumann's contrapuntal art.

With regard to Schumann's four symphonies, the two known as the first and the fourth were both written in his "symphony year" of 1841, the one called second in 1845–46, and the third ("Rhenish") in 1850; it was the publication order that determined today's numbering of them. Schumann gave the title

"Spring" to his *Symphony No. 1* (Op. 38), calling that music the emotion felt in his heart following his marriage to Clara Wieck. The "Rhenish" symphony (Op. 97) is in five movements, and it presents Schumann's picture of Rhenish life. The majestic music of the fourth movement is said to have been inspired by the installation of Archbishop Geissel as cardinal in the Cologne Cathedral. The finale is a scene at a Rhenish village festival.

Schumann's *Piano Concerto in a minor* (Op. 54, 1845) was originally conceived as a two-movement concert piece for piano and orchestra; however, the addition of two more movements was to produce the finest piano concerto since Beethoven. It is definitely not a mere showpiece; its value lies in its musical quality. Cello players have, in turn, found one of the outstanding delights of their Romantic literature in the *Concerto in a minor for Cello and Orchestra* (Op. 129, 1850). Another Schumann work frequently heard is the incidental music to *Manfred* (Op. 115, 1849), based on the dramatic poem by Byron. Unlike Brahms and Berlioz, however, Schumann was not a first-rate orchestrator, and often his awkward or muddy orchestrations obscure the definite contrapuntal element in his symphonic works.

THE WORKS OF CHOPIN

Frédéric Chopin (1810–49). Frédéric Chopin was born near Warsaw, Poland, of a French father and Polish mother. His education, which included lessons in piano and in composition, was acquired in his father's private school. In 1831, Chopin's concert appearances in Paris were so well received that he decided to make that city his permanent home. He made frequent appearances in the *salons,* a feature of Parisian social life, where he mixed freely with the aristocracy, and through his teaching and composition he was able to make a comfortable living. He was always in rather delicate health, and concert tours to London in 1848 and 1849 brought on extreme fatigue and hastened his death. His career and composition, mainly concerned with the piano, is a prime example of Romantic specialization.

The mazurkas and polonaises of Chopin reveal the love of a Polish upbringing he never quite forgot. These together with the waltzes and scherzos retain their dance flavor, but in a concert style and in a new modern form. He expressed technical pianistic problems in much the same way; that is, he presented his studies of Opp. 10 and 25 as full-fledged recital pieces for concert-hall appreciation and enjoyment, the first composer so to do. Chopin himself said that his four ballades had been inspired by the poetry of his compatriot Adam Mickiewicz; the Romantic element is quite prominent in these, and especially in the *g*-minor (Op. 23) and *f*-minor (Op. 52) ballades. However, the listener is perhaps brought closest to Chopin's intimate thoughts through his nocturnes, impromptus, and preludes. Chopin gave credit for the name and form of the nocturne to John Field, but it is certain that the latter never wrote a single nocturne that could rival any one of Chopin's. The affinity of the Romantic composer for the shades of night is well expressed in the Chopin nocturnes, and especially so in the *Nocturne in D♭ Major,* Op. 27, No. 2. Op. 28 provides a prelude in each key of the tonal system (*à la* Johann Sebastian Bach)—twenty-four preludes in all, arranged in the order *C* major, *a* minor, *G* major, *e* minor, and so on through the complete circle of fifths; the preludes have been called the pearls of Chopin's works.

In the larger forms the two piano sonatas (Op. 35 in *b♭* minor, 1839, and Op. 58 in *b* minor, 1844) make any qualified performer only wish that Chopin had written more of them. Op. 35 is deeply serious, almost gloomy; the famous *Marche funèbre* is a part of this sonata. On the other hand, the *Sonata in b minor* (Op. 58) has one of the gayest scherzos that Chopin ever wrote, the *Largo* is a lovely piece of night music, and the finale is a sparkling rondo. The *Fantasia in f minor* (Op. 49, 1840–41) is another of Chopin's fine works, and it stands in worthy succession to the fantasias of Schubert and Schumann. Chopin's style in general may be described as one of exceptional melodic beauty, daring harmonic innovations coupled with an advanced application of chromaticism, and an originality that has neither predecessor nor successor. However, because of his discursive, sectional style, Chopin's sonatas present a very different picture from their tightly knit Classical model, and performers have found it difficult to make them hang together.

The main contributions of Chopin to the larger forms of symphonic literature are his two piano concertos—the one in *e* minor (Op. 11, published in 1833) and the other in *f* minor (Op. 21, published in 1836). Pianists do perform them for their fine qualities as piano music, although the orchestral parts suffer from ineffective writing and scoring, and the numerous attempts to rescore them have met with little success.

THE WORKS OF LISZT

Franz Liszt (1811–86). In Franz Liszt, born in Raiding, Hungary, can be seen a Romanticist truly in keeping with his times. He was a child prodigy and was destined to become one of the world's greatest piano virtuosos. In order to help him as much as possible, his parents moved the family to Vienna, where he could study with Czerny and Salieri, and they moved again to Paris for more study. In 1831 Liszt heard Niccolò Paganini (1782–1840), the great violin virtuoso, and he resolved to transfer Paganini's fabulous pyrotechnics to the piano. A series of successful concert tours followed during the years 1839–48. In 1848 Liszt accepted a post as musical director at the court in Weimar, bringing great cultural acclaim to that city. Later he taught in Rome, and in 1875 he was appointed president of the Academy of Music at Budapest. To his credit and in spite of his busy personal life, Liszt spent much time in his later years in the furtherance of the careers of other musicians, notably that of Wagner.

SOLO KEYBOARD MUSIC

Franz Liszt was a true son of the concert stage. The term "recital" first appeared in an advertisement for an appearance by Liszt (London, 1840); the word was well chosen, for Liszt, the actor, sensed the desire of the Romantic audience for a musical "show," and he responded in kind. His compositions, too, reflect this dramatic attribute: the music is written in an advanced harmonic idiom employing altered chords, the Hungarian minor scale (Example 43), and suggestions of the

Example 43

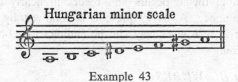

whole-tone scale (Example 51b); the Paganini-patterned virtuoso style has already been mentioned, but the virtuoso description does not mean that all Liszt's music lacks lyrical phrases; the six *Consolations* (1850) are quite melodic and sensitive and the *Années de Pèlerinage* (published in three volumes: *Première Année, Suisse,* 1855; *Seconde Année, Italie,* 1858; *Troisième Année,* 1883) have some lovely things, such as the Petrarch sonnets and the *Sposalizio* (inspired by Raphael's painting *Betrothal of the Virgin Mary*) of the *Italie* book.

Liszt's virtuosity comes to the fore in the *Six Paganini Etudes,* written in 1840 (of which the second, *La Chasse,* and the third, the *Campanella,* are the most popular), and the twelve *Études d'exécution transcendante,* published in final form in 1852. Some other works of this nature are the nineteen Hungarian rhapsodies (a twentieth was never published). Of these the most famous are Nos. 2, 6, and 12, but Liszt's own favorite was No. 13. Two of Liszt's large-scale solo works for piano are the *Ballade in b minor* (1853) and the *Sonata in b minor,* composed in 1852–53. The ballade is in the grand manner of a past age. The sonata is scarcely a sonata at all, since the formal characteristics of a sonata have been all but erased; it makes considerable demands on the listener through its great length and through the fact that it is written without breaks between the movements, yet the piece stands as one of the loftiest works in all of Romantic piano literature and proudly bears a dedication to Robert Schumann.

Liszt also enriched organ literature with at least two fine works: the *Fantasia and Fugue* (1850) on the chorale tune *"Ad nos, ad salutarem undam,"* from Meyerbeer's opera *Le Prophète* and the *Prelude and Fugue on B-A-C-H* (1855). In the latter the four-note theme occurs and recurs in nearly every conceivable manner. A flashy prelude is followed by a somber fugue that in turn gives way (in the ending) to a brilliant fantasia section.

SYMPHONIC WORKS

Except for the *Piano Concerto in E♭* (Op. 22, published in 1857) and the *Piano Concerto in A* (Op. 23, published in 1863) Liszt wrote very little for orchestra that did not have programmatic inspiration. His *Faust Symphony,* written in 1850, presents character studies of Goethe's Faust, Gretchen, and Mephistopheles, respectively, in its three movements. To its last movement Liszt added, in 1857, a male chorus singing the final verses of Part II of Goethe's drama. In a similar way he concludes his *Dante Symphony* (1856) with a Gregorian Magnificat for women's chorus. It has been said that Liszt always kept three books near at hand: his breviary, Dante's *Divina Commedia,* and Goethe's *Faust;* one does not have to look very far to observe their influence on his life and musical works.

A new and major contribution to 19th-century orchestral literature, both in the works themselves and in their influence on later composers, was made by Liszt's symphonic poems. He wrote twelve such compositions within the ten years following 1848, and added a thirteenth (*From the Cradle to the Grave*) about 1882 or 1883. Some of these works were orchestral arrangements of earlier piano pieces, but most were newly created. They are comparatively short, single-movement compositions that do not follow any Classical form, but rather take their shape from a thought pattern generated by the poem, painting, drama, or whatever it was that provided the creative inspiration.

For example, *Ce qu'on entend sur la montagne* ("What One Hears on the Mountain") and *Mazeppa* are based on poems by Victor Hugo; *Prometheus* is based on Johann Herder's *Prometheus; Die Ideale* ("The Ideals") is based on a poem by Schiller; *Tasso* on a poem by Lord Byron; *Hamlet* follows Shakespeare; *Die Hunnenschlacht* ("The Battle of the Huns") was inspired by Wilhelm von Kaulbach's painting; and *Les Préludes* is after the title of one of Lamartine's *Méditations poétiques,* although Liszt affixed a paraphrase of Lamartine's ode to the score only after the symphonic poem had been completed. *Les Préludes* is the only one of the symphonic poems heard today with any frequency. Example 44 shows the open-

(a) Andante

(b) Andante maestoso (1)

(c) Andante maestoso (2)

(d) Allegro marziale animato

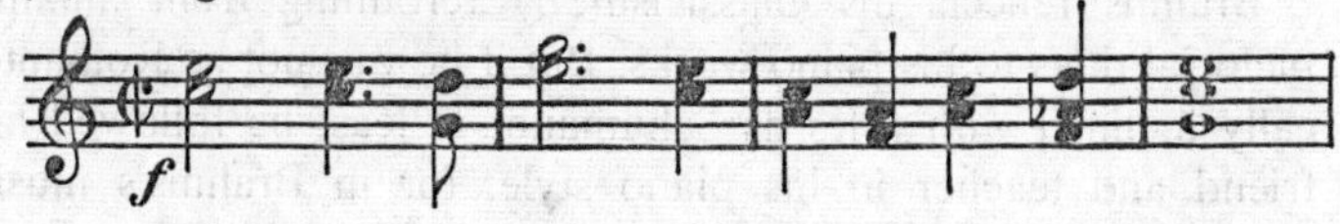

Example 44

ing theme of the work and a number of the transformations the theme undergoes later in the piece.

A further discussion of Liszt's programmatic orchestral works–not classed as symphonic poems–would include the *Hungarian Fantasia* (1860), the *Totentanz* ("Dance of Death"; the final revision was completed in 1859), the *Mephisto Waltz No. 2* (published in 1881), and the *Two Episodes from Lenau's Faust:* (1) "The Night Ride," and (2) "Dance in the Village Inn," commonly known as the "Mephisto Waltz"; the last named is No. 1 of a series of four such waltzes. Liszt, it can be readily seen, was one of the most literary minded of all the Romantics, and the difficulty for the modern listener in many of his works lies in their too great fidelity to their program, a fault that leads Liszt to an extreme emotionalism that the 20th-century listener often finds irritating.

THE WORKS OF BRAHMS

Johannes Brahms (1833–97). Johannes Brahms was born in Hamburg, Germany, where his father played double bass in the Hamburg Opera. Brahms studied with a well-known local musician, Eduard Marxsen, and gave his first public recital at the age of fourteen. A concert tour in Germany with the Hungarian violinist Eduard Reményi made him better known; personal contacts on this tour made it possible for Brahms to play for Liszt and Schumann, who both praised his talents. A warm friendship was to develop between Brahms and Robert and Clara Schumann. For several years Brahms moved freely from city to city concertizing, conducting, and composing; he finally settled down in Vienna in 1878, where his years were both pleasant and productive.

SOLO KEYBOARD WORKS

Brahms reflects his Classicism by refraining from affixing pictorial titles to his piano works. But if he was not as Romantically inclined with titles as Schumann, at least he followed his friend and teacher in his piano style, for in Brahms's music can be found that same disdain for the unessential in pianistic figuration, the same doublings and darkly colored sonorities (Brahms indeed has received criticism for a too heavy texture at times, particularly in some left-hand passages in low tessituras), and the same interesting application of rhythmic cross-currents. He wrote a number of pieces in the forms of the ballade, rhapsody (two great works in Op. 79—in *b* minor and *g* minor), capriccio, and intermezzo. Brahms's three sonatas are early works, the last (Op. 5, 1853), in *f* minor, being the best of the lot. Next to the sonatas the *Variations and Fugue on a Theme of Handel* (Op. 24, 1861) and the *Paganini Variations* (Op. 35, 1863) are most important; the borrowed Handel theme is from that composer's *Suite No. 9 in B♭ Major*. For the organ Brahms left eleven splendid chorale preludes (Op. 122, 1896) modeled along Classical lines and manifesting the utmost restraint.

SYMPHONIC WORKS

In his orchestral works Brahms wrote melody and harmonic material with a high Romantic coloring and yet with a predominantly diatonic basis, and he used, moreover, a variety of cross-rhythms and a well-balanced orchestration. The four symphonies of Brahms are all masterful works using the classic forms and techniques as their bases. Brahms waited until he was forty-three to produce his first symphony, but the result was a work that the conductor Hans von Bülow honored with the title of the *Tenth*—that is, the one symphony artistically capable of following Beethoven's nine symphonies. It was also Von Bülow who coined the three "B's" of music: Bach, Beethoven, and Brahms.

The *Symphony No. 1* (Op. 68, 1876) reveals a first movement in a tragic mood, yet not without its drive and thrust. The second movement is built around two themes; it builds to a high emotional pitch, only to subside at the close. This tranquillity is preserved in the next section of the symphony, which lacks the drive of a Beethovian scherzo. The fourth movement is the apex of the symphony. The *Adagio* introduction leads into one of the loveliest of all horn melodies, and finally the music bursts forth with an exuberant, flowing theme reminiscent of the *Ode to Joy* melody in the final movement of Beethoven's *Symphony No. 9.*

Brahms's *Symphony No. 2* (Op. 73, 1877), with its genial manner and melodious themes stands in direct contrast with the tragic *Symphony No. 1,* although it appeared only a year later. As if always seeking a link with Beethoven, some have called this work Brahms's "Pastorale."

The *Symphony No. 3* (Op. 90, 1883) has also been referred to as Brahms's "Eroica." It is perhaps not as "heroic" as it is "human"; Brahms does come as close to his audience in this symphony as his reserved nature would permit, and here we find the typical yet personal side of the composer.

Symphony No. 4 (Op. 98, 1885) begins with an opening movement that is heavily scored in gray colors and that in turn is relieved by a second movement of great beauty. The third movement, a short and boisterous affair complete with piccolo and triangle, is the only true scherzo movement in any of Brahms's four symphonies.

Throughout the history of instrumental music, composers have turned to the theme-and-variations form to test their imagination and inspiration; in Brahms can be found one of the 19th-century "greats" in the use of this form. The composer employs it in the last movement of the *Symphony No. 4,* using, as his theme, a short eight-bar subject borrowed from Bach's *Cantata No. 150,* announced by the woodwinds and brasses; then without pause, and with only one extension intervening, there occurs a lengthy series of variations in passacaglia or chaconne style. The variations are written partly on the bass of the theme, again on the melody, and sometimes on both bass and melody. All is closed off with a studious coda, which recalls the Bach theme several times.

Brahms also wrote another magnificent set of variations for orchestra, published as a single work under the title *Variations on a Theme of Haydn* (Op. 56a, 1873); a transcription by the composer for two pianos (Op. 52b, 1873) was first performed by Brahms and Clara Schumann in Vienna in August of 1873. Other attractive works for orchestra by this master include the *Academic Festival Overture* (Op. 80, 1880) and the *Tragic Overture* (Op. 81, 1880).

In concerto writing Brahms contributed two excellent works for the piano and an equally splendid concerto for the violin. Brahms wrote the *Piano Concerto No. 1* (Op. 15) when he was twenty-five years old, and his second piano concerto (Op. 83) twenty-three years later; this, of course, accounts for the *Sturm und Drang* of the former and the mature certainty of the latter. Both are quite difficult to perform effectively, and it remains a question of the piano player's subordinating his personal glory to that of the music. Performance difficulties are found as well in the *Violin Concerto in D major* (Op. 77, 1878); following the gracious and lightly flowing Mendelssohn violin concerto, Brahms's work found few sympathetic ears on its initial hearings, but time has brought to this composition a well-deserved popularity. The *Double Concerto in a minor for Violin and Cello* (Op. 102, 1887) shared much the same fate, and even today its seriousness and polyphonic treatment make concentrated listening absolutely necessary.

CHAMBER MUSIC

Brahms, with his twenty-four chamber music compositions, ranks first among the Romantic composers writing in this medium, both in his total output and in his quality of achievement. Brahms's string literature consists of the quartets in *c* (Op. 51, No. 1), *a* (Op. 51, No. 2), and *B♭* (Op. 67); quintets in *F* (Op. 88) and *G* (Op. 111); and the sextets in *B♭* ("Spring") and *G* ("Agathe"). Like Schumann, Brahms wrote a piano quintet (Op. 34, 1864; in *f* minor), and three piano quartets, in *g, A,* and *c.* There are also three sonatas for violin and piano, a *Sonata in F for Cello and Piano* (Op. 99), and a fine *Trio in E♭* for piano, violin, and horn (Op. 40, 1865). Clarinet players are fortunate to have the *Trio in a minor for Clarinet, Cello, and Piano* (Op. 114), the two sonatas for clarinet and piano (*F,* Op. 120, No. 1; *E♭,* Op. 120, No. 2), and especially the *Clarinet Quintet in b minor* (Op. 115, 1891). The piano quartet of Op. 25, in *g* minor, is one of the most popular of Brahms's chamber works; this popularity is no doubt due, at least in part, to the Romantic coloring and mood of the *Intermezzo* and the lively rondo in Hungarian gypsy style which closes the composition.

Brahms revised, rewrote, and destroyed many works, and even made a practice of rewriting compositions for new and different media until he was satisfied that he had the best "sound." For example, the *Piano Quintet in f minor,* Op. 34, started as a string quintet, became a two-piano sonata, and finally emerged in 1864 as a piano quintet; as proof that Brahms finally arrived at the right combination is the fact that this is one of his most famous chamber works.

Another well-known piece of chamber music by Brahms, the *Clarinet Quintet,* Op. 115, was first performed in 1891, in Berlin, by the Joachim Quartet with Richard Mühlfeld as clarinetist. The first movement, in sonata form, is somber in mood–the characteristic coloring of Brahms's late works. The clarinet announces the theme of the slow second movement, a lovely *Zigeuner* (gypsy) tune, imitated by the first violin; the rhapsodic middle section returns at the close to the calm pronouncement of the opening. The next movement begins with a moving theme in an *Andantino* tempo, has a *Presto* middle section, and ends with the original theme and tempo, much as in the second movement. The last movement, marked *con moto,* is an easygoing set of variations, ending with a reference to the close of the first movement. This composition was to mark the conclusion of any kind of fruitful writing for winds in the 19th century.

LIEDER AND OTHER VOCAL WORKS

Over 260 songs came from the pen of Brahms. He knew the voice well, for during his lifetime he served as accompanist for many Lied singers, two of special fame being Frau Amalie Joachim and Julius Stockhausen. Frequently Brahms wrote for the low voice, yet another indication of his predilection for warm, dark coloring in his music. Although written with a firm background of Romantic melody and harmony, his songs breathe an air of restraint and, generally, seriousness. A special trait of Brahms is his building of melodies around a chordal line (often in a descending pattern), as may be seen in his famous *Sapphische Ode.*

Brahms often turned, as did Schubert, to a strophic or modified strophic song form, but unlike Schubert he did very little picture painting in the piano accompaniments, and unlike Schumann he found small place for piano preludes and postludes in his songs. Ludwig Tieck contributed the poems for the excellent song cycle *Magelone* (Op. 33) and late in life Brahms crowned his efforts in this medium with the *Vier ernste Gesänge* ("Four Serious Songs," written for Stockhausen; Op. 121, 1896), based on biblical texts treating of death.

Brahms's *Requiem* was not conceived in the first place for the Catholic service, as its text is in German and instead of following the words of the Latin Mass the text consists of biblical passages chosen by the composer; thus it is known as the *German Requiem.* It is one of Brahms's finest works, and its emotional appeal, clothed as it is in the most splendid garb of Romantic melody and harmony, is calculated to touch the hearts of all who hear it.

In the field of secular Romantic choral music Brahms is the supreme master. Some of his finest works, still sung by choral societies today, include the following (all with orchestral accompaniment): *Rhapsodie* ("Alto Rhapsody," Op. 53, 1869) for alto and male chorus (after a portion of Goethe's *Harzreise im Winter*); *Schicksalslied* ("Song of Destiny," Op. 54, 1871), after Hölderlin's poem and for mixed chorus; *Nänie* (Op. 82, 1880–81) after Schiller and for mixed chorus; and *Gesang der Parzen* ("Song of the Fates," Op. 89, 1882) after Goethe's *Iphigenie auf Tauris* and for six-part chorus. His two sets of *Liebeslieder* waltzes (for four voices with piano accompaniment) are also noted vocal pieces.

THE WORKS OF BERLIOZ

Hector Berlioz (1803–69). Born in southeastern France, near Grenoble, Hector Berlioz, like Mendelssohn, came from a well-to-do family; his father was a physician, and eventually young Berlioz was sent to Paris to study medicine. However, the young man neglected his medical studies and, though he had only a rudimentary education in music, entered the Paris Conservatory. After several unsuccessful attempts he finally won the Prix de Rome in 1830, which gave him eighteen months' study in Italy. Berlioz had always been concerned with the new and the unusual in Romantic music; indeed, so unconventional were some of his creations that their acceptance was slow in coming. The composer aided his cause, and that of others who felt as he did, by accepting in 1835 a position as a music critic in Paris; he was also on the library staff of the Paris Conservatory from 1852 until his death. Berlioz, like Schumann, had a way with the written word as well as with the written note. His literary writings are of considerable worth, with the *Traité d'instrumentation et d'orchestration modernes* (1844) laying the foundation for the modern orchestra.

SYMPHONIC WORKS

Berlioz is the first wholehearted Romantic composing in the symphonic medium. His huge creations are tightly bound to literary backgrounds, and yet he was loath to abandon the Classical forms entirely. His three symphonies–*Symphonie fantastique* (Op. 14, first performed 1830), *Harold in Italy* (Op. 16, 1834), and *Romeo and Juliet* (Op. 17, 1839)–all have movements or groupings in the Classical order. The *Symphonie fantastique* draws its inspirations, at least in part, from De Quincey's *Confessions of an English Opium Eater* and Goethe's *Faust,* the two of which were capable of stimulating the wildest Romantic musical ideas. The work is set forth in five movements entitled "Visions and Passions," "A Ball," "Scenes in the Country," "March to the Gallows," and the "Witches' Sabbath." The unifying *idée fixe*—here a melody signifying the artist's beloved—is heard in all the movements, and in the "Witches' Sabbath" there appears a parody of the plain song *Dies Irae* from the Catholic Requiem Mass.

The *Dies Irae* chant, "Day of wrath, day of mourning," had a morbid fascination for many Romantic composers. Besides Berlioz's use of it in the *Symphonie fantastique,* the chant tune appears also in his *Requiem;* in Liszt's *Totentanz* and *Dante Symphony;* in Moussorgsky's "Trepak" in his *Songs and Dances of Death;* in the *Rhapsody on a Theme of Paganini, The Isle of the Dead, Symphony No. 3,* and the *Symphonic Dances,* Op. 45, all by Sergei Rachmaninov; in Saint-Saens's *Danse macabre;* and in the theme and variations in Tchaikovsky's *Orchestral Suite No. 3* and also in that composer's song "In Dark Hell." Example 45 gives the *idée fixe* as first heard in the *Symphonie fantastique* and the *Dies Irae* (beginning) as found in its original chant form.

(a) Berlioz: *idée fixe*

(b) Chant: *Dies Irae*

8 Di-es I-rae di-es il-la. Sol-vet sae-clum in fa-vil-la

Example 45

Berlioz's *Harold in Italy* is a set of four scenes after Byron's *Childe Harold.* A solo viola is featured in a pseudo-concerto style, and there is also a unifying theme for viola which runs throughout the work. *Romeo and Juliet* is a "dramatic symphony" utilizing vocal soloists and a chorus in conjunction with the orchestra. Thus the work follows the lead of the last movement of Beethoven's *Symphony No. 9,* but carries the vocal idea a step further by using voices in more than the one movement. This composition is a musical re-creation of Shakespeare's play. In this work Berlioz himself considered the "Love Scene" music some of his best writing. The "Queen Mab" scherzo is a splendid piece of orchestration, and the scene laid in Juliet's tomb is excellent dramatic music.

Berlioz also made use of voices in a later "dramatic legend" entitled *Damnation of Faust* (Op. 24, 1846). However, the most popular excerpts from this work today are the instrumental numbers "Minuet of the Will-o'-the-Wisps," "Dance of the Sylphs," and the "Rakóczy March." This work follows Goethe's *Faust,* but Berlioz could not find enough compassion in his heart to pardon the sins of Goethe's hero. Finally, on the basis of its popularity and as a rather concise example of Berlioz's compositional style, we must mention the delightful *Roman Carnival Overture* (Op. 9, 1844).

VOCAL AND OPERATIC WORKS

Berlioz was really the leader in the Romantic urge to use the grandiose and the spatial. His *Requiem* (*Grande Messe des Morts,* Op. 5, 1837) was commissioned by the French Government for use in a memorial service dedicated to those who lost their lives in the Revolution of 1830. (Shades of Delacroix's *Liberty on the Barricade* commemorating the same subject.) The grandiose and the spatial are represented in the *Requiem* through the use of a tenor soloist, a mixed chorus, a large principal orchestra, and four smaller instrumental ensembles, one to be placed in each of the four corners of the auditorium.

Berlioz's *Te Deum* (1849) (recalling Napoleon's triumphal return from the Italian campaign) again reflects the grandiose idea; the first performance required a large orchestra, a double chorus, and a children's chorus of six hundred voices.

Though early French Romantic opera will be discussed as a whole later in the chapter, the operas of Berlioz will be discussed here with the rest of his work. Berlioz's operas are somewhat apart from other works in this genre; indeed, all of Berlioz's music is a kind of law unto itself. His comic opera *Benvenuto Cellini* (Paris, 1838) makes no attempt at a consistent plot development, but unravels instead in a series of broad episodes. His next opera *Béatrice et Bénédict* (Baden, 1862), in two acts, was based on a portion of Shakespeare's *Much Ado about Nothing.*

Berlioz's most important opera, however, is *Les Troyens* (written in 1856–59). Its lengthy five acts were composed to be presented in two parts: (1) *La Prise de Troie* ("The Capture of Troy"), and (2) *Les Troyens à Carthage* ("The Trojans at Carthage"). Berlioz himself wrote the libretto, based on the second and fourth books of Virgil's *Aeneid.* Due to the length and sectioning of the opera, it has a peculiar performance record. Berlioz heard only the second part (Acts III, IV, and V) in performance, this being given a number of times in Paris in 1863; Part I was heard for the first time in Karlsruhe in 1890. In 1898 the whole work was produced, in German, in Cologne. Finally, a complete performance of both parts in the original French was given in Rouen in 1920.

It unfolds the plot in much the same manner used in *Benvenuto Cellini,* with the ballets and musical numbers appearing at spots where they can be appropriately accommodated. Here Berlioz's music, compared with his earlier works, is almost Classical in concept; *Les Troyens* is such a large-scale opera that productions have been few and far between, but when performance is possible the music makes the undertaking completely worth while.

EARLY ROMANTIC OPERA

EARLY FRENCH ROMANTIC OPERA

As we mentioned earlier, Paris was the center of opera production in the early 19th century. The grand opera was developed there, and the lyric opera too. Berlioz's contributions to French opera have already been discussed along with the rest of his work earlier in the chapter.

Giacomo Meyerbeer (1791–1864). Giacomo Meyerbeer's name requires an explanation. Born Jakob Liebmann Beer (in Berlin, of Jewish parents), he assumed the name Meyerbeer as a prerequisite for an inheritance from a wealthy relative; and Jakob became Italianized to Giacomo in order to aid his compositional career. After studies with Zelter, Anselm Weber, and Abbé Vogler he was ready to challenge the famous Gioacchino Rossini.

Meyerbeer's *Robert le Diable* (1831), *Les Huguenots* (1836), *Le Prophète* (1849), and *L'Africaine* (produced in 1865 after the composer's death) were all successful—especially *Les Huguenots*—in his age, but their demand for the most spectacular of settings has worked against their performance in modern times. Meyerbeer's fame derived from his ability to combine a solid German musical heritage with the Italian *bel canto* line and the light charm of French rhythmical movement—all this plus the fine theatrical effects of his operatic librettos by the French playwright Augustin Eugène Scribe (1791–1861).

Charles Gounod (1818–93). Charles Gounod was born in Paris of cultured parents; his father, Jean François Gounod, was a painter of some repute, having won a 2nd Grand Prix de Rome. After study at the Lycée St. Louis, the young Gounod enrolled in the Paris Conservatory. He followed in his father's footsteps as a prize winner by acquiring a 2nd Prix de Rome in 1837; and two years later he won the Grand Prix with his cantata *Fernand*.

After study in Rome he made Paris his home. Gounod's *Faust* (1859) was the most famous example of the lyric opera style. Here Gounod did not attempt the impossible—as did Boito with his *Mefistofele*—in trying to set both parts of Goethe's drama, but confined his opera to Part I. The result was an opera of good proportions to which Gounod's musical talents added melodies and harmonies of a particularly satisfying nature. From a rather long list of well-remembered pieces from the work, the following will be mentioned as displaying its marvelous lyric content: Valentin's *Avant de quitter ces lieux* ("Even bravest hearts may swell"), and the "Waltz" from Act II. Marguerite's "Jewel Song" from Act III, and the "Soldiers' Chorus," which opens Scene 3 of Act IV. The chorus also intones the famous *Dies irae* chant in Act IV, Scene 2.

Gounod wrote only one other opera of lasting interest, *Roméo et Juliette* (1867).

Other French Opera Composers. The lighter side of French comic opera is seen in the works of Daniel François Auber (1782–1871) and Jacques Offenbach (1819–80). Auber's *Fra Diavolo* (1830) and his *Le Domino noir* ("The Black Domino," 1837) were both popular in his time, but little is heard by this composer today save the overture to *Fra Diavolo*. Offenbach composed many operettas for performance in Paris, of which *Orphée aux enfers* ("Orpheus in Hades," 1858) was one of the best. His masterpiece is his only grand opera, *Les Contes d'Hoffmann* ("The Tales of Hoffmann"), produced posthumously at the Opéra-Comique in 1881. Another lesser-known Frenchman of this period was Léo Delibes (1836–91). Although he is best remembered for his ballets *La Source* (1866), *Coppélia* (1870), and *Sylvia* (1876) his opera *Lakmé* (1883)–with a Hindu setting and a slightly Oriental flavor–is also still heard today.

EARLY ITALIAN ROMANTIC OPERA

Gioacchino Rossini (1792–1868). Gioacchino Rossini, the leading Italian composer of the early 19th century, excelled in the writing of grand opera. He was born in Pesaro, Italy, of parents who made their living as performers in provincial theaters; Rossini's mother sang opera, and his father played trumpet and horn in the orchestras of the opera house. Thus, it is not surprising that after his studies in the Liceo Comunale of Bologna, Rossini turned his efforts toward operatic composition.

Rossini is remembered today chiefly for two works: *The Barber of Seville* (Rome, 1816), which compares favorably with the comic operas of Mozart, and *William Tell,* first produced in Paris in 1829. Strangely enough, although *Tell* was a successful opera, Rossini wrote no more operas after 1829, perhaps because of competition from Meyerbeer or perhaps from a failing of his health; it does pose one of music's greatest enigmas. At any rate, *Tell* is a great work in the grand opera tradition and deserves to be seen and heard today. Rossini's musical style features beautiful and free-flowing melodies backed by original harmonizations in clear-cut phrases and well-shaped formal structures; his orchestrations, too, are compact and pleasing.

With respect to other titles in Rossini's long list of operas, the overtures to *La Scála di seta* ("The Silken Ladder," Venice, 1812), *L'Italiana in Algeri* ("The Italian Woman in Algiers," Venice, 1813), *La Gazza ladra* ("The Thieving Magpie," Milan, 1817), and *Semiramide* (Venice, 1823) frequently find a place on current symphonic concerts and recordings.

Rossini also wrote a *Stabat Mater* (written in 1832 and revised extensively in 1841), but like all the liturgical music of the Romantics it was later deemed inappropriate for use in the Church service.

Gaetano Donizetti (1797–1848). Born of a weaver in the city of Bergamo, Italy, Gaetano Donizetti had to overcome parental objections before entering the music school at Bergamo and later the Bologna Liceo Filarmonico. Still, he was to become one of the most prolific Italian composers of his age, composing in both the serious and the comic opera types. The best of the former is *Lucia di Lammermoor* (Naples, 1835), based on Sir Walter Scott's *Bride of Lammermoor;* it is a prima donna's opera, noted for the leading lady's "Mad Scene" (and also for the famous "Sextet"). Outstanding among his comic operas are *L'Elisir d'amore* ("The Elixir of Love," Milan, 1832) and the enduring *Don Pasquale,* first produced in Paris in 1843. Most of Donizetti's operas (about sixty) were written for the Italian houses, and as it was customary for these establishments to demand works on short notice, many of his operas reveal haste of composition through rather monotonous rhythms, harmonies, and orchestrations.

Vincenzo Bellini (1801–35). Vincenzo Bellini came from a musical background. Both his grandfather and father served in their time as organist at the cathedral in Catania, Sicily, the city of Bellini's birth. When the boy grew up he entered the Conservatory of San Sebastiano at Naples, where the opera and church music composer Nicola Zingarelli was one of his instructors. The heart of Bellini's music–like that of most Italian composers–is his melody, and his harmony and orchestration suffer in comparison with Rossini's art. However, his *La Sonnambula* and *Norma* are still known today. The *opera semiseria* entitled *La Sonnambula* (Milan, 1831) is about a young lady who walks in her sleep, which leads to questions about her reputation; but all ends happily. *Norma* (Milan, 1831) is a more famous opera; the libretto concerns Norma, a priestess of a Celtic religious order of ancient Gaul, who is seduced by a Roman officer; the opera ends with her self-sacrifice.

Other Italian Opera Composers. Luigi Cherubini (1760–1842) was a respected composer of the early 19th century. He wrote many works for the stage, of which *Les Deux journées* ("The Two Days," Paris, 1800) is his finest and stands as yet another example of rescue opera. Arrigo Boito (1842–1918) is mentioned several times in this chapter, chiefly for his excellent librettos; outstanding among these were his books for Verdi's *Otello* and *Falstaff,* and for *Gioconda* (Milan, 1876) with music composed by Amilcare Ponchielli (1834–86). However, Boito also enjoyed success as a composer in his own right, as his honorary doctorates of music from both Cambridge and Oxford universities testify. He completed but one opera–*Mefistofele* (Milan, 1868; revised in 1875); this work was actually closer in spirit to Goethe's drama than Gounod's *Faust,* but its success was never equal to that of Gounod's opera.

EARLY GERMAN ROMANTIC OPERA

German Romantic opera achieved its first real development in the works of Carl Maria von Weber. The basis for this Romantic style was the German *Singspiel,* the greatest of which was Mozart's *Magic Flute.* Romantic elements were united with those of the *Singspiel* in the operas of E. T. A. Hoffmann and in Ludwig Spohr's (1784–1859) opera *Faust* (Prague, 1816; after Goethe). Schubert also wrote several works in the *Singspiel* and opera genre, works that unfortunately lacked that all-important spark that gives theatrical life. This literature was of course known to Weber, as were the grand operas of the French and Italian schools, and all these influences can be found in his operas.

Carl Maria von Weber (1786–1826). Carl Maria von Weber was born of musical parents in Eutin, Oldenburg, Germany; his desire for musical training had the blessing of his father, and among his teachers can be found the important names Michael Haydn and Abbé Vogler. In 1817 he took charge of the German Opera Theater at Dresden, and after this time his musical career moved rapidly forward.

Weber's *Der Freischütz* (Berlin, 1821) exemplifies the fundamental traits of German Romantic opera, which consist of the following: (1) romanticizing of plots based on legend and folklore, (2) dramatic presentation of supernatural elements, (3) nature in its wildest forms, and (4) realism of contemporary life gained through the use of German folk songs. The libretto was written by Friedrich Kind and is based on a fantastic tale from Apel and Laun's *Gespensterbuch* ("The Ghost Book"). The title *Der Freischütz* (literally "free shooter") concerns one who shoots magic bullets. The scene is laid in a Bohemian village near the end of the Thirty Years' War (*c.* 1648).

The plot concerns Max, a young hunter, who seeks to win Agathe as his bride in a shooting contest. He enlists the aid of Caspar, who has connections with Samiel, the Evil One. Max obtains some magic bullets with which he means to win the contest, but when he fires the final shot Agathe falls to the ground and Caspar falls dead from a tree. It seems that Samiel had directed the bullet at Agathe, but her goodness made her immune and Caspar was claimed by the devil as a forfeit. All ends happily when Agathe is revived. In the overture the horns —the instruments par excellence of Romantic nature scenes—

depict the somberness of the forest. The diabolical "Wolf's Glen" scene, where the magic bullets are cast, is given an added frightening aspect through some very effective orchestral scoring, and folk choruses and dances exist side by side with Italian arias. A further musical technique is the use of recurring motives.

Two other Weber operas–*Euryanthe* (Vienna, 1823) and *Oberon* (London, 1826, to English words) are known today chiefly through their overtures. No great German composers followed Weber in Romantic opera with any success until Wagner. Schubert's operas were not successful, and Schumann's *Genoveva* (Leipzig, 1850) likewise failed to survive.

THE WORKS OF VERDI

Giuseppe Verdi (1813–1901). Born of an innkeeper in a small Italian village near Parma, Italy, Giuseppe Verdi had little opportunity for serious music study in his early youth. Thus when he later sought admission to the Milan Conservatory he failed to pass the entrance examination. He then studied privately with Vincenzo Lavigna of the La Scala opera house. Verdi achieved some early fame as a composer of opera from his successes at La Scala, where after 1843 his position was assured. Now other opera houses in Europe began to open their doors to him, and in the 1850's the masterpieces for which he is known today first began to appear. Verdi also became involved with the Italian struggle for independence. His admirers and fellow patriots linked his name with that of Victor Emmanuel II, future king of Italy, by the cry *"Viva Verdi,"* which used the letters of Verdi's name as an acrostic to signify Viva "V*ittorio* E*manuele* R*e* D' I*talia.*" In 1869–71 Verdi wrote his *Aïda* for the new theater in Cairo to celebrate the opening of the Suez Canal. Verdi's last opera, *Falstaff,* was written in his eightieth year. He is considered today to be the greatest composer of Italian opera.

Verdi's opera career developed at a most propitious time for himself and for Italian opera in general. Rossini had ceased writing opera, Bellini had died, and Donizetti was ill. The public for Italian opera had been created and there was little native competition. The six masterpieces on which Verdi's fame mostly rests are *Rigoletto* (Venice, 1851), *Il Trovatore* (Rome, 1853), *La Traviata* (Venice, 1853), *Aïda* (Cairo, 1871), *Otello* (Milan, 1887), and *Falstaff* (Milan, 1893). Not so outstandingly famous but still consistently staged are *Nabucco* (Milan, 1842), *Ernani* (Venice, 1844; based on Victor Hugo's *Hernani*), *Macbeth* (Florence, 1847; a performance of the revised score was first given in Paris in 1865), *Luisa Miller* and *Don Carlos* (Naples, 1849, and Paris, 1867, respectively; both libretto sources are from Schiller), *Un Ballo in maschera* ("A Masked Ball," Rome, 1859; based on Eugène Scribe's libretto for Auber's *Gustavus III*), and *La Forza del destino* ("The Power of Fate," St. Petersburg, 1862).

The libretto for *Rigoletto* is based on Victor Hugo's *Le Roi s'amuse*. It was mostly through Hugo's influence that the "happy ending" disappeared from serious opera—that is, after the works of Donizetti. Gilda's tragic demise furnishes *Rigoletto* with a most "unhappy ending." Verdi, the master of melody, wrote tunes for Gilda's *"Caro nome"* and the duke's *"La donna è mobile"* that soon were to be heard played by every street organ grinder, and the "Quartet" stands with the "Sextet" from Donizetti's *Lucia* as one of the two most famous small-ensemble pieces in all of operatic literature.

The play *El Trovador* ("The Troubadour"), by García Gutiérrez, provided the story for Verdi's popular *Il Trovatore*. Verdi always gave the chorus plenty to do in his operas, and from this opera comes the well-remembered "Anvil Chorus."

The background for *La Traviata* ("The Lost One") came from the play *La Dame aux camélias*, by Alexandre Dumas *fils*. The operatic setting of a tragic play of contemporary domestic life was something of an experiment for Verdi, and the immediate public response was not very rewarding. It was not until sometime near the turn of the century, when the singer Gemma Bellincioni—considered by Verdi the ideal Violetta

—began to put real depth into her part, that the opera gained a firm foothold.

Aïda was commissioned for public ceremonies in connection with the opening of the Suez Canal and was first performed in Cairo, Egypt. The book was sketched by the Frenchman A. E. Mariette, an Egyptologist in the Khedive's service, and the Italian libretto was put in final form by Antonio Ghislanzoni. It is a stage manager's delight, full of pomp and majesty, and because of its spectacular show it is often used in the large opera houses to open an operatic season. Yet it is also a work of sound dramatic character, full of fine music and thoroughly human characterization. The *"Celeste Aïda"* aria for tenor voice and the "Triumphal March" seem destined to live on forever.

After *Aïda,* Verdi waited sixteen years before presenting his next opera, *Otello,* which is considered by many to be his greatest work. In 1862, Arrigo Boito had furnished the words for a secular cantata by Verdi entitled *Inno alle nazioni.* Now the two teamed up again to produce *Otello.* Boito, basing the work on Shakespeare's drama, gave Verdi the best libretto he ever had or was to have. At this time the operatic field was all Verdi, as Wagner had died a few years earlier. *Otello* revealed a number of new directions in the composer's personal style as can be seen in its ever-changing flow of musical thought. Boito's libretto presented in sharp focus the jealousy of Otello and the scheming nature of Iago, and Verdi was not slow in writing the finest of musical characterizations around these figures. Iago's *"Credo"* is one of the opera's most eloquent and sinister soliloquies, and the love scene between Otello and Desdemona at the end of Act I, built as it is around the beauties of the night, is wonderfully Romantic music. The final act has Desdemona's beautiful "Willow Song" and "Ave Maria," and also the dramatic murder of Desdemona by Otello and the latter's subsequent suicide; Verdi uses the remembrance motive technique when the orchestra plays the "Kiss Motive" near the end of the opera, recalling its use in the love scene at the end of Act I. The music of the opera is knit together in splendid fashion, and the orchestration reaches supreme heights.

Falstaff, again on a libretto by Boito after Shakespeare's *The Merry Wives of Windsor,* was an astonishing accomplishment for the eighty-year-old Verdi. It represented Verdi's second comic opera, the first having been written early in his career. Great climaxes are reached in the finales of the second and third acts, and the opera is, in all, a thoroughly entertaining and masterful piece of writing. Verdi spoofs perhaps himself and the century in the last scene with a classical fugue to the words *"Tutto nel mondo è burla"* ("all the world's a joke"). With *Falstaff,* Verdi showed that *opera buffa* was not dead, and that much could still be done in the form.

Verdi's *Requiem* (composed in 1874 in memory of the Italian author Alessandro Manzoni) is written in theater style, the only style this composer really knew how to handle effectively; the *Requiem* has been called Verdi's finest "opera," but it is nevertheless a superb combination of flowing Italian melody and outstanding technical construction.

THE WORKS OF WAGNER

Richard Wagner (1813–83). Richard Wagner was born in Leipzig, and his early interest while he was a student centered in Greek, not music. However, around 1825 he began to develop an interest in opera. After 1828 he went to the schools of St. Nicholas and St. Thomas in Leipzig, and he had his first serious training in composition with Theodor Weinlig, cantor of the Thomasschule. Wagner subsequently held several posts as conductor of small civic German opera houses. The success of *The Flying Dutchman* at Dresden in 1843 led to an appointment as music director at the Saxon court, but Wagner became politically involved in a revolution and had to flee Saxony. He thereafter lived in many places, fell in and out of love frequently, and wrote and produced operas and literary works. Wagner had cherished the dream of a theater designed especially to produce his works, and when an offer of such a theater came from Bayreuth he immediately moved to that city and the cornerstone of the Festspielhaus was laid on May 22, 1872. In August of 1876 the dream of Wagner's life was realized; a complete performance of *The Ring of the Nibelung* was given, with notables of music and royalty attending from all over the world.

Wagner wrote very little of any value for orchestra alone. One of the better such compositions is his solidly constructed *Eine Faust Ouverture,* written in 1840 and revised in 1855 and based on Goethe's drama; another is a piece for small chamber orchestra called *Siegfried Idyll,* first played for Wagner's wife Cosima as a birthday present for her on Christmas morning, 1870.

Wagner's name has gone down in musical history as the greatest German opera composer of the 19th century, and indeed one of the greatest of all time. He began with the German Romantic opera and ended up as the creator of the music drama. Wagner's first important opera was *Rienzi* (Dresden, 1842), written very much in the style of Meyerbeer; it is remembered today outside of Germany mainly through its overture. The next year *Der fliegende Holländer* ("The Flying Dutchman") was premiered in Dresden, the musical style seeming now to follow more in Weber's footsteps. Here the libretto, written by Wagner, as were all his librettos, is based on legend–a policy the composer was to continue to follow in his later works. *Tannhäuser* (Dresden, 1845) is a sort of German Romantic opera in grand opera style. From out of this work comes the notable music of the "Pilgrims' Chorus," the "Festal March" of Act II, and the beautiful "Elizabeth's Prayer" of the final act.

Lohengrin, first performed in Weimar in 1850 and conducted by Liszt in Wagner's absence, is the last of the true Romantic Wagnerian operas. By now the opera is beginning to shape into whole, unified acts; the music flows more continuously in a fuller texture, and the "set numbers" of earlier operas are less noticeable. The use of a declamatory style is under development in pieces like Lohengrin's *"In fernem Land";* other especially fine music comes in the "Prelude to Act I" (to describe the Holy Grail as it appears and vanishes) and the rousing "Prelude to Act III." There is also the "Wedding March," which leads the wedding couple, not into the cathedral, as in contemporary marriage ceremonies, but into the bridal chamber.

Munich was the city of the first performance of *Tristan und Isolde* (1865), which many consider to be Wagner's greatest opera. It appears that Wagner based his libretto on the Tristan legend as set down by the 13th-century writer Gottfried von Strassburg. The story is one of the greatest love narratives of all history; it concerns the love of Tristan and Isolde, a love outside the bounds of convention, and one that finally destroys the both of them. The "Prelude to Act I" contains the music of the transcendental love of the pair, a love that can be fulfilled only in their death. The music preluding the second act —during which, while King Mark is away on a hunting party, Tristan and Isolde spend a night of love together—builds with ever-increasing intensity toward a tremendous emotional climax signifying the meeting of the lovers. In Act II the couple invokes the cloak of night in the duet *"O sink hernieder, Nacht der Liebe"* ("O night of love, descend upon us"). In the final act is found one of the finest musical pieces of all German opera in Isolde's *Liebestod* ("Love Death"); her solo begins with the words *"Mild und leise wie er lächelt"* ("Fair and gently he is smiling"), and the orchestra joins hands with Isolde in the outpouring of her grief.

Much has been said about the considerable amount of chromatic writing found in *Tristan* and how this technique helped to destroy tonality and paved the way toward the modern harmonic style. The vagaries of tonality found in many sections of *Tristan* are apparent, and the very opening bars of the "Prelude to Act I" show the unrest generated by the blurred chromatic passage (see Example 46).

Wagner did an about-face in his next opera, *Die Meistersinger von Nürnberg* ("The Mastersingers of Nuremberg"), first produced in Munich in 1868. In this work the tragedy and chromaticism of *Tristan* were replaced by the fun of 16th-

Example 46

century German meistersingers' guilds and by a predominantly diatonic harmony.

Wagner's crowning achievement was the great tetralogy of *Der Ring des Nibelungen* ("The Ring of the Nibelung"). It consists of the following operas: (1) *Das Rheingold* ("The Rhine Gold"; Munich, 1869); (2) *Die Walküre* ("The Valkyrie"; Munich, 1870); (3) *Siegfried* (Bayreuth, 1876); and (4) *Die Götterdämmerung* ("The Twilight of the Gods"; Bayreuth, 1876). The first complete performance of the entire cycle took place on August 13, 14, 16, and 17, 1876, in connection with the opening of the Wagnerian theater at Bayreuth.

In 1851, when Wagner was writing the libretto for *The Ring,* the German master was also busy expounding his ideas concerning music drama in a book entitled *Opera and Drama.* His ideal was the *Gesamtkunstwerk* ("universal art work"), where such individual arts as drama, music, staging, etc., are each subjugated to the whole creation. The legend is the starting point, for it is both entertaining and comprehensible; then the music and staging enter and lift the text to a fuller expression. Unlike Verdi, whose orchestrations are never allowed to cover the melodic line of the singer, Wagner's characters become part of the great ensemble. In other words, Verdi's singers stand *before* the orchestra, Wagner's *within* it. Wagner's music is continuous within the act—"endless melody" as it is called; this continuous-music principle was important to Wagner, as it counteracted the impediment to action that had occurred in the "numbers" opera, and the distraction of spectator applause that had followed the many arias and ensemble pieces.

In the music of *The Ring,* Wagner realized the dream of his *Opera and Drama.* But the continuous-music principle needed some sort of unification, which Wagner provided in two ways: (1) through a large-scale organization of the acts of the operas, usually in a mammoth ternary (ABA) or *Bar* (AAB) form–which, it must be admitted, cannot be *heard* by the listener, and (2) through a highly developed use of the leitmotif. Now the leitmotif had not been invented by Wagner (Weber had used "recurring motives"), but he had used them more or less extensively in his operas from *Rienzi* on, where they had become the material for the development of the polyphonic web of his vocal and orchestral music. But in *The Ring,* in the absence of not only separate airs and "numbers" but nearly all ensembles and choruses as well and in the unifying demands of the tetralogy, their need was even greater. Example 47 illustrates a number of the leitmotifs found in all four operas of *The Ring,* serving as a unification of the plots and music of the tetralogy.

In *Parsifal* (Bayreuth, 1882) Wagner closed out his operatic career and that of the music drama. The musicians who followed Wagner realized the futility of even attempting operas of the size and scope of that composer, but his harmonic practice and orchestral colorings proved very useful as a line of further development, as the next chapter will reveal.

(a) "Ring"

Example 47

(b) "Walhalla"

(c) "Sword"

(d) "Loge"

(e) "Alberich's Curse"

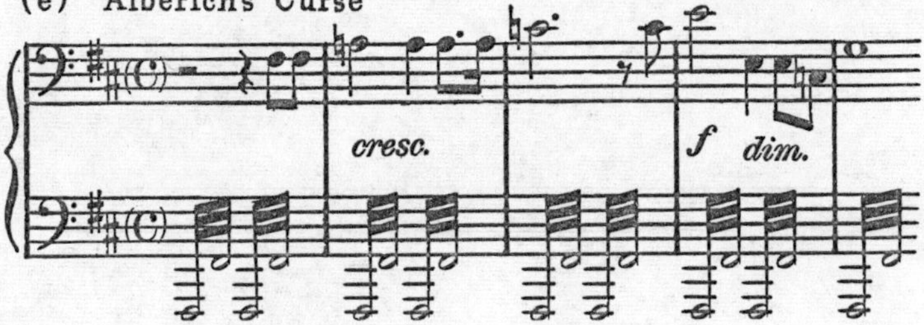

Example 47 (cont.)

PART FIVE

Post-Romanticism and Modern Music

CHAPTER 9

Post-Romanticism and Impressionism

INTRODUCTION

After the Romantic style of music had taken definite shape—that is, after the close of the first quarter of the 19th century—Romanticism became almost entirely the property of German, Italian, and French musicians. In these three countries were to be found the best composers, the best music schools, and the most appreciative and informed listening audience. However, just as the first quarter of the 19th century was to see the build-up to Romanticism, the last quarter was to witness its disintegration. Two factors played important roles in the stylistic change:

(1) The surge of nationalism, which embodied the desire to make music express nationalistic concepts; this spirit of nationalism arose first in Russia, then spread West with varying degrees of intensity into Bohemia, Norway, Denmark, Finland, Spain, Italy, England, and the United States.

(2) The strong French challenge for musical supremacy. The first factor was called post- or late Romanticism, and the second pointed the way to modern music—to a style called Impressionism.

LATE GERMAN ROMANTICISM

SYMPHONIC MUSIC

Anton Bruckner (1824–96). Anton Bruckner, the son of a schoolmaster, was born in Ausfelden. With only meager instruction on the organ he rose to the heights of a virtuoso, holding a number of church positions and eventually securing the post of instructor of organ and harmony at the Vienna Conservatory. In 1875 he was appointed to the faculty of Vienna University as a lecturer in music. His death occurred in Vienna.

Bruckner stands today as a composer who, on the one hand, has many wholehearted admirers and, on the other, a number who will not listen to his works. It was about the same situation in his own day, and the criticism of his music then (and probably his own continual search for perfection) prompted much revision of his scores; indeed, today some of them exist in two or more versions.

Bruckner wrote nine symphonies, the last movement of the ninth being left unfinished at his death. The harmonic structure and solemn grandeur of these symphonies suggest Wagnerian opera in symphonic dress. These two factors and the enormous lengths of the works—and some have criticized them for their uneven quality—have no doubt led to their slow acceptance outside of some parts of Europe. Still, the *Symphony No. 4* ("Romantic," written in 1874, with the scherzo and finale movements revised 1878–80) and the *Symphony No. 7* (1881–83) are becoming a little better known with each passing year. The latter piece is undoubtedly Bruckner's most evenly inspired work; the *Adagio,* a funeral march said to stem from Bruckner's meditations on the last illness of Wagner, is perhaps his greatest piece of writing and does indeed appear to have Wagner in mind.

The Wagnerian scope and size are also evident in Bruckner's religious music—that is, in his symphonic Masses in *d* minor (1864, revised in 1876) and in *f* minor (1868, revised 1890). Also sharing this style are his *e*-minor Mass for eight-part choir and wind instruments (1866, revised in 1885) and his *Te Deum in C* (1881, revised in 1884). These works, like all Romantic liturgical music, are not deemed appropriate for use in Church services.

Gustav Mahler (1860–1911). The last of the great post-

Romantic German symphonists was Gustav Mahler. Mahler studied music at the Vienna Conservatory and history and philosophy at the University of Vienna. He became a famous conductor, and in his lifetime held such important posts as director of the Royal Opera in Budapest, the Vienna Court Opera, and shortly before his death the position of principal conductor of the Metropolitan Opera in New York.

Mahler created nine vast symphonies (a tenth was left unfinished at his death) that mix sections of profound and noble concept with moments of great emotional intensity. The large scope of these works (he was preceded in this respect by Berlioz, Wagner, and Bruckner) demands huge performing resources, exemplified in the popular name "Symphony of a Thousand" for his *Symphony No. 8*. Programmatic influences abound in the symphonies; Austrian folk songs, chorale themes, plainsong tunes, nature scenes, and hints of the supernatural; motives are often used throughout a symphony as unifying devices. In his *Symphony No. 8* the first movement uses the plain-song hymn *Veni creator spiritus* (LU, p. 885), and the last part of Goethe's *Faust* provides the basis for the three following movements.

Besides the *Symphony No. 8,* the symphonies most often heard today are the first, second, fourth, fifth, and ninth. Mahler himself said that the *Symphony No. 1 in D* ("Titan," 1888) had been inspired by a novel by Jean Paul Richter. Each of the five movements bears a programmatic title. The long introduction depicts the awakening of nature at dawn; themes from Mahler's earlier *Lieder eines fahrenden Gesellen* ("Songs of a Wayfarer," composed 1883–84) appear in the first and fifth movements, and the famous French round *Frère Jacques* is parodied in canonic imitation in the slow fourth movement. (Example 48 shows both the French round and the tune as Mahler used it.) Because the second movement (probably an *Andante*) was excised from the score after the Weimar performance of 1894 and has been lost, it is never heard in modern concerts.

Symphony No. 2 in c minor ("Resurrection," 1894) fol-

(a) *Frère Jacques*

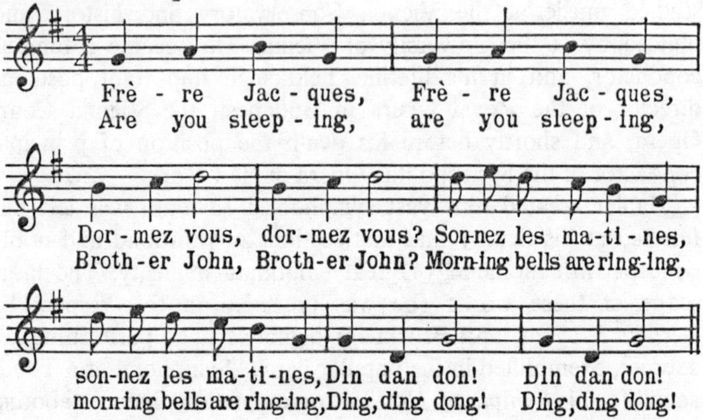
Frè - re Jac - ques, Frè - re Jac - ques,
Are you sleep - ing, are you sleep - ing,
Dor - mez vous, dor - mez vous? Son-nez les ma-ti - nes,
Broth - er John, Broth - er John? Morn-ing bells are ring-ing,
son-nez les ma-ti-nes, Din dan don! Din dan don!
morn-ing bells are ring-ing, Ding, ding dong! Ding, ding dong!

(b) Mahler's parody of *Frère Jacques*

Example 48

lows the practice of Beethoven, Berlioz, and Liszt by introducing voices. This symphony has been described as an allegory of the struggles in the life of man; the answer to his struggles is given by Mahler in the finale setting for soloists and chorus of a Resurrection ode by the German poet Friedrich Klopstock (1724–1803). In the fourth movement a contralto sings *Oh, Little Red Rose,* a song with a text from *Des Knaben Wunderhorn* ("The Boy's Magic Horn"), an early-19th-century anthology of German poetry.

The *Symphony No. 4 in G Major* ("Ode to Heavenly Joy," 1900) is one of Mahler's shortest and most lyrical symphonies.

The ode of the subtitle is a lyric from *Des Knaben Wunderhorn* and is sung by a soprano soloist in the last movement.

Symphony No. 5 in c♯ minor (1902) is called "The Giant" with respect to its length and orchestration; it is also a symphony of five movements, grouped here in three sections.

Symphony No. 9 in D (1909) is Mahler's symphonic swan song and makes obvious references (in the first and last movements) to the *Lebewohl* ("Farewell") theme of Beethoven's piano sonata, Op. 81a. The second movement has music resembling an Austrian peasant dance (*Ländler*), and the third movement introduces a chorale section. The symphony ends as it begins, in a slow, resigned-to-fate mood.

Actually none of the five symphonies mentioned above is Mahler's best-known work. That distinction falls on the excellent song cycle for solo voices and orchestra entitled *Das Lied von der Erde* ("Song of the Earth," 1908), based on six poems translated from the Chinese by Hans Bethge with the title *The Chinese Flute*. Songs for tenor and contralto are interlaced with the symphonic web in a full, integral texture. The six songs are as follows: (1) "The Drinking Song of Earthly Woe," which reveals a cup of bitter tears, (2) "The Lonely One in Autumn," a drab nature scene, (3) "Of Youth," reflections in the water of a happy young group, (4) "Of Beauty," picturing two lovers, (5) "The Drunken One in Spring," again a morbid picture, and (6) "Awaiting a Friend" and the "Farewell of a Friend," in which all happiness is abandoned.

Richard Strauss (1864–1949). The great German composer Richard Strauss was born in Munich, where his father, Franz Strauss, was a competent horn player. Strauss had his early musical instruction with musicians of the court orchestra in Munich, and in the academic year 1882–83 he attended lectures in philosophy at Munich University. In 1883–84 he served as an assistant to the conductor Hans von Bülow, and later he acquired important posts as conductor of the Weimar court orchestra, the Berlin Philharmonic, and the Vienna State Opera orchestra, and also served as guest conductor of many of the other great orchestras of the world. During the years

1883–85, while in Meiningen, Strauss became well acquainted with the poet-musician Alexander Ritter, who interested him in the Wagnerian concept of music and turned him toward the path of the symphonic poem. Strauss's last important work in that field stems from the year 1898, but the dozen or so years following he devoted to the composition of opera and Lieder, so successfully that he now stands as the greatest German composer for voice between the time of Wagner and the present day.

TONE POEMS. Of principal renown among the symphonic poems are *Don Juan* (1888), after a poem by Nikolas Lenau; *Tod und Verklärung* ("Death and Transfiguration," 1889), with a poem by Alexander Ritter affixed to the score after Ritter was well acquainted with Strauss's piece; *Till Eulenspiegels lustige Streiche* ("The Merry Pranks of Till Eulenspiegel," 1895); *Also sprach Zarathustra* ("Thus Spake Zarathustra," 1896), after Friedrich Nietzsche (1844–1900); *Don Quixote* (1897); and *Ein Heldenleben* ("A Hero's Life," 1898). In the symphonic poem a composer may choose one of two means of expression. He may elect to portray in general musical terms a mood or atmosphere, or he may choose to depict a more detailed story or a series of related events. The former usually achieves the best musical result, for the latter often involves the problem of "realism," that is an attempt to depict concrete images by using imitative musical sounds—a process that rarely produces art of great aesthetic value. However, Strauss was able to manage both approaches with about equal success. The first approach was followed, for example, in *Don Juan,* in *Death and Transfiguration,* and in *Thus Spake Zarathustra,* while the second appears in *Till Eulenspiegel* and *Don Quixote.*

Thus Spake Zarathustra is a musical commentary both on Nietzsche's philosophy of the superman and on man's battle with himself. However, Strauss seeks only inspiration from Nietzsche's work and does not try to depict philosophical ideas. He presents the work in nine sections, with titles from Nietzsche's writing scattered throughout the symphonic score, the sections being identified as follows: (1) a powerful orchestral opening declaims Zarathustra's address to the sun,

(2) muted low strings suggest the ghostly forms "Of the Inhabitants of the Unseen World," but faith is reaffirmed in the use of horns and the organ, (3) the organ briefly sings a Gregorian Magnificat in "Of the Great Longing," answered by the Credo plain song in the horns, (4) intense emotions and turbulence speak forth in "Of Joy and Passion," (5) "Dirge" introduces solo cello and English horn, (6) "Of Science" makes use of music's scholarly fugal procedure with further development in (7) "The Convalescent," (8) earthly pleasures are revealed in a waltz in the "Dance Song," and (9) "The Song of the Night Wanderer" comes in after twelve strokes of the midnight bell.

Strauss becomes much more descriptive and realistic in *Till Eulenspiegel.* The source of the program is an old German legend about a rascal called Till Eulenspiegel, who is condemned to die for his pranks but manages to escape his punishment. Strauss changes the script somewhat, and in the symphonic poem Till is hanged. Two themes are assigned as Till's motives: the one is a horn theme of quite a wide range, and the other a bright little rascally clarinet tune (Example 49). Their constant return throughout the music follows the "Rondo" subtitle of the piece. Some of the realistic touches

(a) Horn theme

(b) Clarinet theme

Example 49

occur at such places as the rhythmical hoofbeats of Till's horse as he rides to the market place, and the musical cacophony depicting flying pots and pans and cackling geese when Till crashes the horse into a market stall. The heights of bliss and depths of despair—the two poles of love and courtship as experienced by Till—are portrayed by a long, descending *glissando* on the violin. But the *pièce de résistance* of picture painting is the hanging. The falling trap door is depicted by two notes in the downward interval of a major seventh—played by the tuba—followed by the whine and struggle of the upward-rising clarinet theme; a flute flutter suggests a fight for breath and irregular beats on the timpani signify a few last kicks of the hanged Till's legs (see Example 50).

In spite of their programmatic associations Strauss's symphonic poems seem perfectly acceptable as good music in their

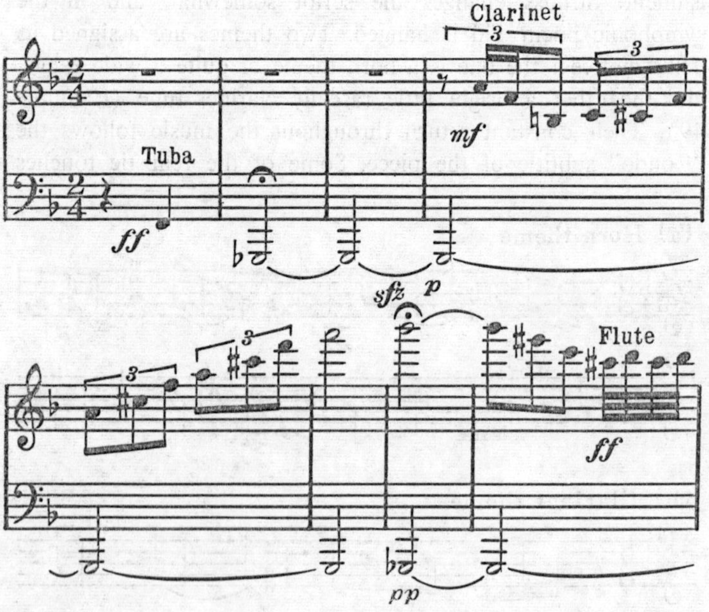

Example 50

own right–that is, music not dependent on a program for its enjoyment. The texture is rich and full and exhibits polyphonic tendencies, and the melodies are built on large lines and show strength and vigor. Strauss was a master of orchestration (he brought Berlioz's *Traité d'instrumentation* up to date as of 1905) and wrote for a large orchestra, introducing new ideas on capabilities and ranges of the instruments, particularly those of the brass section.

OPERAS. Strauss's operatic successes came after the turn of the century. Of his fifteen operas *Salome* (Dresden, 1905), *Elektra* (Dresden, 1909), and *Der Rosenkavalier* ("Cavalier of the Rose," Dresden, 1911) are the most outstanding. *Salome* is a setting of a German translation of Oscar Wilde's one-act play, and librettist Hugo von Hofmannsthal (1874–1929) based his *Elektra* book on Sophocles. The subjects and music of these two operas shocked the theater patrons of the early 20th century. The musical treatment of the subject of sexual perversion in *Salome* and the rather one-sided emphasis on Electra's revengeful nature were almost too much for their first audiences to swallow. Musically speaking, *Salome* may be regarded as a continuation of the Wagnerian tradition of chromatic writing, but with bolder harmonies creating greater dissonance; in *Elektra* passages of lush Romanticism alternate with sections that approach atonal treatment.

In the comedy *Der Rosenkavalier*–also with a libretto by Von Hofmannsthal and considered by many to be Strauss's finest and most spectacular opera–the composer matched the gay, delightful atmosphere of 18th-century Vienna in the time of Maria Theresa by switching from the dark harmonies of *Salome* and the overpowering and often stridently dissonant orchestral score of *Elektra* to charming waltzes and lilting melodies in a lighter musical texture. One should take note, however, that these waltzes are more in the style of Johann Strauss, Jr., than in that of the 18th century. Incidentally, Octavian's soprano part in *Der Rosenkavalier* is a "trouser role"–a female singing a male role, a practice not uncommon in operas of the late 18th and of the 19th centuries, probably having its basis in the *castrati* roles of the early operas.

The trend away from Wagnerian chromaticism toward a Classical diatonicism, which had its beginning in *Der Rosenkavalier,* is more markedly found in Strauss's *Ariadne auf Naxos* ("Ariadne on Naxos"; Stuttgart, 1912). Hofmannsthal wrote the libretto for *Ariadne,* and the books for Strauss's *Die Frau ohne Schatten* ("The Woman Without a Shadow"; Vienna, 1919) and *Arabella* (Dresden, 1933) as well.

SONGS. The songs of Richard Strauss, written for the most part before 1900, reflect, on the one hand, the richness of the Wagnerian technique and, on the other, the passionate lyricism of the Florestan of Schumann's *Davidsbund. Allerseelen* ("All Souls' Day") is most characteristic of Strauss's song style; and *Befreit* ("Made Free"), *Freundliche Vision* ("Friendly Vision"), and *Traum durch die Dämmerung* ("Dream in the Twilight") are Lieder of much beauty. Among his other songs that have remained in favor are to be found *Die Nacht* ("The Night"), *Ständchen* ("Serenade") *Zueignung* ("Dedication"), and *Morgen* ("Tomorrow").

Max Bruch (1838–1920). Max Bruch took little part in the movement toward the new contemporary style, and continued throughout his career to write orchestral and stage works in the Romantic vein. Nevertheless, today's artists perform and speak well of his *Concerto No. 1 in g minor* (Op. 26, 1866) for violin and orchestra, his *Kol Nidrei for Cello and Orchestra* (Op. 47, 1880), and a few other works.

Max Reger (1873–1916). The name of the German musician Max Reger is known particularly to organists who play his *Fantasy and Fugue on B-A-C-H,* Op. 46, his *Variations and Fugue on an Original Theme,* Op. 73, and selections from his many chorale preludes, fantasias, and preludes and fugues. But a few symphonic works have also gained distinction, such as the *Variations and Fugue on a Theme by J. A. Hiller* (Op. 100, 1907) and the *Variations and Fugue on a Theme by Mozart* (Op. 132). As a composer, Reger's Classical and polyphonic leanings can be seen in the forms and titles of his principal works.

ART SONG

Hugo Wolf (1860–1903). Although Hugo Wolf wrote one complete opera (*Der Corregidor;* Mannheim, 1896) and an *Italian Serenade* (1892) for small orchestra (in which the principal melody is an Italian folk song), he is particularly remembered for his Lieder. Wolf began music lessons in piano and violin with his father and later entered the Vienna Conservatory (where, incidentally, his bad conduct caused him to be expelled). He seemed always, throughout his lifetime, to be in dispute with someone or other, and he finally suffered a mental breakdown in 1897 which plagued him the last six years of his life. In his song writing is to be found the influence of Wagner in the "symphonic" nature of some of his piano accompaniments, also in his involved contrapuntal and chromatic style. However, Wolf never allows the vocal line to be dominated by the accompaniment, as often happens in Wagner's operas. It was Wolf himself who called his works "Songs for voice and piano," thus indicating a more important role for the piano than the older accompaniment designations. Wolf's songs are actually small-scale music dramas, gems of mood handlings and characterizations all written in the white heat of inspiration. Like Schumann, he often employed the prelude, interlude, and postlude in the piano part to heighten the mood, but unlike Brahms he made no use of the folk-song type of melody, and seldom used the strophic form.

Wolf concentrated on the works of only a few poets, and he respected their part in the creation of song by acknowledging their names on his manuscripts. The principal Lieder of the composer are represented in five large collections; three of these are identified outright by the name of the authors of the poems, as may be seen in the following table.

TABLE XIX

Title	Published Date
(1) *"Gedichte von Eduard Mörike"*	1889
(2) *"Gedichte von Eichendorf"*	1889
(3) *"Gedichte von Goethe"*	1890
(4) *"Spanisches Liederbuch, nach Heyse und Geibel"*	1891
(5) *"Italienisches Liederbuch, nach Paul Heyse"* (Pt. I)	1892
"Italienisches Liederbuch, nach Paul Heyse" (Pt. II)	1896

Nos. 4 and 5, above, are songs set to German translations from the Spanish and Italian, and all five collections represent a grand total of 214 songs.

OPERETTAS AND OPERA

The large and emotional Wagnerian operas of the 19th century were balanced by the German operettas—clever and colorful works in a lighter vein with spoken dialogue—and also by the *Märchen-oper* ("fairy-tale opera").

Johann Strauss, the **Younger** (1825–99). Perhaps the most famous example of the operetta is the ever-popular *Die Fledermaus* ("The Bat") by Johann Strauss, "The Waltz King." *Die Fledermaus* was first staged in Vienna in 1874 and has remained to this day one of the masterpieces of its kind. Strauss started as an entertainer with a band of fifteen players at a restaurant in Heitzing. He wrote, in addition to his stage works, dance pieces totaling 498 opus numbers; of his waltzes, *The Blue Danube* (1867), *Tales from the Vienna Woods* (1868), *Roses from the South* (1878), and *The Emperor Waltz* (1888) are known throughout the world.

Franz von Suppé (1819–95). Another famous operetta composer was Franz von Suppé. He obtained a measure of success almost equal to that of Offenbach; concerning his operettas, most of which were first produced in Vienna and are known today chiefly through their overtures, the following are important: *Dichter und Bauer* ("Poet and Peasant," 1846), *Die* *schöne Galatea* ("The Beautiful Galatea," 1865), *Leichte Cavallerie* ("Light Cavalry," 1866), *Fatinitza* (1876), and *Boccaccio* (1879).

Engelbert Humperdinck (1854–1921). Engelbert Humperdinck provided the world with one of the most charming of fairy-tale operas with his *Hänsel und Gretel* (Weimar, 1893). It is still regularly produced today during the Christmas season, and children and adults alike flock to hear the lovely melodies and to see the beautiful dances. He also wrote one other famous fairy-tale opera, *Die Königskinder* (1910).

NATIONALISM IN LATER 19TH-CENTURY MUSIC

The movement toward national expression in music in the later 19th century began as a reaction primarily against German music, which had so successfully held the center of the stage throughout the century. This national urge gained momentum especially in those countries that lacked a fully developed musical tradition, and it revealed itself particularly in composers' deliberate use of their country's folk songs and native rhythms, and in their choosing scenes from national history or contemporary life as subjects of their operas and symphonic works.

RUSSIAN MUSIC

Early National Composers. The ground swell of the movement occurred in Russia through the efforts of Michael Glinka (1804–57) in his operas *A Life for the Tsar* (St. Petersburg, 1836) and *Russlan and Ludmilla* (St. Petersburg, 1842). Alexander Dargomyzhsky (1813–69) added his backing with *Russalka* (St. Petersburg, 1856) and *Kamennyi Gost* ("The Stone Guest," after Pushkin's like-named poem), the latter being scored by Rimsky-Korsakov and first produced posthumously in St. Petersburg in 1872. These works, drawing their inspiration for the most part from Russian backgrounds and peoples, laid the foundations for Russian national opera.

Glinka was followed by a group of musicians which came to be known as the "Russian Five" or the "Mighty Five."

The Five. They were: Alexander Borodin, César Cui, Mily Balakirev, Modest Moussorgsky, and Nicolai Rimsky-Korsakov.

Alexander Borodin (1833–87). Alexander Borodin is well known for a few works such as his opera *Prince Igor* (posthumously performed in St. Petersburg in 1890), the two symphonic works *Symphony No. 2 in b minor* (1876, called *"Bogatyr,"* or "Giant," after the heroic character of the music) and *In the Steppes of Central Asia* (1880), and a *String Quartet No. 2 in D* (1885). *Prince Igor* was left unfinished at the composer's death, and was completed by Rimsky-Korsakov and another Russian composer, Alexander Glazunov, (discussed later); but the famous "Polovtsian Dances" from Act II are by Borodin. Borodin incorporated the stylistic traits of Russian folk song into his scores, but chose also to blend in with these Oriental rhythms, melodies, and instrumental colorings.

César Cui (1835–1918). César Cui was the weakest member, musically speaking, of the "Five" and has left the world little of lasting value.

Mily Balakirev (1837–1910). Mily Balakirev is remembered today chiefly through two works. One is a symphonic poem entitled *Russia;* this music was written in 1864 and published in 1869 as "1000 Years," but was revised and rescored in 1882 under the present title. The other is *Islamey* (1869) for piano, an Oriental fantasia that offers many performance difficulties.

Modest Moussorgsky (1839–81). The most inspired and musically gifted of the group was Modest Moussorgsky, but certain deficiencies in compositional technique and degrading personal habits hindered his artistic career. His finest orchestral work is the symphonic fantasy *Night on Bald Mountain* (1867), after Nicolas Gogol's (1809–52) *St. John's Eve.* The suite for piano entitled *Pictures at an Exhibition* (1874, later orchestrated on a commission from Serge Koussevitzky by Maurice Ravel) is well known today. Moussorgsky was also one of Russia's finest song writers. Excellent material is to be found in his cycles *Sunless* (1874; six songs), *Songs and Dances of Death* (1875–

77; four songs, of which the famous *"Trepak"* is No. 3), and *The Nursery* (1868–72; seven children's songs); his *Mephistopheles' Song of the Flea* (1879) is one of the great airs based on Goethe's *Faust*.

His masterpiece–the greatest Russian opera–is *Boris Godunov,* first performed in St. Petersburg in 1874. It is based on a play of the same name by Alexander Pushkin (1799–1837) and on Nicolai Karamzin's (1766–1826) *History of the Russian State*. The opera was revised and reorchestrated by Rimsky-Korsakov in 1896, and in 1941 a third version, with yet another orchestration, was arranged by Dmitri Shostakovich. *Boris Godunov* was cast by Moussorgsky in a loose series of scenes, with little formal plot development. Of tremendous importance is his declamatory style (seen at its best in the "Clock Scene" at the end of Act II and in the "Farewell and Death of Boris" in Act IV), in which a lean but forceful musical texture brings out all the emotional power of the libretto lines.

Outstanding among Moussorgsky's other operas is *Khovantchina* (St. Petersburg, 1886); this opera, too, reveals a concern with Russian history, based, as it is, on a story from the era of Peter the Great. And in a line of summary on Moussorgsky it might be noted that this composer does not often quote Russian folk tunes literally (as he does in the coronation scene of *Boris Godunov*), but the modal qualities and melodic characteristics and repetitive rhythms of these songs permeate his music, as indeed they do in most all works by the national Russian composers.

Nicolai Rimsky-Korsakov (1844–1908). The last composer of the "Five" is Nicolai Rimsky-Korsakov. He was an assiduous collector of Russian folk songs, the influence of which is to be seen in the melodies and harmonies of the classical scores of the artist's own compositions. Rimsky-Korsakov was the best technician and orchestrator of his group, and his symphonic works are consistently interesting and colorful. His *Foundations of Orchestration,* in two volumes, was published posthumously in St. Petersburg in 1913 with illustrations from his own works, and his book on harmony is widely used in Russian schools.

Rimsky-Korsakov's principal symphonic works include the *Symphony No. 2,* Op. 9 ("*Antar,*" written in 1868 and revised 1875 and again in 1897); *Capriccio espagnol* (Op. 34, 1887), an elaboration of popular Spanish melodies; *Scheherazade* (Op. 35, 1888), based on episodes from *The Arabian Nights;* and the *Russian Easter Overture* (Op. 36, 1888). The principal melodic material of the last-named work comes from the *Obikhod,* a book of canticles of the Russian Orthodox Church. Two melodies from this collection are heard in the introduction: "Let God Arise" in the woodwinds, and "An Angel Cried Out," given by solo cello, and these melodies are developed during the course of the composition.

After 1894, Rimsky-Korsakov turned oftener to the opera form. His best-known works in this medium—both with librettos by Vladimir Bielsky—are *Sadko* (Moscow, 1898) and *Le Coq d'or* ("The Golden Cockerel," first performed posthumously in Moscow in 1909). The latter is the only opera by Rimsky-Korsakov performed with any frequency outside of Russia today; it is based on a satirical fairy tale written by Pushkin. But excerpts from *Sadko* (especially the "Sea Episode") and suites from the operas *Snow Maiden* (St. Petersburg, 1882) and *Tsar Saltan* (Moscow, 1900) are still heard with some regularity. Of all the composer's works just mentioned the *Russian Easter Overture* is perhaps the most Russian, whereas the *Scheherazade* and *The Golden Cockerel* each combine Russian and Oriental qualities.

LESS NATIONAL COMPOSERS. Not all the Russian composers of the period so interested themselves in deliberately expressing a national spirit. The composers mentioned below, while unmistakably Russian, are much less nationalistic. They are Anton Rubinstein, Peter Ilyich Tchaikovsky, Alexander Glazunov, Sergei Rachmaninov, and Reinhold Glière.

Anton Rubinstein (1829–94). Anton Rubinstein was the first Russian musician to become famous both as a performer and as a composer. He was one of the great piano virtuosos of the 19th century, second only to the fabulous Liszt. He wrote a number of Russian operas and several piano concertos; his solo piano pieces *Kamennoi Ostrow, Melody in F,* and *Romance* became drawing-room favorites, and his *Ocean Symphony* found a place (during his lifetime) on many orchestral programs in Europe and the United States.

Peter Ilyich Tchaikovsky (1840–93). Born of a well-to-do family, Peter Ilyich Tchaikovsky received a solid education in jurisprudence. But when he reached the age of twenty-one he undertook the study of composition with Anton Rubinstein at the St. Petersburg Conservatory, and after graduation accepted the post of professor of harmony at the Moscow Conservatory. A wealthy widow named Nadezhda von Meck (whom Tchaikovsky never met face-to-face) was to aid his career for many years with commissioned works for large fees and an annuity of six thousand rubles.

Tchaikovsky's principal works in the field of absolute music include the symphonies *No. 4* (Op. 36, 1877), *No. 5* (Op. 64, 1888), and *No. 6* (Op. 74, 1893; the "Pathétique"); the *Violin Concerto in D major* (Op. 35, 1878); and the almost too well-known *Piano Concerto in b♭ minor* (Op. 23, 1875). But the composer is perhaps at his very best in programmatic works such as the symphonic fantasia *Francesca da Rimini* (Op. 32, 1876; after Dante) and the symphonic poems *Romeo and Juliet* (a final revision made in 1880; after Shakespeare) and *Manfred* (Op. 58, 1885; after Byron). The ballet music from *Swan Lake* (Op. 20, 1876) and *Sleeping Beauty* (Op. 66, 1889), along with the ever-popular *Nutcracker Suite* (Op. 71a, 1892), contain some of Tchaikovsky's most charming music. In the medium of opera his *Eugen Onegin* (Moscow, 1879) and *The Queen of Spades* (St. Petersburg, 1890), both based on works by Pushkin, still hold the boards.

Tchaikovsky's *Overture-Fantasy Romeo and Juliet* follows Shakespeare's play rather faithfully, but within the confines of the sonata form. The work begins with a woodwind chorale tune depicting the good Friar Laurence. Next a turbulent orchestral section suggests the feud between the Capulet and Montague houses. Following this is Romeo's passionate love music in a long, sweeping line for English horn and muted violins, accompanied by pizzicato strings and horns in syncopated rhythms. Juliet returns her love as illustrated in a lovely, "rocking" theme for muted and divided strings. But this love bliss is shattered by the return to reality in the feud music. As the tension rises, the amorous themes break in again as the couple's love struggles against family hate. But the timpani (often the instrument of death and trouble in musical literature, symbolically speaking) and a sudden silence (a rest in music is many times as dramatic as sound) foretell the unhappy future. The great tragedy and death of the lovers is painted by a violent cascade of sound in the orchestra. Finally a chorale announces the reconciliation of the feuding houses. The story is told, and a timpani roll writes *finis* to an ancient legend of a splendid but impossible romance.

With regard to Tchaikovsky's fifth and sixth symphonies, *No. 5* (in *e* minor) opens with a clarinet theme ("Fate") that is expanded into a lengthy introduction. The recurrence of this theme in each of the following movements has bestowed the nickname "Fate" symphony upon this work. The second movement has in it one of the most famous French-horn themes of all orchestral literature, and a graceful waltz replaces the traditional 19th-century scherzo as a third movement. The "Fate" theme changes triumphantly from minor to major to open the finale, and this theme is used again later in a majestic close to the entire composition.

The *Symphony No. 6* is a picture of Tchaikovsky's eternal pessimism. Typical is a first-trombone passage in the opening movement–the use of a melodic phrase from the Russian burial service. The second movement lightens in mood and texture, using a lilting 5/4 meter; and the third is a stirring march, using as a thematic foundation an eight-bar oboe phrase found in the march introduction. All the gloom of the initial movement returns in the fourth and final movement, and once this morbid outcry is spent the symphony concludes in a whisper of sound.

Alexander Glazunov (1865–1936). Alexander Glazunov is

remembered for his *Symphony No. 6 in c minor* (Op. 58, 1896), the ballet *The Seasons* (Op. 67, 1900), and a fine *Violin Concerto in a minor* (Op. 82, 1904–15).

Sergei Rachmaninov (1873–1943). Sergei Rachmaninov wrote two piano concertos that are still frequently performed, *No. 2 in c minor* (Op. 18, 1901) and *No. 3 in d minor* (Op. 30, 1909); a symphonic poem *The Isle of the Dead* (Op. 29, 1907) inspired by Arnold Böcklin's painting; and the *Symphony in e minor* (Op. 27, 1907).

Reinhold Glière (1875–1956). Reinhold Glière was an avid collector of Eastern European folk songs–a fact that was (not surprisingly) to influence his musical composition. Romanticism and Russian nationalism are successfully fused in his third symphony *Ilya Murometz* (1911), this work being a description of the life of a legendary Russian hero. After the Russian Revolution, Glière adhered faithfully to the party line, and his esteemed ballet *The Red Poppy* (first performed in Moscow in 1927) praised and glorified the political policies of the U.S.S.R. He twice won the Stalin prize, in 1948 for his *String Quartet No. 4* and again in 1950 for the ballet *The Bronze Horseman.*

Alexander Scriabin (1872–1915). One Russian composer–Alexander Scriabin–stands alone. His later works are very colorful and original, and he is particularly famous for a "mystic chord" that could be spelled from the root upward as C-F♯-B♭-E-A-D and that served as a basis for all his mature compositions. He is noted for the two symphonic pieces *Poem of Ecstasy* (Op. 54, 1908) and *Prometheus: The Poem of Fire,* with piano, organ, chorus, and color keyboard (Op. 60, 1910; the color keyboard was a device built to project upon a screen ever-changing colors according to the spectrum scale). He is noted also for ten piano sonatas (none over twenty minutes long) and especially for the last six such sonatas (written 1908–13). The most famous of all the sonatas is *No. 9* (Op. 68, 1913), called the "Black Mass," as against *No. 7* (Op. 64, 1911), which is the "White Mass."

BOHEMIAN (CZECH) MUSIC

Bedřich Smetana, Antonin Dvořák, and Leoš Janáček are the three most important Czech nationalistic composers.

Bedřich Smetana (1824–84). Smetana's *Bartered Bride* (Prague, 1866) was Bohemia's first folk opera and remains the greatest work of its genre from that land. And in his symphonic compositions this composer was one of the first to demonstrate how Western harmony, melody, and techniques of thematic development could be successfully combined with folk songs and dances. This he showed in his cycle of symphonic poems *Má vlast* ("My Country," composed during the years 1874–77), of which the second number is the popular *Vltava* ("The Moldau"). Another fine work by Smetana is the autobiographical string quartet *Aus meinem Leben* ("From My Life," 1877).

Antonin Dvořák (1841–1904). Antonin Dvořák used Bohemian folk songs and rhythms (for instance, in such as the *Slavonic Dances,* Opp. 46, 1878, and 72, 1886), but his style was still basically that of German Romanticism. He knew Brahms and his music, and during his lifetime he visited England and the United States. In 1892 Dvořák came to New York, where he served as director of the National Conservatory for three years. It was at this time, during a visit to the Bohemian colony at Spillville, Iowa, that he completed his *Symphony in e minor* (Op. 95, "From the New World") and the *American Quartet* (Op. 96, 1893), which suggest Negro and Indian melodies, respectively. More Slavic in nature is the *Piano Quintet* (Op. 81, 1887), in which folk rhythms receive full play in the last two movements. Dvořák's symphonies have recently been renumbered as follows *No. 1 in c* ("Bells of Zlonice," Op. 3, 1865); *No. 2 in B♭* (Op. 4, 1865); *No. 3 in E♭* (Op. 10, 1873); *No. 4 in d* (Op. 13, 1874); *No. 5 in F* (Op. 76, 1875, revised in 1887); *No. 6 in D* (Op. 60, 1880); *No. 7 in d* (Op. 70, 1885); *No. 8 in G* (Op. 88, 1889); and *No. 9 in e* ("New World," Op. 95, 1893). The listening public of today will hear with any regularity only Nos. 5–9. Master violinists and cellists of the present day find pleasure in playing, respectively, Dvořák's *Concerto in a minor* (Op. 53, 1880) and *Concerto in b minor* (Op. 104, 1895); the Op. 53 violin concerto uses Bohemian folk material in the slow movement and in the finale, but the cello work (written during Dvořák's stay in the United States) has some themes that reflect the style of the Negro spiritual.

Leoš Janáček (1854–1928). Leoš Janáček is certainly the most nationalistic of this Czech trio of composers; he is still not as widely known as the first two men, although the performance of his music is on the upswing; Janáček's masterwork is the opera *Jenufa* ("Her Foster Daughter," Brno, 1904), in which the melodies and rhythms bear a close relationship to speech inflections. Other notable compositions by this composer are a symphonic rhapsody *Taras Bulba* (1918), based on Gogol's novel of like name and a *Glagolitic Mass* (1926), also called the *Slavonik Mass* or *Festival Mass,* to a text in old Slavonic.

Bohuslav Martinů (1890–1959). A name prominent in more recent Czech musical history is that of Bohuslav Martinů. His compositions have successfully fused traditional dance music and folk tunes with the modern idiom; his style is neo-Classical, but with more than a trace of Romanticism. Martinů's love for his homeland is heard in the somber tones of his *Concerto for Two String Orchestras* (1940), written after the betrayal of Czechoslovakia at Munich, and in the *Memorial to Lidice* (1943). A compilation of his compositions includes five string quartets and other chamber music, six symphonies and miscellaneous symphonic pieces, ten operas, ten ballets, several choral works, and songs and piano pieces.

NORWEGIAN AND DANISH MUSIC

Edvard Grieg (1843–1907). Norway's greatest composer is Edvard Grieg. The feel of his native land, its forests and fjords, is present in all his music. Although Grieg made little actual use of Norwegian folk songs and folk dances, his art often sounds closely related to authentic folk materials. Perhaps he is at his best in the ten books of *Lyric Pieces* for piano, composed during the thirty-four years between 1867 and 1901; these often portray some facet of Norwegian life. He also composed a *Piano Concerto in a minor* (Op. 16, 1868; revised 1907), which Liszt praised. On February 24, 1876, the play *Peer Gynt* by Henrik Ibsen (1828–1906), with incidental music by Grieg, was produced in Christiania (now Oslo). Grieg arranged two suites from this music: the first as Op. 46, in 1888, and the second as Op. 55, 1891. The first suite, with its movements entitled "Morning," "Ase's Death," "Anitra's Dance," and "In the Hall of the Mountain King," has been the most popular.

Carl Nielsen (1865–1931). Denmark's foremost composer of the late 19th and early 20th centuries was Carl Nielsen. His carly compositional style followed the art of his teacher Niels Gade (1817–90), who is said to have founded the modern Scandinavian school of composition by fusing Danish folk melodies with the Germanic style. The music of Liszt and Grieg, as well, appears to have influenced the young Nielsen, but later his compositions show the traits of French Impressionism, the somewhat involved texture of late-19th-century chromaticism, and the aversion to holding to a single tonal center. Nielsen created harmonizations for many Danish folk songs, and it is interesting to note how he rejects chromaticism in the climactic passages of, say, his six symphonies and turns instead in these passages to a diatonic formula reminiscent of folk-song style.

FINNISH MUSIC

Jean Sibelius (1865–1957). Jean Sibelius took his musical training at the Helsinki Conservatory and also in Berlin and Vienna. But upon his return, in 1891, to Finland he leaned away from German Romanticism toward a national expression. Yet, although the dates of many of his compositions extend well into the 20th century, his style remained basically that of post-Romanticism.

As might be expected, Sibelius's nationalistic tendencies find their fullest flower in his symphonic poems. *En Saga* (Op. 9, written in 1892 and revised in 1901) has no definite program and is nationalistic only through Sibelius's inherent Finnish qualities. *The Swan of Tuonela* (Op. 22, 1893) is the third of four *Legends* taken from the *Kalevala,* the national epic of Finland. Tuonela is a land of death, the hell of Finnish mythology. Around this land is a swift black river on which a swan floats and sings (a swan sings only at the time it dies). In the symphonic poem a gentle melody played by the English horn serves as the swan theme; upon its last return Sibelius does a small bit of picture painting by having the violinists tap the strings with the backs of their bows in imitation of the flapping of the swan's wings.

In its defiance of tyranny, *Finlandia* (Op. 26, written in 1899 and revised the next year) became a virtual second Finnish national anthem. It was once thought that this work was composed around folk songs, but the material is the composer's own. In fact Sibelius is not known to have used any actual folk songs in his scores, but only their modal structures and colorings. *Pohjola's Daughter* (Op. 49, 1906) is again based on the *Kalevala.* Väinamöinen, a minstrel from Pohja, courts "the daughter of the North" by performing heroic deeds, in the course of which he suffers a grievous wound. Fortunately he recovers, and Sibelius's music ends peacefully.

The last symphonic poem, *Tapiola,* Op. 112, was written in 1925. Tapio is the name of an ancient forest god of Finland, and Sibelius paints here, in a somewhat Classical style, the dark and brooding forests of his native land.

Sibelius wrote seven symphonies. The first two reflect the influences of Tchaikovsky in their sweeping melodies and emotional warmth. After the *Symphony No. 3* (Op. 52, 1907) is seen a leaner texture, a simplification of harmonic vocabulary, and a change in melodic treatment to a greater use of episodic subjects and motives.

In his later works Sibelius tends to build motives into themes, instead of the earlier Romantic practice of breaking down themes into motives for use in developmental procedures.

He stays pretty much away from dissonant harmonies and unrelated tonal centers, but an exception to this general statement can be found in the *Symphony No. 6* (Op. 104, 1923). The symphonic form becomes more compressed in the course of his seven symphonies, until a symphony in one movement is reached in his final work (Op. 105, 1924) in this genre. *Symphony No. 2 in D major* (Op. 43, 1901) and *Symphony No. 4 in a minor* (Op. 63, 1911) remain today the most popular and most frequently performed of all his symphonies.

A single concerto by Sibelius is the *Violin Concerto in d minor* (Op. 47, 1903), a lyrical and rhapsodic work in a warm Romantic style. The celebrated *Valse Triste* (Op. 44) was written as incidental music for Järnefelt's play *Kuolema,* first presented in 1903. Not to go unnoticed is his fine *String Quartet in d minor* ("*Voces intimae,*" Op. 56, 1909).

Sibelius was not at his best as a song writer, and yet works like *Black Roses, In the Field a Maiden Sits, The Tree,* and *Was It a Dream?* appear on present-day song recitals from time to time.

SPANISH MUSIC

As part of the national movement, the Spanish composers Isaac Albéniz, Enrique Granados, and Manuel de Falla turned to the colorful and exciting rhythms and melodies of their native land.

Isaac Albéniz (1860–1909). Isaac Albéniz wrote his best works for the piano, and among these is found a suite of twelve pieces entitled *Iberia* (1906–09, published in four books of three pieces each). The individual selections of *Iberia* use dances and songs of Spain and portray scenes of Spanish life.

Enrique Granados (1867–1916). Another Spanish composer of this period, Enrique Granados, wrote in a Romantic idiom replete with dashing native rhythms. His masterpiece *Goyescas,* first written for piano, but with the identical music being later used in the opera of the same name (New York, 1916), was inspired by the works of the Spanish painter Goya.

Granados's *Danzas españolas* ("Spanish Dances") have also contributed to his fame.

Manuel de Falla (1876–1946). Manuel de Falla, being something of a mystic, sought to suggest the essence of Spanish life in his music rather than to picture its realism. Thus it is not surprising to find also the influences of the French Impressionists in his composition. His principal works are an opera *La Vida breve* ("Life Is Short," Nice, 1913), two ballets *El Amor brujo* ("Wedded by Witchcraft," Madrid, 1915) and *El Sombrero de tres picos* ("The Three-Cornered Hat," London, 1919), and a symphonic work *Nights in the Gardens of Spain* (1915). *El Amor brujo* has had many performances in a suite arrangement, and *The Three-Cornered Hat* is based on a short story of Spanish life by the Spanish writer and statesman Pedro Alarcón (1833–91). De Falla's most Impressionistic work is the *Nights in the Gardens of Spain,* in three movements for piano and orchestra.

ITALIAN MUSIC

Italian music of the late 19th century is primarily operatic. There is less national coloring except perhaps in the use of the *verismo,* or "realistic," style, in which everyday situations are presented in an attempted realistic manner.

Pietro Mascagni (1863–1945). Pietro Mascagni is remembered today for but a single work, the one-act opera *Cavalleria rusticana* ("Rustic Chivalry," Rome, 1890); it is based on a tale with a Sicilian background by Giovanni Verga (1840–1922).

Ruggiero Leoncavallo (1858–1919). Ruggiero Leoncavallo is another composer whose fame rests on one opera, this time the two-act *I Pagliacci* ("The Clowns," Milan, 1892); the plot revolves around a performance being given by traveling players in a village in Calabria (southwestern Italy). Of worldwide fame are the baritone Prologue and Canio's aria *"Vesti la giubba,"* which closes Act I.

Umberto Giordano (1867–1948). Umberto Giordano should be mentioned here, if only for his grand opera *Andrea Chénier*

(Milan, 1896). The libretto is based on the period of the French Revolution; André Marie de Chénier (1762–94) was a French poet of some repute who espoused the revolution in its early years, but later criticized Robespierre and subsequently was guillotined. In his opera Giordano made use of songs of the revolution, including *La Marseillaise* (words and music by the artillery officer Claude Rouget de Lisle in 1792).

Giacomo Puccini (1858–1924). The most important Italian opera composer following Verdi was Giacomo Puccini. He came from a long family line of musicians, and in due time he was sent for his musical education to the Istituto Musicale of Lucca, where he became a capable performer on the piano and organ. Sometime later financial assistance from a relative and from Queen Margherita made it possible for Puccini to attend the Milan Conservatory; there he studied with the famous Amilcare Ponchielli, who not only taught the young composer how to write for the stage, but also introduced him to the right people as an aid to his budding career.

Puccini ranged far afield for his opera librettos; only one of his famous operas has an Italian background. His first success was *Manon Lescaut* (Turin, 1893), with a plot after the novel *Histoire du Chevalier Des Grieux et de Manon Lescaut* (1731), by Antoine Prévost d'Exiles, known as Abbé Prévost (1697–1763).

His next opera was *La Bohème,* first produced at Turin in 1896. It deals with bohemian life in Paris as described in the famous novel *Scènes de la vie de bohème,* by Henri Murger (1822–61). The tenor aria "*Che gelida manina*" ("How cold is your little hand") and Mimi's "*Mi chiamano Mimi*" ("They call me Mimi") from this opera have both gained wide popularity.

The action of *Tosca* (Rome, 1900), based on the celebrated play by Victorien Sardou (1831–1908), takes place in Rome near the turn of the 19th century. One of the greatest songs of the opera is the soprano aria "*Vissi d'arte, vissi d'amore*" ("I lived for art and love"), as sung by Tosca in Act II.

In 1898 the American novelist John Luther Long (1861–

1927) wrote a short story for *Century Magazine* entitled "Madame Butterfly." It was adapted for the stage by David Belasco and was subsequently used as the basis for an opera by Puccini, produced at La Scala, Milan, in 1904. Its debut was not impressive, but in time this opera became one of Puccini's greatest successes. Butterfly's aria *"Un bel dì vedremo"* ("One fine day we shall see") of Act II has become one of the most famous songs of operatic literature.

A few other Puccini operas, of lesser importance, might still be mentioned. A touch of *verismo* is blended with romance in *La Fanciulla del West* ("The Girl of the Golden West"); this opera, on an American subject drawn from a play by Belasco, was given its première performance in 1910 at the Metropolitan Opera House in New York. Also opening at the "Met" (in 1918) was the triptych (*Il Trittico*) of one-act operas entitled *Il Tabarro* ("The Cloak"), *Suor Angelica* ("Sister Angelica"), and *Gianni Schicchi*. Each of the three had its own special style and character, the first being a realistic melodrama, the second a miracle play, and *Gianni Schicchi* (the most popular) reflecting the spirit of 18th-century Italian *opera buffa*. *Turandot* (Milan, 1926), fashioned after a play by the writer Gasparo Gozzi (1713–86), lacked the final scene at the time of Puccini's death, and the task of completing this work fell to the eminent opera composer Franco Alfano (1876–1954).

Italo Montemezzi (1875–1952). The early decades of the 20th century witnessed the fading of realism in Italian opera, and a tendency toward a surge of neo-Romanticism in a curious blend of Italian *bel canto* with German Wagnerianism and French Impressionism. This new trend is especially prominent in the operas of Italo Montemezzi, and especially in his *L'amore dei tre re* ("The Love of Three Kings," Milan, 1913) and his *La Nave* ("The Ship," Milan, 1918). *L'amore dei tre re* has been called the finest Italian tragic opera since Verdi's *Otello* and has become a part of the repertoire of opera houses the world over.

Ildebrando Pizzetti (1880–). Pizzetti's operas have also been written in the neo-Romantic harmonic idiom, with traces of Impressionism still present. The Wagnerian handling of the leitmotif has been altered in Pizzetti's works to a mosaic of themes not given to recurrence. Dramatic touches of skilled theatrical writing are evident early in his career in both his *Fedra* (Milan, 1915) and the biblical *Debora e Jaele* (Milan, 1922). His most famous work is *Fra Gherardo* (Milan, 1928); also highly regarded is his *Assassinio nella cattedrale* ("Murder in the Cathedral," Milan, 1958), based on a drama written in 1935 by T. S. Eliot dealing with the assassination of St. Thomas à Becket.

Ottorino Respighi (1879–1936). Although Respighi wrote nearly a dozen works for the theater, he is best remembered for his symphonic poems *Le Fontane di Roma* ("The Fountains of Rome," 1917), *I Pini di Roma* ("The Pines of Rome," 1924), and *Feste romane* ("Roman Festivals," 1929). These titles suggest the national approach, but in reality the style is one of Debussian Impressionism, Strauss post-Romanticism, and bright flashes of Rimsky-Korsakov instrumental color all put together by one of the finest Italian orchestrators of the early 20th century.

ENGLISH MUSIC

Sir Edward Elgar (1857–1934). During this period in England it was Sir Edward Elgar who came as close as any other English musician to being a national composer. His most popular work today is probably the *"Enigma" Variations* (Op. 36, 1899) for orchestra, the fourteen variations representing fourteen of Elgar's intimate friends. To identify each, he set initials or a nickname before the corresponding variation. The term *"Enigma"* comes from the belief that there is supposedly a hidden theme somewhere in the work; but, imaginary or real, it has never been identified.

Another work for orchestra is the overture *Cockaigne* (Op. 40, 1901), subtitled "In London Town," which paints in musical tones the city of London in the time of King Edward VII as seen through the eyes of two strolling lovers. Between 1901 and 1907 Elgar wrote four *Pomp and Circumstance* marches (Op. 39), a fifth being added in 1930. The first of these, in *D* major, is famous the world over, and the melody of the second part of this march has been associated with the text "Land of hope and glory." Many consider Elgar's oratorio *The Dream of Gerontius* (Op. 38, 1900) to be his masterpiece; it is based on a dramatic poem of Cardinal John Henry Newman (1801–90), a monologue describing a soul's departing from the body.

Arthur Sullivan (1842–1900). Just about this same period Arthur Sullivan was creating a special brand of comic opera. After 1871 he teamed with W. S. Gilbert, the playwright whose scintillating verses when coupled with Sullivan's delightful music produced a truly British light opera that has provided entertainment for vast numbers of listeners in English-speaking countries. Outstanding among the "Gilbert and Sullivan" operas are *H. M. S. Pinafore* (1878), *The Pirates of Penzance* (1879), *Iolanthe* (1882), *The Mikado* (1885), *The Yeomen of the Guard* (1888), and *The Gondoliers* (1889). These operas were often performed at the London court, and gained their creators such distinction that both men were knighted.

Frederick Delius (1862–1934). To the disgust of Frederick Delius's merchant father (who would never listen to a note of his son's music), young Delius stubbornly insisted on a career in music, and finally secured parental permission for study in Leipzig. While living in that part of the world, he met Grieg, a meeting that was to shape to a degree the future musical style of the young Englishman. But Delius was a distinct personality, and the Grieg stylistic influences as well as the devices of Impressionism found in his music (Delius lived in France for forty-six years of his life) are blended with his own often dissonant chromatic idiom in a style of complete individualism. Delius found a champion in the great English conductor Sir Thomas Beecham, who made the world familiar with the symphonic works *Over the Hills and Far Away* (1895); *In a Summer Garden* (1908); the English rhapsody *Brigg Fair* (1907), using as its main theme a folk song of English extraction; *On Hearing the First Cuckoo in Spring* and *Summer Night on the River,* the two first presented at the same concert in Leipzig in 1913; and the vocal work *Sea Drift* (1903), for baritone soloist, chorus, and orchestra on a poem by Walt Whitman.

AMERICAN MUSIC

Edward MacDowell (1861–1908). Edward MacDowell, through study and residence in Germany, was greatly influenced by German Romanticism. As the holder of the first university chair of music–now named after him–in the United States (at Columbia University, New York, 1896–1904), he espoused American nationalism but not on the basis of the then current Russian or Bohemian methods. For all that, MacDowell himself never really came to grips with nationalism, his attempts in that direction lying in his *Suite No. 2* ("Indian") for orchestra (Op. 48), first performed by the Boston Symphony in 1895, and in some piano works in the collections *Woodland Sketches* (Op. 51, 1896) and *New England Idyls* (Op. 62, 1902). In the field of absolute music he is best remembered for his *Piano Concerto No. 2* (Op. 23), first performed in New York City (1889) with the composer as soloist and Theodore Thomas conducting; and notable also is his *Piano Sonata No. 4* ("Keltic," Op. 59, 1901), which is dedicated to Grieg.

Charles Ives (1874–1954). Charles Ives chose not to engage professionally in the field of music, but to combine the insurance business with composing. This way he felt he could write as he pleased, and his musical integrity could not be impugned. And write as he pleased is exactly what he did. Musical passages involving polytonality, cross-rhythms, tone clusters, dissonances, wide skips of melody, quarter tones, and strange rhythmic patterns are set against other passages in the common harmonic practice, sometimes even using Presbyterian church hymns. He was not only the first modern American composer, but also one of the most original composers of his period in the world.

But today Ives is known for only a half-dozen or so compositions. His *Symphony No. 3,* written in 1904 and revised in 1911, was first performed in 1945; it was awarded the Pulitzer Prize in music in 1947. There are definitely national touches amid the originality of his compositions, as can be seen in such works as his *Sonata No. 2* for piano ("Concord, Mass., 1840–1860"), completed in 1915, and the symphonic work *Three Places in New England* (1914).

Charles Martin Loeffler (1861–1935). Born in Alsace, Charles Martin Loeffler lived in many countries of Europe and studied music in Berlin and Paris before he finally settled in the United States in 1881. He and Charles Griffes represent the major American composers identified with Impressionism. Loeffler's style embodies modal sounds in shifting harmonies in a loosely constructed texture, and his art has been credited with breaking the chain of American dependence on German 19th-century music. His most enduring work is *A Pagan Poem* (after Virgil), a piece that started in 1901 as chamber music but was reconstructed by the composer during 1905–06 for piano and orchestra.

Charles Tomlinson Griffes (1884–1920). In comparison with Loeffler, Charles T. Griffes had a greater talent but a shorter life span. French Impressionism and Oriental influences are quite strong in his music; Griffes's programmatic pieces for piano and for orchestra show his fondness for the exotic and the fanciful. He too studied in Berlin; upon his return to the United States he accepted a position as music teacher at the Hackley School for Boys at Tarrytown, New York, where he remained until his death. Griffes's music has withstood changing times fairly well. Among his still-popular works may be found *The White Peacock* (the first of *Four Roman Sketches* written for piano [1917] and later transcribed by the composer for orchestra [1919]), *Poem* for flute and orchestra (1918), and *The Pleasure Dome of Kubla Khan* (after Samuel Coleridge), first performed by the Boston Symphony Orchestra in 1919.

FRANCE AND IMPRESSIONISM

SYMPHONIC MUSIC

As an instructor of organ at the Paris Conservatory, César Franck founded a French school that has as its core a polyphonic compositional style geared to Classical forms, and featuring a symphonic and leitmotif treatment of lyric drama.

César Franck (1822–90). Born in Liège, Belgium, he spent the creative part of his musical life in Paris. He entered the Paris Conservatory as a student in 1837, where much later in his career (1872) he returned to take up the post of professor of organ. His fame was to be made as organist of St. Clothilde, a position he held from 1858 until his death. Franck contributed at least one fine work to solo piano literature with his *Prelude, Chorale, and Fugue* (1884), but is perhaps best remembered as a composer for the organ. Present-day organists choose much of their Romantic literature from his *Six Pieces* (including the *Grande pièce symphonique*), his *Three Pieces* (including *Pièce héroïque*), and the *Three Chorales* (1890).

With such works as the *Piano Quintet in f minor* (1879), the *Violin Sonata in A* (1886), and the *String Quartet in D* (1889), Franck founded the modern French school of chamber music composition. All these compositions make use of cyclical themes–themes from the early movements reappearing either verbatim or transformed in later movements. Franck's *Violin Sonata* is one of his finest works; the piece remains fresh and interesting from start to finish, and the canon of the final *Allegretto poco mosso* movement is splendid.

Franck's *Symphonic Variations* (1885) for piano and orchestra is an example of a new and freer style introduced into the variation form in the late 19th century. A departure from the customary procedure is the introduction of a second theme in the work; a combination of variations on this second theme with those of the first theme gives the entire composition the character of a set of double variations. Franck's *Symphony in d minor* (1888) was treated badly by both the members of the orchestra and the listening audience on its first hearing, but the work has continually grown in popularity, and today it is considered a masterpiece among Franck's compositions.

Vincent d'Indy (1851–1931). Franck's most famous pupil was Vincent d'Indy, who as director of the Schola Cantorum (founded 1894 and opened in 1896) continued teaching the principles of his master. D'Indy's lyric drama *Fervaal* (Op. 40, Brussels, 1897) shows Wagnerian influences also, as can be seen in the fact that the composer wrote the poem used in the work and in the music itself. He had great admiration for Wagner's music; he was present when the first complete performance of *The Ring* was given at Bayreuth, and he also made frequent trips to Munich to hear all of Wagner's operas presented there.

Symphonic works for which he is noted include the *Symphony on a French Mountain Air,* with a prominent part for piano (Op. 25, 1886); a *Symphony in B♭ Major* (Op. 57, 1903); the symphonic variations *Istar* (Op. 42, 1896), a reverse presentation in which the variations are given first and a simple statement of the theme concludes the work; and a symphonic poem *Summer Day on the Mountain* (Op. 61, 1905), extolling the countryside of the Cévennes, where D'Indy liked to spend his summers. A final work occasionally performed is the *Violin Sonata in C* (Op. 59, 1904).

Paul Dukas (1865–1935). Paul Dukas was a composer who wrote somewhat in the same style as Franck and D'Indy. He is remembered today chiefly for his symphonic poem *L'Apprenti sorcier* ("The Sorcerer's Apprentice," 1897), a work that has gained great popularity.

Édouard Lalo (1823–92). The Spanish descent of the French composer Édouard Lalo comes to the fore in the sparkling Spanish rhythms inherent in his music. Skilled in performance on the violin and the viola, this composer had talent for composition that is best revealed in his world-famous *Symphonie espagnole* for violin and orchestra, first performed by Sarasate in 1875. Of importance, too, is his *Violin Concerto* (1874) and his *Concerto in d minor for Cello and Orchestra* (1877);

an opera *Le Roi d'Ys,* based on a Breton legend and combining scintillating rhythms with colorful harmonies, was a smashing success at its Paris première in 1888 and has since remained in the repertory.

Emmanuel Chabrier (1841–94). Another Frenchman, Emmanuel Chabrier, was a composer of several light operas, but again it was a trip to Spain that produced the inspiration for his most famous work *España* ("Spain"), a rhapsody for orchestra introduced in Paris in 1883. A number of his piano works are also popular. Best known among these are the *Marche française* (1888), which reached its definitive form when the composer orchestrated the piece and renamed it the *Joyeuse marche* in 1890, and the *Bourrée fantasque* (1891), written in homage to Chabrier's province of Auvergne (where some believe the bourrée dance form originated); this piece, too, was later scored for orchestra by Felix Mottl, and again by Charles Koechlin.

Ernest Chausson (1855–99). A pupil of Franck, Ernest Chausson wrote a number of stage works in the late-19th-century style, but found his greatest success in the symphonic medium. Chausson's finest and most enduring work is the *Symphony in B♭ Major* (1898), written with a high degree of French refinement and emotional restraint. Also popular with violinists is the *Poème* for violin and orchestra (1897), which leans toward the Impressionistic style and yet is not to be associated with it.

Camille Saint-Saëns (1835–1921). In late-19th-century French composition Camille Saint-Saëns took a path somewhat different from that of Franck and his pupils. Saint-Saëns's eclectic style involved a thicker texture in harmonic and orchestral techniques, encased in a polyphonic fabric, a style unfamiliar to a French public that seemed to prefer a lighter music. Thus his recognition was rather slow in coming in his homeland, and as a matter of fact his opera *Samson et Dalila* (Op. 47) was first performed at Weimar (in German) in 1877. However, by the end of his life Saint-Saëns was regarded as a symbol of French traditionalism. Actually his influence was considerable as a teacher of piano at the École Niedermeyer (where one of his pupils was Gabriel Fauré), and also as one of the founders of the Société Nationale de Musique (1871) established to encourage French composers in their art. Some of Saint-Saëns's best symphonic works are the *Piano Concerto No. 2 in g minor* (Op. 22, 1868); a *Concerto for Cello and Orchestra* (Op. 33, 1873); four symphonic poems, notably *Danse macabre* (Op. 40, 1874); the *Concerto in b minor for Violin and Orchestra* (Op. 61, 1880); and the *Symphony in c minor* (Op. 78, 1886, with organ and two pianos).

Gabriel Fauré (1845–1924). Although firmly grounded in the art of composition by Saint-Saëns, Gabriel Fauré did not use the heavier textures of his teacher. He employed instead a light and airy fabric in an original style faintly touched with modality and dissonance, a vague forerunner of Impressionism. Thus his music gained favor more quickly in France than had that of his master; yet it is this very factor in his art–an art that often approaches the *salon* style in its light texture–that has worked against its ready acceptance outside of his native country. Nevertheless, a number of Fauré's compositions are prominent in the present-day scene.

Fauré's *Requiem* (Op. 48, 1887) is frequently performed, and the *Violin Sonata in A* (Op. 13, 1876), the *Piano Quintet in c minor* (Op. 115, 1921), and the *String Quartet in e minor* (Op. 121, 1924) are well regarded in the field of chamber music. In the symphonic field the incidental music (Op. 80) to *Pelléas et Mélisande,* of Maurice Maeterlinck (1862–1949), was first performed in London in 1898. Of particular significance are his songs, in which the precise moldings of the melodic line are in the best traditions of French song literature. Artful settings of poems by the Frenchman Paul Verlaine (1844–96) are found in the *Cinq mélodies* (Op. 58, 1890) and in the cycle *La Bonne chanson* (Op. 61, 1892). In all his works Fauré preferred Classical clarity to virtuosity, and this he passed on to his famous pupil Maurice Ravel and to one of the greatest of contemporary musical pedagogues, Nadia Boulanger (1887–).

ART SONG

Henri Duparc (1848–1933). Franck considered Henri Duparc one of his most gifted students. He stands with Fauré as the creator of the modern French art song. Add the name Debussy to this pair and the trio probably comprises the three greatest masters of French song of all time. Duparc's health failed in his thirty-seventh year, and he did not compose after that age; since he had always worked slowly, his fame today rests on some fifteen songs. Among these Classical control is maintained in *Chanson triste* ("Sad Song") and *Extase* ("Ecstasy") in spite of the Wagnerian richness of the latter; *Le Manoir de Rosemonde* ("The House of Rosemonde") has its fine dramatic moments; and *Soupir* ("Sighing") represents a passionate outpouring of the composer's soul. *L'Invitation au voyage* ("Invitation to the Voyage") has been called one of Duparc's most perfect songs, for here Baudelaire's imaginative poetry is wonderfully heightened through an association with a rapturous musical lyricism.

LATE FRENCH ROMANTIC OPERA

Continuing Charles Gounod's style of lyric opera, Ambroise Thomas (1811–96) composed his melodious *Mignon* (Paris, 1866), based on Goethe's *Wilhelm Meister*. Received into the opera repertory, it gained world-wide performance.

Jules Massenet (1842–1912). In the same sentimental vein Thomas's pupil Jules Massenet contributed *Hérodiade* (1881), *Manon* (Paris, 1884), on the same subject as the previously mentioned *Manon Lescaut,* by Puccini, and *Thaïs* (Paris, 1894). Thaïs, heroine of the historical novel by Anatole France (1844–1924), was famous for her great beauty and her great vices. Massenet's "Meditation" for violin and orchestra from *Thaïs* is known to young and old.

Georges Bizet (1838–75). From the pen of Georges Bizet came the opera *Carmen* (Paris, 1875), perhaps the most popular opera in the repertoire; it is based on a story by Prosper Mérimée. A Spanish plot and music embodying Spanish melodies and dance patterns (although written by a French musician, which leads Spanish musicians to remark occasionally that there is nothing at all Spanish about the opera) make up a work that takes a first step toward the realistic type called *verismo*. It is doubtful if a more colorful and entertaining opera has ever been written. An earlier opera *Les Pêcheurs de perles* ("The Pearl Fishers," Paris, 1863), more in the style of Gounod, still receives performances in Europe. Two orchestral suites from the incidental music for Daudet's play *L'Arlésienne* (1872) and the youthful *Symphony No. 1 in C Major* constitute Bizet's major successes in the symphonic medium.

Gustave Charpentier (1860–1956). The next step toward naturalism (combined with nostalgia, symbolism, and sentiment) in French opera occurs in Gustave Charpentier's *Louise* (Paris, 1900). The sounds and happenings of city life in Paris are presented in a moving story set to delightful music. This opera stands as Charpentier's one great contribution to the art of music and is a world-wide favorite of opera-house audiences.

DEBUSSY AND IMPRESSIONISM

Impressionism may be defined as a type of realism in which the primary aim is to portray the artist's immediate sensory reaction or "impression" rather than the objective characteristics found in the observance of a scene or event. Thus a musical work of Impressionism is always a kind of program music, albeit the program is rarely other than a mere suggestion. As with the rest of Impressionistic art, the heart of Impressionistic music can be found in the terms "color" and "light"–in melody, rhythms, harmony, and often in orchestration. The Symbolist poets Verlaine, Maeterlinck, and Mallarmé not only attempted to express ideas and emotions by symbolic words, but also insisted that the musical sounds (color) of the French language be preserved. The Impressionistic painters, of whom Claude Monet was the leading representative, thought in terms of the immediate and over-all impression of the subject on the mind of the artist, and believed that light, shade, and the reflection of light were of the greatest importance with relation to the coloristic qualities of the subject.

The short brush strokes used by Impressionistic painters in placing color on their canvasses are reflected in music in the short melodic lines of narrow range. In orchestral works the frequent change of instruments sounding these melodic bits matches the many colors of the Impressionistic painter's art. Musical works in this style add further melodic color through their use of pentatonic, modal, and whole-tone scale patterns. Rhythms tend not to be sharp and clear-cut, but flow onward without a strong pulse and in a slightly irregular manner produced by subdivided beats and vaguely concealed syncopations.

The Impressionistic style does not negate traditional harmony, but the chords are freely altered and move in a manner that is not functional in the common practice. This technique,

(a) Phrygian Mode (transposed)

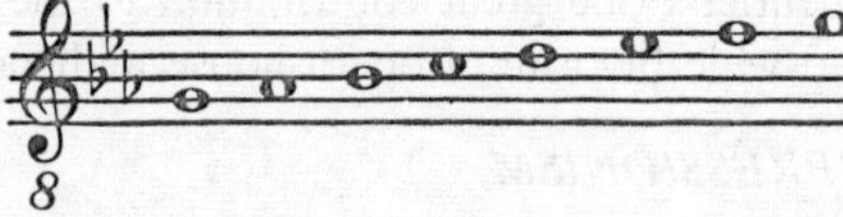

Application: Debussy, *String Quartet*

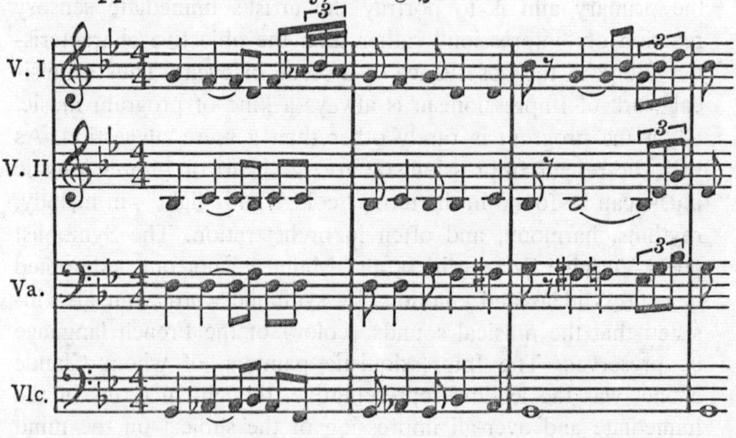

Example 51: Compositional techniques of Debussy.

(b) Whole-tone Scale

Application: Debussy, *String Quartet*

Example 51: Compositional techniques of Debussy (cont.)

(c) Pentatonic Scale

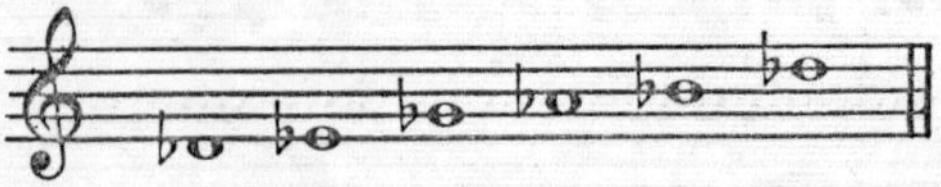

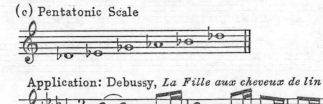

Application: Debussy, *La Fille aux cheveux de lin*

* *passing tone*

(d) Chord Stream: Debussy, *La Fille aux cheveux de lin*

Example 51: Compositional techniques of Debussy (cont.)

together with the fact that unresolved dissonances freely follow one another, tends to blur and disrupt the traditional forward progress of the harmonies and often renders the musical phrase vague and distorted. In orchestral music certain patterns and orchestrations add to the haze and the blur, and in piano music a liberal use of the damper pedal is used to achieve the same result. Again, a favorite harmonic technique is the "chord stream," in which chords erected predominantly in intervals of the fourth and fifth are sideslipped up and down in the fashion of the old *organum* practice. (See the technical illustrations in Example 51.) Unity of form is not demanded, nor is it desired, in Impressionistic music, and thus the form is suggested by whatever program is being followed, however slight. Rarely is any Classical form in evidence, save perhaps for the broad general outlines of ternary (ABA) design.

Claude Debussy (1862–1918). Musical Impressionism found its first and, for the most part, only true representative in the hands of Claude Debussy. He was born in St. Germain-en-Laye, and as a pianist he was prepared for study in the Paris Conservatory, which he entered at age eleven, by Mme. Mauté de Fleurville, a pupil of Chopin. In the conservatory he continued the study of piano with Marmontel, and it is of interest also that he won first prizes in the solfeggio class of Lavignac three years in succession.

For a time after graduation he was in the employ of Mme. Nadezhda von Meck, Tchaikovsky's patroness, and although he played Tchaikovsky's music for her, he never seemed to take to the great Russian. In 1884, Debussy won the Grand Prix de Rome, but his compositional efforts in Rome were displeasing to the academy jury. On his return to Paris he became associated with a group of French poets of the symbolist school.

In 1888 he journeyed to Bayreuth to hear Wagner's *Parsifal,* and he made a return visit the next year. However, his interest in Wagner's music soon died out, and he turned from the German master to his own French heritage, particularly the music of Couperin and Rameau. Debussy, moreover, was impressed by the colorful qualities inherent in a Javanese *gamelan* orchestra that he heard perform at the Paris Exposition of 1889. It was about this time that he set about developing his individual style of Impressionism concerned with mood, atmosphere, and color. It was only in the twilight of his career that his music took on a neo-Classical tinge and austere quality. Debussy's death, from cancer, came during the shelling of Paris by the Germans in 1918.

In turning to the music of Debussy, it must be understood that, although he is set forth as the leader of this movement, not all of his music will show the principles of the style hitherto set down. The style of any musical work lies in its sound, and any composer may from time to time use one and then another variance in stylistic practice. However, with Debussy, the Impressionistic style is first glimpsed in the *Prélude à l'après-midi d'un faune* ("Prelude to the Afternoon of a Faun," 1894), based on the poem by Mallarmé, and it continues in the *Nocturnes* (1899) and in the sea sketches *La Mer* (1905). All these are for orchestra.

In piano literature Debussy's Impressionism shows up to best advantage in the *Estampes* (1903), the *Images* (first series, 1905; second series, 1907), and especially in the *Préludes* (first book, 1910; second book, 1913). Impressionistic techniques are also found here and there in the *Suite bergamasque* (1890–1905), of which the third of the four pieces is the celebrated *Clair de lune,* and in the *Children's Corner* (1908), which Debussy dedicated to his daughter "Chouchou."

Debussy's opera *Pelléas et Mélisande,* set to the play by Maeterlinck, represents the nearest to perfection in the fusion of drama and music that the operatic stage has ever known. Using no arias or ensemble numbers, the composer matched a text treating of shadowy characters in a fanciful world of symbolism almost word for word with music of a free-flowing, declamatory nature. The work stands today as the one great Impressionistic opera.

Other fine works by this master are the formal *String Quartet* (1893) and the *Violin Sonata in A* (1876). Debussy continues the splendid tradition of French song literature with the *Ariettes oubliées* (1888) and the *Fêtes galantes* (1892 and 1904), both collections setting poems by Verlaine; the *Cinq poèmes* (1889) on works by Charles Baudelaire (1821–67); the *Chansons de Bilitis* (1897), on prose poems by Pierre Louÿs (1870–1925) written in 1894; and the *Trois ballades* (1910), settings of ballads by the first and one of the greatest French lyricists, François Villon (1431–?).

Maurice Ravel (1875–1937). Ravel studied with Fauré at the Paris Conservatory. In 1901 he won the Second Prix de Rome, but ensuing efforts to win the Grand Prix were unsuccessful. Weak in body, he was rejected for military service in World War I, but did serve his country in the ambulance corps until his ill health forced him into a hospital. The rest of his life was spent in a quiet existence; Ravel had a few pupils and no connections with any faculty of any school. He made a few tours as pianist and conductor in Europe, and in 1928 he appeared professionally in the United States.

Ravel used a number of the techniques of Impressionism: unresolved dissonances, pandiatonicism (where *all* notes of a diatonic scale are considered consonant in harmonic relationship with one another), augmented triads and seventh and ninth chords (often with chromatic alterations), and including pictorial passages. He also shared other ideas with Debussy. However, he never forsook his inclination toward clear-cut melodic lines, precise rhythms, functional harmonies, and control through underlying Classical forms. In this respect Ravel joined hands with a fellow countryman Paul Cézanne (1839–1906), who felt the need to add to Impressionistic painting something solid and durable, as in the old masters. Because of their formal aspects both Ravel and Cézanne are sometimes labeled post-Impressionists.

Ravel stands closest to Impressionism in his piano works *Jeux d'eau* (1901), a pictorial painting of a water fountain using many chords of the ninth, *Miroirs* (1905), and *Gaspard de la nuit* (1908); and Impressionistic elements are found to some extent in the suite *Rhapsodie espagnole* (1907) for orchestra, and in the ballet *Daphnis et Chloé* (completed in 1912) from which an arranged orchestral *Suite No. 2* is very popular. As might be expected, Classic leanings are more prominent in the piano piece *Sonatina* (1905) and in the chamber works *String Quartet in F* (1903) and *Piano Trio in a minor* (1914).

Other well-known compositions by Ravel are the piano solo pieces *Pavane pour une infante défunte* (1899), *Valses nobles et sentimentales* (1911), and *Le Tombeau de Couperin* (1917); the *Pavane* has various English translations and stories connected with it, but this seems pointless since Ravel himself declared that he chose the name merely for the alliteration and pleasurable sound in the title. Still other famous works include the piano duet *Ma Mère l'oye* (the "Mother Goose" suite, first written as a children's duet in 1908, and arranged into ballet form and orchestrated in 1912); and the *Introduction and Allegro* for harp, string quartet, flute, and clarinet (1906). Later symphonic works include the dance music *La Valse* (1920), using Viennese waltz rhythms, and *Boléro,* commissioned by Ida Rubinstein and performed at her dance recital in Paris in 1928; *Tzigane,* written for violin and piano in 1925, but with the piano accompaniment orchestrated by the composer soon after its completion; a *Piano Concerto in G major* (1931); and a *Concerto in D for the Left Hand* (1931) written for and first performed by the one-armed pianist Paul Wittgenstein. Ravel eventually orchestrated a good number of the above piano pieces and compositions not written strictly for the orchestra for concert presentation, and he is also noted for his many fine choral selections and songs.

Impressionism came about from the disintegrating post-Romantic and national schools and served as a stylistic connecting link between the Romantic art of the 19th century and the modern music of the 20th. It became a part in one degree or another of the style of many composers at the turn of the century; prominent in a list of such composers would be: the Spaniard Manuel de Falla, the Italian Ottorino Respighi, the

Englishman Frederick Delius, and the Americans Charles Martin Loeffler and Charles Griffes. Impressionism was the dominant style for only a relatively short time. Ravel's attempt at the solidification of its primary tenet–vagueness–proved to be the beginning of the end. A definite reaction set in against Impressionism and against all types of Romanticism as well. The nature of the new trend will be discussed in the next and concluding chapter.

CHAPTER 10

The Twentieth Century

INTRODUCTION

Most 20th-century music has been conceived in a spirit of searching and probing, the basic musical style of the age being one of radical change. Still, something of the old has been maintained. For one thing, the modern composer is more aware than his predecessors of the musical traditions of the past, and, for another, the concept of national music as found in the 19th century has shown itself to be especially infectious. It seems, however, that in the history of Western music the completion of each span of three centuries from the Gothic age on has produced a radical change in style, a change so striking and so different that the word "new" was called for. The year 1300 marks the beginning of the *ars nova,* 1600 the *nuove musiche,* and 1900 the *neue Musik* ("new music").

Asymmetrical rhythms, multimeters, atonal style, polytonality, contrapuntal techniques described as linear or dissonant, new definitions of structural density, total serialization, and stylistic procedures related to Expressionism and neo-Classicism have all been briefly mentioned in Chapter 2. These and other characteristics of contemporary music will now receive a more complete study in this chapter.

RHYTHM. Modern composers have long felt cramped by what they call the "tyranny of the bar line." Thus they have tried to gain a freer flow of rhythm by frequent changes of meter within a composition, by shifting accents within the measure, by writing measures without secondary accents or even without accentual rhythms altogether, by substituting asymmetrical divisions of rhythmical patterns within measures for the regular beat divisions used in earlier music, by using compound and newly created meter signatures, and even by omitting bar lines entirely. Moreover, serial technique has been extended of late to include rhythm as well as pitch and interval regulation. American jazz rhythms have also found a place in important works by Satie, Stravinsky, Milhaud, Gershwin, and Copland —in compositions written by most of these men in the early decades of this century. As a reaction to the overblown Romanticism of the late 19th century, a return to primitive rhythms (in a style variously called primitivism, barbarism, or dynamism) can be found in such works as Bartók's *Allegro barbaro* (1911) for piano, Stravinsky's ballet *Rite of Spring* (1913), and in the driving *ostinato* rhythms of much of the music of Bartók and Prokofiev. Add to this the modern composer's continuing interest in the irregular rhythms of European folk song, and the complex and fascinating picture of musical rhythm in our time is largely complete. (This writer has long felt that an understanding of 20th-century rhythms is the ideal way to begin the journey to a complete enjoyment of modern music.)

MELODY. Most melody in today's music differs radically from the traditional concept of a smooth vocal-styled line arranged in a symmetrical and repetitious phrase pattern. The tensions of contemporary life are reflected in modern music's angular lines, which often appear unvocal or antivocal at first glance. The vocal performer of this new music may be tempted to rebel at what is expected of him, but he will also find here a fresh and stimulating challenge to his musicianship. This applies to vocalists (and instrumental accompanists as well) who wish to perform Expressionistic works like Arnold Schoenberg's *Pierrot Lunaire* (1912), or the same composer's opera *Moses and Aaron* (from the early 1930's) or Alban Berg's opera *Wozzeck* (1925), or the songs of Anton Webern.

HARMONY. The harmonic background of 20th-century music often reflects a blend of the old and the new. The techniques of pandiatonicism, the use of parallel chord movements in chord streams, the employment of chords with added nonchord tones, chordal structures erected by intervals of fourths rather than thirds, unusual or synthetic scales, and nonfunctional chordal progressions all stem from late-19th-century music (many from French Impressionism) and they are further developed in the 20th century. Debussy, for one, reintroduced Renaissance modality, and later composers made use of these ecclesiastical modes either along with or mixed with tonal elements or in polymodal combinations. Modal writing in the Elizabethan style can be found in Ralph Vaughan Williams' work—for example, in his *Fantasia on a Theme by Thomas Tallis* (1910) and in his *Mass in g minor* (1923). But tonality has not disappeared entirely from 20th-century music (Paul Hindemith was a strong advocate of a tonal center in music); and a new approach to this system has been discovered in polytonality (Darius Milhaud's music is a foremost example; polytonality in his *Piano Sonata No. 1,* composed in 1916, produced several harmonic planes running concurrently). Skyscraper chords—an example of one would be the simultaneous erection of the 1-3-5-7-9-11-13 steps of the scale—and tone and chord clusters in modern music have become so complex that vertical combinations involving these devices often lose their identity as "chords" and must be referred to as "densities."

NEO-CLASSICISM. The link with the past is strongest in the work of composers sometimes called neo-Classicists. A feature of this style is a sparing use of chromaticism with a resulting tendency to employ the diatonic idiom in which a semblance at least of tonality is retained. Musical textures here tend to thin out, perhaps due to the frequent use of dissonant counterpoint. The neo-Classic composers use the passacaglia or chaconne, *concerto grosso,* fugue, sonata form, and variation forms in general. Clarity (exemplified by the music of the French *Les Six*), balance, and order are all insisted upon. This clarity and balance is reflected in orchestrations that emphasize line, avoid doublings of parts, and specify definite coloristic timbres; more attention is paid to attractive and telling parts for the brasses and woodwinds, and much more is made of the rhythmical and coloristic possibilities inherent in the percussion section. Examples of this style are Igor Stravinsky's *Octet for Wind Instruments* (1923), *Oedipus Rex* (1927), and *Symphony of Psalms* (1930); Paul Hindemith's opera *Mathis der Maler* (first performed in 1938); and Benjamin Britten's *Peter Grimes* (1945).

EXPRESSIONISM. The Expressionistic style, on the other hand, marks the greatest cleavage with the past. Arnold Schoenberg was the leader in this style, with his pupils Alban Berg and Anton Webern comprising his most notable disciples. Around 1908, Schoenberg abandoned tonality and his early post-Romantic style (patterned after Wagner and Brahms) at one and the same time. He set out on the path of atonality and urged a completely new approach to all elements of music, with one exception–the retention, as a unifying principle, of the classical forms of music. The old tonal concept (based on a diatonic scale of seven notes of the twelve found within the octave) now gives way to a system using all twelve tones in which these tones are related only to one another and not to a single, tonic note. Schoenberg's *Five Orchestral Pieces* (1908) and *Pierrot Lunaire* (1912) and Webern's *Six Pieces for Orchestra* (1909) and *Five Pieces for Orchestra* (1913) may be cited as outstanding examples of atonal style. Schoenberg firmly established his system of composing with twelve tones in the early 1920's, his *Five Piano Pieces* (Op. 23, 1923) being the first work in this system. Other examples by Schoenberg include the *Variations for Orchestra* (1928) and *Moses and Aaron*. Berg and Webern adapted the system to their respective needs, as seen in Berg's *Lyric Suite* (1926) and Webern's *Symphony for Chamber Orchestra* (1928). Another fine adaptation was realized by Stravinsky in his ballet *Agon* (1957). The latest development of the system extends the "classical" serial technique to include color, rhythm, and duration of tones, dynamics, density, and the timing of entrances into the musical process; recent compositions of Boulez, Stockhausen, and Křenek are prime examples, for they use as a point of departure the serial techniques of Webern.

OTHER CHARACTERISTICS OF MODERN MUSIC. The invention of the electronic tube in 1906, the subsequent construction of electronic musical instruments, and the still later discovery of the process of recording sound on tape have all had their influence on contemporary music. In 1923 the French composer Arthur Honegger attempted to depict the mechanized age of that day with a musical description of a railroad locomotive in his *Pacific 231*. Shortly after 1950, a group of musicians in Paris, with a somewhat similar purpose, set about to tape-record actual sounds of everyday life for incorporation into musical art. This experimentation came under the name *musique concrète*. At about the same time Otto Luening and Vladimir Ussachevsky began experimenting at Columbia University in New York with the manipulation of taped sounds derived from conventional vocal and instrumental sources. This work at Columbia has been advanced in recent years through the use of sounds produced by an electronic synthesizer. A third school of electronic music is centered in Cologne, Germany, where Karlheinz Stockhausen and others have shown an interest in applying serial techniques to sounds originated by an electric generator. The application of all such experiments as these to musical art is yet to be fully determined.

The contribution of folk song to rhythmical evolution has already been mentioned, and of course folklore has added new ideas to the elements of melody and harmony as well. Hungarian melodies, rhythms, and the scalar background of Hungarian folk songs lend charm to the music of Béla Bartók and to that of Zoltán Kodály, as heard in the latter's *Dances of Galanta* (1933) and *Peacock Variations* for orchestra (1939). German folk songs can be found in Carl Orff's *Carmina Burana* (1936), and English street cries and folk songs in Ralph Vaughan Williams's *Symphony No. 2* (1914) and in Gustav Holst's suites for the band written in 1909 and 1911. Russian nationalism is reflected in much the same way in the ballets *Firebird* (1910), *Petrouchka* (1911), and the *Rite of Spring*

(1913), by Igor Stravinsky, and in the compositions of other Russians such as Dmitri Shostakovich and Aram Khachaturian. Carlos Chávez reaches into Mexican folklore for Indian tunes, rhythms, and instruments in his *Sinfonía india* (1936), and Heitor Villa-Lobos uses like material from his Brazilian heritage in his musical works identified as *chôros.* Aaron Copland and Roy Harris have also furthered the course of nationalistic music to some extent in the United States.

As one can readily see, the composers of the 20th century have a great many varied interests and styles. Therefore, we feel that the only reasonable organizing pattern in which to treat them is by nationality. This does not mean that all these composers are especially national; some are, some are not, but it is a convenient way to deal with them.

AUSTRIA

Three Austrians, Arnold Schoenberg, Alban Berg, and Anton von Webern, have acquired a measure of importance and influence in 20th-century music equal to or greater than that of any other national group. Since Vienna was for some time their city of residence, these three working together have been called by some a Second Viennese School, which is indeed a great honor when remembering that the First Viennese School (or the Viennese School proper) was composed of three of the greatest names in music–Haydn, Mozart, and Beethoven.

Arnold Schoenberg (1874–1951). Arnold Schoenberg was born in Vienna. As a boy he had instruction on the violin and cello, and at the age of twenty he took some lessons in counterpoint with Alexander von Zemlinsky; but on the whole he had only a little formal training in music. In 1910 he was appointed to the faculty of the Vienna Academy, and the next year his *Harmonielehre* was published–a book that included both traditional harmonic theories and some of the new approaches of the 1910 period. Schoenberg's career was interrupted by World War I service in the Austrian Army. It was in the years following this war that he developed his individual system of composing with twelve tones. The composer gained respect for his creative leadership, and in 1925 attained a position of importance as professor of composition in the Prussian Academy of Arts in Berlin. When the nazis came to power, Schoenberg was dismissed from his post and shortly thereafter came to the United States, as Bartók and Hindemith did later. Subsequently he taught at the University of Southern California and the University of California at Los Angeles; he became an American citizen in 1941, and he died in Los Angeles at the age of seventy-seven.

Zemlinsky's appreciation of the music of Brahms and Wagner found ready acceptance in the young Schoenberg, whose *Verklärte Nacht* ("Transfigured Night," Op. 4, 1899) for string sextet was written in the Wagnerian tradition. This composition, arranged by the composer for string orchestra in 1917 and revised in 1943, has consistently remained Schoenberg's most popular and most frequently performed work, a fact that proves that the way of the musical pioneer is most difficult and often the least acceptable to the immediate listening public. The *Gurre-Lieder* (songs from the mythical castle of Gurre) was begun in 1901 and finally completed in 1911. Reminiscent of Mahler's scope, it is seldom performed because of its vastness, requiring as it does five soloists, three male choruses, an eight-part mixed chorus, a narrator, and a very large orchestra.

The closing years of the first decade of the 20th century saw Schoenberg moving toward an atonal, dissonant, Expressionistic style of composing music. This meant, with Schoenberg, a subjective approach to the expression of his musical emotions, which he believed required the complete negation of the traditional principles of tonality. Schoenberg himself, however, disliked the term "atonality," with its meaning of the total absence of tonality, and preferred another term "pantonality"—that is, a method in which each chromatic tone is of equal importance and thus *all* tonalities are deemed present. But "atonality" was nevertheless to remain the designating term for this style. The *Five Orchestral Pieces* (Op. 16, 1908) is one of the early important examples of atonality. The style invokes a degree of discontinuity in content and in color, and although the work is written for a large orchestra its emphasis is on the coloristic use of individual instruments. The third piece of the five—*"Sommermorgen an einem See"* ("A Summer Morning by a Lake")—is especially interesting for its reliance on color, which here is supreme, with all other elements of music in complete subordination; change of orchestral timbre is even substituted for change of pitch. Such a concept has been called *pointillism,* a term borrowed from painting where art works in this style are produced by the accumulation of many, many varying dots of color on the canvas. The paintings of the Frenchman Georges Seurat (1859–91), especially *La Grande jatte,* is a perfect example of this style.

A second well-known Schoenberg work from this period is *Pierrot lunaire* ("The Moonstruck Clown," Op. 21, 1912). This atonal work is for a smaller group—voice, violin (or viola), cello, flute (or piccolo), clarinet (or bass clarinet), and piano—and sets to music twenty-one symbolic poems by Albert Giraud (1860–1929), which were translated into German by O. E. Hartleben. The voice part employs a technique known as *Sprechstimme,* something of a middle ground between speech and song. Schoenberg did not write actual notes for the singer, but used a symbol on the staff of the vocal part to indicate "approximate" pitch.

Schoenberg evidently worried about the vagaries of his atonal style, and with traditional Germanic thoroughness came up with a system of control in the early 1920's which he called a method of composing with twelve tones. The composer never published an analytical description of his twelve-tone technique (also called serial or dodecaphonic technique), but others have defined its basic principles as follows: first a row of twelve tones is established, each tone or note being a different pitch in a given chromatic scale. This tone row, or series of notes, is actually made available in four forms: the original series, a retrograde or reverse order of the original row, an inversion of the original row, and a retrograde presentation of this inversion. The row can be employed in practice both melodically and harmonically, with the stipulation that the melodies and notes of the chords must follow the series of the tone row in use, and that there be no repetition of a tone (except immediate repetition, considered only as an extension of that tone) until the entire series has been transversed, since a return to a note might suggest that pitch to the ear as a possible tonal center.

A series may be used in any transposition, that is, starting on any tone (pitch) but retaining the correct intervallic sequence; thus transposition in connection with the four rows opens up the possibility of forty-eight different series. (Mathematicians have calculated that when all possible rows of twelve tones in forty-eight positions each have been used, the number of different tone rows will reach the staggering total of 479,-001,600!) *Tessitura* is no object; any tone in the row may be sounded in any octave, but in practice modifications of many types are bound to occur; in certain situations, such as in the application of the trill as an ornament or in the use of a pedal point, repetition of a note of the series does take place; and sometimes a twelve-tone composer will work over subdivisions of the row, or he may willfully modify the entire system. In 1923 Schoenberg wrote his *Five Piano Pieces,* Op. 23, of which the fifth piece is his first twelve-tone composition. Example 52 gives the tone row in its four basic forms, and shows how the composer shaped the series in the opening bars of the piano piece.

The *Variations for Orchestra* (Op. 31, 1928) represents the first application of the twelve-tone technique in a composition for full orchestra. (The tone row which serves as the basis of this work may be seen in Example 7 of this book.) Here the technique is masterfully applied, and a structural lightness and delineation of color line is maintained in spite of the large forces employed. Important compositions written by Schoenberg after he came to the United States include the *Violin Concerto* (Op. 36, 1936), a *Piano Concerto* (Op. 42, 1942), and the *Theme and Variations for Band* (Op. 43a, 1943). The last named–it was transcribed by the composer in 1944 for orches-

(a) Original Tone Row

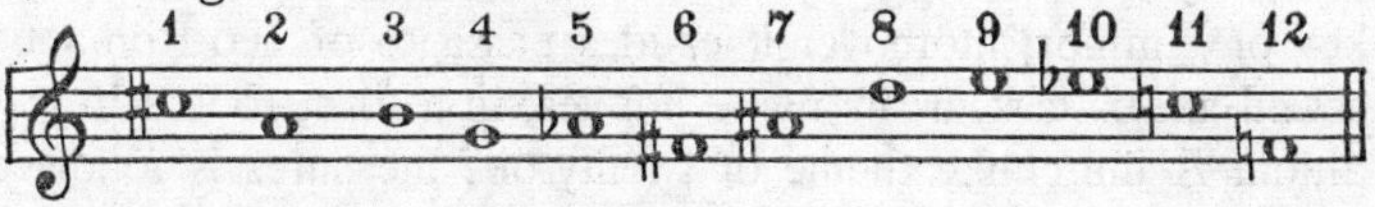

Inversion of the Original Row

Retrograde of the Original Row

Retrograde of the Inversion

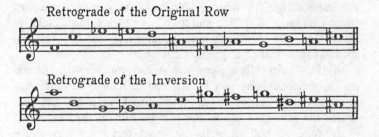

(b) Application: Schoenberg, Five Piano Pieces, Op. 23 (No. 5)

Example 52

tra (Op. 43b)—has proved to be one of the most popular of the late works. It is about the only one of his mature works to have any definite tonal bearing, focusing as it does around the key of *g* minor; moreover it exudes passages of neo-Romantic sound and is cast, as its name implies, in a form rooted in tradition. A marchlike theme of twenty-one measures is followed by seven variations on that theme.

Schoenberg's opera, *Moses and Aaron,* set to a libretto by the composer, was begun very early in the 1930's and was never actually completed. Schoenberg, as late as the last year of his life, hoped to finish the work, but stated that the short last act could be spoken if he were not able to compose the musical setting. The first performance was a radio broadcast from Hamburg in 1954, and the first staging took place in Zurich in 1957. Although it is incomplete, what is there is a splendid specimen of Expressionistic opera.

In 1904 both Alban Berg and Anton von Webern became pupils of Schoenberg, and for the rest of their lives they were to remain close friends and disciples of that composer. Both accepted the principles of the atonal style, and the theories of the twelve-tone method as well, once that technique was established. Berg and Webern were to spend all of their musical lives in and around Vienna, teaching privately, lecturing, and accepting conducting opportunities when they were offered.

Alban Berg (1885–1935). Alban Berg's masterpiece is the opera *Wozzeck* (Berlin, 1925), based on scenes the composer arranged from a play written about 1830 by Georg Büchner (1813–37). The plot is a rather sordid affair. Wozzeck is a poor army soldier, mistreated by his superiors, and experiencing added trouble at home, where his common-law wife Marie is having an affair with the drum major. As Wozzeck's troubles pile up he gradually loses his reason, murders his wife, and in a highly emotional state accidentally drowns himself. The real loser is the small child of the couple, left alone in the world. But whereas Büchner's play is not a particularly delightful story, Berg's atonal and expressionistic setting has produced the finest opera of its genre.

The range of expression in this work is extraordinary; the normal speaking voice and the normal singing voice are used, with the addition of falsetto and *Sprechstimme*. Orchestral instruments and a few choral passages paint some fascinating and moving pictures: there is the military march of Act I; the waltz music at the tavern and the chorus of sleeping soldiers in Act II; and in the final act Marie's murder, Wozzeck's drowning, and the pathetic final scene in which the child of Wozzeck and Marie happily rides his hobbyhorse, unmindful of the tragedy that has befallen his parents.

The atonal style of the opera is warmed from time to time by the inclusion of tonal elements, and the scenes of each act are connected by interludes. Berg furthermore strives for some underlying unity by basing the scenes on some traditional form, as noted in Table XX.

TABLE XX

Act	*Scene*	*Form*
I	1	Suite: Prelude, Pavane, Gigue, Gavotte, and Aria
	2	Rhapsody
	3	Military March and Lullaby
	4	Passacaglia with twenty-one variations
	5	Rondo
II	1	Sonata form
(a sonata)	2	Fantasy and Fugue
	3	Slow Movement (*Largo*)
	4	Scherzo
	5	Rondo with Introduction
III	1	Invention on a theme
	2	Invention on a tone (the note B)
	3	Invention on a rhythm
	4	Invention on a chord
		(The following interlude is an invention on a key; the music moves from *d* minor into atonal regions.)
	5	Invention on a note pattern

A second opera, *Lulu,* was left unfinished at the time of Berg's death. It has been performed recently with success.

In the field of absolute music two compositions by Berg are

well known: the *Lyric Suite* (1926, his first work in the twelve-tone method) for string quartet, which, incidentally, has a fast movement very comparable to the second movement of Bartók's later (1928) *Fourth String Quartet;* and the increasingly admired and very moving *Violin Concerto* (1935).

Anton von Webern (1883–1945). Although Anton von Webern barely made a living as a musician during his lifetime, since about 1950 his compositions have attracted a great deal of attention. He wrote in the most compact manner imaginable; entire compositions are over in minutes, and some movements can be timed in seconds. Webern's complete works (thirty-one compositions) have been fully recorded–a lifelong career that can be heard in less than three hours.

Webern's atonal music has a tendency to sound quite disjointed, employing as it does wide melodic intervals, many rests, a low dynamic level, and a great reliance on the pointillistic technique. This technique is especially prevalent in the *Six Pieces for Orchestra* (Op. 6, 1909) and again in the *Five Pieces for Orchestra* (Op. 10, 1913). Whereas in adopting the principles of the twelve-tone technique Alban Berg had incorporated his own dramatic and neo-Romantic ideas into the system, Webern chose a firmly knit construction based on a concise, almost mathematical, ordering of intervallic note patterns–a terse utterance that has served as a point of departure for most of the serial music of the past several years. Webern used his individualized twelve-tone technique in the *Symphony for Chamber Orchestra* (Op. 21, 1928); scored for two horns, clarinet, bass clarinet, harp, and strings, the first movement is constructed in the form of a double canon; here the canonic theme is instrumented in pointillistic style, with each instrument playing only one or two notes of the subject with a resulting constant color change.

HUNGARY

Béla Bartók (1881–1945). Béla Bartók has become well established as one of the finest of 20th-century composers. He received a thorough training in piano and composition at the Academy of Music in Budapest, and shortly after his graduation was appointed an instructor there (1907). After World War I he served along with Ernst von Dohnányi and Zoltán Kodály on the board of directors of the academy. Bartók had a great interest in the folk-song literature of Central and Eastern Europe. He collected folk materials not only in Hungary, but also in Romania, Arabia, Egypt, and Turkey, and these tunes and their modal settings found great favor in his compositions. For some thirty years Bartók led the life of a teacher, composer, and concert artist, mostly in Budapest. However, in 1940 he came to the United States, forced out of his homeland by his hatred of Nazism. His years in the States were not fortunate ones; he was sick with leukemia, which brought about his death in 1945, and he was practically destitute. His works found their true popularity only after his death.

Like many composers writing at the beginning of the 20th century, Bartók came under the influence of Impressionism, as can be seen in his early works. Near the end of the first decade of the century there was also a vogue of the primitive in all art forms. In music it was represented by percussive, driving rhythms coupled with dissonant tone clusters, and Bartók's popular *Allegro barbaro* (1911) for piano is in this style. However, his most important works stem from the 1920's and 1930's. A quick survey of his stylistic pattern over these years can be found in the pedagogical works for piano, six volumes grouped under the title *Mikrokosmos* and written during the period 1926–37. They begin with easy pieces and gradually move toward the advanced grades. Bartók includes the modal forms and styles that he found in the folk songs of Eastern Europe, polytonality, rhythmical complexities, and dissonances of various kinds. He often uses scales not heretofore found in classical music, bringing in unusual key signatures–in Example 53 see the scale on which piece *No. 41* of Volume II is based. It is certainly not a scale found in the major and minor system, nor is it one of the Church modal scales.

The large works from this period include the *Piano Concerto*

(a) The Scale

(b) Application: Bartók, Mikrokosmos, Vol. II (No. 41)

Example 53

No. 2 (1930–31), *Music for Strings, Percussion and Celesta* (1937), and the *Violin Concerto* (1937–38). These are all compositions of the highest order. The *Piano Concerto No. 2* makes considerable use of the primitive style, giving a driving, rhythmic feeling of excitement to the music. The *Violin Concerto* is a masterwork that makes use of full-blown melodies in a warmer style, yet the dynamic rhythms are still present. The *Music for Strings, Percussion and Celesta* is one of Bartók's best-known and best-liked works. The composer draws sounds and colors of great beauty from an instrumentation of two string quartets, percussion, double basses, and celesta. The fugal first movement is among the finest compositions of contemporary contrapuntal art.

Bartók's six string quartets are surely among the best works in this medium written in the 20th century. *Quartet No. 1* was composed in 1910, *No. 2* in 1917, *No. 3* in 1927, *No. 4* in 1928, *No. 5* in 1934, and *No. 6* in 1939. *No. 4* is one of the most popular. It is done in the Expressionistic style of this period, yet in a somewhat restrained manner; the organization is that of a five-movement arch form. Clusters of tones dominate the first movement, and the second is a wonderfully fast collage of sound from muted strings; the third movement has qualities that have been dubbed Bartók's "night music," the fourth is played entirely pizzicato by all four instruments, and the last movement is dancelike in character. String glissandos add their characteristic color in several of the movements. A *Divertimento for String Orchestra,* composed in 1939, should also be mentioned. It is full of abrupt rhythms and choice dissonances, all brought to splendid, climactic conclusion in the third and final movement.

Throughout most of his career Bartók surrounded his folk songs and other melodic types with dissonant harmonic and polyphonic structures to which he added strong rhythms often backed by *ostinato* passages. But tonality seemed to be always the basis of his music, and as he came to the last years of his life he chose a less dissonant style, making the works of this time sound even more tonal. One of the best and most popular of the late works is the *Concerto for Orchestra* (1943). It is in five movements, the last section being a lively Hungarian rondo with a fugue in the middle. Another well-respected work is the *Piano Concerto No. 3,* written in 1945, the final year of the composer's life.

Zoltán Kodály (1882–). Zoltán Kodály was Bartók's colleague on the Budapest Academy faculty, and he shared with Bartók a desire to collect folk songs of Hungary and use them in musical compositions and arrangements. In 1923 a celebration of the fiftieth anniversary of the union of Buda and Pest took place, and Dohnányi, Bartók, and Kodály were each asked to write something for the occasion. Bartók's composition was the popular *Dance Suite,* and Kodály gained his first real fame with the *Psalmus Hungaricus* (for chorus and orchestra) as his contribution. Kodály's opera *Háry János* was well received when first performed in Budapest in 1926, and an orchestral suite in six movements from this opera is quite popular today. The opera is named after a character in Hungarian folklore known for his tall tales. Other works that show Kodály's concern for the melodies and rhythms of Hungarian folk songs and dances are the *Marosszék Dances* (1930), the

Galanta Dances (1933), and the *Peacock Variations* for orchestra (1939), based on the folk song "Fly, Peacock, Fly."

GERMANY

Some of the most original contributions to 20th-century musical art are to be found in the contemporary works of German composers. Our discussion here will be in terms of the works of Paul Hindemith and Carl Orff. Of these, Hindemith will be considered as a composer in the neo-Classical manner, and Orff as a proponent of national style.

Paul Hindemith (1895–1963). Born in Central Germany in the town of Hanau, Paul Hindemith played in dance bands in his early youth. He studied violin and composition at the Frankfurt Conservatory, and later toured Europe with a string quartet in which he played the viola. In 1927 he assumed the instruction of a master class in composition at the Hochschule für Musik in Berlin, but a mounting conflict with the Hitler regime compelled him to leave the country. At this time (1935) he accepted an invitation from the Turkish Government to organize a system of musical education there. In 1940 he became a valued member of the faculty of Yale University in New Haven, Conn.; and the academic year 1950–51 found him lecturing at Harvard. The composer returned to Europe in 1953 to make his home in Switzerland, where he taught at the university of Zurich.

In all his writings Hindemith remained a practical musician. He was a champion of *Gebrauchsmusik* ("Music for functional, everyday use")–music that is not too difficult and yet is constructed in a sound manner. He made a serious effort to provide literature in the contemporary vein for certain instruments, some of which badly needed this kind of help. Thus he enriched modern music by concertos for cello, clarinet, harp and woodwinds, horn, organ, piano, trumpet and bassoon, and violin; in like manner, he composed sonatas for piano and bassoon, cello, clarinet, flute, oboe, trombone, trumpet, and violin. The solo *Sonata No. 3 for Piano* (1936) is well regarded, and organists often play the *Three Sonatas for Organ* (1937–40). The *Symphony in B♭* (1951) is one of the finest compositions yet written for band; the linear contrapuntal nature of much of Hindemith's music is aptly illustrated in a fascinating fugal movement in this band piece.

The neo-Classical in Hindemith can be seen most clearly in a series of compositions that have appeared from time to time under the general heading of *Kammermusik* ("chamber music"), and which show a reverence for Baroque forms and polyphonic conceptions. Bach's *Well-Tempered Clavier* is echoed in Hindemith's *Ludus Tonalis* ("Tonal Diversions," 1943) for piano, which consists of twelve fugues, each in a different key, the fugues being joined one to another by interludes, and the whole set being preceded by a prelude and followed by a postlude made up of a reversed version of the prelude. Against this is the *Suite 1922,* for piano, with its reflections of the jazz age.

An old wine in a new bottle might well describe the opera *Mathis der Maler* ("Matthias the Painter") written by Hindemith in the early 1930's. This composition concerns the life and works of the painter Matthias Grünewald (*c.* 1460–1528), and especially the artist's paintings on the Isenheim altarpiece. Production of the opera was delayed for political reasons in Germany (it was not performed, in fact, until 1938 in Zurich), which led Hindemith to arrange (in 1934) an orchestral suite of three extensive instrumental portions, which he brought out as the *Symphony: Mathis der Maler;* in this form the music has become probably the most frequently heard of Hindemith's works.

The three movements portray, in turn, three different scenes on the Isenheim altarpiece. The first movement (the overture of the opera) is the "Angelic Concert"; it has some joyful lilting music in it, and also introduces an old German hymn tune *Es sungen drei Engel* ("There sang three angels"), first played by the trombones in bar 8 (see Example 54). The second movement is the "Entombment," the music of which can be explained by a later theoretical work of Hindemith. A few years after he wrote this movement, in 1937 and 1939, Hinde-

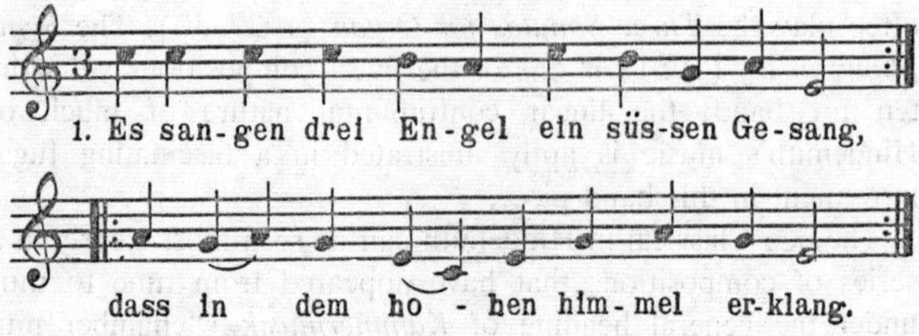
1. Es san-gen drei En-gel ein süs-sen Ge-sang,
dass in dem ho - hen him-mel er-klang.

Example 54

mith published two volumes entitled *Unterweisung im Tonsatz,* in which he explained his manner of composing. He advocated the free use of the twelve tones of the chromatic scale in a harmonic web based on tension and relaxation gained through varying degrees of dissonance, yet still related to a tonal center. The "Entombment" would seem a perfect example of his theory; as the short movement progresses the dissonant structures and the tension build as if to advance the question whether Christ's death was so very necessary after all, but gradually the music subsides to a quiet, resigned acceptance of what must be, ending in a final, tonic triad. This music serves as an intermezzo near the close of the opera. The last movement—from the sixth scene of the opera—is after the painting "The Temptation of St. Anthony." Here the composer uses dissonance in shock waves as the old saint battles temptation. But his salvation is assured when, near the end, the woodwinds proclaim the plain-song sequence for Corpus Christi—the *Lauda Sion Salvatorem* (Example 55).

A few other successful works by Paul Hindemith are his *Symphonic Metamorphoses on Themes of Weber* (1945), an orchestral suite *Nobilissima Visione* (1938), adapted from the ballet *Saint Francis* written for Diaghilev and his Ballet Russe, and the song cycle *Das Marienleben,* on poems by Rainer Maria Rilke (1875–1926). The last named, a set of songs on the life of the Virgin Mary, was composed in 1923, but revised in 1948 to conform with his new melodic and harmonic theories.

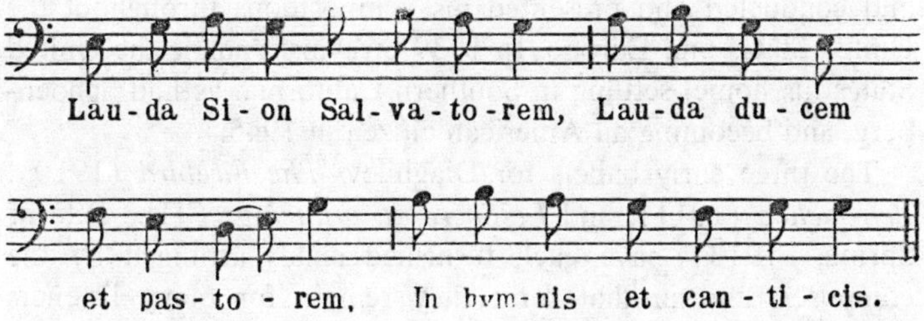
Lau - da Si - on Sal - va - to - rem, Lau - da du - cem
et pas - to - rem, In hym - nis et can - ti - cis.

Example 55

Carl Orff (1895–). There is less to say about Carl Orff. His works are more concerned with German history and background. Two operas–*Der Mond* ("The Moon," Munich, 1939) and *Die Kluge* ("The Wise Woman"; Frankfurt, 1943)–are rather well known; both are based on fairy tales by the brothers Jacob (1785–1863) and Wilhelm (1786–1859) Grimm.

Orff is most famous, however, for his scenic cantata *Carmina Burana* ("Songs from Burana," 1937), a decidedly dissonant and polyphonic setting of old 13th-century, monodic student songs discovered at a monastery in Bavaria. Not so well known are the second scenic cantata, entitled *Catulli Carmina* (1943), and the third of the series *Trionfo di Afrodite* (1953).

RUSSIA

Igor Stravinsky (1882–). The greatest Russian-born composer living today–and one of the greatest musical artists of the world in this century–is Igor Stravinsky. (As we stated earlier, it is only a convenient pattern to organize the discussion of modern composers by nationality. Stravinsky, although born near St. Petersburg, cannot in any real sense be considered a national or Russian composer.) Abandoning the law for music, Stravinsky became a pupil of Rimsky-Korsakov, and in 1910 he began a successful series of collaborations with the Russian ballet impresario Sergei Diaghilev in Paris. The years of World War I found him living and composing in Switzerland. After the war he worked again with Diaghilev, and composed and conducted and presented his compositions throughout the United States and Europe. In 1939 Stravinsky made the United States his home, settling in Southern California, as had Schoenberg, and becoming an American citizen in 1945.

The three early ballets for Diaghilev–*The Firebird* (1910), *Petrouchka* (1911), and *Le Sacre du printemps* ("The Rite of Spring," 1913)–have each furnished suites arranged by the composer, and in that form they remain for many listeners Stravinsky's most popular pieces. There are actually three orchestral suites from *The Firebird* (or, in the French, *L'Oiseau de feu*). The second is the best known; it is the one that best captures in its orchestration the colorful music of Stravinsky's teacher Rimsky-Korsakov. In particular, the "Dance of the Kastchei" and the "Finale" sections of the six-part suite exercise great rhythmic ingenuity. The ballet itself has a Russian legendary background: the adventures of Ivan Czarevitch, in which the Firebird figures prominently.

Petrouchka is the setting of a Russian carnival scene. The plot revolves around the affairs of three puppets–Petrouchka, the Ballerina, and the Moor–as brought to life through the magical powers of the Charlatan. The suite is rather long and features, among others, the following: Russian Dance (bold rhythms, parallel movement of chords, and a percussive piano part); Dance of the Moor (colorful orchestral sonorities); Dance of the Ballerina (to a sentimental waltz tune); Dance of the Nursemaids; a dancing bear (complete with tuba growls and an organ-grinder's melody); Dance of a Drunken Merchant (accompanied by tambourine-playing gypsy girls); Dance of the Coachmen and Grooms; and the Dance of the Mummers. Bitonality is present in the famous "Petrouchka Chord"–the simultaneous use of a *C* major and *F*♯ major triad (Example 56). The piece emphasizes throughout the tritone note relationship between the notes *C* and *F*♯.

The springtime religious rites of pagan Russian tribes in *Le Sacre* presented Stravinsky with the challenge to exalt the primitive, and he met this challenge head-on. The composer produced a brutal score replete with polymeters, off-beat *sforzandi,*

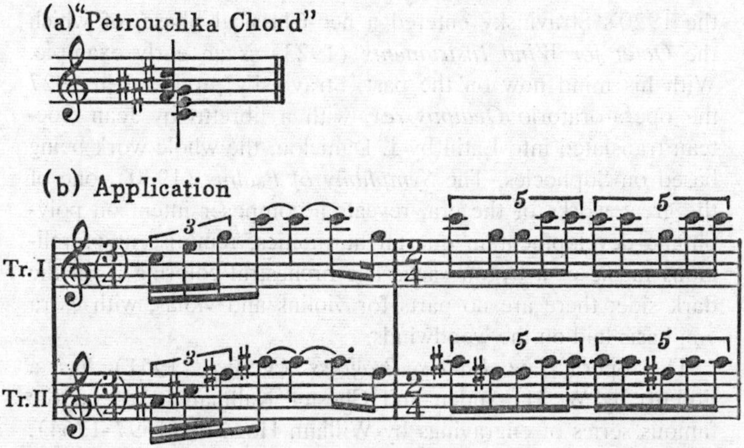

Example 56

wild rhythms, percussive sounds, and blocks of dissonant sounds in previously unheard-of orchestral *tessiture*. The first presentation of the ballet in Paris caused a riot, and real acceptance of the work was slow in coming. Today, however, *Le Sacre* is considered one of Stravinsky's finest pieces, and it is the one great work of the early 20th century. It matched in 1913 a similar glorification of the primitive in painting which was found in the art works of Pablo Picasso (1881–), and many other parallels may be found between the respective styles of these two men throughout their careers.

Toward the end of World War I, Stravinsky began to cut down on his use of forces. Thus the stage work *L'Histoire du soldat* (1918) manages with but a narrator, two dancers, and an orchestra of one violin, a clarinet and one bassoon, a cornet and a trombone, one string bass, and percussion instruments. American jazz influences are seen also at this time in *L'Histoire* and in the *Ragtime* (1918) for eleven instruments. The *Symphonies of Wind Instruments,* in memory of Debussy, was completed in 1920.

As changeable in musical styles as Picasso was in art styles, in the 1920's Stravinsky entered a neo-Classical phase, of which the *Octet for Wind Instruments* (1923) is an early example. With his mind now on the past, Stravinsky produced in 1927 the opera-oratorio *Oedipus rex,* with a libretto by Jean Cocteau translated into Latin by J. Danielou, the whole work being based on Sophocles. The *Symphony of Psalms* (1930), one of the great works of the era, reveals a composer intent on polyphonic development in quartal harmonies, reminiscent of religious music of a bygone age. The orchestral coloring is on the dark side; there are no parts for violins and violas, with extra emphasis laid on the woodwinds.

The opera *The Rake's Progress* (Venice, 1951) has a libretto by W. H. Auden and Chester Kallman based on the famous series of engravings by William Hogarth (1697–1764). Perhaps Stravinsky took a look at Hogarth's dates, for the music is very much in the style of an 18th-century "numbers" opera, with real Italian arias and *recitativo secco* to harpsichord accompaniment. In the 1950's the composer developed (along with many others) an interest in the twelve-tone technique of Anton von Webern. (The American composer Copland used a modified twelve-tone approach in his *Piano Quartet* of 1950). This interest is reflected particularly in the *Canticum sacram ad honorem Sancti Marci nominis* (written for performance in St. Mark's Cathedral, Venice, in 1956), the outstanding ballet *Agon* (1957), and in *Threni–id est Lamentationes Jeremiae Prophetae* ("Threnodies: Lamentations of the Prophet Jeremiah," 1958). *Threni* was the first Stravinsky work to be composed entirely in the twelve-tone technique; here Webern's influence is discernible in the pointillistic instrumental colorings, in canonic procedures, in the extremely angular melodic progressions, and in the sparsely written textures. Nevertheless, and in spite of whatever he may assume from others, Stravinsky remains an artistically individual composer. His rhythmic vitality and other personal qualities are still apparent in a late work, *The Flood,* a ballet pantomime with narrative and melodramatic passages, written for television and performed as a part of his eightieth-birthday celebration in 1962.

COMPOSERS IN THE SOVIET UNION. Two other 20th-century Russian composers of particular importance fashioned their careers almost entirely in their native land. Thus Sergei Prokofiev and Dmitri Shostakovich have found their compositions regulated and criticized by the Soviet regime, at least to some extent. Also Aram Khatchaturian enjoys great acceptance both at home and abroad. Music of extreme modernism and dissonant character has not been held commendable to the masses in Soviet Russia; Stravinsky's works, for example, have until recently lacked government sanction in the land of his birth, and the twelve-tone technique and the atonal style are not practiced there. Yet, in spite of restrictions, Prokofiev and Shostakovich and Khatchaturian have produced high quality works of musical art.

Sergei Prokofiev (1891–1953). Sergei Prokofiev, in particular, has quite a few compositions that are regularly performed. His *Symphony No. 1* (called "Classical," Op. 25, 1918) is an attempt to cloak the 18th-century symphonic form in modern harmonies and melodies, and it has found general public approval. His *Symphony No. 5* (Op. 100, 1944) and *Symphony No. 6* (Op. 111, 1947) have also been successful. Of five piano and two violin concertos, the *Piano Concerto No. 3 in C Major* (Op. 26, 1921) and the *Violin Concerto No. 2 in g minor* (Op. 63, 1935) are well known. His opera *The Love for Three Oranges* (Op. 33) had its first staging in Chicago in 1921, but is best remembered today in a suite (Op. 33a) from this opera, of which the "March" is a great favorite. Other notable works include an orchestral suite *Lieutenant Kije* (Op. 60, 1934) from music set to a satirical film on Czarist militarism, and the wonderful *Peter and the Wolf* (Op. 67, 1936) for narrator and orchestra, written for the educational instruction of children with regard to the instruments of the orchestra.

Dmitri Shostakovich (1906–). The successes of Dmitri Shostakovich are found primarily in his symphonic compositions. He has written eleven symphonies, and of these the first (Op. 10, 1925), fifth (Op. 47, 1937), and the seventh (Op. 60, 1941) are the most noted. *Piano Concerto No. 2* (Op.

101, 1957) is also highly regarded. The *Piano Quintet* (Op. 57, 1940) is a valuable contribution to chamber music, and there is an opera, *Lady Macbeth of Mzenska,* Op. 29 (Moscow, 1934) on a novel by Nikolai Leskov (1831–95). The ballet *Age of Gold* (Op. 22, 1930) participates in a bit of satirical comment on fascism and capitalism, and is best known through a suite and particularly for the "Polka" and "Russian Dance" in this suite; the "Polka," with its "wrong-note music," presents a caricature of the Geneva Disarmament Conference.

Aram Khatchaturian (1903–). A professor at the Moscow Conservatory, Aram Khatchaturian is the last in this discussion of Russian composers. His style includes Russian folklore material in a melodious framework of rhapsodic improvisation with touches of orientalism. Khatchaturian has obtained a measure of international success with his *Concerto for Piano and Orchestra* (1936); his *Concerto for Violin and Orchestra* (1940); and the *Concerto for Cello and Orchestra* (1946). Of especial importance is the ballet *Gayane* ("Happiness," 1942), from which two suites have been extracted; his "Saber Dance" from this ballet was once quite the rage in the United States.

FRANCE

Erik Satie (1866–1925). A reaction to Impressionism appeared in the music of the Frenchman Erik Satie. Something of a mystic, a member of the Rosicrucian Society, and quite eccentric in his manner, Satie's reaction to Impressionism was expressed in caricature as seen in the titles of his piano pieces *Trois morceaux en forme de poire* ("Three Pieces in the Shape of a Pear," for piano duet, 1903) and *Embryons desséchés* ("Dried Embryos," 1913). (*Trois morceaux* was Satie's reply to a critic's statement that his music lacked "form.") His ballet *Parade* (1917) involved the collaboration of Cocteau, who furnished the scenario, the work of the choreographer Léonide Massine (1896–), and the then cubistic Picasso, who designed the staging. The composer's orchestra approximated the instrumentation and sounds of a village dance band, and his *Ragtime du paquebot* ("Steamship Ragtime") from this ballet was his contribution to the jazz craze.

Albert Roussel (1869–1937). Albert Roussel began composing under the influence of French Impressionism and the exotic memories of his travels to Indo-China as a student in the French Naval Academy. He resigned from the navy in 1894 and four years later entered the Schola Cantorum in Paris, where he studied under Vincent d'Indy. A voyage to India in 1909 made possible his discovery of the legend of Queen Pâdmâvatî, which became the basis for his opera bearing her name, first performed in Paris in 1923. Of his early works, a suite from the ballet *Le Festin de l'araignée* ("The Spider's Feast," 1912) has proved very popular with the listening public. In the 1920's Roussel embraced neo-Classical tendencies in his art–traditional French clarity of texture clothed in Classical forms. His second (1921), third (1930), and fourth (1934) symphonies, the *Suite in F* (1926), the *Sinfonietta for Strings* (1934), and the *Cello Concertino* (1936) are all created in this vein.

"Les Six." Jean Cocteau was a very gifted and influential man–a writer of plays, ballet scenarios, and novels, a poet, and an artist. He had definite ideas on music, too. Cocteau was drawn to Bach, but disliked Beethoven, Wagner, and Debussy. This man of letters worked closely with five of the young Paris musicians of his day: Francis Poulenc, Arthur Honegger, Darius Milhaud, Louis Durey, Georges Auric, and a feminine member Germaine Tailleferre. A newspaper article entitled *The Russian Five and the French Six and Erik Satie,* published in 1920 by the French critic Henri Collet, was to bind these six musicians rather unfortunately together in the panorama of music history. Of the six, only Poulenc, Honegger, and Milhaud have enjoyed the satisfaction of prominent and lasting musical careers.

Francis Poulenc (1899–1963). Cocteau had no use for the blurred line of Impressionism. He demanded an art that was original, of course, but it also had to have simplicity (which he particularly liked in Satie), clarity, and order; and, to be French, it needed cleverness, wit, and charm, too. Francis Poulenc perhaps came the closest to being Cocteau's perfect disciple, for the majority of his compositions are in no way pretentious and most have a certain Gallic tongue-in-cheek quality. He was a great writer of songs, and here his French clarity and easy mobility of line are especially evident. Ravel and Satie he took for his models, and the texts are from Pierre de Ronsard, Cocteau, and others. Poulenc also wrote many piano pieces (of which the *Mouvements perpétuels,* 1918, is a great favorite) and some effective chamber music. An excellent contribution to contemporary concerto literature is a work for organ, string orchestra, and timpani composed in 1938. Two operas have had some success: *Les Mamelles de Tirésias* ("The Breasts of Tiresias," Paris, 1947)—a comic opera that approaches surrealism—and a serious, religious work *Les Dialogues des Carmélites* (Milan, 1957) set to a worth-while libretto by Georges Bernanos (1888–1948).

Arthur Honegger (1892–1955). Arthur Honegger never tied himself very closely to Cocteau's theories. Really, this composer was not of French heritage at all, for he was born of Swiss parents. Unlike Poulenc, he found his best medium to be the larger forms, using musical scores that flirted with atonality and polytonality as an adjunct to a fundamentally tonal concept. Quite a number of Honegger's compositions exhibit motoristic rhythmical propulsion, as may be found in *Pacific 231* (1923)—a description of a steam locomotive. A dramatic presentation of *Le Roi David* ("King David") was first performed in Switzerland in 1921; two years later Honegger re-orchestrated the work for concert-form presentation, and as an oratorio the piece has been most successful. The oratorio-drama *Jeanne d'Arc au bûcher* ("Joan of Arc at the Stake," 1935) is also commanding current performance. The composer's five symphonies are well-constructed works, with the *Symphony No. 3* (*"Liturgique,"* 1946) and the *Symphony No. 5* (*"Di tre re,"* 1951) being especially favored today. Honegger has written an operatic setting of Cocteau's version of *Antigone* (Brussels, 1927), songs and much film music, and organists who play his *Fugue et choral* (1917) only wish that he had written more for their instrument. Again the jazz age of the 1920's is reflected in this composer's *Concertino for Piano and Orchestra* (1924).

Darius Milhaud (1892–). One of the most prolific and important of 20th-century French composers is Darius Milhaud; he has to his credit nearly four hundred works of many types and based on many topics. Milhaud prepared for his career at the Paris Conservatory, where Dukas and D'Indy were two of his professors. During World War I he served as a secretary to the French diplomat and writer Paul Claudel and accompanied him to a legation post in Brazil. Shortly after the end of hostilities Milhaud returned to France.

The artist's compositions were soon to show the fruits of his travels, for in 1921 there appeared the popular *Saudades do Brazil* ("Nostalgia for Brazil"), twelve dances after various localities in Brazil for orchestra (also available for piano), and also the ballet *Le Boeuf sur la toit* ("The Ox on the Roof," 1919), a work that showed definite South American influences. The year 1922 saw Milhaud in the United States lecturing at Harvard, Columbia, and Princeton Universities and performing his own works. His next and particularly famous work was the ballet *La Création du monde* ("The Creation of the World," 1922), in which jazz elements are conspicuously employed, and the orchestra is a seventeen-piece jazz ensemble patterned after a band Milhaud had seen and heard in Harlem, New York. An instrumental suite in five parts has been derived from the ballet score.

Two operas of importance by Milhaud are *Christophe Colomb* (Berlin, 1930), to a libretto by Claudel, in which Milhaud's predilection for polytonal writing is particularly strong, and *Bolivar* (Paris, 1950) about the famous South American liberator Simón Bolívar (1783–1830). The strength of Milhaud's religious faith is revealed in his *Sacred Service*

(1947) for use in the synagogue and in his five-act opera *David,* produced in Jerusalem in 1954 as part of the three-thousandth-anniversary celebration of the land of Israel. French folklore inspired the *Suite française,* which appeared in both band and orchestral instrumentation in 1944; there is also a *West Point Suite* (1952) for band. The composer has written many songs, setting among others the words of Claudel, Mallarmé, Cocteau, and Ronsard.

During World War II Milhaud taught at Mills College in California. He is a famous teacher as well as composer of music, and one of his American pupils has been Dave Brubeck, the jazz musician. Milhaud has said of his creative talents that he likes to open the windows and that he prefers not to live in a matchbox, and this largely reflects the way he lives, for during the past several years he has been alternating the winter seasons between Paris and California, and teaching and composing during the summers at Aspen, Colorado, under the auspices of the Aspen Music Festival.

Olivier Messiaen (1908–). One of the latest of important names in French music is that of Olivier Messiaen. Once a student at the Paris Conservatory, he accepted a professorial position at that institution in 1947, and serves as well as the organist of Trinity Church in Paris. His interests as a composer range in material from Gregorian chant to Hindu rhythms, expressed in a most original and often mystical manner. Complex rhythms and harmonies are a part of his nature, and he appears to be constantly searching for new musical sonorities. He has written very well for his instrument (the organ) in such compositions as *Le Banquet céleste* (1928)—twenty-five measures in length, at a very slow tempo—*L'Ascension* (1933), and *La Nativité du Seigneur* (1935), the last named being nine Christmas meditations; and he also has works for orchestra that include *Hymne au Saint Sacrement* (1932) and *L'Ascension* (1934). The composer has explained his method of working in a two-volume treatise *Technique de mon langage musical* ("Technique of my Musical Language," 1944).

ENGLAND

Ralph Vaughan Williams (1872–1958). The most outstanding composer England has yet produced in this century is Ralph Vaughan Williams. The son of a minister, his early education was at Charterhouse, a "public school" in London. The composer's professional training was taken primarily at the Royal College of Music and at Cambridge University. He also studied on the Continent with Max Bruch and briefly with Maurice Ravel. Vaughan Williams served as an artillery officer in the British Army in World War I, and after his discharge from this service he became a teacher of composition at the Royal College of Music in London. Except for brief visits, chiefly to the United States, London remained his home for the rest of his life.

Vaughan Williams' English background shows through in a great many of his compositions. This side of his nature is expressed also in his membership in the English Folk Song Society and his active participation in the editing of the hymnal of the Church of England. Stylistically, Vaughan Williams is not what one would call a "tough" modern, although his later works are not without dissonant expression. His melodic treatment is basically diatonic, and this and his counterpoint in the modal manner can be taken as indicative of his interest in folk song and Elizabethan music. Much use is made harmonically of triadic construction, with the frequent appearance of parallel movement of such triads.

The composer is remembered first and foremost as a symphonist, his most famous works of this kind being his nine symphonies and the *Fantasia on a Theme of Thomas Tallis* (1910). The name Thomas Tallis immediately recalls the 16th century and that composer's part in the early music of the English church; Vaughan Williams' setting of the tune by Tallis is for a double string orchestra–that is, for a quartet of strings plus a string orchestra.

The *Symphony No. 2* (1914, revised 1920) has become a part of the basic symphonic repertoire. It is subtitled "A London Symphony," and the composer has appended a program for each movement and the music becomes a colorful portrayal of scenes in the city, with the river Thames as the focal point. The tune "Sweet Lavender" is heard in the second movement, and near the end of the work the striking of Big Ben is imitated by the plucking of the harp string.

Symphony No. 3 (1921), called the "Pastoral," receives its name for its mood, which is one of great calmness and quietude. In direct contrast, the *Symphony No. 4* (1932) shows Vaughan Williams in his most "modern" attire. Angular melodies and dissonant, complex structures are prominently displayed. One last comment on the symphonies is reserved for *Symphony No. 6* (1947); the work opens with a grand chorale and closes with a contrapuntal finale played at a low dynamic level throughout.

Outstanding among his work for the stage are the operas *Hugh the Drover,* first performed in London in 1924, and *Sir John in Love* (London, 1929), based on Shakespeare's *Merry Wives of Windsor*. Vaughan Williams' setting of the "Greensleeves" folk melody from *Sir John* has become famous. In the field of religious music, his *Mass in g minor* (1923) is a virtual re-creation of the spirit of the Renaissance Mass.

Gustav Holst (1874–1934). A contemporary and personal friend of Vaughan Williams, Gustav Holst shared with the latter a love of English folk melodies. Early in his career Holst became interested in the pre-Buddhist religious rites of India; this interest was transformed into a musical creation entitled *Choral Hymns from the Rig-Veda* (Op. 26–with texts translated by the composer–written during the years 1908–12). He is best known for the orchestral suite *The Planets* (Op. 32, 1916), in which the composer writes movements entitled "Mars," "Venus," "Mercury," "Jupiter," "Saturn," "Uranus," and "Neptune." Each movement pictures that planet's position in the cult of astrology; for example, for Mars there is martial music to signify the aspect of war, and for the association of pleasure and happiness with Jupiter the composer introduces a melody of folklike character as a part of a village dance.

Benjamin Britten (1913–). The operas of Benjamin Britten have found listening audiences in many parts of the world. Probably the two best known are *Peter Grimes* (Op. 33, London, 1945) and *The Turn of the Screw* (Venice, 1954). The libretto of the first is after a poem *The Borough,* by the English poet George Crabbe (1754–1832), and is a story of the hard life of a lonely, poor fisherman whose fellow-villagers turn against him when two of his assistants are lost at sea and he is held responsible. Strong orchestral music in the modern manner reflects the emotional upheavals of the text, and choruses and ensembles take an important place alongside the solo numbers. The scenes of the opera are connected by orchestral interludes, and four of these have been formed into a concert suite called *Four Sea Interludes* Op. 33a; they are popular on orchestral programs along with a fifth interlude, *Passacaglia,* Op. 33b.

The Young Person's Guide to the Orchestra (Op. 34, 1946) has been mentioned earlier in this book as music for an instructional film, but it is also often found programmed on symphony concerts. In *A Ceremony of Carols* (Op. 28, 1942) for boys' chorus and harp is seen a somewhat different side of Britten's nature, as a bit of the Middle Ages becomes a part of his style.

LATIN AMERICA

Two Latin American musicians of considerable importance are the Mexican Carlos Chávez and Heitor Villa-Lobos, Brazil's most famous composer.

Carlos Chávez (1899–). Not often one to quote folk melodies directly in his music, Carlos Chávez has nevertheless been able to blend both early Indian and later Spanish and Mexican elements into his highly rhythmical and rather severe style. The best of his symphonies are the *Sinfonía Antígona* (1933) and the *Sinfonía india* (1936). The former originated as incidental music for Jean Cocteau's play *Antigone,* based on the drama by Sophocles; this explains the melodies using Greek scales that Chávez mixes with Indian and Mexican melodic patterns and rhythms. The *Sinfonía India* is a very colorful work, using instruments and melodies found in the early Indian culture of Mexico. Furthermore, the rhythmic flavor of this composer's art makes interesting the *Xochipilli Macuilxochitl* (1940) for traditional Indian instruments, and the *Toccata* (1942) for percussion instruments. Chávez is also distinguished for his conducting–he founded the National Symphony Orchestra of Mexico City and was its conductor for many years —and as an educator in the field of music.

Heitor Villa-Lobos (1887–1959). Heitor Villa-Lobos was another 20th-century artist who collected folk songs. His formal education in music was not extensive, and thus his compositions are closely tied to his studies of folk music. His most popular works are under grouping titles called *chôros* and *Bachianas brasileiras*. The *chôros* is a Brazilian street dance using pointed rhythms and tuneful melodies; Villa-Lobos wrote fifteen pieces under this title, sometimes for a solo instrument and other times for an instrumental ensemble and perhaps vocal chorus; for example, *Chôros No. 1* (1920) is for guitar solo and *Chôros No. 7* (1924) is for a small orchestra. The *Bachianas brasileiras* are an effort by the composer to united Brazilian folklore with the classical style, that is, by the setting of folk materials in a Bach-like contrapuntal fabric. There are nine suites under this heading, written between the years 1930 and 1945. *Bachianas brasileiras No. 1* (1930) is for eight cellos, and *No. 2* (1930) for orchestra, as is *No. 4* (1930–36); the most popular is *No. 5* (1938–45) for soprano and cellos; *No. 6* (1938) makes use of flute and bassoon, and *No. 7* (1942) and *No. 9* (1945) were written for strings. A tremendously prolific composer, Villa-Lobos has written a grand total of some two thousand works, in which are incorporated the color and excitement of Latin rhythms. He was also famous as an educator and held a position as superintendent of musical education, during which time he was instrumental in instituting the study of Brazilian songs and dances in the public schools of the land.

THE UNITED STATES

American jazz has become a vital part of the world's music. It came into being in the early 20th century and made use of many diverse elements: the Afro-American work songs, blues, and spirituals; ragtime piano music, which appears to have come from the cakewalks and other tunes of the minstrel shows; and British and American folk songs and religious music. New Orleans has always been considered the focal point of the origin of jazz, and it was there that Negro brass bands played for all sorts of functions, including funerals at which solemn music was heard on the way to the cemetery and "hot" music on the way back. Gradually these bands began to play for dancing in the honky-tonks of the city, and ragtime, blues, and marches for brass band began to sound together as jazz.

In 1917 "King" Oliver (1885–1938) moved his band to Chicago, and in 1922 Louis Armstrong (1900–) followed him. The latter is still one of the greatest names in jazz today. *Muskrat Ramble* and *Tiger Rag* were two well-known pieces from this period, often played by "combo" groups of some five to seven musicians. In New York, the large band of Fletcher Henderson (1898–1954) necessitated a written-out score, as the earlier and smaller bands had all played in an improvisatory manner, and Duke Ellington (1899–) started his successful jazz career about this time.

The era of "swing" began in the 1930's, introduced by the band of Benny Goodman (1909–) and including other famous swing artists like Harry James (1916–) and "Count" Basie (1904–).

In the early 1940's a jazz style called "bop" made its appearance, with "Dizzy" Gillespie (1917–) and Charlie "Yardbird" Parker (1920–55) as its chief protagonists.

Next to appear was a type called "cool" jazz, a more intimate style designed for listening rather than for dancing, and often played by school-trained musicians such as Dave Brubeck

(1920–). At present there is much experimentation taking place along with an academic flavoring in the medium.

George Gershwin (1898–1937). An interesting amalgamation of jazz melodies and rhythms with classic art occurred in the more serious music of George Gershwin, a successful writer of Broadway musical comedies. The jazz basis of his works can be clearly seen in his *Rhapsody in Blue* (1924), his *Concerto in F* for piano and orchestra (1925), his *American in Paris* (1928), and in his folk opera *Porgy and Bess* (Boston, 1935). Indeed, jazz has played a part in a number of the classical works of many fine 20th-century composers, as will be noted from time to time in the remainder of the chapter.

Aaron Copland (1900–). Perhaps the most important American composer of the century is Aaron Copland. At least his works are now commonly played and recorded, and his influence is spread even further through his books. Born in Brooklyn, New York, Copland studied in Paris with Nadia Boulanger, after which he made New York City his home. He has lectured extensively at many schools, including Harvard College, and has made appearances as a pianist and as a conductor. Some of his earlier compositions, such as *Music for the Theater* (1925), reveal a wealth of dance rhythms.

At one time in his career Copland thought that perhaps an American style might be erected on a jazz background; some of his works of the 1920's—especially the *Piano Concerto* (1926), in which are found jazz rhythms, including the Charleston—attempted this, but he soon abandoned the effort. In fact, the early 1930's found the composer adopting a quite dissonant and difficult style, as in his *Piano Variations* (1930). The composer himself has pointed out that in this work he put the simplest version of the theme second so that he could open with a more striking pronouncement of it, thereby indicating the dynamic quality of the music. However, Copland soon felt that he was losing contact with his audience, and he turned to a more appealing type of composition. After a visit to Mexico City, he wrote *El Salon Mexico* (1936), a colorful piece of music containing a number of Latin American melodies, with their rhythmic associations.

All his life Copland has been interested in the furtherance of a national concept in his art. His *Lincoln Portrait* (1942) especially points up this idea, as do also the ballets *Billy the Kid* (1938), *Rodeo* (1942), and *Appalachian Spring* (1944). *Billy the Kid* outlines the life history of the famous outlaw and uses the cowboy songs "Git along, little dogie," "Old Chisholm Trail," "Bury me not on the lone prairie," and a cowboy's song to his horse, "Goodbye, old paint"–songs known to most citizens of the United States.

Appalachian Spring, for which the composer won the Pulitzer Prize in 1945, was written for Martha Graham, the choreographer and dancer. The scenario concerns the activities revolving around a Shaker wedding in the hills of Pennsylvania. The composer has arranged an attractive suite for orchestra from the ballet music, a feature of which is a group of five variations on a Shaker hymn tune, first played by a solo clarinet, called "Simple Gifts" (Example 57). As a final mention of Copland's artistry, the especially fine setting of *Twelve Poems of Emily Dickinson* (1950) is here cited.

Roy Harris (1898–). Roy Harris is a second American composer whose music shows something of a nationalistic bent, although he is best known for his *Symphony No. 3* (1938), which is not specifically connected with the American scene. Many of his compositions bear titles related to Americana, written in a style that is not very dissonant, often modal, basically contrapuntal, and sometimes polytonal. His *Symphony No. 4* (1940), subtitled "Folksong Symphony," is for chorus and orchestra, and uses folklore materials and jazz rhythms.

Although the *Symphony No. 3* has long been considered nonprogrammatic, the composer has revealed to this writer that he actually did have a program in mind when he composed this work. Harris was deeply troubled at that time with the turn of world events and the increasing rise of Hitler's power. He strongly felt that his third symphony might well be his last, and with this in mind he determined to write into the work a "his-

'Tis the gift to be sim-ple,'tis the gift to be free,'Tis the
gift to come down where we ought to be, And
when we find ourselves in the place just right,'Twill be in the val-ley of
love and de-light. When true sim-pli-ci-ty is gain'd, To
bow and to bend we shan't be a-sham'd, To turn, turn will
be our de-light Till by turn-ing, turn-ing we come round right.

Example 57

tory of musical art." Thus the piece opens with monody, heard in the cellos, then gradually moves when the violins enter into a form of faux-bourdon. Ornamentation is added to the melody as the strings ascend, with a clearer statement of the theme given over to the woodwinds. From here the music moves into a freer expression of counterpoint, but in very clear harmonic textures, and finally into the pastorale, where the strings sound a double-inverted canon in polytonal harmonic texture as a background for the woodwinds. This treatment leads finally into concentrated contrapuntal designs and into a fugue, which enters in the timpani and then moves into stretto and lastly to a final restatement of the first subject in canon as a background for the working out of elements of the fugal subject in stretto style. A coda completes the symphony.

Ernest Bloch (1880–1959). Ernest Bloch is one of a number of world-famous composers who are American by adoption, although his Jewish racial background and the fact that he was born and raised in Switzerland gave certain special characteristics to his music. He lived for many years in the United States and died here. He served as director of the Institute of Music in Cleveland (1920–25), and in the same capacity at the San Francisco Conservatory during the years 1925–30. He wrote an epic symphonic rhapsody, entitled *America,* in 1927, but is at his best in the traditional forms, such as his *String Quartet No. 1* (1916), the *Sonata No. 1 for Violin and Piano* (1920), and the *Quintet for Piano and Strings* (1923). Bloch's Jewish heritage is beautifully expressed in the *Israel Symphony* (1912–16); the *Baal Shem* (1923), for violin and piano, based on Jewish legends and later orchestrated; the *Sacred Service* ("*Avodath Hakodesh,*" 1933); and in his *Schelomo* ("Solomon," 1916), a rhapsody for cello and orchestra, his most widely performed composition.

Noted Composers as Teachers. A trio of composers have been active creators of music as well as directors of prominent American music schools: Howard Hanson (1896–), at the Eastman School of Music, and Walter Piston (1894–), at Harvard, and William Schuman (1910–), at the Juilliard School of Music and, since 1962, president of the Lincoln Center for the Performing Arts, in New York City. Hanson writes in a neo-Romantic style of which his *Symphony No. 2* (1930), nicknamed "Romantic" by the composer, is a good example. Piston is a master craftsman in his chamber music and several symphonies, and has been called a neo-Classic composer. Along with his ballets, symphonic works, and choral pieces Schuman has contributed original compositions for a new and upcoming medium of the 20th century–the symphonic band.

Samuel Barber (1910–). Samuel Barber is best known for his *Adagio for Strings* (1936), arranged by the composer from his *String Quartet No. 1,* and also for his opera *Vanessa* (1956).

Roger Sessions (1896–). In spite of performance and listening difficulties inherent in his music, Roger Sessions has achieved the position of an eminent composer. His oftenest-heard work is an orchestral suite (1923) arranged from his incidental music to the play *The Black Maskers,* written by the Russian novelist Leonid Andreyev (1871–1919); his *Symphony No. 2* (1946) and *Symphony No. 3* (1957) are also both fine works.

Virgil Thomson (1896–). Virgil Thomson has had a measure of success with his ballet *Filling Station* (1938) and an opera, *Four Saints in Three Acts* (Hartford, Connecticut, 1934), set to words by Gertrude Stein.

Gian-Carlo Menotti (1911–). Although Gian-Carlo Menotti was born in Italy and has retained his Italian citizenship, he has been most important on the scene of American opera. His works are composed to his own librettos, and show a fresh and individual style. Most important are *The Medium* (New York, 1946), *The Telephone* (New York, 1947), and *The Consul* (New York, 1950). A charming Christmas story, *Amahl and the Night Visitors,* was first heard on Christmas Eve, 1951, as presented on television by the National Broadcasting Company, and has subsequently become an annual Christmas production.

Elliott Carter (1908–). Elliott Carter is something of a musician's musician, and has gained prominence on the basis of only limited production, but a production still of excellent craftsmanship. An abstract but highly controlled style features a concept he calls "metrical modulation," in which the metronomic timing of a note value (for example, a quarter note) in one passage differs from the timing of the same-value note in succeeding passages. Carter's two string quartets (1951 and

1959) are considered important additions to the literature of that medium.

THE ROAD AHEAD

There are some who have maintained ever since the invention of the twelve-tone technique that it was too restrictive in scope, that it was a fad, and that it would not endure. It has endured and in fact has acquired strength and backing from rather unexpected quarters, Stravinsky being a striking example. Copland has previously been cited as showing some interest in the technique, and he did contribute a strict twelve-tone work, *Connotations for Orchestra,* to the opening concert (September 23, 1962) in Philharmonic Hall of New York's Lincoln Center for the Performing Arts. Others who have written in the serial manner are Sessions, Barber, Britten, the Greek composer Nikos Skalkottas (1904–49, a student of Schoenberg), and the Italian Luigi Dallapiccola (1904–). Many other composers of equal or lesser stature around the world, save in Russia, have also become followers in the technique.

That the twelve-tone technique is very much alive today is further demonstrated by developments within the system itself. These developments spring in part from Webern's technique and Messiaen's experimentation with "rhythmic rows," and presently the aspect of pitch control originally applied to melody and harmony has been passed on to time (rhythm), timbre, dynamics, etc.–that is, to all aspects ("parameters") of the creative process. Well-known composers of today who seem most interested in this new development are Messiaen and his pupils Pierre Boulez (1925–) and Karlheinz Stockhausen (1928–) in Europe, and Ernst Křenek (1900–) and Milton Babbitt (1916–) in the United States.

Total serialization has been combined with experiments in electronic music at the West German Radio studios in Cologne, where the leading musical figure is Stockhausen. Music is a product of its age, and the 20th-century invention of the electronic tube, the electric organ, and tape-recorded sound have affected the art. Electronic music has opened up all sorts of new vistas in dynamics, rhythm, pitch, and timbre. In Cologne the Germans built up complex sound masses out of electronically conceived sinusoidal sounds—that is, pure sounds with their overtones filtered out.

In Paris a like experimentation goes on under the title *musique concrète*. However, the French composers, headed by Messiaen and Boulez, gather their material from nature and the sounds of man, combining and mixing these sounds as they see fit.

Otto Luening (1900–) and Vladimir Ussachevsky (1911–), along with Sessions and Babbitt, are engaged in similar activities which are centered at Columbia and Princeton universities in the United States. Working with tape recorders, they have electronically transformed the sounds of traditional musical instruments and the human voice into altogether new and striking tonal sonorities. With the development of the RCA Electronic Synthesizer, rhythmic patterns, pitches, and timbres are now available that far transcend the possibilities of present-day musical instruments.

Two new attitudes in the presentation of some music of today have brought the performer into a somewhat closer relationship with the composer. One kind of composition passes to the performer the right of partial improvisation; the second type may be called aleatory or "chance" music. The latter is particularly interesting. For example, both Stockhausen and Boulez have written works consisting of many relatively short segments, with permission granted to the performer to play these sections in any order that he may see fit.

Hand in hand with these musical experimentations goes a more conventionally created music. Here the greatest interest is centered on seeking and following new avenues of rhythmical expression. The pioneering aspect of the New Music of the 20th century seems to be a continuing thing, and we are still awaiting the amalgamation of these experiments into a full and articulate musical language that will help to shape the course of the music of the future.

Index

(Page numbers in **boldface** signify major references to the subject. Page numbers in *italics* signify illustrations.)